KIERKEGAARD IN
POST/MODERNITY

KIERKEGAARD IN POST/MODERNITY

Edited by
Martin J. Matuštík
and Merold Westphal

Indiana University Press

Bloomington and Indianapolis

"Kierkegaard's View of the Unconscious" by C. Stephen Evans originally appeared in Birgit Bertung, ed., *Kierkegaard: Poet of Existence* (Copenhagen: Reitzel, 1989) and is reprinted in this volume by permission of C. A. Reitzel, Ltd.

The paper used in this publication meets the minimum requirements of American National Standard for Information Sciences— Permanence of Paper for Printed Library Materials, ANSI Z39.48-1984.

Manufactured in the United States of America

Library of Congress Cataloging-in-Publication Data

Kierkegaard in post/modernity / edited by Martin J. Matuštík and Merold Westphal.
     p. cm. — (Studies in Continental thought)
    Includes bibliographical references (p.   ) and index.
    ISBN 0-253-32888-8 (cloth : alk. paper). — ISBN 0-253-20967-6 (pbk. : alk. paper)
    1. Kierkegaard, Søren, 1813–1855—Influence. 2. Philosophy, Modern—20th century. 3. Postmodernism—Religious aspects— Christianity. 4. Religion—Philosophy. I. Matuštík, Martin Joseph, date. II. Westphal, Merold. III. Series.
B4377.K4555 1995
198'.9—dc20   94-46241

1 2 3 4 5 00 99 98 97 96 95

Contents

Introduction

Merold Westphal and Martin J. Matuštík

KIERKEGAARD, like Nietzsche, deserves to be a full partner in contemporary philosophical conversations. To that end, this volume places him in dialogue with a variety of twentieth-century themes and with such thinkers as Buber, Derrida, Freud, Gadamer, Habermas, Heidegger, Kristeva, Levinas, Sartre, and Wittgenstein. Such a listing would not be exhaustive even if we added the names of those thinkers who receive less extended attention; but then, claims to totality are not exactly what a book of this sort needs.

In one respect the current situations of Kierkegaard and Nietzsche are quite similar, but in another quite different. In both cases there is a continuous flow of scholarly studies throwing fresh light on thinkers we thought we had pretty well mastered long ago. But if we turn from exegetical and interpretative scholarship to current philosophical debates, Nietzsche seems to be a resource drawn upon more easily and more frequently than Kierkegaard. Why is this so?

Proffered explanations seem to us inadequate to justify this situation. Consider, first, the fact that Kierkegaard has long been viewed as the father of existentialism and that existentialism is not the hottest ticket in town these days. This would be a good reason for concluding that he is not *à la mode* IF it could be shown a) that the issues raised by existentialism can safely be viewed as "solved" and thus no longer in need of attention, and b) that the texts which in one way or another bear the name of Kierkegaard do not overflow the concept of existentialism, but are for all practical purposes exhausted by it. In both cases, however, just the opposite thesis would seem to have the stronger claim on our credence. Nietzsche, too, was a father of existentialism, but we have learned not to hold it against him.

A second factor is the lingering suspicion that while Kierkegaard is a major religious thinker, he is not really a philosopher. Insofar as this view stems from the assumption that to be taken seriously a philosopher must either be secular or abstract from his or her religious identity, it can be dismissed as a prejudice rooted in very dubious Enlightenment conceptions of the autonomy of human thought.

But not every religiously important thinker is philosophically important, so no positive conclusion would seem to follow from such a dismissal. It is the task of the essays that follow to identify some of the ways in which Kierkegaard is an important interlocutor for contemporary philosophical conversations, but the fact that such secular thinkers as Heidegger and Sartre, and, more recently, Habermas and Derrida, have found it useful, even necessary, to engage themselves with his thought gives strong *prima facie* reasons to resist claims, overt or unspoken, that he is not really a philosopher. Heidegger even goes so far as to say in *Being and Time* that "there is more to be learned philosophically from his 'edifying' writings than from his theoretical ones," with the exception of *The Concept of Anxiety*, of course (Heidegger, *Being and Time*, 235n. vi).

Some of the contributors to this volume are sympathetic in one way or another to Kierkegaard's religious interests. Others are not. But all find at least some part of his corpus to be worthy of the closest attention, and none finds it necessary to pretend that he was not at one and the same time a religious and a philosophical thinker.

A third factor is the long-standing interpretation of Kierkegaard as an irrationalist. But two things have changed dramatically. On the one hand, a closer look at Kierkegaard's critique of Reason has shown that it is not an invitation to believe p and not-p at the same time, and that it does not contain, any more than does Nietzsche's critique of Reason, the theses that sometimes make it attractive to sophomores, such as:

1) Hard thinking and careful conceptual distinctions are unnecessary.

2) Everything is permitted—all beliefs and all practices are equally appropriate.

On the other hand, contemporary philosophy finds itself engaged in a similar critique of foundationalist (Cartesian) or totalizing (Hegelian) interpretation of human thought that make exaggerated claims about its capacity and baptize themselves (a curious rite) with the honorific title of Reason. While there remains great disagreement about how to find the middle ground between the hubris of such claims, sometimes rebaptized with the pejorative title of Logocentrism, and the cynical nihilism sometimes portrayed as the only alternative (*après nous le déluge*), there is a widely shared unwillingness to be intimidated by the name of Reason, especially when it is the self-designation of a quite particular interpretation of what it means to be reasonable.

In such a context it is easier to see the *Auseinandersetzung* of the Absurd and the Paradox to Reason and the System for the kind of critical philosophy it is, a challenge to a reason that is not only human, all too human, but also a quite specific, substantive account of the human logos. *Almost all of the chapters in this volume can be read as contributions to the critique of Logocentrism, even when that is not how they would primarily describe themselves.* Sometimes this involves explicit argument against a Reason that claims too much for itself, while sometimes it involves the practice and articulation of a humbler mode of rationality.

Finally, there is the perception of Kierkegaard as representing an anti-social, apolitical individualism that is worse than useless in the search for community, communication, and cooperation in a world where violence, hatred, and neglect signify on a daily basis not only their absence but the cost of their absence. But just as it is becoming clear that Kierkegaard's "irrationalism" is a protest against a contingent interpretation of reason's necessity, so it is becoming clear that his "individualism" is a protest against a particular mode of human togetherness that he calls by such names as Christendom, the public, the present age, and even, anticipating Nietzsche, the herd. This individualism turns out to be the flip side of a thoroughly relational conception of the self, and is beginning to be seen as having interesting ramifications for social theory and practice. *Almost all of the chapters in this volume can be read as contributions to the ongoing task of critical social theory, even when that is not how they would primarily describe themselves.* In several cases this involves critical social theory in the narrower sense, signifying conversations in which the work of Habermas plays a central role. But in the wider sense of the term it also includes the feminist discourses addressed in several chapters and a variety of other ways in which Kierkegaard in dialogue turns out to be a social philosopher.

The collection opens by situating what Schrag calls the "Kierkegaard-effect" at the contemporary crossroads of modern and postmodern cultures. Schrag raises key issues that we encounter in most of the contributions gathered in this volume: Given that Weber describes modernity as split into the three culture spheres of science, morality and law, and art, should we follow Habermas's neo-Kantian, fallibilist, and communicative rereading of Hegel, which strives for unity under the postmetaphysical conditions of modernity? Or should we prefer Rorty's postmodern rejoinder that the wrong turn occurred in taking Kant's critiques of fragmented reason too seriously? And whichever path we take, what role do Kierkegaard's existence spheres, especially the religious, play in this present postmodern-modern impasse?

While several dialogues with Kierkegaard in this book involve thinkers writing earlier in this century, others engage our more recent contemporaries. In the former grouping, we can follow the "Kierkegaard-effect" in post/modernity from Heidegger and Buber to Sartre, Gadamer, and Wittgenstein. In the latter we witness Kierkegaardian encounters with Lacan, Irigaray, Kristeva, Theunissen, Derrida, Habermas, and Levinas, often drawing into the conversation one or more of the old "masters of suspicion," Marx, Nietzsche, and Freud. Each chapter seeks to create a conversation that will produce light as well as heat.

Within the first trajectory McBride's return to Sartre's positive, yet decisively secular debts to Kierkegaard is both historical and conceptual. Similarly, Huntington tries to sort out what was illuminated and what was obscured by Heidegger's fundamental ontology. Whereas Huntington questions anew whether or not Heidegger is existential in an ethico-political sense, McBride argues that in spite of manifest differences, both Sartre and Kierkegaard move from a moral critique of conventionalism, self-deception, and the spirit of seriousness, to an attack on the established order. Keying off Gadamer's Heideggerian notion of language as a game of questions that plays us and our answers, Dunning shows that Kierkegaard and Gadamer share a notion of the ethical as an existential task. Pursuing the language theme so central to Heidegger and Gadamer, Roberts argues that Kierkegaard, like the later Wittgenstein, is a moral grammarian who views forms of life as depth grammars. The philosophical task, then, is to elucidate and differentiate the operative grammar rules that are already guiding our embedded practices of various virtues. Perkins urges us to leave aside Buber's one-sided Kierkegaard, the anti-social religious individualist, and encounter him along with Buber as a communicative and socio-political thinker. Like Sartre, Kierkegaard takes a radical distance from the conventions, but he does so for the sake of an existentially responsible and deliberative politics. The goal of reflection is not isolation but a new kind of involvement.

Several chapters that open up new fields of contemporary dialogue with Kierkegaard take him as a partner in current feminist and psychoanalytic conversation. While McBride suggests that Kierkegaard and Sartre are rare among the "dead white males" in their attention to the sex and gender problematic, Huntington proposes to complement the French psychoanalytic feminists—their extensions of Heidegger to critique the symbolic of domination—with Kierkegaard's suspicion of motives. Brown carries a three-way discourse among Kierkegaard's Haufniensis, Nietzsche, and Irigaray on the role of anxiety in identity formation. Whereas Kierkegaard's and Nietzsche's authorships—creating others or one's future self—can provide some secular relief from anxiety by covering over one's fear of madness and woman, Brown discloses the limits of such strategies by displaying how Irigaray allows for self-creation without such fictitious unifications of the fragmented self. Because both Kierkegaard and Freud depict the dynamic unconscious as a result of willed repression, Evans can regard the unconscious in dynamic clinical and existential categories. A Kierkegaardian self, restored from division through self-relation to the wholly other, becomes a locus of responsible freedom incommensurable with the Freudian framework of cultural superego and biological instincts. Since deception and domination are existential and historical terms alike, Evans's focus on Kierkegaard's religious therapy complements those contributors who read Kierkegaard through Marx's ideology critique. Lorraine turns to Kristeva's Lacanian and Kierkegaard's "amatory discourse of self-transformation" to project a cosmopolitan community that welcomes strangers within its borders. In this space of identity in difference we can re-think the social categories of gender, race, class, and ethnicity and enter into a dialogue with others as individuals. Likewise Berry envisions a new feminist dialogue with Kierkegaard even though he is one of those dead white male mentor figures "in our head" who happens to come from a patriarchal tradition of the West. She appeals to Kierkegaard's indirect, non-authoritarian, and receptive style: it welcomes the other's agency as the truth of her subjectivity, and it invites to multiple dialogues across cultures and races, among feminists and womanists, in liberation theologies and secular struggles for justice alike.

The last five chapters engage current controversies surrounding the "Kierkegaard-effect" in critical and postmodern social theory. Habermas's place in these dialogues with Kierkegaard is *sui generis*, i.e., both in his own contribution and as a primary source for several other conversations in this collection. Since his 1987 Copenhagen lecture, Habermas has returned to Kierkegaard on several occasions in his criticisms of nationalism and of the positive theological receptions of communicative action theory. The present chapter is unique in content and style, and we have tried to preserve its existential vocabulary and manner as a more felicitous rendition of a side of Habermas not widely known to Anglo-American readers of his thought. He addresses the German reception of Kierkegaard through Heidegger and through Theunissen's development of Buber's philosophy of dialogue; at the same time he responds indirectly to some questions raised by Schrag as well as Marsh and Matuštík.

Habermas defends Kierkegaard's existential ethics as compatible with Marx's critique of the present age, yet he complains that Heidegger, Theunissen, and many postmodern appeals to difference replace the religious absolute with a negative discourse of alterity. Habermas welcomes existential descriptions of damaged life, but only in a form of negative philosophy that would motivate our positive communicative and liberating praxis. In contrast to Habermas, on the one hand, Marsh argues that Kierkegaard needs critical theory in order to flesh out fully the implications of a radical religious interiority, but that economic, socio-political, and cultural critiques of society also need a Kierkegaardian religiosity in order to be adequately critical. On the other hand, Caputo presents Derrida's recent work on Kierkegaard as that of a knight of faith: Kierkegaard is a deconstructionist ahead of his age. In distinction from Levinas's teleological suspension of the religious for the sake of ethical obligation, Derrida's deconstructive justice offers an Abrahamic sacrifice bereft of the consolation of the ethical. Matuštík argues that Kierkegaard's category of the individual differs from both liberal individualism and its opposing communitarianism, on the one hand, and lies between Derridean deconstruction and Habermasian proceduralism, on the other. Kierkegaard's individual both dissents against established secular and religious orders and acts on behalf of personal and social liberation. Westphal shows that Kierkegaard and Levinas are united above all in their protest against humanity's self-deification and in their willingness to let the God who is never simply present or simply absent reveal the lack of absolute self-evidence for any "decent" theodicy. Levinas suspends the positively religious in order to protect it from its tendency toward holy war, whereas Kierkegaard suspends the communal ethics of *Sittlichkeit* to protect it from a complacency that involves the same absolutizing of "our" form of life that turns violent in holy war. For Levinas, ideology critique involves interrupting the religious with the radical ethics of the face to face encounter with the other, while for Kierkegaard it involves interrupting the ethical with the radical religion of revelation.

Finally, a word of caution. Kierkegaard insisted that we attribute to him nothing of what his pseudonyms say. He had his reasons for such a request, which has been more honored in the breach than in the observance. The practice in these chapters embodies the usual diversity, sometimes attributing pseudonymous works to their pseudonyms, sometimes not. We recommend in reading them, and as a general practice except where biography is at issue, that "Kierkegaard" be taken to stand for a body of texts brought into the world by Søren Kierkegaard because he wanted readers to engage seriously with the points of view expressed in them, paying more attention (subjectively) to their own relation to those points of view than (objectively) to his.

References to the Kierkegaardian corpus are given in the text with the help of the sigla given immediately hereafter. Readers seeking full bibliographical data on sources cited briefly in the endnotes are referred to Works Cited.

Sigla

AN   *Armed Neutrality* and *An Open Letter*, trans. Howard V. Hong and Edna H. Hong. Bloomington and London: Indiana University Press, 1968.

Br   *Breve og Aktstykker vedrørende Søren Kierkegaard*, 2 vols., ed. Niels Thulstrup. Copenhagen: Munksgaard, 1953-1954.

C   *The Crisis [and a Crisis] in the Life of an Actress*, trans. Stephen Crites. New York: Harper and Row, 1967.

CA   *The Concept of Anxiety*, trans. Reidar Thomte in collaboration with Albert B. Anderson. Princeton: Princeton University Press, 1980.

CD   *Christian Discourses*, including *The Lilies of the Field and the Birds of the Air* and *Three Discourses at the Communion on Fridays*, trans. Walter Lowrie. London and New York: Oxford University Press, 1940.

CI   *The Concept of Irony* together with "Notes on Schelling's Berlin Lectures," trans. Howard V. Hong and Edna H. Hong. Princeton: Princeton University Press, 1989.

COR   *The Corsair Affair*, trans. Howard V. Hong and Edna H. Hong. Princeton: Princeton University Press, 1982.

CUP   *Concluding Unscientific Postscript*, 2 vols., trans. Howard V. Hong and Edna H. Hong. Princeton: Princeton University Press, 1992.

EDVS   *Edifying Discourses in Various Spirits*, trans. Howard V. Hong and Edna H. Hong. Princeton: Princeton University Press, 1993.

EO   *Either/Or*, 2 vols., trans. Howard V. Hong and Edna H. Hong. Princeton: Princeton University Press, 1987.

EPW   *Early Polemical Writings*, trans. Julia Watkin. Princeton: Princeton University Press, 1990.

EUD   *Eighteen Edifying Discourses*, trans. Howard V. Hong and Edna H. Hong. Princeton: Princeton University Press, 1990.

FSE   *For Self-Examination* and *Judge for Yourselves*, trans. Howard V. Hong and Edna H. Hong. Princeton: Princeton University Press, 1990.

FT   *Fear and Trembling* and *Repetition*, trans. Howard V. Hong and Edna H. Hong. Princeton: Princeton University Press, 1983.

JC   *Philosophical Fragments* and *Johannes Climacus*, trans. Howard V. Hong and Edna H. Hong. Princeton: Princeton University Press, 1985.

JFY   *For Self-Examination* and *Judge for Yourselves*, trans. Howard V. Hong and Edna H. Hong. Princeton: Princeton University Press, 1990.

JP   *Søren Kierkegaard's Journals and Papers*, 7 vols., eds. and trans. Howard V. Hong and Edna H. Hong. Assisted by Gregor Malantschuk. Index, 7, by Nathaniel Hong and Charles Baker. Bloomington and London: Indiana University Press, (vol. 1) 1967; (vol. 2) 1970; (vol. 3) and (vol. 4) 1975; (vols. 5–7) 1978.

JSK   *The Journals of Søren Kierkegaard*, trans. Alexander Dru. London and New York: Oxford University Press, 1938.

KAUC   *Kierkegaard's Attack upon "Christendom,"* 1854–1855, trans. Walter Lowrie. Princeton: Princeton University Press, 1944.

LD   *Letters and Documents*, trans. Hendrik Rosenmeier. Princeton: Princeton University Press, 1978.

LY   *The Last Years*, trans. Ronald C. Smith. New York: Harper and Row, 1965.

NSBL   *The Concept of Irony* together with "Notes on Schelling's Berlin Lectures," trans. Howard V. Hong and Edna H. Hong. Princeton: Princeton University Press, 1989.

OAR   *On Authority and Revelation, The Book on Adler*, trans. Walter Lowrie. Princeton: Princeton University Press, 1955.

P   *Prefaces: Light Reading for Certain Classes as the Occasion May Require*, trans. William McDonald. Tallahassee: Florida State University Press, 1989.

Pap   *Søren Kierkegaards Papirer*, 16 vols., 1st edition, eds. P. A. Heiberg, V. Kuhr, and E. Torsting. Copenhagen: Gylendal, (vols. I–XI^3) 1909–1948. 2nd edition, ed. Niels Thulstrup, photo-offset with two supplemental vols. Copenhagen: Gylendal, (vols. I–XIII) 1968–1970, and index, ed. N. J. Cappelørn. Copenhagen: Gylendal, (vols. XIV–XVI) 1975–1978.

PC   *Practice in Christianity*, trans. Howard V. Hong and Edna H. Hong. Princeton: Princeton University Press, 1991.

PF   *Philosophical Fragments* and *Johannes Climacus*, trans. Howard V. Hong and Edna H. Hong. Princeton: Princeton University Press, 1985.

PV   *The Point of View for My Work as an Author*, including the appendix " 'The Single Individual' Two 'Notes' Concerning My Work as an Author" and *On My Work as an Author*, trans. Walter Lowrie. London and New York: Oxford University Press, 1939.

R   *Fear and Trembling* and *Repetition*, trans. Howard V. Hong and Edna H. Hong. Princeton: Princeton University Press, 1983.

SLW   *Stages on Life's Way*, trans. Howard V. Hong and Edna H. Hong. Princeton: Princeton University Press, 1988.

SUD   *The Sickness unto Death*, trans. Howard V. Hong and Edna H. Hong. Princeton: Princeton University Press, 1980.

SV   *Søren Kierkegaards Samlede Værker*, 14 vols., eds. A. B. Drachmann, J. L. Heiberg, and H. O. Lange, 1st edition. Copenhagen: Gylendal, 1901–1906.

TA   *Two Ages: The Age of Revolution and the Present Age. A Literary Review*, trans. Howard V. Hong and Edna H. Hong. Princeton: Princeton University Press, 1978.

TDIO   *Three Discourses on Imagined Occasions*, trans. Howard V. Hong and Edna H. Hong. Princeton: Princeton University Press, 1993.

WL   *Works of Love*, trans. Howard V. Hong and Edna H. Hong. New York: Harper and Row, 1962.

1 | The Kierkegaard-Effect in the Shaping of the Contours of Modernity

Calvin O. Schrag

I. The Culture-Spheres of Modernity and the Role of Religion

IT HAS BECOME increasingly common in the literature to define modernity against the backdrop of three quite distinct culture-spheres, identified respectively as science, morality, and art. Max Weber spoke of this division of spheres as a "stubborn differentiation." Jürgen Habermas accepts, and pretty much without qualification, this triadic compartmentalization of culture; traces its origins in the philosophy of Kant; tracks its developments in the philosophy of Hegel; and then sketches a critical theory of communicative action designed to overcome the unfortunate separation of the spheres. The assessment of the differentiation of science, morality, and art into distinct spheres as unfortunate, of course, is already a value judgment. And it is this that the proponents of postmodernity, who comprise Habermas's more formidable opponents, never tire of pointing out. For the postmodernists diversity, plurality, and difference are to be celebrated and emulated, while projects of unification and totalization are to be discouraged. For the modernist, on the other hand, unity is good and diversity is bad, and that is why the differentiation of the culture-spheres is a "problem" to be overcome.

The problem, it is alleged, has its source in the philosophy of Kant. In his three *Critiques* Kant addressed the role of reason in the areas of science, morality, and art respectively. What Kant left unattended, however, was how these three areas of cultural endeavor might be unified. Is there some manner of grounding the foundations peculiar to each of the spheres in a more encompassing foundation, a final grounding, a *Letztbegrundung*, from which the knowledge claims in each of the spheres arise and to which they return for their validation? Kant raised this question but did not have the available resources to answer it. Hence, it became a challenge bequeathed to his successors. Hegel was quick to take up the gauntlet, and it would indeed appear that he had the conceptual resources for achieving the sought-after unification. If it can't be done with seventy-three categories (as delineated in Hegel's *Logic*), then it probably can't be done!

Although Hegel seemed to be qualified to do the job, in the end he botched it. And he botched it, says Habermas, by taking the wrong turn. If Hegel would have stuck with his *Jügendschriften*, the works that he wrote during his stay in Jena, he could have fashioned a response to Kant's problem by utilizing the notions of community, love, and freedom—which were central to these early writings. Apparently he was in a position to consolidate these early themes into a kind of Habermasian universal pragmatics of communicative rationality! Unfortunately he recoiled from such a project and then took the wrong turn by placing his bets on a subject-centered rationality, which enabled him to fashion a philosophy of identity in which all opposites are brought under the umbrella of the Absolute Idea.[1]

In this move by the later Hegel, the unification of the differentiated culture-spheres was indeed effected, but only at the expense of marginalizing the concretely situated individual. It was principally up to Feuerbach, Marx, and Kierkegaard—the most resourceful anti-Hegelians of their time—to show how in different ways the Hegelian philosophy of identity, with its claims for unity and final synthesis, was not an answer to a *real* problem—namely the self-understanding of flesh-and-blood individuals in their concrete sensory-biological, socio-economic, and ethico-religious situatedness. The three anti-Hegelians were of one mind in their assessment that after the dust had settled in Hegel's grandiose synthesis of opposites, the ironic fact remained that the synthesis had occurred only in Hegel's head. In the actual context of the self's historical existence, estrangement and alienation still remained very much in force. Marx called to the world's attention the fact that workers continued to be alienated from their entrepreneurs, from other workers, and ultimately from themselves. Kierkegaard had much to say about the existential reality of sin as an estrangement of the self from itself and from God. To speak of a synthesis in which alienation and estrangement are sublated into a higher unity is comically to place oneself at the end of history.

Habermas, who has certain sympathies with the anti-Hegelians, intends to correct the wrong turn taken by the later Hegel and begin again where the early Hegel left off, this time working out a theory of social reconstruction in which a communicative rationality is substituted for the subject-centered rationality of modernity. For Habermas this does not mean that modernity itself was somehow wrong-headed from the bottom up. Rather, what is needed is a critical reconstruction of modernity from within. This reconstruction, if properly programmed, will solve the problem of the differentiation of the three culture-spheres, bequeathed to us by Kant, by tapping the resources of a communicative rationality that is able to bind the validity claims that are operative in each of the spheres.

Now other interpreters of the current philosophical scene put a quite different spin on the problem of modernity, suggesting a response other than that of Habermas. This is notably the case for one of America's indigenous post-modernists, Richard Rorty. Whereas Habermas indicts the later Hegel for making the wrong turn in his efforts toward a reunification of the three culture-spheres, Rorty is of the mind that the wrong turn can be traced to those philosophers who took Kant too seriously and inherited a problem that was more artificial than real. "On this view," muses Rorty, "the wrong turn was taken when Kant's split between science, morals, and art was accepted as a *donné*, as *die massgebliche Selbstauslegung der Moderne*."[2] What is at issue for Rorty and his new pragmatism is the obsession in modernity with a foundationalist grounding of our knowledge claims. Clearly, knowledge claims and moral and aesthetic judgments will continue to be part of the conversation of humankind. The point is that it is futile to search for a theoretical back-up and universal grounding for these claims and judgments.

We want to frame our discussion of Kierkegaard against the backdrop of the animated polemic on the fortunes and misfortunes of modernity that has been so much in the philosophical news of late. More specifically, we want to investigate what a Kierkegaardian response to the "stubborn differentiation" of the three culture-spheres might look like, given Kierkegaard's own triadic differentiation of the three stages or spheres of existence—the aesthetical, the ethical, and the religious. In what manner, if indeed any, do Kierkegaard's three existence-spheres relate to the three culture-spheres?

To address these issues it is mandatory to go back to Kant, either to take him seriously, as does Habermas, and see how the differentiation problematic unfolds across the span of the three *Critiques*, or to travel the road with Rorty and see the problem created by Kant as an artificial one. In any event, Kant provides much of the plot in any telling of the story of the travails of modernity.

The space for the three culture-spheres of science, morality, and art, we are told, was carved out from Kant's *Critique of Pure Reason*, *Critique of Pure Practical Reason*, and *Critique of Judgment*, respectively. What remains untold in this story is the role played in Kant's consummate philosophy by his work *Religion within the Limits of Reason Alone*. Could one not read this later work by Kant as comprising his "fourth" Critique, in which he sought to provide a space for the sphere of religion as in his three *Critiques* he initiated discourses about the spheres of science, morality, and art? Or is religion for Kant simply an extension of morality, somehow reduced to it, falling out as a *moral* religion in which the object of worship becomes the moral law as resident in every rational creature?

That religion displays for Kant a certain integrity and irreducibility is already evident, it would seem, from a reading of his second *Critique*, in which the existence of God and the immortality of the soul assume their importance as postulates of practical reason, ensuring the realization of the universal moral law. In the third *Critique* another perspective on the theistic governance of the world is opened up through a consideration of the evidence of teleological forces and a tracking of the experience of the sublime. Kant's book on religion, *Religion within the Limits of Reason Alone*, which might function as his "fourth" *Critique*, could then be understood as a consolidation of the forays into religion in the preceding three *Critiques*, culminating in a "critique of rational faith," in which the accusative grammar of critique receives expression in an attack on doctrinal dogmatism and the genitival grammar marks the self-reflexivity whereby faith becomes critically aware of its positive resources as distinct from belief as intellectual assent.

If indeed Kant's ruminations on religion set the stage for a fourth culture-sphere in the annals of modernity, could Kierkegaard's contribution to the modern age be properly understood as that of supplying the script and the actors for the stage that Kant had set? Did religion as the fourth culture-sphere of modernity have to wait until the writings of Kierkegaard to achieve self-consciousness? How does the multi-faceted discourse of Kierkegaard, including a variety of pseudonyms and a variety of literary styles, fit into the discourse of modernity? More specifically, do Kierkegaard's three existence-spheres—the aesthetical, the ethical, and the religious—have any bearing upon the topography of modernity's three culture-spheres? Might one use Kierkegaard's understanding of religion as an existence-sphere to "complete" the project of modernity? If so, what specific role would religion have vis-à-vis the economies of science, morality, and art? In dealing with these questions much will hang on the distinction between an "existence-sphere" and a "culture-sphere."

II. Existence-Spheres and Culture-Spheres

In Kierkegaard's elucidations of the aesthetical, the ethical, and the religious there is a shift in terminology from "stages of life" to "existence-spheres" as one moves from *Stages on Life's Way* to *Concluding Unscientific Postscript*. Although in the end not all that much hangs on this difference of terminology, the language of "existence-spheres" is preferable because it avoids the imagery of a succession of levels of development that attaches to the grammar of stages. Also, it signals the peculiar qualification of aesthetics, ethics, and religion as manners or modes of existing. And these manners or modes of existing are more like cross-sections of possible life styles within the concrete history of the self than like developmental stages that progressively succeed each other.

To see how Kierkegaard's existence-spheres line up with the culture-spheres of modernity we need to achieve some clarity on the Kierkegaardian use and understanding of "existence." Kierkegaard introduced a novel usage of the term "existence" by having it apply uniquely to *human* existence. It functions as a determination of the human self as a process of becoming within the finite structures of time and space. "To exist" is the peculiar and distinctive *way to be* characteristic of human beings, a way to be that is always a becoming. C. Stephen Evans provides some needed illumination on this point.

> As is probably known by anyone who has studied Kierkegaard at all, he uses special terms for "existence" and "exist" (*eksistens* and *eksistere*) which focus on the distinctiveness of human existence. Human beings do not merely exist in the sense of being actualized in space and time as do rocks and plants, nor merely in the still broader sense of merely having some kind of 'being.' Human existence is a *becoming*; moreover, a special type of becoming.[3]

In giving this particular spin to the notion of existence, Kierkegaard stands as the principal precursor of the existential ontology of Heidegger, for whom "existence" also was a unique determinant of *Dasein's* way to be, a becoming in the primordial sense of arriving from a past and moving into a future. The difference between Kierkegaard and Heidegger, and it is a difference that is of some importance, is that Kierkegaard's interest resided in the *concretely* existential, in what Heidegger would call the *ontisch* and *existenziell* as distinct from the *ontologisch* and *existenzial*. This is all part of Heidegger's wider project which, in *Being and Time* at least, can be seen as a program of ontologizing and secularizing Kierkegaard's understanding of existence as it pertains to the lived-through experiences of the self in its aesthetical, ethical, and religious self-consciousness.[4]

We are going to approach the manners or modes of existing in the aesthetical, ethical, and religious spheres as displaying different experiences of temporality and alterity. The three existence-spheres are to be distinguished in terms of the different relations to time and to the other.

The aesthete's experience of time is that of time and history externalized. The aesthete does not yet apprehend time as being constitutive of her/himself as *existing*, as being inserted in the world as a concretely becoming historical subject. Time for the aesthete is something external and objective, an orderly serial succession of nows. In this succession of nows it is the present now that is privileged. This is particularly the case for the young lover in the "Diary of a Seducer," who is at once a prototype of Don Giovanni and an archetype of aesthetical consciousness. The young lover, like Don Giovanni, lives for pleasure, a pleasure that is experienced in the immediate instant. For the aesthete the passing present nows become potential erotic instants. But an erotic instant quickly passes by, sinks off into the past, and is forgotten—as the aesthete awaits yet another instant of pleasure to come her/his way. In such a way of life all reality is squeezed into the erotic instant as a passing present. The aesthete has neither a past to remember nor a future to anticipate. All that matters is the present now as a potential erotic instant.

As the young lover takes over specific attitudes toward time, s/he also assumes a certain stance with respect to the other. The other is a possession that is acquired through an arduous conquest, a prize that is won and now belongs to the aesthete, if, indeed, only temporarily. There is here a recognition of the other, but clearly only the other as *other-for-me*; as an objectified and faceless other; as an other who is subject to my domination and control; as an other caught in the gaze of a Sartrean *regard*. Always a means toward an end, but never an end in itself, the other is a possession that is disposable at will.[5]

In the scenario of the ethical existence-sphere both the experience of time and the attitude toward the other undergo transformations. The chief determinant of the ethical sphere is choice—not first and foremost the choice of this or that, but rather the fundamental *choice of oneself*. This is the long and short of Judge William's message to the young aesthete. "On the whole, to choose is an intrinsic and stringent term for the ethical" (EO, II, 166). This choice of oneself, exhibited in the *act* of choosing, which antedates the distinction between good and evil, is the basic requirement for the achievement of ethical selfhood, whereby the self first *becomes* a self, and gathers up its life in its responsivity to the claims of other selves.

The ethical sphere of existence brings with it a new understanding of temporality. The present is no longer apprehended as an erotic instant, as in the life of the aesthete, but is transformed into an *opportune moment*, a time for decision, the "right time" to become who we are.[6] Whereas the aesthetic self is unable to choose itself and make commitments to another self, moving from one romantic involvement to another, the ethical self lives a life of commitment and constancy. It is Judge William, Kierkegaard's archetypical ethical personage, who exemplifies the life of decision, choosing himself time and again, committing himself to marriage, so that he can repeat the constancy of his love by remembering the past and vowing to remain faithful in the future. At issue here is a quite different attitude toward temporality than that which we found in the life of the aesthete. The past is no longer, as it is for the young lover, a series of successive seductions that have gone by and are now forgotten; it is rather a past to be remembered and commemorated, a past to be repeated, moment after moment, as the husband envisions the constancy of his love for the future. Whereas the three dimensions of time (past, present, and future) remain dispersed and fractionated in the life of the aesthete, in the life of the ethical person the dimensions of time are unified, rendering possible the integrity of ethical existence.

In concert with the new configuration of time in the ethical sphere, we find that a new stance in the relationship with the other appears. The objectivization and depersonalization of the other, so prominent in the aesthetic sphere, is recast against the backdrop of social and civic responsibilities. The ethically chosen self finds that it has not only duties for and to itself but also duties for and to others as it is shaped by concrete reciprocal relations with its natural and social surroundings. Judge William does seem to be quite explicit on this point. Describing the self that has ethically chosen itself, he puts the matter quite straightforwardly:

> The person who has ethically chosen and found himself possesses himself in his entire concretion. . . . Here the objective for his activity is himself, but nevertheless not arbitrarily determined, even though it became his by his own choosing. But although he himself is his objective, this objective is nevertheless something else also, for the self that is the objective is not an abstract self that fits everywhere and therefore nowhere but is a concrete self in living interaction with these specific surroundings, these life conditions, this order of things.
>
> *The self that is the objective is not only a personal self but a social, a civic self.* (EO, II, 262) (Italics mine)

Speaking from his concrete situatedness as a married man, Judge William uses the relation of husband and wife to be in some manner exemplary of wider social and civic responsibilities and duties. The ethical existence-sphere does not simply mark out the requirements for a personal or individual ethic. The ethics at issue has to do, from bottom up, with a *social* ethics, in which aims and purposes, duties and obligations, in various and sundry ways inform the manner of existing and style of life that defines the ethical.

The existence-sphere of religion is usually considered to involve the most radical modulation within the interstices of the three spheres. This sphere is also the most important for the purposes of the current project of investigating whether religion might qualify as the fourth culture-sphere of modernity, and what role Kierkegaard might play in all this. At this juncture matters become complicated both because of Kierkegaard's distinction between religiousness A and religiousness B, and because of the evident slackness in the concept of "culture-spheres."

III. Religiousness A and Religiousness B

Our interpretation of the difference in the two forms of religiousness, A and B, yields the following two-fold thesis with regard to the matter at issue: 1) religiousness A can be understood to embody the fourth culture-sphere that has been glossed by the makers of modernity, and 2) religiousness B provides a critical principle and transcending perspective on the culture-spheres as culture-spheres, including religion as a culture-sphere along with those of science, morality, and art. The first task in the supporting of this two-fold thesis is that of discerning the line of demarcation between the two forms of religiousness.

Religiousness A is named in the *Postscript* by Climacus as the "religion of immanence." As the religion of immanence it is "the dialectic of inward deepening; it is the relation to an eternal happiness that is not conditioned by a something but is the dialectical inward deepening of the relation, consequently conditioned by the inward deepening, which is dialectical" (CUP 556). The measure that remains applicable here is directly related to the moral demands of inward self-actualization. Thus one speaks properly of religiousness A as a conjugated "ethico-religious sphere." As the religion of immanence, A still proceeds hand in glove with the project of the ethically existing subject in process of "becoming subjective" and appropriating "truth as subjectivity" through the turn toward inwardness. To be sure, in religiousness A there is already a God-relationship, but as Climacus points out this is a relationship within the dialectic of an inward appropriation. It is not, as we shall see is the case in religiousness B, a God-relationship which is initiated by God breaking into the region of immanence from the outside.

In laying out the defining features of religiousness A, we find that it does indeed qualify as a candidate for a fourth culture-sphere of modernity. As the religion of immanence it is a phenomenon within the cultural life of humankind, illustrating an inmixing not only with the ethical sphere but also with the aesthetic sphere.[7] Religiousness A can exist quite happily in paganism as well as in Christianity.[8] It is a religious consciousness that issues from a dialectic of inwardness that is able to express itself in a variety of religious forms, be they pagan or Christian, Buddhist or Islamic, Jewish or Hindu.

The feature of religiousness A that needs to be emphasized is that it moves within the bounds of moral consciousness and its requirement for choosing oneself—which Judge William already had defined as the stringent expression of the ethical. Hence, we do well to speak of a commerce between the ethical and the religious, of an ethico-religious existence sphere, somehow mediating ethics and religion. However, religiousness A cannot simply be reduced to the formative factors within the ethical sphere proper. Religiousness A is not simply morality with a touch of religious fervor. It displays a certain integrity as a distinct and irreducible culture-sphere.

Specifically, what religiousness A brings to the ethical situatedness of the existing subject in the process of becoming subjective is the determinant of guilt. Again, Climacus is quite explicit in making this point. "The totality of guilt-consciousness is the most upbuilding element in Religiousness A" (CUP 560). The ethically existing subject in its baptism into religiousness A becomes aware of its being-guilty, of a rather profound dis-relationship with itself as a social and civic self, of deep fissures and fractures within the immanental structures of its finitude. Proceeding in tandem with this guilt-consciousness is a problematization of the moral self-assurance in the ethical sphere; a recognition of the insufficiency of the subject's moral efforts towards rectifying its misdeeds; and a questioning of the power of the human will to do that which it ought.

Another feature of religiousness A has to do with its cultural predicates, including churches, parsonages, parsons, doctrines, rituals, ceremonies—indeed the whole gamut of institutionalized beliefs and practices that are the object of reference when one speaks of "Christianity," "Christendom," or the "Christian religion." That the Christian religion and the institutionalized church has played a role, and continues to play a role, in Western culture is clearly a sociological fact that needs to be recognized. Kierkegaard does indeed recognize this fact, even though he is of the mind that Christendom has gravitated into a situation of crises. This is, according to Kierkegaard, particularly the case in nineteenth century Denmark, where the preoccupation with externals by the Danish state church had virtually eclipsed the original mission of the early Christian community, making it exceedingly difficult, if not impossible, to become a Christian in Christendom.[9]

In sorting out and consolidating Kierkegaard's descriptions of religiousness A we thus come upon something like a culture-sphere, involving beliefs and practices that are given a cultural expression in their institutionalization and their effect upon a wider public. Although this cultural expression of religion, and specifically in the form of acculturated Christendom, is not judged as negatively as it was by Nietzsche (for whom the church was the veritable embodiment of the Antichrist), Kierkegaard never tired of harpooning the Christian establishment for its manifold shortcomings. The principal difference between Kierkegaard and Nietzsche on this point resides in the fact that whereas Nietzsche attacked religion, and specifically the Christian religion, from the "outside," Kierkegaard forges his attack from the "inside," striving desperately to become a Christian in Christendom—or indeed *in spite of* Christendom!

An explication of religiousness A as comprising, at least in one of its expressions, a culture-sphere, returns us to our earlier question about the place of Kant's *Religion within the Limits of Reason Alone* within the developments of modernity. Does not this work on religion by Kant secure a place for religion as a culture-sphere, along with the spheres of science, morality, and art? And to this we can now add another question: Does Kierkegaard's delineation of religiousness A exhibit sufficient similarities with Kant's definition of religion to endorse a more pronounced visibility of religion as a fourth culture-sphere in modernity?

That Kant recognized the efficacy of religion in the shaping of cultural configurations and trends can hardly be denied. Indeed, for Kant the significance of the Protestant Reformation consisted in its liberation of critical religious thought from the heteronomous constraints of an absolute church (as the French Revolution remained for Kant the quintessential symbol of the liberation of humankind from the fetters of an absolute state). Yet Kant like Kierkegaard, had reservations about organized religion in general and ecclesiastical institutions in particular. Kant, like Kierkegaard, inveighs against the trappings of clericalism that reduce religion to a form of fetish-worship.[10] Both Kant and Kierkegaard have a fine sense of the inherent tendencies in religion as a culture-sphere to lapse into clericalism and hollow ceremonialism.

There are, however, both for Kant and Kierkegaard, positive features that travel with a religion within the limits of reason and the cultural configuration of religiousness A. These features have to do with the definition of religion as immanental and closely allied with morality. Kierkegaard's characterization of religiousness A as the "religion of immanence" resonates with Kant's definition of "religion within the limits of reason alone." In both descriptions the God-relationship is seen as initiated from the side of the subject—Kierkegaard's existential subject appropriating the truth of the God-relationship within a dialectic of inwardness, and Kant's volitional subject striving to live in accordance with a moral law that is legislated from the interior of the moral self. Both Kierkegaard's religiousness A and Kant's religion within the bounds of reason see religion as linked with morality. Kierkegaard speaks of a conjugated "ethico-religious sphere" and Kant's project falls out as a program of "moral religion." Both emphasize the phenomenon of guilt, occasioned by a disrelationship of the self with itself (Kierkegaard) and by a will that has a "propensity to evil" (Kant).[11] Kant's religion within the limits of reason alone, like Kierkegaard's religiousness A, is basically a religion of immanence, proceeding from the inwardness of an intensified moral consciousness.

However, the crucial and most decisive move in Kierkegaard's economy of the existence-spheres is the transition from religiousness A to religiousness B. And it is at this juncture that the Kant-Kierkegaard connection becomes more tenuous.[12] Religiousness B punctuates the decisive moment in the life of the existence-spheres by marking out the advent of the incursion of the eternal into the temporal, the descent of the divine into the historical, disclosing the ground of edification in a source other than that of the self.

> In Religiousness B, the upbuilding is something outside the individual; the individual does not find the upbuilding by finding the relationship with God within himself, but relates himself to something outside himself to find the upbuilding. (CUP 561)

The decisiveness of religiousness B consists in the transmutation of the inwardness of religiousness A as the religion of immanence by reversing the vectors in the God-relationship. In religiousness A the movement is from self to God, finding God in the depths of the self. In religiousness B the movement is from God to the self. The relationship is initiated from the side of God, who deems it fit to become incarnate in time and history so as to effect an eternal happiness which even the most intensified inwardness could not achieve through its own efforts. In religiousness B the guilt-consciousness of religiousness A is refigured as sin-consciousness, as a disrelationship with God, the effects of which are so far-reaching that no amount of moral striving can bring about the needed restoration.

Peculiar to religiousness B are renewed stances of the existing subject with respect to time and to the other. The new temporality characterizing the sphere of religiousness B is that of time qualified by eternity, time as the kairotic moment for God's intervention within historical becoming. It is this paradox of "God in time," disclosing the decisive action from the side of God, becoming present on the scene of historical action, becoming incarnate in human form, that alone can provide an answer to the basic and underlying question posed by Climacus: "How can something historical become decisive for an eternal happiness?"

As time undergoes a transfiguration in religiousness B as a consequence of the impingement of eternity upon it, so also is the other seen in a new light. Not only is the neighbor someone who is nearby—co-sharing with me a social space in which our moral self-actualization in becoming subjective is to proceed—the neighbor from the perspective of religiousness B is the other with whom I share a common sin-consciousness, co-implicated in the travail of human suffering, and delivered through a free and forgiving act of God. Against this background of human suffering and redemptive grace, a transvalued morality is set into place. This is a transvalued morality because it is no longer the deontological ethics of duty espoused by Judge William in *Either/Or* nor is it a teleological ethics based on universal ends and norms. It is a morality transvalued in and through the "works of love."[13]

The role and function that religiousness B performs in Kierkegaard's doctrine of the existence-spheres is quintessential. Although religiousness A, as we have seen, delineates the space for religion as a culture-sphere situated alongside or in dialectical relation with ethics and aesthetics as complementing culture-spheres, religiousness B is, properly speaking, not a culture-sphere at all. Its function relative to the occurrent culture-spheres is that of reining in any propensities that a particular culture-sphere might have towards hegemony and totalization. It provides, if you will, a sheet-anchor against any idolatric claims on the part of science, morality, art, and religion. Implied here is a distinction between "a religion" and "being religious." Religion as "a religion," as a culture-sphere that assumes a particular social configuration—be it one that finds its center in a church, a synagogue, a mosque, or a Buddhist temple—is but one historically conditioned sphere of human endeavor among others. To be sure, all of these spheres of human endeavor display a certain integrity and intrinsic positivity and are to be heard. Even the voice of the aesthete makes a positive contribution toward cultural self-understanding. Things go awry only when the aesthete absolutizes the aesthetic way of existing in the world and voices a claim for its ultimacy.

Things are no different for religion as a culture-sphere, as a religion of immanence taking on a cultural form, as a manifestation of religiousness A. If a particular religion, or a particular sect within a religion, makes a claim for ultimacy and absoluteness, we have idolatry of the most pernicious kind. A religion unable to recognize its social origins and historical contingencies is destined to make of itself an idol. It is religiousness B, which is a matter of *being religious* rather than adhering to the doctrines and practices of a particular religion, that provides the measure against the recurring idolatric tendencies across the spectrum of culture-spheres. And it is important to remember that just as science, morality, and art are able to make hegemonic claims for ultimacy, so can an established religion. It is thus that religiousness B can be understood as a "critical principle," a principle of protest against the absolutizing of any sector of the cultural accomplishments of the human race.

IV. Rescripting the Map of Modernity

We are now in position to consolidate our observations of the preceding sections and conclude with some general remarks about the Kierkegaard-effect in the shaping of the discourse of modernity, and particularly as the effect relates to the culture-sphere problematic.

Through a cross-reading of Kant's *Religion within the Limits of Reason Alone* and certain texts of Kierkegaard we have found that in these two representatives of modernity there is indeed a recognition of the role of religion in the shaping of the consciousness and culture of the modern age. Taking our cues from the contributions of Kant and Kierkegaard, we suggested including religion as a fourth culture-sphere of modernity. This would entail at least an emendation, if indeed not a more critical revision, of the generally accepted Weberian/Habermasian three culture-sphere theory of modernity.

To tell the story of modern culture without an acknowledgement of the social effects of religious movements and organizations would be as myopic as rehearsing the narrative of medieval culture without reference to the role of popes and princes in the struggles of church and state, each vying for ascendancy. Whatever judgment one might render of the positive and negative consequences of religious institutions in the history of medieval and modern culture is of course another matter, but to fail to recognize the profound impact of religion on the wider social fabric of cultures past and present is to leave out that which is very much a part of the story.[14] Kierkegaard and Kant had shown, each in their own way, how religion might well qualify as a fourth culture-sphere in modernity.

However, what we found to be of even greater consequence was Kierkegaard's understanding of religiousness B as a critical principle, as a principle of protest, protesting the self-elevation of any one of the culture-spheres to a status of ultimacy. Religiousness B comprises the vertical dimension of transcendence that stands in judgment of the horizontal succession of immanent culture-spheres. In the language of Paul Tillich (whose debt to Kierkegaard was considerable), religiousness B points to the "dimension of depth," to the religious as the state of being ultimately concerned, which Tillich distinguishes from the horizontal dimension of historical becoming, on which religion as a cultural form, as a set of beliefs and institutions, is one content of culture among others. It is this dimension of depth that at once informs the variegated cultural contents with meaning and stands in judgment of any absolutizing and infinitizing of their relative and finite status.[15] It is thus that the space of Kierkegaard's religiousness B, like that of Tillich's dimension of depth, provides a standpoint for rigorous cultural critique, which Kierkegaard carried through with consummate skill in *The Present Age* and *The Attack on Christendom*. From all this there emerges the portrait of Kierkegaard as a critic of culture, and what distinguished him from other religiously oriented critics of his day was his clear perception that the critical principle that issues from religiousness B needs to be used against religion itself.[16]

Our investigations of Kant and Kierkegaard on the role and cultural status of religion provide a context for assessing Habermas's take on religion in his two-volume *The Theory of Communicative Action*. In volume one Habermas approaches the phenomenon of religion in connection with his discussion of the world of myth and the trappings of magic in primitive society, with the intention of demonstrating the role played by religion in the rationalization process within Western culture specifically and world cultures more generally. Religion subject to the process of rationalization is progressively demythologized, releasing its potential for a rational comprehension of the world. Making significant purchases on the modern progressivistic theory of history, Habermas sees this process of rationalization of religious world views moving toward an enlightenment in which the discourse of religion undergoes a demythologization and is taken up into a "communicative rationality" that binds the culture-spheres of science, morality, and art.[17]

In volume two of *The Theory of Communicative Action* this process of demythologization of religion is supplemented with an account of the *linguistification* of religion, whereby religion works out its potential for rational discourse. Using Durkheim's sociological account of religion as a point of departure, Habermas proceeds to interpret the socially integrative function of religion through the adventures of the linguistic turn in late modernity. The rituals, ceremonies, symbols, and myths, which according to Habermas allowed only an expressive function for the religious consciousness, pass over into the rationality of communicative action, whereby "the authority of the holy is gradually replaced by the authority of an achieved consensus."[18] Through this linguistification of the sacred and the holy "the rationality potential in communicative action" is released, and "the aura of rapture and terror that emanates from the sacred, the *spellbinding* power of the holy, is sublimated into the *binding/bonding* force of criticizable validity claims."[19]

What this all amounts to is a somewhat facile reduction not only of religious beliefs and practices but the experience of the holy to a state of pre-rational communicative action. For Habermas the function of myth and symbol remains restricted to a pre-rational lifeworld. This denigration of the power of myth and symbol may well comprise the most serious problem in Habermas's linguistic turn. Myth and symbol, which basically comprise the "language" of religion, are prejudged as feeble, pre-scientific, and pre-rational efforts toward an understanding of the world. The linguistic demythologization of these pre-scientific religious myths proceeds in such a manner as to coordinate the three culture-spheres with three forms of speech acts and three forms of validity claims. The culture-sphere of science makes use of constative speech wherewith to validate the "truth" of propositions; the culture-sphere of morality has the franchise for regulative speech acts through which the "rightness" of norms is validated; and the culture-sphere of art works with expressive speech acts to convey the "truthfulness" of self-disclosure. For language to count and be accountable, for discourse to be genuine discourse about something, for speech to be a proper vehicle for conveying truth, rightness, and truthfulness, speakers need to be girded with the armor of argumentation, and the meaning of what speakers say is determined by the three-fold grid of validity claims.

Within such a scheme of things it is not all that difficult to see why for Habermas religion can have no indigenous space and no distinctive grammar. Religion, ensconced in myth, is at best an embryonic communicative action waiting to be born, a pre-cognitive understanding of the world waiting to be pruned of its mythic and symbolic trappings. As a potential culture-sphere, religion ends up falling somewhere between morality and art. The salvageable ethical features of religion become rationalized and find their proper residence in the culture-sphere of morality. The uses of myth, symbol, and metaphor in the history of religion (and elsewhere) become linguistified as ornamentations for the expression of the aesthetical and fall into the culture-sphere of art. Falling between the two chairs of morality and art, it is difficult to discern what positive role religion and the religious play for Habermas. Indeed, it would appear that when all the dust has settled, the force of the better argument takes the place of the power of the Divine Will and consensus stands in as a secularized version of the Kingdom of God.

Given Habermas's enchantment with the ordinary language approach and speech act theory, as proposed principally by J. L. Austin and John Searle, it is somewhat puzzling that he overlooked the resources in this tradition for an analysis of the economy of religious language, irreducible to the language of science, morality, and art.[20] Such a perspective on language use would allow the installation of religious language as appropriate currency in talk about religion both as a culture-sphere and as a quality of being religious.

We have seen how Kierkegaard's distinction between religiousness A and religiousness B does both of the above, i.e., it enables a recognition of religion as a component within the cultural life of humankind, and as an existential quality of being religious in responding to a transcending alterity, against which all immanent culture-spheres are measured. It is in this distinction that the Kierkegaard-effect in the shaping of the contours of modernity principally resides. The effect finds a place for a *fourth* culture-sphere, reminiscent at least in part of Kant's definition of religion within the limits of reason alone. More importantly, however, the Kierkegaard-effect of religiousness B opens to a vision beyond the religion of immanence (religiousness A), and all other immanent culture-spheres. The function that religiousness B performs, relative to the status of the demarcated culture spheres, is that it supplies the critical principle that relativizes the culture-spheres and protests any claims for ultimacy that might at different times and in different ways be voiced by each.

Notes

1. Habermas, *The Philosophical Discourse of Modernity*, pp. 40 and 74.
2. Rorty, "Habermas and Lyotard on Postmodernity," p. 167.
3. Evans, *Kierkegaard's "Fragments" and "Postscript."*
4. For a detailed examination of Heidegger's ontologization of Kierkegaard's elucidation of concrete existence and his doctrine of truth as subjectivity, see Schrag, *Existence and Freedom.*
5. For a helpful discussion of the role of the other in the life of the aesthete, see Dunning, *Kierkegaard's Dialectic of Inwardness*, p. 180.
6. There are numerous references to Aristotle in Kierkegaard's writings. In *Either/Or* Aristotle is credited with basing the concept of justice upon the idea of friendship, which Judge William finds to be more satisfactory than basing justice upon duty. Having studied Aristotle's ethics, Kierkegaard surely came upon Aristotle's notion of *kairos* as qualitative or ethical time, the right or appropriate time, distinct from the quantitative time of chronological succession. Kierkegaard clearly saw the relevance of the notion of *kairos* for fleshing out both the ethical and religious existence-spheres.
7. Climacus makes this point quite dramatically when he portrays religious consciousness as "at times a jumbled, noisy pathos of all sorts, esthetics, ethics, Religiousness A, and Christianity" (CUP 555).
8. "Religiousness A can be present in paganism, and in Christianity it can be the religiousness of everyone who is not decisively Christian, whether baptized or not" (CUP 557).
9. "Christendom is a prodigious illusion," writes Kierkegaard in *Point of View*, producing that ironical state of affairs in which everybody has a claim to being a Christian. "Yet all these people, even those who assert that no God exists, are all of them Christians, call

themselves Christians, are recognized as Christians by the State, are buried as Christians by the Church, are certified as Christians for eternity!" (PV 22–23). See also KAUC, particularly pp. 29–32: "The religious situation."

10. "*Clericalism*, therefore, is the constitution of a church to the extent to which a *fetish-worship* dominates it; and this condition is always found wherever, instead of principles of morality, statutory commands, rules of faith, and observances constitute the basis and the essence of the church," Kant, *Religion within the Limits of Reason Alone*, pp. 167–68.

11. Kant, *Religion*, pp. 23–27.

12. Green in his book, *Kant and Kierkegaard: The Hidden Debt*, has argued the rather bold thesis that Kierkegaard was essentially a Kantian who, for a variety of reasons, made a particular effort to conceal his indebtedness to the Königsberg philosopher. Whether one agrees or disagrees with Green's basic argument, and I for one find it to be somewhat overextended, it needs to be noted that he has made an important contribution to Kierkegaard-scholarship by calling our attention to some rather remarkable similarities in the texts of the two thinkers. Unfortunately, he tends to gloss the pivotal role played by religiousness B, which sets forth one of the more important differences between Kierkegaard and Kant.

13. For Kierkegaard's most direct communication of his transvalued morality, see his WL. In this volume Kierkegaard carries through a detailed exegesis of the Biblical injunction "Love thy neighbor as thyself," showing how the love of one's neighbor is quite commensurate with a proper regard for oneself. In the love relationship both self and other are enriched, against the backdrop of God's unconditional love for both. Kierkegaard's detailing of the requirement to suspend the ethical, framed in terms of universal teleological norms, so as to set forth the particularity of the God relationship that first makes an ethic of love possible is found in FT. For a discussion of the problem of the relation of religious faith and ethics in Kierkegaard's existential reading of the Biblical saga of the intended sacrifice of Isaac by Abraham, see Schrag, "Note on Kierkegaard's Teleological Suspension of the Ethical."

14. Troeltsch's two-volume work, *The Social Teaching of the Christian Churches*, remains one of the classic treatments of the relation of the Christian religion to society from its earliest beginnings into the twentieth century.

15. See Tillich, "The Lost Dimension in Religion." In this essay, Tillich puts matters as follows: "I suggest that we call the dimension of depth the religious dimension in man's nature. Being religious means asking passionately the question of the meaning of our existence and being willing to receive answers, even if the answers hurt. Such an idea of religion makes religion universally human, but it certainly differs from what is usually called religion. It does not describe religion as the belief in the existence of gods or one God, and as a set of activities and institutions for the sake of relating oneself to these beings in thought, devotion and obedience," p. 42.

16. Kierkegaard's understanding of religiousness B as a platform for cultural critique is reminiscent of the self-understanding displayed by the eighth-century prophets of ancient Israel in their condemnations of an abstract ceremonialism that had made its way into the popular religion of the day. One is reminded particularly of the memorable denunciation by the prophet Amos: "I hate, I despise your feasts. . . . I will not accept your burnt-offerings . . . take away the noise of your songs. . . . And let justice roll down like waters, and righteousness like a mighty stream" (5:21–24). This link with the ancient prophets should encourage a reading of Kierkegaard against the backdrop of the tradition of "prophetic religion," which sought out idols in the most unsuspecting places. Unlike the tradition of "priestly religion," which was conservative and intent on preserving the status quo, "prophetic religion" was revolutionary in character, intent on addressing the need for social justice to correct the sundry ills and misconceptions that made their way into occurrent beliefs and practices.

As the prophetic principle of protest against idolatric tendencies and social evils was effectively used by the ancient prophets, so also it became an effective instrument in the Protestant movement of the sixteenth century, in which the principle was levied against the Medieval church and its claims for ultimacy and absoluteness on matters of faith and morals. However, this principle of protest, such a central feature of prophetic religion, had to be reactivated when the developing orthodoxy in Protestantism failed to use the principle against itself and proceeded to absolutize its doctrinal and creedal formulations. It may well be that the most durable contribution of Kierkegaard on the religion and culture issue is his recovery of the prophetic and protestant principle as the basis for any viable critique of the modern age.

17. Habermas, *The Theory of Communicative Action*, volume 1. See particularly chapter 2 of part I: "Some Characteristics of the Mythical and the Modern Ways of Understanding the World," and chapter 2 of part II: "The Disenchantment of Religious-Metaphysical Worldviews and the Emergence of the Modern Structures of Consciousness."

18. Ibid., volume II, p. 77.

19. Ibid.

20. It is basically such an analysis that informs Ian T. Ramsey's provocative and insightful work, *Religious Language: An Empirical Placing of Theological Phrases.*

2 | Sartre's Debts to Kierkegaard
A Partial Reckoning
William L. McBride

F ROM APRIL 21 to 23, 1964, UNESCO sponsored a Kierkegaard colloquium in Paris. The theme was "Kierkegaard Vivant," and Sartre was the first of the main speakers.[1] The paper that he presented on that occasion, "L'Universel singulier," is of a genre—a scholarly philosophical "*communication*" presented as one of several colloquium papers—that is relatively rare among Sartre's publications. Rare, too, is the level of appreciation that Sartre conveys, in this talk, for an individual with whose thought he is, on the surface, in such profound disagreement—and in fact in disagreement on the very issue that, for Kierkegaard, ultimately meant everything, the issue of Christian faith. Of course, as we shall see, there is an important sense in which Sartre appropriates Kierkegaard for his own purposes; but such a move, I would argue, along with Sartre, is an inevitability: the present volume is filled with such appropriations, for that is just the way in which the life of the mind is carried on. A careful reading of "L'Universel singulier," involving the examination of many themes in, and additional texts of, Kierkegaard, Sartre, Merleau-Ponty, and others, would easily fill a monograph. I shall pick out only a few themes, not all of them drawn from the text in question, by way of illustrating Sartre's deep indebtedness to Kierkegaard—and ours. (In choosing the language of "indebtedness," I am indirectly acknowledging the different but equally eccentric attitudes towards *money* that characterized both writers.)

A quick perusal of some popular and philosophical literature from the period of existentialism's first becoming widely identified as a distinctive way of thinking, the mid-1940s, recalls many of the claims and counterclaims about the Sartre/Kierkegaard connection (or disconnection, depending on the claimant) that became familiar and exciting to me in my undergraduate and graduate student days between one and two decades later. It is clear, from a number of references, that Jean Wahl (whose *Etudes Kierkegaardiennes* had been published in 1938) played a salient role in France in delineating the contours of this "movement" and naming its alleged stars—Kierkegaard, Nietzsche, Heidegger, and Sartre above all, with important but somewhat subordinate roles being played by Merleau-Ponty, de Beauvoir, Jaspers, and a few others, including the very obscure (but in fact historically quite significant) French contemporary of Kierkegaard, Jules Lequier, and the "ancestor," Pascal. Wahl even contributed a summary article, entitled "Existentialism: A Preface," to the *New Republic* in fall 1945.[2] (This could not have been very long after Sartre and de Beauvoir had learned, for the first time, that the label "existentialist" was being applied to them and had decided, after strong initial reluctance, to accept it.) In this early literature, then, we already find discussions of the existentialist tendency to introduce philosophy into literature and thus to bring these two genres or disciplines together; of the "concept" of dread (a rather ironic use of the word "concept" as Sartre, citing Wahl, points out); of freedom; and of a number of related points on which resemblances between Kierkegaard and Sartre are patent. We also find the obvious distinction being drawn between religious and atheistic existentialism, and we find early polemics, based of course on the then-extant work of Sartre, and in particular on *Being and Nothingness*, objecting to any attempt to yoke the memory of Kierkegaard, the supreme moralist and despiser of philosophical systems, with the a- or immoralist ontologist that Sartre appeared to be. Among the most vehement polemicists was the great Kierkegaard scholar Walter Lowrie, who claimed that Sartre was certainly nothing like Kierkegaard and pronounced himself offended at having had to read parts of Sartre's writings;[3] Robert D. Cumming came to Sartre's defense while expressing regret at Lowrie's remarks.[4]

Sartre's thought evolved a great deal over the decades, a phenomenon that is, of course, also observable over Kierkegaard's regrettably much shorter lifespan. "L'Universel singulier" was presented much closer to the end than to the beginning of the active part of Sartre's career and life, at a time when he was still attempting very hard to work out the relationship between his own thinking, for which he no longer hesitated to accept the label "existentialist" from those who insisted on applying labels, and Marxism.[5] That the influence of Kierkegaard on Sartre's earlier formation, and hence on existentialism as a whole, was capital is a commonplace that strikes me as not in need of demonstration at this juncture. The themes that I shall discuss here, then, all of them having important implications for present-day discussions as well as for discussions of the 1960s, are on the whole not those that were highlighted in the 1940s—or at least now appear in a somewhat different guise. They are: transcendence and history, ethics and politics, and seduction and feminist thought.

A. Transcendence and History

I have chosen the word "transcendence" here to refer, open-endedly, to that dimension (of what? of "reality"? of "existence"? of "life"?—all philosophically problematic terms, among which there is no need to make a selection for the moment) that is other than, different from, beyond, the immediate empirical, positivistically enumerable data. It was a word used both by Kierkegaard, though not to excess,[6] and by Sartre, though decreasingly in his later writings. Simone de Beauvoir made the paired contrast terms, transcendence/immanence, central to her theoretical framework in *The Second Sex* (by way of contrasting the social roles historically assigned to men versus women), a work of which, for its philosophical bases, she over-generously attributed the inspiration to Sartre (and to Hegel), notoriously underestimating her own originality—including the originality of her peculiar, but not unfruitful, use of the notion of transcendence. "Transcendence" appears, *inter alia*, in the title of Sartre's very early essay, *The Transcendence of the Ego*. A brief reflection on the significance of this opens up some fundamental perspectives on the contours of mainstream twentieth century Continental European philosophy.

This Sartrean essay is above all a critical dialogue, from start to finish, with the thinker whose primarily methodological insights so profoundly influenced Heidegger, Sartre, Merleau-Ponty, and, in short, at least two generations of philosophers, Edmund Husserl. At the end of *The Transcendence of the Ego*, the basic purpose of which is to argue that the individual "ego" or "self" is a *construct* of human consciousness rather than a primordial reality of (any particular) consciousness as such—and hence that this constructed ego is "transcendent" to ongoing existential human reality—Sartre deplores the philosophical and even political implications of Husserl's assertion of the need for a "transcendental ego," a central concept in the latter's later thought. Just how did the notion of transcendence function for Husserl? Although I admit that the following is something of an oversimplification, I find it useful for present purposes to quote at length from Herbert Spiegelberg's classic history of *The Phenomenological Movement*:

> The title "transcendental," of which Husserl grew increasingly fond and which clearly indicated his growing identification with Kant, is nevertheless rarely explained and is only in part identical with any of its traditional meanings. In the *Ideen* the implication seems to be that what is transcendental about phenomenology is that it suspends (*ausschalten*) all transcendental claims (i.e., assertions about reality other than that of consciousness itself). The fullest explicit discussion of the term occurs in Husserl's last publication, the *"Crisis of the European Sciences and Transcendental Phenomenology."* Here, he wants to assign it a wider meaning . . . according to which a transcendental philosophy "reaches back to . . . the ultimate source of knowledge," with the implication that this source is to be found in the ego. In other words, it expresses Husserl's commitment to a radical subjectivism for which subjectivity is the source of all objectivities. . . . [7]

One way—it is only one way among many possible ways, but that is in keeping with the profoundest tendencies of contemporary thought—of recounting the story of the later intellectual developments of so many philosophers who had been strongly influenced by Husserl in their early years is to focus on the tension between this radically subjective point of departure and the felt need to escape from its a priori constraints toward a transcendence of one sort or another—toward a "real" transcendence rather than the pseudo-transcendence of the "transcendental ego." Heidegger's *Sein*, both in its early incarnations, still heavily ontological in orientation, and in the wilder forms of his later years; Merleau-Ponty's efforts at rediscovering what envelops us, beyond individual subjectivities, through such devices as the expression "the flesh of the world" that dominates his last, unfinished work; Jaspers's more straightforward though vague allusions to *Tranzendenz*; and, yes, Sartre's groping efforts at reconceiving history as ongoing "totalization" rather than as a "totality" that could allegedly be grasped in what Merleau-Ponty pejoratively denominated a *"pensée de survol"* can all be seen as expressions of this felt need to escape the Husserlian cage of "radical subjectivism." Husserl had left the impression, as Descartes had done centuries before him, that the site of this cage as starting-point for reflection was apodictic. In fact it was not, nor was the descriptive/explanatory reasoning employed to try to establish this supposed apodicticity by any means irrefutable. But it was difficult for those who had been attracted, as Sartre had been, to Husserlian phenomenology because of its ability to lead philosophy away from the predominantly abstract idealist atmosphere of the early twentieth century "towards the concrete,"[8] fully to acknowledge this.

And so there emerged the hybrid—a term that I am not intending pejoratively, but only by way of indicating its unacceptability to purists of all stripes—known as "existential phenomenology." Or, if one prefers, "phenomenological existentialism." What was its relationship with the ur-existentialism of Søren Kierkegaard (who, however, as Lowrie and many others have quite rightly pointed out, never once in his life, whether on paper or, to the best of our limited knowledge, even to himself said "I am an existentialist")? On the surface, a relationship of great similarity: what Western thinker ever surpassed Kierkegaard in stressing the importance of *the subject*? Yet all of Kierkegaard's efforts at compelling his readers to reflect profoundly on subjectivity would from his point of view have been vain, even monstrous, if they had had the effect, comparable to that of Husserlian phenomenology, of blocking in advance all access to what I have called transcendence. On the contrary, of course: for Kierkegaard, it was from the standpoint of the individual subject, and *only* from that standpoint, that the leap to the Absolute, to absolute transcendence, became a possibility.

Why, then, would this way of thinking have seemed so attractive to the later Sartre, the Sartre of 1964? After all, the writer of *Being and Nothingness* had made clear his own atheism and had used, if I may be permitted some slight exaggeration, the bastardized version of Husserlian methodology employed in that work as a sort of cocoon to guarantee or even "prove," with a bravado air of certainty, the *im*possibility of an "In-Itself-For-Itself"—a really existing, conscious, but un-self-questioning Being, *quod omnes Deum nominant.* In his autobiography, begun some years earlier but published in the same year as that of his UNESCO paper on Kierkegaard, Sartre famously recounts that he had easily concluded one morning, as a student waiting for some class-mates on the way to high school and deciding to think about the topic as a means of whiling away the time, that God does not exist.[9] But, he goes on more significantly to say, many of the trappings of religious belief remained with him for years and gave him the sense of grandeur and self-importance as *"l'élu du doute"* (the Elect of doubt) that one can discern in his novel, *Nausea,* and in such passages of *Being and Nothingness* as the brief "proof" of God's non-existence to which I have just alluded. In fact, he claims eventually to have learned, "Atheism is a cruel and marathon undertaking; I think I have seen it through to the end."[10] Thus it is clear that Sartre remained a self-avowed athe-ist throughout the numerous stages of his intellectual evolution, and indeed at several points in "L'Universel singulier" he reaffirms his distance from Kier-kegaard on this issue of religious belief. Why, then, to repeat, is his general evaluation of Kierkegaard so favorable?

The answer to this turns on the expression employed in Sartre's title, the singular universal. "Kierkegaard," he says by way of concluding a lengthy paragraph of more than four pages which begins with the words "We are all Adam" and traverses the domains of history and psychoanalysis, Marxism, Hegelianism, and Christianity, "was perhaps the first to have shown that the universal enters History as singular, to the extent to which the singular estab-lishes itself there as universal."[11] Sartre is here attributing to Kierkegaard what is perhaps the single most important new theme or set of themes, by compari-son with the philosophical climate of *Being and Nothingness,* of his own major later works: his two-volume *Critique of Dialectical Reason,* along with its in-troductory essay, *Search for a Method* (first published in spring 1957 in Polish as *Marksizm i Egzystencjalizm*), in which Kierkegaard is featured quite promi-nently, and his three-volume incomplete masterpiece of the 1970s concerning the singular universal that was Gustave Flaubert, *The Family Idiot.* The "his-torical" moments that most concerned Kierkegaard, the appearance of Adam and the Incarnation that are central to Christian theology, were of course not those that usually interested Sartre the most. But he saw in Kierkegaard's ap-proach to the paradoxes surrounding the role played by the individual in his-torical time—the treatment of the phenomenon which was so badly, even ludi-crously, botched by Plekhanov within the Marxist tradition,[12] for example—a road to insight that had not been achieved by either of the other great nine-teenth-century philosophers of history, Hegel or Marx himself. And in the es-say on the singular universal Sartre applies these insights above all to the individual, Søren Kierkegaard himself, the mid-nineteenth century Dane with all the well-known limitations, accidents, and hang-ups of his personal life, who nevertheless incarnated and expressed universal,[13] transcendent themes. As he says,

> The paradox, for [Kierkegaard], is that we discover the absolute in the relative. A Dane, son of a Dane, born at the beginning of the last century, conditioned by Danish culture and History, he discovers Danes who are his contemporaries, formed by the same History, by the same cultural traditions. In addition, he can at the same time *think about* the historical circumstances and traditions that have produced them and that have produced him himself.[14]

In fact, along the way in this remarkable essay Sartre attributes to Kierkegaard nothing less than a whole new way of thinking, taking as its starting-point the concrete individual at birth;[15] this way of thinking permits us as persons reflecting on the historical past to be *contemporaneous* even with Adam, for example,[16] and asserts that "all knowledge (*savoir*) concerning the subjective is in a certain sense a false knowledge,"[17] since the starting-point of thought, lived experience (*le vécu*), occurs as *non-savoir*. Sartre stresses the importance of trying to understand Kierkegaard, despite the virtual impossibility of the task, as he must have understood himself—as a Christian, in his surroundings, with the burning awareness of his father's blasphemy. By contrast, Sartre casts suspicion on those contemporaries of Kierkegaard's who claimed to have become unbelievers and who in fact ended up holding "a Christian *pseudo-atheism*."[18] If Sartre has any reproach to make to Kierkegaard in this essay, it is not his religious faith but rather his "neglect of the *praxis* that is rationality."[19] Sartre gently attributes this failure to Kierkegaard's felt need to concentrate on defending the reality of human contingency against the hegemony of Hegelian philosophy.

"Is there," we may ask about Sartre's thinking about Kierkegaard as Sartre asks about Kierkegaard's reflections on the historical circumstances and traditions (referred to in the longer citation above) that had produced him, "deviation or appropriation?"[20] And we may answer as Sartre does, "Both." Of course, Kierkegaard would have been astonished by some aspects of Sartre's interpretation of his ideas, though not at all by others. The same can be said, however, about Kierkegaard's probable reactions to virtually all of his interpreters. What is important from the standpoint of the evolution of twentieth-century thought, however, is the sense in which this later Sartrean reappropriation of Kierkegaard reinforced Sartre's own strong qualms, which he had held even during the years of his closest affiliation with Marxism, about the claims of "orthodox" Marxism, and of all other philosophical orthodoxies for that matter, to *knowledge* (*savoir*) about the nature of history;[21] caused him, in a way that clearly anticipated major tendencies of postmodernism,[22] to give up on whatever faith he might still have held during his early years in the viability of a closed ontological system (however deviant in type from the great systems of the past his own in *Being and Nothingness* was); *and*, to return to the beginning of our discussion, allowed his thought to break out of the closed circle imposed by Husserlian phenomenological methodology, toward *something like* transcendence. In Sartre's own words:

> In each of us he gives himself and refuses himself, as he did during his lifetime; he is my own adventure and remains, for others, Kierkegaard, the Other, at the horizon, witness for that Christian that faith is a becoming which is always at risk, witness for me that the process of *becoming-atheist* is a long, difficult undertaking, an absolute relationship between two absolutes, man and the universe.[23]

Note should be taken of the resemblance between Sartre's references to his own atheism here and in his autobiography, previously cited. Here, however, the emphasis is different, decidedly metaphysical in the broad sense in which Kierkegaard, too, is a strongly metaphysical thinker—that is, someone who entertains the possibility of absolutes, transcendences, beyond all experienced horizons, and who, moreover, ventures beyond the entertainment of their mere possibility to generate a personal faith in their existence. No one can doubt for a moment, of course, that the names of Kierkegaard's and Sartre's respective absolutes, along with the thinking and cultures that produced them, are radically different; but it is interesting and important to observe their affinities and intersections, which have been felt though not often articulated by religious and non-religious thinkers alike. (It is revealing, for example, to consider the large number of Sartre scholars with significant present or former religious commitments.)

Some sense of these affinities was already captured in a lecture given in November 1961, well before Sartre composed "L'Universel singulier," by the late John Wild, whose importance in developing interest in existentialist thinking in the United States was comparable to that of Jean Wahl (roughly two decades earlier) in France. Wild, summarizing earlier lectures in the same series given by William Earle (on Kierkegaard, Nietzsche, and Sartre) and James Edie, and prophesying a certain "rebirth of the divine" in future Western thought, begins by declaring traditional dogmatic Christian approaches to be dead and then turns to "three interpretations of transcendence." The first, a kind of caricature (by implication, not by name) of Sartre's early philosophy, according to which "there is no transcendence, or absolute, of any kind,"[24] and the second, which Wild calls "immanentism" and associates with Hegel, among others, are then examined and found lacking by him. Finally, he turns to a third way of understanding transcendence, strange and unfamiliar and therefore not to be named, with the following Wildian formulation of which neither Kierkegaard nor Sartre would, I believe, have altogether concurred, but which captures important elements of the intellectual connections that I have been attempting to bring out in this section:

> According to this way of understanding, there is something radically tran-scending us and separated from us, which is nevertheless both present in and absent from our history. When present, however, it never merges with man but rather maintains a certain distance. From this distance, it may excite men and lure them on to acts of self-transcendence without interfering with their freedom and responsibility, nay, rather eliciting and strengthening these, if man will listen to the call. But whether he listens or not, it is up to him, for he is responsible.[25]

B. Ethics and Politics

For reasons that John Wild gives very clearly at the conclusion of the above citation, it is essential to make reference to ethics and politics in considering Sartre's debts to Kierkegaard. Both Kierkegaard and Sartre placed the strongest emphasis on human freedom and individual responsibility as the starting point for their ethical reflections, reflections which are of utmost concern to both of them as thinkers, though their respective contexts and conclusions are of course very different. As for political thinking, which became increasingly pre-dominant in the last years of Sartre's life, whereas its comparative absence from Kierkegaard's writings and activities was, as I have noted, the object of Sartre's one major criticism of him in "L'Universel singulier"—well, more of that anon.

We no longer need merely to speculate about possible ways in which Kier-kegaard's influence on Sartre's thinking about "dreadful freedom" may have been exerted. Since the posthumous publication, ten years ago, of extant por-tions of Sartre's extensive *War Diaries*, one very salient route of this influence is beyond dispute: he was carefully reading and making notes, including direct line-by-line citations, on *The Concept of Anxiety* during his posting near the front at Morsbronn in December 1939. In this part of his diaries he observes the degree of borrowing, such as the precise phrase "to be in dread of noth-ing," that Heidegger had made of Kierkegaard, reflects on the difference of meaning that "nothing" here has for the two of them, and engages in further musings that anyone familiar with *Being and Nothingness* can see as leading toward the central insights of that work.[26] Simone de Beauvoir was also famil-iar with *The Concept of Anxiety* (she was also, in fact, the source of much of Sartre's reading material during this so-called "phony war" ["*drôle de guerre*"] period), and it is clear from his references to Adam in his essay of a quarter-century later that that book remained a principal referent in Sartre's understanding of Kierkegaardian thought.

The category that runs like a red thread through *The Concept of Anxiety* is, to be sure, sin—though not, Kierkegaard makes quite clear particularly at the end of the book, sin as understood by "dogmatics," or moral theology, but rather sin as a psychologically operative phenomenon. Given this, and given the correlative fact that Kierkegaard conceives the highest possible dialectical conception of sin within this sphere to be *guilt* (CA 103–10), how are we to understand the great attraction of this work for Sartre, since he did not accept the concept either of sin or of guilt as its correlative, and in fact from all the evidence seldom experienced any of those deep feelings of guilt that obviously reigned over Kierkegaard's psyche throughout his adult life?[27] (Is it mere accident that the single strongest exception to this generalization of which I am aware occurred some two months after Sartre's careful study of *The Concept of Anxiety*, when he engaged, while on leave back in Paris, in behavior with two women, including a thoroughly dishonest repudiation of Simone de Beauvoir, which he soon came deeply to repent?[28]) The answer, very schematically put and without the benefit of the sort of extended psychological speculation that would be needed to complete the picture, is that Sartre more or less discounted the religious or proto-religious aspects of Kierkegaard's analysis, attributing them at first vaguely, and then eventually (as, for example, in the 1964 essay) more explicitly, to the author's historical time and place, while recognizing the great worth and validity of the descriptions of anxiety themselves and of the implications that they hold for the notion of moral responsibility.

In Sartre's defense with respect to this appropriation of Kierkegaard's thought, I must confess never to have been satisfied with Kierkegaard's fundamental assertion that the content of *The Concept of Anxiety* remains in the sphere of psychology and thus pre-dogmatic or (as I have just expressed it) proto-religious; the assertion strikes me as disingenuous, given the book's content. In fact, Kierkegaard throughout this work makes use of the previous, complex historical appropriation, by a succession of Christian churches, of a term, ἁμάρτημα, that in classical Greek carried something closer to the connotations of "fault" or "flaw" than those of "sin" in more modern language. That Kierkegaard, well trained as he was in ancient Greek literature, was aware of this is shown by his numerous observations concerning the "inferiority" of that culture with respect to the concepts of sin and guilt, as well as by the disparaging remark that he makes at one point (CA 26) concerning the Greek Orthodox Church's term for "original sin"—ἁμάρτημα πρωτοπατορικόν (first-fatherly sin)[29]—by comparison with the much more refined concept of it to be found in "the profound Protestant piety." If, then, we put into question the claim to universal conceptual validity that is implied at least by the *style* of *The Concept of Anxiety*—one of the most easily assimilable to mainstream traditional philosophy (with its penchant for making such claims) of all of Kierkegaard's works despite its Christian theological trappings—and recognize just how historically specific it is in its details, then we may be led to respect the singularity of both Kierkegaard *and* Sartre with respect to their respective treatments of the universal problem/phenomenon of ethics. We may also find it easier to locate their affinities.

Neither Kierkegaard nor Sartre was satisfied with autonomous ethical systems, of which Kant's philosophy serves for both as a sort of archetype. Both Kierkegaard and Sartre were, to be sure, attracted or rather tempted by the spirit of Kantianism in ethics. Commentators have rightly found strong Kantian elements in Judge William's position in volume II of *Either/Or* and in his "Reflections on Marriage" in *Stages on Life's Way*,[30] as well as in Sartre's famous short lecture/essay, "Existentialism Is a Humanism." But both thinkers felt a fruitful ambivalence toward the whole idea of ethics as understood by philosophical orthodoxy.

Kierkegaard, despite his strong personal eccentricities, took on the whole a fairly conventional attitude, in practice, towards moral conduct; it is only because this was so that, given the important status of marriage engagements in his society, his decision to effect a rupture of his engagement with Regina Olsen caused him such infinite self-questioning as we find, for example, in the "Guilty? Not Guilty?" section of the *Stages*, as well as in his diaries and elsewhere. An important part, though ultimately not the dominant one, of his own personality *was* Judge William. On the theoretical side, it is important to recognize that the position attributed by Kierkegaard to Judge William is not just warmed-over and occasionally caricatured Kant, with a few local Danish twists added; that it is something more than this is true not only by virtue of the inspiration that William obviously draws from Christian sources, which already makes Judge William's ethic more "theonomous" than either heteronomous or strictly autonomous,[31] but also by virtue of the emphasis that William places, particularly in the section entitled "Equilibrium" or "Balance" in *Either/Or*, on the role of individual personality as "the absolute . . . the unity of the universal and the particular" (EO, II, 265). Thus, in some of the formulas that Kierkegaard ascribes to this ultra-respectable pseudonymous character, we have a first hint, though only a hint, of the radically new Kierkegaardian idea of what Sartre was to call the "singular universal." (Needless to say, the philosophical connotations of the word "universal" as used by Judge William, on the one hand, and by Sartre in the essay discussed in the first section of this chapter, on the other, are different from one another in important ways, although I do not have the space adequately to sort out those differences here.) Quite notoriously, in any event, Kierkegaard insisted that this comfortable "equilibrium" of Judge William's needed to be ruptured in favor of an awareness of one's ineluctable guiltiness before the Absolute and of the "teleological suspension of the ethical."

To suspend or bracket ethics is not equivalent, of course, to discarding "it"—ethical questioning, an ethical standpoint—altogether. The hyphenated expression, "ethico-religious" (*ethisk-religieuse*) in the title of the 1847 publication, *Two Minor Ethico-Religious Treatises*, that Kierkegaard published under the pseudonym "H.H." remained a valid characterization of his own point of view to the end. Nevertheless, his recognition that conventional ethics, even when practiced with the presumed near-perfection of a Judge William, was not enough and in fact was inevitably tainted with pompous self-conceit no doubt exerted an important influence over the thinking of Sartre as well as of Heidegger, Camus, and many others. The later existentialist moral critique of bourgeois conventionality and self-deception, or bad faith, obviously had its roots in Kierkegaard.

Sartre, as is well known, experienced enormous difficulty in producing an ethical position that would satisfy him. Yet he was always, like Kierkegaard, haunted by ethical questions. The superficial quip that Sartre's worldview remained at the level of Kierkegaard's aesthetic stage is clearly inapplicable to someone who, for example, at the outset of the very same diary entry (Dec. 18, 1939) in which he goes on to note the impact on him of his reading of *The Concept of Anxiety*, expresses in some detail the sense in which he believes the war to be his responsibility as well as that of all others who are living[32]—an insight that he was to reproduce in one of the shortest and most dramatic sections, entitled "Freedom and Responsibility," in *Being and Nothingness*.[33] In the concluding sentence of that long tome he promised *"un prochain ouvrage"* on ethics,[34] but nothing so labeled was ever published during his lifetime. We now know that he indeed made a massive effort, which he ultimately set aside as unsatisfactory, in that direction: it has been published posthumously as *Notebooks for an Ethics*, a long, uneven manuscript on which Kierkegaard's thought exerts no very clear influence. It was composed during the immediate post-war years. Thereafter, Sartre began his period of closest affiliation with Marxism and even, for a time, with Communist-sponsored causes, though never with the Party itself. There were indications that, from this perspective, he no longer regarded an authentic ethics to be a genuine possibility, for reasons based on the Marxist theory of ideology, and indeed he later characterized this period of his life as one of "amoralist realism."[35] In subsequent years, however, ethical concerns again came to be uppermost in his mind, a point about which he was very clear in his reminiscences. Perhaps the high-water mark of the later Sartrean ethic was a long paper that he presented at the Gramsci Institute in Rome in late May 1964, just one month after his UNESCO Kierkegaard paper. (One of the many commonalities between

Kierkegaard and Sartre was, quite obviously, their enormously prolific character as writers!)

Only certain portions of the Rome paper have as yet been published, but Robert Stone and Elizabeth Bowman, who are in possession of a copy, have provided us with some sense of its contents.[36] Still writing within a broadly Marxist framework at this point, and speaking to a comparatively friendly audience of Italian Communist Party intellectuals (the comparison is with more rigid French, Russian, and "Eastern Bloc" Party ideologues), Sartre insists on the need for a Marxian ethics and, relying heavily on analyses of the evolution of Algerians' attitudes and experiences through the time of their recently-concluded war of liberation from French rule, focuses especially on the concepts of (human) need and of *praxis*. As far as I am aware, he does not invoke Kierkegaard's name in the course of this manuscript, and it may be recalled that his one significant criticism of Kierkegaard in "L'Universel singulier" had centered, precisely, on the latter's alleged neglect of the dimension of *praxis*. But there are two truly underlying themes, as I have argued in my book on Sartre's political theory, to be found throughout his later philosophical work, namely, freedom and socialism; and Kierkegaard is unquestionably one of his major inspirations concerning the first of these, freedom. The Gramsci Institute lecture was dedicated to rescuing Marxism from the heavy hand of Marxist-Leninist determinism in favor of human freedom on the road to developing a Marxian ethics; Sartre's later repudiation of Marxism itself turned on his new perception that this could not adequately be done.[37] It can thus truly be said that, by the end of his career, Sartre had in some significant measure rejected one of the two great figures whom he had linked together, in the final paragraph of "L'Universel singulier," as "those dead-alive people [who] condition our base position (*ancrage*)," Marx, while never repudiating the other, Kierkegaard.[38]

But it also must be acknowledged that the later Sartre's orientation turned increasingly in a direction that many commentators claim not to find in Kierkegaard himself, the socio-political. Even if we set aside Kierkegaard's strong distaste for socialism, on the ground that there are different socialisms and the one that he found so distasteful would not have met with applause from Sartre, either, nevertheless the fact remains that freedom in the later Sartre is above all the freedom of *praxis*, human activity within a social milieu, hence no longer as individualistic as Kierkegaardian freedom is typically thought to be. Moreover, the later Sartre, in his *Critique of Dialectical Reason*, contends that there can even be such a thing as free "group *praxis*," as incarnated in the French mob that stormed the Bastille—an extremely un-Kierkegaardian idea. (Kierkegaard, as we know, had nothing good to say about "the mob.") Finally, in the fragmentary "last words" of Sartre that were published in three installments in *Le Nouvel Observateur* just before his death, we even find something approaching what many would consider an equally un-Kierkegaardian notion of genuine human community.

These short pieces, which consist of a transcribed dialogue between Sartre and the close confidant of his final years, Benny Lévy, and were given the title, "Hope, Now," by the newspaper editors, begin with an odd exchange concerning Kierkegaard, in which Lévy elicits from Sartre an acknowledgement that he had never personally experienced despair but had written much about it in earlier years because Kierkegaard had done so and Kierkegaard was then "*la mode.*" Basically, Sartre says, Kierkegaard had influenced him greatly. "That's curious," replies Lévy, "because you really don't like Kierkegaard." Sartre's reply is, "Yes, but I nevertheless underwent his influence."[39] Aside from the fact that this early part of "Hope, Now" dramatically demonstrates Sartre's awareness of Kierkegaard's enormous influence on him, I think it would be unwise, for a number of reasons, to read too much into the dialogue either concerning Sartre's stance, at the end of his life, towards his previous thought, or even concerning his personal feelings about Kierkegaard! What is perhaps most interesting about these "last words" for present purposes is their occasional but clear religious overtones, attributable in large measure to the strong interest in Judaism taken by Lévy.[40] At the time of his death, Sartre had "mellowed"; he had by no means lost interest in political matters, but he was no doubt more skeptical than at any time since his pre-World War II days concerning the value of allegiances to particular political movements. His disillusionment with politics was considerable, as it is almost bound to be ultimately for any passionate ethicist who lives long enough.

If we take a backward look now at Kierkegaard's trajectory with respect to this same set of issues, "ethics and politics," we should note, first, that he was always much more engaged, throughout his writings, with the social question of *community* than most commentators credit him with having been[41] and, second, that the struggle against the Established Church at the end of his life did, even by Walter Lowrie's own account and *pace* what Lowrie actually *says* about it,[42] take on political overtones. (Ecclesiastical politics, when one is dealing with an Established Church, is *eo ipso* at the same time politics *tout court*; moreover, Kierkegaard's veritable "last words," as Lowrie himself eventually came to realize,[43] included a populist appeal to "the plain man" (KAUC 287–88), many exemplars of whom did indeed attend his funeral.) Of course, for Kierkegaard the idea of community connoted above all a *religious*, or at least a religiously-determined, community, as it had for Hegel at the conclusion of the *Phenomenology of Spirit*. At the end of his life, Kierkegaard had become more convinced than ever that the notion that any such larger community, called "Christendom," actually existed was a pernicious illusion.

Taken together, these concluding observations yield mixed results concerning Sartre's indebtedness to Kierkegaard in the areas of ethics and politics. Paradoxically enough, Kierkegaard by the end of his (much shorter) life had become, in the sense that I have indicated, more "politicized" but also, if anything, more "individualistic" than ever before, whereas the later Sartre took much greater interest than the earlier in the impact of the social on the individual. Common to both at the times of their respective deaths was great disillusionment with "institutions"—the Church and the Movement Left, respectively—with which they had more or less identified at earlier times, even while retaining their very pronounced individualities. Characteristic of both of these individualities was an extremely intense sense of moral commitment. There can be no doubt that in Sartre's case this sense of commitment, which had not been highly developed in his earlier years and later evolved in certain un-Kierkegaardian political directions, in part in response to war experiences of a sort that Kierkegaard never underwent, nevertheless owed much of its edge and form to the existentialist insight into the responsibility of the free individual that Sartre learned from his readings in and about Kierkegaard.

C. Seduction and Feminist Thought

For Kierkegaard, the ultimate expression of the irresponsible use of freedom is the figure of the seducer. This figure can take a range of forms, from the comparatively unreflective Don Juan to the demonic author of "Forførerens Dagbog." Sartre's *Being and Nothingness* contains long phenomenological analyses of "Love, Language, Masochism," and other forms of "concrete relations with another" that are justly famous and have occasioned almost endless controversy, but that in any case are so revealing of his early philosophy as to make plausible the claim that "without the possibility of seduction, sexual or otherwise, Sartrean ontology loses all meaning."[44] Moreover, the two writers share the fate of being objects of considerable hostile criticism from various contemporary feminists—Kierkegaard for the numerous texts in which he treats Woman as a somewhat fantastical and in many ways subordinate Other to men, Sartre for his conflictual conception of love and his somewhat bizarre negative manipulation of female imagery in his psychoanalysis of "the viscous" in *Being and Nothingness*,[45] among many other reasons.

At the same time, it should be recognized that Kierkegaard and Sartre together stand out, among the Dead White Males who have dominated Western philosophy up to the present time, in the amount of attention that they pay in their writings to serious, extensive considerations of the complexity and importance of sex and gender relationships in human life. (There are others, such as Rousseau and, it could perhaps be added, Plato, whose *Symposium* of course serves as the principal historical referent for the "In Vino Veritas" portion of

Kierkegaard's *Stages on Life's Way*. But the numbers are few.) And if there are important senses in which it is likely to be said about both of them, by critics of this aspect of their writings, that they "didn't get it," it seems to me reasonable to be skeptical about whether *anyone* can be confident of having done so—so complex and filled with paradox are the philosophical issues in this area. "Seduction" well names the central site of these complexities and paradoxes. I cannot be sure just what, if anything, Sartre learned directly about seduction from Kierkegaard's writings about it, but, as I shall attempt to show, there is a broader sense of the word with respect to which Sartre's indebtedness is, once again, considerable. In making this case, I shall have recourse to both textual and personal aspects of their approaches to the topic, as well as to historical antecedents.

Just what is meant by seduction? Literally understood, the equivalents for this word appear to have a roughly similar connotation in a number of languages—Danish, French, English, German, etc.—to wit, that of leading astray, or misleading. While the use of the word in a sexual context is perhaps the most common and the one that is foremost in Kierkegaard's writings, if not also Sartre's, it can play a powerful role in other contexts as well. One of my favorite examples of this in the Western philosophical literature occurs at the culminating point of Rousseau's *Discourse on the Origin of Inequality*, where he imagines "le riche," the generalized individual of the state of nature who has accumulated possessions but maintains them precariously because of a lack of institutional guarantees for his possession, to have conceived "le projet le plus réfléchi qui soit jamais entré dans l'esprit humain" (the subtlest scheme ever to have entered the human mind). This supremely well-reflected upon project was to persuade the masses in his community to place the united force of the community as a whole behind his position of dominance. It was the moment of the invention, through clever, misleading speech, of the institution of private property, which Rousseau was to go on to denominate as "usurpation" and Proudhon, in the next century, simply as theft. After reconstructing the imagined speech, replete with rhetorical flourishes and concluding with the promise of "concorde éternelle," Rousseau continues:

> Il en fallut beaucoup moins que l'équivalent de ce discours pour entraîner des hommes grossiers, *faciles à séduire*. . . . Tous coururent au-devant de leurs fers, croyant assurer leur liberté.[46] (Emphasis mine) (Far less than the equivalent of this speech would have been needed to win over crude, easy-to-seduce men. All ran headlong to their chains, thinking to guarantee their freedom.)

This non-sexual employment of the term "seduction" in a crucial passage by one of Western literature's most boastful and at the same time anxiety-ridden seducers is, it seems to me, rich in significance: to be seduced is to run to one's chains in the expectation of assuring one's liberty. But may this not be a meta-phor for human projects in general? *Quaeritur.*

As far as Kierkegaard's "Diary of a Seducer" is concerned, no amount of commentary can begin to do justice to the original text, which so brilliantly captures the dialectic of the aesthetic attitude in a very advanced form. Among the most important features of the Seducer's project are its ludic quality, the background anxiety that is never far from breaking through, and the emphasis that is placed on making it seem to Cordelia as if she were the one, rather than he, who was making the decisive moves. Since the Seducer remains lucid throughout concerning his ultimate goal of conquest, or actual domination, followed instantly by abandonment, he could conceivably, as totally lucid, be characterized as fundamentally "authentic" in a Sartrean sense even though from Judge William's conventional ethical standpoint his pursuit is, of course, thoroughly reprehensible. But there are in fact many passages throughout the Seducer's diary that reek of the attitude that Sartre was to analyze at length as inauthentic "bad faith," lying to oneself—so many as to constitute an histori-cal anticipation of that analysis. From the religious standpoint, the Seducer's entire enterprise is, to be sure, one of bad faith from start to finish—a bad faith that may be said, in a way that for Sartre is no mere play on words, to block any possibility of a Kierkegaardian leap of faith.[47] Finally, to note an extremely obvious point that nevertheless needs to be noted as explicitly as possible, many of the Seducer's moves are patterned after those already made by his real-life creator in the latter's relatively brief but fateful relationship with Regina Olsen, as numerous entries in his own diary render abundantly clear. Ah, but Kierkegaard's motivation was religious, it will be pointed out. Yes. . . . .

The vast majority of the treatments of Woman in Kierkegaard's pseudony-mous works, for instance by the various aesthetic voices (including the Se-ducer's) in volume I of *Either/Or*, by Judge William himself, and by the speakers at the banquet in *Stages* . . . , strongly presuppose an essentialism concerning "Her"—that is, the familiar Platonic/Goethean view that there is an "ewig Weibliche" in which each individual woman participates. The various voices differ, of course, on the precise nature of that womanly essence. Implicit par-ticularly in many of the voices that reflect the aesthetic attitude in its "purest" form is the further assumption that Woman is the eternal object-victim of se-duction, Man the eternal seducer-victimizer. Or, to sharpen the claim and put it in the harsher language of one important strand of contemporary feminist thought, which is itself at least on the verge of essentialism even if sometimes qualified by the perception that this need not be so in all possible human so-cieties, "Male and female are created through the erotization of dominance and submission. The man/woman difference and the dominance/submission dynamic define each other."[48]

What makes this kind of position, when taken as a philosophical assertion about Woman, problematic from an existentialist standpoint is that it tends to put into question both women's individualities and their freedom. The unbridled sexist language and commentary that Kierkegaard attributes to certain of the participants in "In Vino Veritas" reduces women not only to commodities, but even to nearly—i.e., "essentially"—identical commodities, lacking any of the element of the *singular* from Sartre's expression "the singular universal." And if, as the Seducer at times appears to imply, the techniques of seduction that he has mastered are virtually guaranteed of success, then the free choice of the male, such as himself, virtually effaces the element of choice on the female's part, leaving her with only an illusion of being free. Moreover, sexual seduction must then be regarded, as in my experience of discussions of the topic it often is, as an exclusively masculine activity.[49]

That Kierkegaard himself did not concur with this last-mentioned assumption is clear from the fact that he actually projected, in his diary, writing a "Hetaerens Dagbog" and/or arranging, in the course of a second "Diary of a Seducer," for a meeting between the latter and a courtesan; together, they would create a society to study the difference between seductions originating with men and those originating with women (JP, V, 5676 and 5705 / PAP, IV, A, 128 and 181). (It would have been fascinating to read an hetaira's diary as composed by Kierkegaard, but it is probably just as well for his intellectual reputation that he did not write one; it is very interesting to note that his thinking about female seducers ran in the direction of hetairas and courtesans.) As for the issues of women's individuality and freedom, it seems to me that Kierkegaard was very ambiguous about them in much that he wrote concerning the one woman to whom he was closest in his life, Regina; at least it can be said that he was never confident about what her reactions would be, which implies that he acknowledged her freedom. He even expressed fear that she might take her life when he broke with her and thus render him, in effect (to his way of thinking), guilty of murder.

When Kierkegaard decided, in August 1849, to review, in his diary, the history of his relationship with Regina, he began by quoting from the *Aeneid*, "Infandum me jubes, Regina, renovare dolorem."[50] (You are bidding me, Queen, to revive uspeakable sorrow.) What attracted Kierkegaard about this famous line, the commencement of Aeneas' lengthy narrative, to Queen Dido and her court, of the unspeakably sorrowful events surrounding the Fall of Troy and Aeneas' subsequent "odyssey," was the play on the word "Regina" which enabled Kierkegaard to personalize it. But it is interesting to consider, as well, what light the original story—with which Kierkegaard, thoroughly steeped as he was in the Classics, was very well acquainted—may shed on Kierkegaard's relationship with "his" Regina, as well as on the question of seduction itself. In Vergil's poem, Dido is portrayed as a female leader, *dux*, of a large expedition that had escaped from Tyre, where her brother, Pygmalion, who had been revealed to her in a dream as her first husband's murderer, held harsh sway; aided by the further revelation of a secret gold hoard, they set sail with her in command—"dux femina facti" (I, 364)—and eventually founded the new city of Carthage, where she became queen. After Aeneas' party arrives and he recounts his tragic story, she falls deeply in love with him, with the connivance of Juno and Venus. These goddesses then arrange for a violent storm to drive the two of them to "find the same cave" (IV, 165) during a hunting expedition; thenceforth Dido calls Aeneas husband, even though it had not been a formal marriage, and, Vergil editorializes, "hoc praetextit nomine culpam" (with this name she covered over the fault—IV, 172). Eventually, with the connivance of other heavenly powers and in particular with the sending of a mandate by Jupiter through his messenger, Mercury, to resume the voyage to Italy to found Rome, Aeneas makes secret preparations to desert Dido and Carthage. When she learns of this, she pleads with him to stay, at least for a while, but he refuses. She kills herself as his ships set sail.

Aeneas, "pius Aeneas" as Vergil so often calls him, is in this central episode portrayed as more seduced than seducer at the outset—though of course it is in fact the wiles of the goddesses that effect the liaison—but in the end he plays the traditional Seducer's role of cad, supposedly out of religious motivation. It does not seem far-fetched to identify affinities between Aeneas and Kierkegaard, especially since the latter has called our attention to them. Happily for all concerned, however, Regina, unlike Dido, went on with her life. In any event, the deep-level misogyny of Vergil's framework, typical of so much of our male-dominated Western culture, is pervasive: it was Dido, hospitable and kind as she had been towards Aeneas, who was nevertheless "at fault," and it is not only she but also Vergil's divine villainess, Juno, who suffer crushing defeat at the end, thus foreshadowing—the political agenda of the epic—the historical annihilation of Carthage itself by Aeneas' arrogant descendants ("populum . . . belloque superbum"—I, 21), beloved of the fates.

Sartre's extended account of human relationships in *Being and Nothingness* cannot, of course, rely on invocations of necessitarian fate or of divine intervention. When it comes to the matter of love, the account is not as thoroughly negative as the further phenomenological analyses of such behaviors as masochism, hate, and sadism might lead the reader retrospectively to think it had been, and as it is often caricatured in secondary literature. After indicating the sense in which the "look" of one human being at another constitutes a primitive kind of possession, he points out that this idea of possession, which had been central to the motivation of the "world-historical" seduction effected by the wealthy in Rousseau's philosophy (an important though usually unacknowledged influence on Sartre), and which is frequently equated with love in popular literature, cannot by itself adequately explain the phenomenon of love; for love requires the mutual *freedom* of both parties to be sustained. Analyzing the common lover's demand for exclusivity in a relationship, Sartre refers to the familiar expression, "being made for one another," which carries the implication that it was ultimately God who brought this about; he shows the role of the concept of "God" as a limiting principle here. He concludes this section with the observation that being "wanted in [the] least details by an absolute freedom [i.e., the beloved] that [our existence] simultaneously conditions — and that we ourselves want with our own freedom" constitutes "the basis of the joy of love, when it exists: to feel ourselves justified in existing."[51] In other words, Sartre presents love, the free choice of oneself by another, as the best path to overcoming the sentiment of being *de trop*, superfluous.

However, he goes on to observe, there is "a conflict" in the project of loving, not only because two freedoms are involved, but also, more specifically, because the beloved must inevitably perceive the lover against a background of other objects in the world and thus cannot restrict his or her own freedom, or perspective on the world ("look"), to the point of preventing it from transcending, or going beyond, the lover. It is for this reason, Sartre says, that the lover must try to engage in *seduction* of the beloved, "and his/her love is not distinguishable from this enterprise of seduction."[52] He characterizes seduction as making oneself into a *fascinating object* to the other, such that the other will, ideally, become conscious of his or her own nothingness vis-à-vis the lover, filling his or her outlook on the world, so to speak, with the massive objectness of that seductive person. This analysis, in turn, leads to a discussion of language (taken in the broadest sense — gesture, etc.), of which seduction is one very important type of expression, as fundamental.

I have always tended to regard Sartre's analysis here, despite all the criticisms of it for failing to recognize the alleged possibility of a "true union of souls," as basically sound. Seduction considered in a broad sense, I take him to be implying, is a pervasive part of most if not all positive interpersonal, dyadic relationships (as well as of many negative ones), for reasons that are more ontological than psychological.[53] That is, one must always try to make oneself "fascinating," *somehow* attractive to others, in order to obtain their attention and, if one wishes, persuade them to pursue a course that one favors. And, since we live in time and the potential conflict between attending to one individual and attending to other objects that coexist in every individual's world is inescapable, such efforts must be perpetually renewed. From this ontological standpoint, the question of one's precise *motivation* (which may range, e.g., from sheer egoistic self-gratification, as in the case of Kierkegaard's aesthete, to giving the Other joy or wisdom or healing care) becomes secondary. It may only be in an individual's relations with God, if there is a God, that the element of seduction is entirely dispensable in the domain of "être-pour-autrui."[54]

Insight into the pervasiveness of the dialectic of seduction is not really new with Sartre. I suggest that his indebtedness to Kierkegaard here, as in the case of the other topics that I have been considering in this chapter, is very strong. Although Kierkegaard portrayed his Seducer proper as a complete "bastard," he also displayed a constant awareness, throughout his writings, of the need for an element of seduction and of the ludic[55] in everyday life (that is the whole point of Judge William's emphasis on "the *aesthetic* validity of marriage," for example), as well as of the seductiveness of his own brilliant gift of language. Indeed, he viewed the entire enterprise of his pseudonymous works as one of seducing, in a broad sense, his readers into orienting themselves towards taking a leap of faith. Of course both Kierkegaard and Sartre are themselves indebted, in this regard, to Plato's profound musings about the disreputable (as he depicted it) seductiveness of the Sophists versus the genuinely positive seductiveness of Socrates and of the Wisdom for which he quested—the "seductiveness of philosophy." But I am inclined to think that Sartre went further and showed greater understanding than his predecessor, Kierkegaard, of the moral dilemmas involved in "seducing" an Other while not suppressing that Other's freedom.

It is on this ground that some of the important issues of contemporary feminist thought are being played out, often in the language of "empowerment." To empower someone has been said to mean exerting "transformative" power over that person in order to encourage the latter to transcend this situation and eventually "take charge"; examples cited include teacher-student and parent-child relationships. I think that this language, while it may point to some important aspects of the dialectic of freedom and "seduction" that I have been discussing, is inexact and misleading, particularly when applied to those many interpersonal relationships between adults in contemporary society in which the disparities between the relative "power" of each party are less clear-cut and sometimes less relevant.[56] (Certain strains of feminist literature, in their justifiable commitment to calling attention to the overwhelming prevalence of male dominance in our society and culture, have tended to underplay the existence of more ambiguous relationships—to underplay, for example, the ways in which men are sometimes "objectified" by women as well as women by men, and to overlook as well the ways in which "objectification" can sometimes be positive.[57]) The goal of one or both parties in concrete dyadic human relations may be—indeed, according to an existentialist ethic of freedom ideally *ought* to be[58]—to augment the other's individuality and self-expression even while (in fact, by means of) maintaining the privileged character of the relation. That the chances of failure, of deception, of self-deception, and often of all three of these are extremely high, particularly when sexual tensions and disparate physical risks are also involved along with the inevitable psychological ones, should go without saying: historical examples such as the Dido-Aeneas and Søren-Regina relationships are legion. Sartre's analysis of love and seduction, filled with Kierkegaardian overtones and interpreted along lines that I have been suggesting, is very helpful in showing why this is so, and why nevertheless, *pace* many commentators on the early Sartre, a reaction of total despair is also inappropriate.

This is not to suggest—far from it!—that Sartre in his personal life, particularly in his relationships with women, offers a splendid model for imitation. By the end of his life, he was known to be providing financial support to several women, at least some of whom had the background and talent for independent intellectual development that, it could be argued, failed fully to blossom as a result of his apparent seductiveness toward them. It could further be (and has been) argued, as I myself suggested at the beginning of my discussion of Transcendence, that his longest-term and, at least for most of his life, closest partner, Simone de Beauvoir, failed to develop deserved confidence about her own originality as a philosopher as a result, in part, of her being so "fascinated" by him. By the same token, de Beauvoir's seductions of others, at least of other women, sometimes had very disempowering consequences.[59] Sartre even went so far as to acknowledge candidly, in an American magazine interview,[60] that he would probably not personally feel very comfortable in the feminist world of sexual equality to which he subscribed intellectually. But the fact that he *did* subscribe to it intellectually, together with the fact that his relationship with de Beauvoir truly was egalitarian in many respects, should not be forgotten.

Crude, often appalling daily examples remind us, if we need to be reminded, that overwhelming numbers of instances of alleged "consent" to another's "seductive persuasion" in fact amount to simple coercion by the dominant party, more often than not male, in dyadic human relationships of both overtly sexual and numerous other kinds, and that this has been true throughout history. Nevertheless, to reduce "seduction" completely to "coercion," or to claim that "seduction" as used in the sexual sense and "seduction" in its broader senses are entirely equivocal terms, is, I think, to falsify reality and more specifically to misconstrue the subtle, enormously complex dialectic of freedoms that both Kierkegaard's and Sartre's treatments of seduction help to illuminate. Viewing the issues in this light shifts emphasis away from the conventional, bourgeois ethic of a Judge William, according to which what does and does not constitute the immoral sort of seduction is clearcut, while the subtler but very real suppression of women's freedom within a traditional marriage like his is justified and even lauded as being in keeping with God's Law. Instead, as both Kierkegaard and Sartre in different but I think not entirely incompatible ways tried to seduce conventionally-minded readers into realizing, what is required is an anguished respect for the freedom of each human individual as an absolute that is in relation to another Absolute, be it God or historical universe, and a recognition that the interaction between ourselves and others which defines the human condition is fraught with infinite possibilities and infinite perils for them, for us, and for that Absolute relation itself—as our two thinkers' interestingly flawed lives well illustrate.

Notes

1. The proceedings were published in 1966 under the title, *Kierkegaard Vivant*. René Maheu, the Director General of UNESCO (then in its palmier days), gave the welcome. Other papers were presented by Gabriel Marcel, Karl Jaspers, Jeanne Hersch, Enzo Paci, Lucien Goldmann, Jean Beaufret on behalf of Martin Heidegger, and Jean Wahl. Two long roundtable discussions, which are also published in this volume, follow. Among the additional participants in these discussions were Emmanuel Lévinas and Jean Hyppolite; Sartre, whose paper was the focus of considerable attention, absented himself from the discussions, much to the annoyance of some of the others. Even greater annoyance was expressed at the fact that Heidegger did not come in person and sent a paper that made no mention of Kierkegaard; it was explained, however, that this arrangement had been accepted by Maheu as a Heideggerian tribute to Kierkegaard nonetheless. Jaspers's paper was apparently presented in German, and he is not listed as a roundtable discussant.

The version of Sartre's paper from which I shall be citing appears in *Situations*, IX, pp. 152–90. There, apparently through typographical error, the wrong date is given—April 24 instead of 21—in the text on p. 154 (Sartre is stressing the contemporaneity of Kierkegaard by invoking the actual date of his lecture), and at the end reference is made to a "Journée Kierkegaard." Presumably, for the editor of this *Situations* volume, only the first day of the colloquium, the day on which Sartre spoke, counted!

2. Wahl, *New Republic* CXIII, Oct. 1, 1945, pp. 442–44.

3. "I may say here, though it is not strictly apropos in this connection, that one who knows Sartre's works will readily recognize that it must be a grim experience for an elderly clergyman to be obliged to read them. Although not much learning can be utilized in this short article, I felt compelled by my training in German *Grundlichkeit* to read all of them, and everything that has been written about them, as far as such books are available here."

After complaining about the difficulty of even obtaining these books from the Princeton library, since they were always on loan because, apparently, French professors had made them required reading, even while Sartre's popularity was supposedly slumping severely in Paris, he continues:

"I do not confound obscenity with immorality, nor would I characterize Sartre as immoral merely because he professes to have no system of ethics. But one can hardly account for the sudden popularity of a dreary philosophy which had waited in vain for thirty years to receive some appreciation, unless one attributes it to the literature produced by Sartre; and one can hardly believe that a literature of this sort could attain so great a vogue, had it not been so indelicate and the *dramatis personae* so indecent. The effect is at once abhorrent and fascinating, like a profound glimpse into one's own soul ('a descent into hell,' as Hamann called it), combined with the consoling reflection that everybody else is as bad or worse. Yet it is disconcerting to discover that men, like dogs, prefer to feed upon vomit, offal, and carrion." Lowrie, " 'Existence' as Understood by Kierkegaard and/or Sartre," 398–99.

4. Cumming, "Existence and Communication," 79–80.

5. Schilpp, ed., *The Philosophy of Jean-Paul Sartre*, "Interview with Jean-Paul Sartre," 22.

6. Typical of Kierkegaard's usage is the text "Of the Difference between a Genius and an Apostle," in which the immanence/transcendence distinction is employed to elucidate this very difference. Another example is the reference to the ordeal of Job in *Fear and Trembling* (FT 210), where Kierkegaard assigns the category of *ordeal* to the sphere of transcendence, which is said to be utterly beyond the aesthetic, ethical, and dogmatic. There are, of course, many more such instances.

7. Spiegelberg, *The Phenomenological Movement*, 112–13. My largest debt for the following reconsideration of the relationship between the Husserlian phenomenological tradition and questions of transcendence is owed, however, not to Spiegelberg's book, but to conversations with Ivanka Raynova. Her book, *From Existentialist Philosophy to Post-Personalism* (a translation of its Bulgarian title), deals with many of these issues, with special additional focus on Emmanuel Mounier's personalism, though some of the conclusions that it draws are very different from my own.

8. *Vers le concret* was the title of Wahl's book of 1932, which Sartre (in *Search for a Method*) singles out as having been especially influential on his own generation of young philosophers.

9. Sartre, *Les Mots*, p. 209.

10. Ibid., pp. 210–11 (my translation).

11. Sartre, "L'Universel singulier," 177–81. (This and all subsequent translations from "L'Universel singulier" are mine.) Caws, in his *Sartre*, prefers usually to translate the French expression as "the universal singular," but most English-speaking Sartre scholars do not follow him in this.

12. Plekhanov, *The Role of the Individual in History*.

13. See the following section for reference to the particular use made by Kierkegaard of the term "universal" as a characterization of the ethical stance epitomized in the person of Judge William; it is not at issue here.

14. Sartre, "L'Universel singulier," 171.

15. Ibid., 169.

16. Ibid., 186.

17. Ibid., 156.

18. Ibid., 172.

19. Ibid., 189.

20. Ibid., 171.

21. In *Search for a Method*, written eight years earlier, Sartre had already used the same language of *savoir* to refer to the sclerosis of orthodox Marxism and its need to learn from the Kierkegaardian existentialist tradition, as well as from the social science disciplines, in order to overcome this sclerosis. But in his discussion of 1964, no doubt under the influence both of external events and of his re-reading of Kierkegaard, he expresses much more skepticism about the very pretension to *savoir*.

22. See McBride, "Sartre and His Successors," 78–92.

23. Sartre, "L'Universel singulier," 189.

24. Earle, Edie, and Wild, eds., *Christianity and Existentialism*, 176.

25. Ibid., 179–80.

26. Sartre, *The War Diaries: November 1939–March 1940*, 131–34.

27. It should, however, be acknowledged that Sartre's play, *The Flies*, very interestingly explores these notions, or rather notions resembling them, as they might have been played out in the pre-Christian setting of ancient Greece.

28. See Sartre, *Lettres au Castor et à quelques autres, 1940–1963*, 104–12 (letters of Feb. 28 and 29 and Mar. 1, 1940). His remark at the beginning of the last of these concern-

ing de Beauvoir's apparent forgiveness of him makes her appear almost saintly in this respect. For an excellent brief discussion of this episode, see Barnes, "Sartre's War Diaries," 99–101.

29. The editors gleefully note (CA 230) that Kierkegaard misspelled the second word, substituting an omicron for the omega.

30. See, for instance, the reference to "Kant's honest way" in SLW 152.

31. See Connell, "Judge William's Theonomous Ethics," in Connell and Evans, eds., *Foundations of Kierkegaard's Vision of Community*, 56–70.

32. Sartre, *The War Diaries*, 127–28.

33. Sartre, *L'être et le néant*, IV, 1, III, 638–42.

34. Ibid., 722.

35. See McBride, *Sartre's Political Theory*, 190. The reference is to Gavi, Sartre, and Victor, *On a raison de se révolter*, 79.

36. Stone and Bowman, "Dialectical Ethics: A First Look at Sartre's Unpublished 1964 Rome Lecture Notes," 195–215.

37. Schilpp, ed., *op. cit.*, 21.

38. Sartre, "L'Universal singulier," 190.

39. *Le Nouvel Observateur*, March 10, 1980, p. 27 (my translation).

40. See McBride, "Community: The Dialectic of Abandonment and Hope in Light of Sartre's Last Words," 218–31.

41. This does not apply, to be sure, to the contributors to *Foundations of Kierkegaard's Vision of Community*!

42. "Political activity was completely foreign to [Kierkegaard] in later years." Lowrie, *A Short Life of Kierkegaard*, 90.

43. "In my *Short Life of Kierkegaard* I picked out, rather arbitrarily, what I was pleased to consider S. K.'s 'last words.' Yet the last words he actually wrote have perhaps a better claim to be thus signified. Especially his pathetic confession of a lifelong suffering, and his address to the 'plain man,' deserve to be treasured as the last words of an intellectual tragic hero." (KAUC, xiv, Lowrie's introduction.)

44. Gordon, footnote 4 (p. 15) to unpublished ms., "Commentary on Phyllis S. Morris's 'Sartre and de Beauvoir on Objectification,' " presented at the May 1993 meetings of the Sartre Society of North America at Trent University, Peterborough, Ontario.

45. Sartre, *L'être et le néant*, IV, 2, III, 690–708.

46. "Far less than the equivalent of this speech would have been needed to take in men [so] crude, easy to seduce. . . . All ran straight ahead to their chains, thinking to guarantee their freedom." (My translation.) Rousseau, *Discours sur l'Origine de l'Inégalité parmi les Hommes*, 78.

47. For Sartre, one key to understanding "bad faith" is to recognize the sense in which faith itself is what he calls a "metastable" phenomenon. See "La 'Foi' de la Mauvaise Foi," *L'être et le néant*, I, 2, III, 108–11.

48. MacKinnon, "Feminism, Marxism, Method, and the State: Toward Feminist Jurisprudence," 56.

49. This assumption was tacitly shared by many participants, for example, at a (different) session of the 1993 meetings of the Sartre Society of North America, mentioned in note 44 *supra*, which persuaded me to analyze the topic here.

50. Lowrie points this out in *A Short Life of Kierkegaard*, 135, but does not say anything more about the possible relevance of the story of Aeneas and Dido. The reference is to line 3 of the Second Book of the *Aeneid* (henceforth cited as [II, 3]).

51. Sartre, *L'être et le néant* III, 3, I, 439 (my translation).

52. Ibid. The gender of Sartre's pronouns referring to the lover and the beloved

throughout the larger portion of the text in which this section falls is masculine, even when, for example, in speaking of body parts in later passages referring to *desire*, it is clear that he is taking a male perspective. In translating the section from which I am citing, Barnes uses "he" and "his," in keeping with the literal French. Several pages later, however, she deliberately switches to feminine pronouns where Sartre refers to "autrui" and "l'autre," because, she says in a footnote, "the feminine sounds more natural in English." *Being and Nothingness*, 390. I believe that my usage of "his or her" or "his/her," which was not current when Barnes undertook her remarkable translation, is more in the spirit of what Sartre actually intended, at least in this section.

53. There are interesting parallels to be developed between "seduction," or "mis-" leading (someone) away from what is metaphorically understood as the correct path, and "deviation," or straying from the path oneself. "Deviation" has generally negative connotations in the writings of Aristotle and other philosophers, psychologists, and sociologists, as well as in much of ordinary language. However, it also has other, more positive uses: " 'Deviation' is one of the major motive powers for the whole development of human society." Ding, *An Examination of the Concept of Socio-Political Deviation*, 258.

54. Of course, if God had a place as an actual Existent within Sartre's philosophy, "autrui" (best translated as "another" rather than "others") would not be an appropriate pronoun to apply!

55. The centrality of the notion of *play* within Sartre's philosophy, as well, is brought out very well by Bell in her excellent book, *Sartre's Ethics of Authenticity*. However, in her analysis of his treatment of love (and seduction) on pp. 77–78, I think that she places excessive emphasis, relative to what Sartre implies, on the inevitability of failure in such relationships.

56. Particularly interesting treatments of these ideas are to be found in Wartenberg's *The Forms of Power*, esp. chap. 9, "Transformative Power," 183–201, and Kuykendall's "Toward an Ethic of Nurturance: Luce Irigaray on Mothering and Power," which Wartenberg cites. My own critique of Wartenberg, "Power and Empowerment: Reflections on Thomas Wartenberg's *The Forms of Power* and the Feminist Movement," presented at the School of Varna in summer 1992, is unavailable in published form in English.

57. This point is developed very well in Phyllis Morris's thus far unpublished paper, "Sartre and Beauvoir on Objectification: A Feminist Perspective."

58. The meaning and philosophical justification of the assertion, made frequently by both Sartre and de Beauvoir, that none of us can be truly free until there is a certain modicum of freedom for every living person, are issues that lie beyond this chapter's necessarily limited range of exploration; there is an abundant literature concerning them.

59. The recent publication of Lamblin's *Mémoires d'une jeune fille dérangée* has heightened this impression. Bianca Lamblin is the person referred to as "Louise Védrine" in the Sartre-de Beauvoir correspondence.

60. Sartre, "What's Jean-Paul Sartre Thinking Lately?", 286.

3 | Heidegger's Reading of Kierkegaard Revisited

From Ontological Abstraction to Ethical Concretion

Patricia J. Huntington

HEIDEGGER'S *Being and Time*, long considered one of the pathbreaking works of the twentieth century, offers us an ambiguous legacy. This is nowhere more evident than in the question of Heidegger's relation to Kierkegaard. The reception of *Being and Time* in the United States, France, and Germany heralded Heidegger as a leading figure in developing the philosophical underpinnings of existential philosophy. *Being and Time* was initially considered a crucial supplement to and extension of general existentialist and specifically Kierkegaardian themes. Accordingly, Heidegger was understood to supply the ontology implicit but undeveloped in Kierkegaard's description of human rationality as a concrete, historical, and lived practice. And, further, *Being and Time* evinced an extension of the Kierkegaardian *existential* goal of personal integrity or self-honesty in thought (what Heidegger calls authenticity), to include a *methodological* aspect. Kierkegaard's challenge to think from within the concretion of one's personal situation informed Heidegger's attempt to concretize philosophy by overcoming the ahistorical and abstract methods of western ontology.[1]

Even within this initial reception, questions arose concerning the categorization of Heidegger as an existential thinker. Not only did Heidegger explicitly attempt to distance his work from existential thought, but also the question of being (ontology), which focuses on giving an objective description of how language constitutes the meaning-context of human interactions, did not pertain to existential issues of personal existence.[2] It is now widely held that *Being and Time*, specifically Heidegger's conception of authentic resolve, suffers from the competing logics of existential (and/or factical) concretion and a tendency toward formal abstraction. Whereas Heidegger's marxist critics, who have long charged that *Being and Time* simply abstracts from the historical, material, social, and personal features of concretion (Habermas, Adorno, Lukács), have levelled similar attacks against Kierkegaard; nonetheless, still other scholars, such as Daniel Berthold-Bond, suggest that Kierkegaard's personal view of authenticity offers a corrective to Heidegger's methodological abstraction from social and material concretion.[3]

In the following, I wish to follow Berthold-Bond's line of work by elaborating further some of the differences between Kierkegaard's personal conception of ethical life (authenticity) and Heidegger's methodological concern to thematize an authentic ontology of being. To the extent that early Heidegger reduces authenticity to a formal-methodological and cognitive practice, I argue, *Being and Time* does not evince a strong appropriation of Kierkegaard's existential thought. To the contrary, by ontologizing Kierkegaard's existential categories, Heidegger depletes the latter's thought of its ethical import, central to the focus on personal edification. For this reason, I believe *Being and Time* constitutes not a development and extension of Kierkegaard's thought but rather a significant transmutation.

Heidegger's abstraction from Kierkegaard's notion of inwardness accounts, in significant measure, for the twin problems of stoicism and decisionism that suffuse his early thought and, in this instance, drive his involvement in National Socialism. Whereas Heidegger has been correctly accused of valorizing the will for will's sake and seizing arbitrarily upon a conservative revolutionary pathway, Kierkegaard has been labeled, equally, yet often incorrectly, a supporter of irrationalism, blind voluntarism, and bourgeois conservativism.[4] I wish to show that Heidegger's embroilment in decisionism emerges from collapsing Kierkegaard's sharp distinction between ethical inwardness (sincerity of motives) and morality (justification of a course of action). Finally, given that some versions of Derridean deconstruction evince remnants of Heideggerian stoicism and decisionism, I will close with indications of how a dialogue between Kierkegaard and deconstruction would be fruitful for contemporary debates between critical modernism and postmodernism.

Heidegger's Ontologizing of Kierkegaard's Existentialism

Let me begin by indicating how existential interpretations of *Being and Time* well portray the potential (albeit unrealized) advance over Kierkegaard hidden in Heidegger's thought. Theoretically, Heidegger demarcates his project of overcoming the metaphysics of presence from existential philosophy. Whereas existentialists offer only "ontic-existentiell" descriptions of humans in their historical, sociological and psychological situations, phenomenology supplies the missing "ontological-existential" analysis presupposed by such theories.[5] Calvin Schrag illuminates early Heidegger's relationship to Kierkegaard as follows:

> Kierkegaard is primarily concerned with existence as it is experienced in man's concrete ethico-religious situation. Heidegger is interested in deriving

an ontological analysis of man. But as Heidegger's ontological and existentialist descriptions can arise only from ontic and existential experience, so Kierkegaard's ontic and existential elucidations express an implicit ontology.[6]

By deriving the transcendental structures of human being, Heidegger's ontological-phenomenological analysis aims to provide the universal explanatory framework for the kinds of life choices and possibilities depicted in, but not philosophically analyzed by, Kierkegaard's work.

Heidegger's ontology of being is indebted to the Kierkegaardian notions of *Existenz*, repetition, and ethical identity (authenticity), among other concepts. Kierkegaard thematizes human being in terms of existence (*Existenz*); hence, personal identity or subjecthood has no fixed essence but rather must be constituted through deliberate self-fashioning (CUP 348ff.; SUD 13). Given that existence is temporal, nothing from within our historical passage proper guarantees unity and constancy of personal identity. In *Either/Or*, Kierkegaard depicts the failure to become a self as an aesthetical mode of life. The aesthete is a curious spectator who, observing life from a distance, wavers between boredom and curiosity because s/he flees the concrete responsibility of engaging his/her freedom and instead drifts across time as if a series of dissociated but static nows (EO, I, 26, 42, 289).

Kierkegaard's concept of ethical life, or what adapting Heideggerian terminology can be called personal authenticity, counteracts the abstract dissipation of aesthetical life through self-determination. Kierkegaard depicts the failure of aesthetical life in concrete terms: by refusing to govern who s/he becomes, the aesthete lets her or himself be determined from without by the "public," the "crowd," or that set of ideas endorsed by the community (TA 90; PV 110). Becoming myself holds ethical overtones for Kierkegaard in part because it denotes the activity of assuming responsibility for who I become, for my life choices. What is definitive for ethical existence, however, is the development of critical self-awareness, "raising [one's] consciousness to the second power." Repetition, the temporal activity of constantly resolving upon my possibilities, is not an abstract act of perpetual self-creation. Rather, it opens up the interior *Bildungsprozess* by which I acquire increasing self-consciousness and, correlatively, a critical relation to my culture or the "crowd" (R 229, 307, 315, 324).

Heidegger transposes Kierkegaard's existential themes into ontological categories. He provides a transcendental structural account of human being (Dasein) as becoming or *Existenz* in terms of "temporal ecstases" (past, present, future). Ontologically speaking, Dasein is a "potentiality-for-being" because its possibility for self-knowledge (personal identity) is given to it from out of the past, projected onto the future, and can be appropriated in the present. The task of existence entails the constant retrieval (repetition) of the possibility of self-creation. Heidegger's account of inauthentic life presupposes that *Mitsein* or "Being-with" others is constitutive, ontologically, of human being; thus, prior to developing the ability to undertake self-creation, we find that our self-understanding is always already fashioned out of identification with the "they" or "*das Man.*" Echoing Kierkegaard, Heidegger distinguishes authenticity and inauthenticity as, respectively, the life of "dispers[ion] into the 'they' " and "choosing to make this choice . . . from one's own Self." In effect, Heidegger attempts to provide an ontological explanation for how Dasein can have a situated, yet critical relationship to its world.[7]

Against this rough sketch we can now explain why Heidegger's ontologizing of Kierkegaardian themes can be considered a development of the latter's work. Heidegger saw that one crucial implication of Kierkegaard's ethical consciousness is that authentic life does not transpire in a cultural and historical vacuum. Becoming critically related to my sense of identity is not only personal, but instills in me the capacity for questioning my heritage. In an early piece, John Caputo argued compellingly that Heidegger's genius consisted in recognizing that personal authenticity (self-consciousness) must be accompanied by "methodological consciousness."[8] *Being and Time*, then, can be said to extend the concept of authenticity to incorporate both a personal-existential and a phenomenological-methodological moment. The Kierkegaardian idea of retrieving a self-relation not adopted passively from *das Man* opens up the vista of the critical reassessment of Western metaphysics only implicit in Kierkegaard, but envisioned in *Being and Time* as a systematic *Destruktion* of Western ontology.[9]

Extending the Kierkegaardian exhortation to "become oneself," Heidegger claims that philosophy cannot be authentic, methodologically speaking, if it does not render its presuppositions explicit to itself. As Caputo clarifies,

> On the existential level, authentically being oneself (*eigentliches Selbstsein*) is the counter-tendency to inauthentically being like everyone else (*das 'Man'*). On the hermeneutical level—that is, on the level of a thematic interpretation such as is undertaken by the author of *Being and Time*—an authentic interpretation of Dasein in terms of existence and temporality is the counter-tendency to a falling interpretation of Dasein in terms of presence. Our prethematic fallenness (as existing beings) is mirrored in a fallen ontology.[10]

By Heidegger's reckoning, 2500 years of Western ontology have been inauthentic because Dasein, a historical mode of existence, has been theorized in static categories. Since, for Heidegger, thinking is a mode of being and not purely objective reflection, such fallen ontologies are no simple errors of representation. Inauthentic modes of conceptualization take root in forgetfulness or a practical failure to assume responsibility for critically assessing our philosophical inheritance from the bottom up.

It could be argued, then, that Kierkegaard's existential authenticity remains incomplete without the *Destruktion* of traditional metaphysics. Further, by exposing the inability of metaphysics to yield an authentic ontology, the *Destruktion* envisions a full scale conceptual revolution. New authentic categories would countermand the weight of our heritage of fallen ontologies, thereby begetting a renewal in Western ethos on a collective scale. Our lived possibilities for authentic existence would be secured, according to Heidegger, by this revolution.[11]

Such existential interpretations well portray the hefty ambition of *Being and Time* and, in fact, provide fruitful and productive readings of that work. Nonetheless, Heidegger fails to weave together the two threads of existential and methodological consciousness into a single fabric. As I hope to show, Heidegger's manner of ontologizing Kierkegaard's ethical view of authentic repetition abandons rather than incorporates the Kierkegaardian quest for personal edification.[12] Without the stages of interior growth in critical awareness, Heideggerian authenticity becomes limited to an abstract, *cognitive* achievement as opposed to *attitudinal* transformation. The results of this loss of ethical interiority, I believe, are minimally two. First, as is well noted, Heidegger's thought becomes embroiled in stoic consciousness. Second, he collapses Kierkegaard's notion of the ethical mode of existence into morality proper, thereby rooting morality in a decisionistic paradigm.

Heidegger's De-Ethicization of Kierkegaard

What appears at first glance only a minor modification of Kierkegaard by Heidegger—weaning authenticity of its motivational and attitudinal aspects— proves ultimately a marked divergence in their respective philosophies. Heidegger's deliberate efforts to sever psychological matters from epistemology lead him to underplay the role of interiority in how I engage, assume complicity with, or position myself in relation to reigning world-views. This formal side of Heidegger conflicts with the existentialist thrust of Kierkegaard's authorship; for the latter centers on a hermeneutics of suspicion and calls us to a revolution in consciousness and a correlative capacity for ideology critique.

Heidegger's analyses of inauthenticity and authenticity rely heavily upon the Kierkegaardian critiques of the "public" (*das Man*), "chatter" (idle talk), "anonymity" (ambiguity), "inquisitiveness" (curiosity), and "leveling" (fallenness). The Heideggerian concept of authenticity thus appears at first glance to be a perfect correlate to Kierkegaard's ethical stage of life (TA 90, 97, 103– 105).[13] However, the problem of self-identity is not an ontologically neutral issue for Kierkegaard; he is not concerned abstractly with the sheer act of appropriating possibilities and the need to repeat that act. Authenticity for Kierkegaard is first and primarily an ethical issue; it pertains, accordingly, to motivational life, to the possibilities of self-deception and blind support for cultural ideologies. The problem of authentic self-possession centers on the attainment of a *specific* unity between the life of ideation (possibility) and that of motivation (actuality), and not merely on willing self-unity (CUP 314, 323ff.). Hence, resolute existence is no valorization of the will. Rather, the value of commitment consists in that it gives birth to interiority or critical awareness; and, correlatively, true commitment presupposes critical awareness (cf. TA 92).

Here, I wish to suggest that Heidegger's elimination of motivational analysis renders his conception of self-determination abstract. Accordingly, a tension arises in *Being and Time* between Heidegger's insistence that authentic choice is concretely realized in social situations and the fact that, as Karsten Harries puts it, "resolve calls man to a form of life, not to a particular life."[14] Whereas for Kierkegaard authenticity calls me to embark on the ethical life of critical self-awareness (achieving a coincidence between how I actually live and how I represent my motives and actions to myself), Heidegger tends to restrict authenticity to a cognitive attempt to question the philosophical paradigms of tradition (effecting a coincidence between the categories of ontology and the fact that human life is historical). This difference in accent—psychological-existential and ontological-methodological—substantively differentiates their respective philosophies. Let me characterize these substantive differences in two ways. First, whereas Kierkegaard's model of authentic life is *dialectical*, Heidegger's proves *oppositional*. Second, Kierkegaard does not, as does Heidegger, single out the ethical (or ethico-religious) individual as an exception to public norms.

I will begin with Kierkegaard's *dialectical* view of the relation between personal identity (self-consciousness) and community (social context). Although he recognizes that subjectivity is intersubjectivity (CA 28), Kierkegaard still argues that my relation to others, to cultural beliefs, to public norms and normative discourses hinges upon my self-relation. The theory of indirect communication claims that the relation of a subject to others is never a facile, direct cognitive mediation of alter and self (CUP 74f.). Though never realized outside of a particular mode of relating to others and a specific view of my world, critical self-knowledge is acquired indirectly and not through direct and immediate reflection upon my situation. The ability both to adopt a critical view of my world and to listen or relate sincerely to others requires that I undertake the life of self-analysis and overcome my own naivete about my personal motives. Countering my own capacity for evil and my own entanglement in despair and sin informs my ability to grasp the world critically (CA 31; CUP 242, 246; TA 91, 99).[15]

Even though Kierkegaard's model of dialectical inwardness posits a surd on the side of interiority, this does not generate solipsism or a bifurcation of self-world. To the contrary, it allows him to differentiate the existential-modal relation, individual-crowd, from the ontological fact that subjectivity is always concretely bound up with community, others, a public world in general. Unlike the notions individual and crowd, which qualify subjective and communal life, self and community proper are not antithetical terms. Kierkegaard distinguishes the "crowd" from the possibility of a true community of "individuals" as "neighbors" (PV 60, 118). The crowd, then, is always abstract; it is that form of community which, though perhaps moralizing, obtains *"en masse"* a precritical relationship to its moral code and in this fashion "renders the individual completely impenitent and irresponsible" (PV 112; cf. TA 62–63, 91–95).

According to Kierkegaard, it is the "herd" (crowd) which cannot be social. Genuine community obtains only "dialectically" through indirect relations.

> When individuals (each one individually) are essentially and passionately related to an idea and together are essentially related to the same idea, the relation is optimal and [binding]. Individually, the relation separates them (each one has himself for himself), and ideally it unites them. . . . Thus the individuals never come too close to each other in the herd sense, simply because they are united on the basis of an ideal distance. (TA 62–63)

Whereas genuine community exhibits a true cohesion of individuals who think and act for themselves, the "herd" fails to achieve such cohesiveness.

> On the other hand, if individuals relate to an idea merely *en masse* (consequently without the individual separation of inwardness) . . . we have a tumultuous self-relating of the mass to an idea . . . gossip and rumor . . . and apathetic envy become a surrogate of each for all. Individuals do not in inwardness turn away from each other, turn outward in unanimity for an idea, but mutually turn to each other in a frustrating and suspicious, aggressive, leveling reciprocity. (TA 63)

When relations deteriorate into indifference and apathy, the crowd is born. Though an abstract entity, the crowd does not simply uphold the status quo but transmutes into a dangerous force that pulls everyone away from genuine individuality, thereby subverting the possibility of community (TA 86, 90–91). In this light, Kierkegaard's valorization of the individual as distinct from the crowd should be confused neither with stoic abstraction from the social world nor with repudiation of community. Ethical authenticity constitutes a pull away from the crowd only because it counteracts blind adherence to convention, not sociality and morality.

Kierkegaard's exceptional individual would best be depicted as an exile within community. To be exiled within one's community (as was Kierkegaard) is to somehow be a part of a communal world yet distinguished within it in an isolating way (PV 94–99). The ethical "individual," who resolves upon respon-

sibility for her/his choices, is separated off from the "crowd," but only qualitatively speaking. That separation occurs not in abstraction from my circumstance, but instead through intensifying participation in the community, such
that, even were I to adhere to the same principles as others, my mode of action
would be critical and engaged as opposed to passive and disingenuous. The
individual suffers social isolation because s/he takes seriously the ideas that
everyone else merely parrots. Further, by questioning the crowd's facile and
blind adherence to a pre-given set of public norms, the individual challenges
others to awaken from their immediate and uncritical acceptance of the status
quo (PV 115). Thus, the individual portrays the high personal and social stakes
involved in developing critical awareness; for it is not the individual who repudiates community, but rather the crowd which subjects the individual to social
opprobrium and threatens to destroy her/him. As Kierkegaard puts it, "The
Crowd is untruth. Therefore was Christ crucified. . . . " (PV 114); and further,
"the [crowd] is unrepentant" (TA 95, cf. 91–92).

Because Heidegger does not ground authenticity in the surd of dialectical
inwardness, his model of the relation between the authentic self and the public
world is construed *oppositionally*. *Being and Time* labors under the difficulty
of a fuzzy distinction between the public realm as such and the inauthentic
they-self, between the communal and social character of existence and the
"crowd." Heidegger's attempt to theorize the movement toward critical self-
knowledge as a qualification of how I relate to others (the they) thus fails.
Against his claims that authenticity yields "empathy" and the ability to care
for others, Heidegger posits authenticity as radical aloneness, as the "non-re-
latedness" of self to others.[16] Berthold-Bond clarifies the link between this conceptual problem and Heidegger's entanglement in stoic consciousness:

> Heidegger came to take on the guise of what Hegel refers to as "Stoicism"
> in his *Phenomenology*. The stoical consciousness, for Hegel, is motivated by
> a yearning for freedom, but a yearning which despairs of having its freedom
> acknowledged in the social and political world, a world in which it feels for-
> saken, just as the Heideggerian analysis of the experience of anxiety portrays
> Dasein as feeling lost and "not-at-home" in its everyday world. Hence the
> stoic practices the movement of withdrawal, and turns inward into the free-
> dom of *thought*. In thought, the stoic achieves his or her freedom because
> "in thought . . . I am not in an *other* but remain simply and solely in com-
> munion with myself" — words which are echoed in Heidegger's portrait of
> the radical individualization and "non-relatedness" to others which occurs
> in anxiety, being-towards-death, guilt, conscience, and resoluteness.[17]

Without a sharp distinction between inauthentic participation in "everydayness" and social life per se, freedom and self-determination function as *coun-
terpositions* to the public world of norms (Wolin) and in abstraction from political freedom (Lukács). Contrasted with Kierkegaard's exceptional individual

who is rejected by the crowd, the Heideggerian individual rises above the world of public debate which s/he stoically regards as an impediment to her/his personal autonomy and freedom.[18]

This brings us to a crucial difference between Heidegger and Kierkegaard. Since, according to Kierkegaard, personal authenticity cannot be coerced or dictated *en masse* through conventional morality (that results in the crowd), the correlate to the ethical individual in the public realm is not merely a community of individuals. Kierkegaard clearly fails to flesh out the social theory implied in his work; nonetheless, the complement in the realm of group-identity to the ethical individual, as Jürgen Habermas astutely points out, would be "abstract procedures and principles" that generate "conditions for communal life and communication among different, equally entitled and coexisting forms of life." Habermas clarifies,

> The weight of the "decision" [for Kierkegaard] . . . is meant primarily to stress the autonomous and conscious character of the act of taking hold of oneself. The only thing that can correspond to this on the level of the appropriation of intersubjectively shared traditions, is the autonomous and conscious character of a publicly conducted debate."[19]

Put otherwise, to recover an ethical capacity by no means necessitates the rejection of the very norms that the crowd I resist embraces. By the same token, it does reveal the need to question, legitimate, and embody a set of norms without absolutizing those claims, i.e., without lapsing into a herd-like communitarianism. To become a critical individual thus gets at the heart of those questions first rendered explicit by modern philosophy, e.g., how do we justify our world-views, our institutions, our moral paradigms.

Heidegger's oppositional model of the self-public relation, however, cannot sustain the egalitarian and democratic ramifications of Kierkegaard's view of authenticity. Instead, the oppositional consciousness of the stoic reinforces a tragic heroic view of life. Having collapsed the isolation of the authentic person into one of *ontological* or *numerical* distinction, as compared with Kierkegaard's *dialectical* and *exilic* view, Heidegger slurs the boundary between a qualitative and an essentialist view of excellence. Against the Kierkegaardian view that natural talent alone never distinguishes me, but only growth in self-awareness, Heideggerian authenticity invokes a Greek sense of an ontologically or naturally grounded elitism: Humans are distinguished by virtue of pre-given personality traits and abilities, not by the egalitarian principle that each is capable of the most supremely developed self-awareness that upholds Kierkegaard's conception of excellence. It is not, then, surprising that during the thirties Heidegger valorizes special heroes—"poets, thinkers and statesmen"—and spiritually superior nations, such as Greece and Germany. These "creators" and creative entities are born to a superior authority to see and embody what the public cannot, namely the higher purpose of humanity (cf. EO, II, 291ff.).[20]

Ethical versus Tragic Guilt

Here I want to pave the way for addressing the issue of decisionism by commenting on differences between Kierkegaard's existential and Heidegger's ontological views of conscience and guilt. As the last section implies, Heidegger's ontology does not simply round out Kierkegaard's existential work with a supplementary, but *strictly structural* analysis of Dasein's constitution. Rather, it imports *substantive* ontological claims, such as the elitist and tragic aspects of the Greek world-view, that dramatically conflict with the modern orientation of Kierkegaard's work. Even given a significant overlap of thematic issues, their respective philosophies finally veer off in different directions; this can be elicited from their views on guilt.

Heidegger misreads Kierkegaard, in part, because he is a good reader. He sees that Kierkegaard's ethical conceptions of conscience and guilt are not simply premoral but transmoral.[21] Adherence to conscience centers not on *what* I choose to do, evaluated from the moral point of view, but rather on *how* I inhabit my situation. The Kierkegaardian conception of conscience is modelled after Socrates' interior voice or *daemon*, and not the Freudian view of conscience as the internalization of public norms. While Kierkegaard would not deny that humans internalize public norms, he wants to identify a specific *ethical* as opposed to moral register built into temporal existence. That register signals our ability to be in violation of or estranged from ourselves in a premoral sense. As Schrag puts it,

> Conscience contributes to self-awareness the revelation of the hiatus between what the self is and what it might have been and might be. Conscience performs, as does anxiety, with which it is closely related, a disclosing or revealing function. . . . On the one hand, it discloses the estrangement of the self from its genuine possibilities and thus brings to light the reality of guilt; and on the other hand, it opens the way for authentic or committed existence.[22]

Conscience registers dysfunction in my self-relation, i.e., a disunity between what motivates my action and how I represent my actions and my identity to myself (SUD 20–21; cf. EO, II, 256). As the register for this disunity, despair indicates an ethical (i.e., motivational), not a moral failure (SUD 87–96).

Heidegger keys off what appear to be the ontological implications of Kierkegaard's notion of despair when he theorizes conscience as an inner (as opposed to external) measure built into the temporal structure of Dasein. Since, for Heidegger, "thrownness" is a constitutive feature of temporal being, "falling" and "being-guilty" are not simply modal qualifications of how we live but rather a priori ontological and necessary structures of Dasein's historical being. To be thrown means that, prior to discovering the possibility of taking over my existence, I have already fallen; I am absorbed in and distracted by the "they" such that my identity has been co-opted by some culturally received viewpoint. Were conscience not an inner "voice" registering this self-estrangement, there could be no possibility of freedom, i.e., overcoming inauthentic preoccupation with everyday affairs.[23]

Heidegger's concept of fallenness has merit: in outlining Dasein's inclination toward self-concealment, it reveals an important aspect of finitude, namely that we win through to self-knowledge in a struggle with our desire for immediate existence (absorption in the they). That Dasein is a priori "guilty" of inauthenticity reveals the "nullity" or groundlessness of existence, viz., that "Dasein constantly lags behind its possibilities." Not only must Dasein struggle for liberation, there is no final or pure state of authentic being.[24] Still, by making conscience, guilt, and fallenness necessary ontological features of human existence as opposed to stressing the ethical import of motivational life, guilt assumes a tragic and thus substantively different tonality than it holds for Kierkegaard.

On the one hand, Heidegger notes that ontological guilt is the very precondition of being able to grasp moral responsibility. Hence, "being-guilty" sounds like a transmoral concept. Precisely because, as a free potentiality-for-being I "never have power over [my] ownmost being from the bottom up," I am responsible for constantly taking over my own basis.[25] On the other hand, because Heidegger's theory of guilt suffers from the same abstraction that inheres in his ambiguous formulation of authenticity, the ethical significance of becoming my own basis seems lacking. Where does authentic resolve deliver me? Not to anything like Kierkegaard's life of inwardness or growth in critical awareness. Heeding the call of conscience proves empty. As authentic, we finally see that we are guilty. We grasp that freedom is a burden and a task; however, this "moment of vision" is purely formal, abstract, and "indefinite." It neither frees me from guilt nor guarantees right action; it cannot even inform my critical life.[26]

The abstract and antinormative features of Heidegger's work suggest that his concept of authenticity lapses into premoralism. In other words, unlike Kierkegaard's ethical conscience, which is transmoral, Heideggerian conscience cannot qualify or supplement moral discourse in any way. Furthermore, the Heideggerian thesis that guilt is a necessary ontological feature of freedom already sounds the tragic note of existence and funds an attitude of fatalism. It allows the fact that humans can never achieve pure authenticity (human finitude) to justify a stoic and passive acceptance of tragedy, namely that no matter how morally responsible I become, a collision of goods must inevitably prevail. As I think Kierkegaard anticipated, this perspective opens the door to pawning social responsibility off on being (unconcealment) proper.[27]

Against the ontological and premoral viewpoint, Kierkegaard proclaims the existential and transmoral (ethical) import of guilt. Although guilt and sin (fallenness) are elements of the human condition, Kierkegaard would not reduce the fact of this condition and its implications to an ontological claim. That I inherit "hereditary sin" is neither a question of piously sharing in collective guilt nor an excuse for disavowing responsibility for the failures of my life choices (as with Heidegger's political engagement) (CA 28–29). At issue for Kierkegaard is the manner by which humans disavow moral responsibility by *actively* willing ignorance (despair). Even if Kierkegaard's thesis that self-identity must be created cannot avoid the implication that fallenness is an ontological structure of human existence, he emphasizes the existential significance of the fact that I am born into sin (inauthenticity). Existentially speaking, the fact that I can fall never implies that I must fall. Hence, Kierkegaard defines despair as a possibility of our nature, but not a necessity (SUD 15). And, similarly, he discusses sin as a quality of life as opposed to an ontological condition; accordingly, "the individual participates in [sin] by the qualitative leap" and not through Adam, i.e., by being born into a world wherein the crowd prevails (CA 32–33).

That sin and guilt are not acquired first or necessarily through external acts, thus, does not imply that sin is an ontological condition. It is more accurate to claim that sin remains an "act" for Kierkegaard: an inward act of willed complicity with the age, the crowd, or some circumstance. For this reason, Kierkegaard defines despair and sin not as privations, but rather as "positions" (SUD 96). Although this complicity may not lead me to violate the laws of my society, I remain, existentially speaking, guilty and even sinful to the extent that I willfully refuse to develop an ethically differentiated consciousness. The ethical struggle against my own false and demonic motives cannot be reduced to Heidegger's tendency to locate the enemy outward, in the gravity of culture and tradition.[28]

Guilt for Kierkegaard is inexorably existential; hence, freedom and guilt are dialectical. That is, my ability to discern, understand, critique, derive, legitimate norms, and thus to size up and seize upon a given course of action from the moral point of view is related directly to the degree of critical self-awareness into which I have evolved. That is not to say that I cannot be rightly judged guilty or innocent of a crime independent of my self-comprehension and motives; however, it is to claim that in order to become a morally and politically responsible citizen, I must enter the inward journey of ongoing motivational self-analysis. Social responsibility cannot be critical without the life of interiority; hence, the ethical is transmoral.

Again we find ourselves before the chasm that separates Kierkegaard's ethical conception of inwardness and Heidegger's ontological viewpoint. When Kierkegaard depicts the task of taking over my guilt and my despair as an ongoing project worked out through the stages of life, he demonstrates that the life of self-examination and refinement of the ethical capacity for moral responsibility has no terminus. To the extent that humans need ever more refined awareness, they are always guilty. Accordingly, there is no genuine guilt, for Kierkegaard, without *knowledge* of it. By contrast, when Heidegger proclaims the universal nature of "being-guilty," he tends to project guilt and/or errancy outward. Or, minimally, it is but a short step from *Being and Time* to Heidegger's philosophy of the thirties, wherein he attributes errancy to unconcealment proper. Because "Dasein constantly lags behind its possibilities" it necessarily suffers the limits of its current historical consciousness as dictated by being (destiny). Kierkegaard, however, emphasizes the need to grow in *knowledge* of my actual guilt and actual failings in order to get beyond the tragic viewpoint that wanes passively before the inevitability (destiny) of guilt.

Placing the accent on the ontological feature of guilt, then, appears to betray Kierkegaard's authorship. And, as we might expect, Kierkegaard challenges the Heideggerian ontological claim that *"being-guilty* is more primordial than any *knowledge* about it."[29]

> Because it is an existing person who is to relate to himself, but guilt is the most concrete expression of existence, the *consciousness* of guilt is the expression for the relation. The more abstract the individual is . . . the more he distances himself from guilt, because abstraction places existence in the sphere of indifference. . . . The difficulty, however, is certainly something else, because, inasmuch as the guilt is explained by existing, the existing person seems to be made guiltless; it seems that he must be able to shove guilt onto the one who placed him in existence or onto existence itself. In that case, the guilt-consciousness is only a new expression for suffering in existence. . . . (CUP 528)

Heidegger's tendency to attribute blame for his participation in National Socialism to destiny seems consistent with his de-ethicization of Kierkegaard's concept of guilt. In this light, the very fact that Kierkegaard refuses to derive an ontology begins to appear as a deliberate reinforcement of his implicit philosophical view that existence overrides being or ontology. The Heideggerian turn toward ontology abstracts from the transmoral question of cultivating the ethico-existential conditions of sincere embodiment of the moral point of view. It becomes premoral, i.e., ethically neutral; and for this reason it is also incapable of supplementing moral theory.

Heidegger's Category Mistake

Richard Wolin (unlike early Marcuse and following Habermas) recently argued that Heidegger's political engagement resulted directly from his existentialist philosophy. Wolin carefully points out that the adoption of *Existenzphilosophie* by Heidegger did not occur in a cultural vacuum. Rather, it presupposes a "generational crisis" that witnessed the "total devaluation of traditional meanings and inherited beliefs." Thus, the "Heideggerian variant" of *Existenzphilosophie* "tends to be inherently destructive of tradition" and polemical against public norms. Even so, Wolin tends to implicate all existential philosophies, and not just the "Heideggerian variant" as inherently decisionistic valorizations of heroic will. To his mind, thinkers like Kierkegaard and Nietzsche provide Heidegger his twin theses: that the exceptional person overrides the norm and that the demise of tradition leaves Western humanity in a meaningless void which can only be overcome by combatting the normalcy of everyday life. While this may be true of Nietzsche, the above commentary suggests that Kierkegaard avoids Heidegger's problem of decisionism.[30]

Following Martin Matuštík's recent work on Kierkegaard, I suggest that Heidegger makes a "category mistake" in which he slurs over the boundary between an existential *mode* of action (the *how*) and the *substantive* choice one makes in action (*what* one enacts).[31] This category mistake inheres in Heidegger's stoic and oppositional conception of the authentic and resolute life, thereby embroiling him in the problematic decisionism at the heart of his political involvement in National Socialism. Heidegger's abstract account of authentic resolve, because empty, provides no material criteria for political action. Worse, as oppositional, it rejects democratic procedures for generating criteria for normative theory and political praxis. For this reason, Heidegger finally turns to destiny (an abstract as opposed to materially concrete reading of history) to justify his course of action.

Kierkegaard's ethical notion of authenticity, instead of replacing questions of normative theory and praxis with the *Bildungsprozess* of interiority, maintains a sharp distinction between the ethical (sincerity of motives) and the normative (justifying a course of action). Although ethical life has a certain practical fulfillment unto itself (growth in critical awareness), this practical capacity does not dislodge, but rather prepares me for sincere participation in discourses of legitimation. Conversely, by reducing authenticity to a roughly cognitive and methodological achievement, Heidegger's *theory* of authentic being (ontology) stands in sore need of *practical* fulfillment. This becomes clear in his 1928 lecture course, *The Metaphysical Foundations of Logic*, when he claims that fundamental ontology ("the analysis of Dasein and of the temporality of being") can only be fulfilled in the ontic. In effect, the theory of authentic being must be realized through a practical revolution in the ethos of Western humanity. However, in the absence of any criteria for legitimating action, as Wolin argues, "the National Socialist movement presented itself as a plausible material 'filling' for the empty vessel of authentic decision."[32]

The charge of decisionism pertains to any view that decision (or willed resolve) constitutes the final basis for determining a course of moral or political action, independent of public discourse, existing systems of law, and procedures for legitimation. In effect, the decision "grounds" itself out of its own heroic greatness. Sovereign authority, embodied for example by Heidegger's "creators," and not procedural justice determine that greatness.[33] The problem of decisionism, however central to Heidegger's tragic heroic, elitist, and authoritarian world-view, is not a necessary consequence of existential theories of authenticity, such as Kierkegaard's.

By bringing up the issue of a category mistake, I am claiming that Heidegger and Kierkegaard have two conflicting concepts of *mode*. As dialectical, ethical agency is strictly a modal qualification for Kierkegaard, characterizing how I engage in or relate to theoretical and practical activities. It is difficult to discuss the ethical independent of actual moral and social practices because I never enter into the life of inwardness independent of real life choices. However, that Kierkegaard's pseudonymous authorship depicts concretely the stages of edification and accepts provisionally yet without justification Christian dogma, does not support the assumption that the authorship offers a systematic philosophical response to questions of moral and religious theory. To mistakenly think that Kierkegaard's existential ethics supplies a fully developed moral theory (even Christian moral theory) would be to confuse the ethical problem of developing responsibility for my motivational life with prescribing moral content (what I ought to do). In effect, it would be to fall prey to a category mistake.

Heidegger, indeed, falls prey to just this category mistake because he implicitly transmutes Kierkegaard's existential notion of modality into an ontological concept. Taken as an ontological category, mode or the *how* of human existence is not restricted to the individual's manner of engaging her/his circumstance. Instead, mode expands to encompass the broad web of the social, linguistic, and political features of a people's basic way of being (i.e., an ontological category). Although a structural category referring to the temporal character of existence, "being" is also substantive to the extent that it never exists outside an actual configuration of cultural life. Hence, it connotes the ethos of an historical age of Western humanity.

Existential readings of *Being and Time*, which take Heidegger to incorporate Kierkegaard, find Heidegger's turn to a collective as opposed to individual notion of Dasein, in the latter portions of *Being and Time* and in his subsequent thought, an anomaly.[34] On this reading, Heidegger's work of the thirties would mark a radical break with *Being and Time*; in effect, the concept of authenticity laid out in *Being and Time* would counter his turn to an elitist vision in which individuals submit their wills to the collective destiny of Germany. However, I am arguing that the slippage from individual to collective Dasein is built implicitly into Heidegger's ontologizing the Kierkegaardian concept of modality.

Although the shift to a collectivist focus certainly aggravates the aforementioned deficiencies of *Being and Time*, it, too, was inherent in his transmutation of authenticity into an abstract methodological achievement. That is, cast in terms of deriving an authentic fundamental ontology, the critique of past philosophical paradigms as grounded in inauthentic social practices necessarily demanded practical realization through a revolution in cultural ethos (mode of life). Since this could only be achieved on a collective scale, the objective of *Being and Time*, viz., to countermand the metaphysics of presence, harbored a political intent from the outset. And, moreover, the problem of decisionism follows from Heidegger's ontologizing the concept of modality to the extent that he rejects the validity of all previous forms of collective existence (as rooted in inauthentic ontologies), while nonetheless demanding a spiritual and moral renewal of the German people. As this renewal can find no justification on the basis of our material past, it had to be granted futurally by destiny.[35]

For this reason, I find Kierkegaard's notion of self-becoming at odds with that of Heidegger. That Kierkegaard recognizes a necessary disjunction between who I currently am (necessity) and who I can become (possibility) is not finally an ontological concept of freedom. Ontological freedom is abstract, from a Kierkegaardian perspective, in that it allows me to cast life fatalistically, as a battle with history to wrest my future possibilities from destiny. Existential freedom, however, posits a necessary disjunction between inwardness (ethical life) and the social and moral claims of society and of the historical age on me. Without the surd of interiority built into human nature, no separation could occur of personal conscience from blind adherence to and internalization of the rules of my society. That growth in ethical capacity must be ruled by possibility (i.e., have no terminus) constitutes an existential condition of challenging the accepted norms of my society, hence of non-dogmatic normative theory and praxis. Thus, I would argue that Kierkegaard's teleological suspension of the ethical in favor of the ethical-religious only applies to ethical edification (interior life) and does not imply an actual (heroic) transgression of moral accountability.[36]

In the end, Heidegger and Kierkegaard move in antithetical directions. Unlike Kierkegaard's ethical life, which constitutes a precondition of moral and social responsibility (transmoral), Heidegger's methodological conception of authenticity is deeply antinormative. Ethical life finds rich fulfillment through inward transformation; moreover, in taking over responsibility for monitoring the growth of my own conscience and assessing my own motivational life, the ethical functions as a practical a priori for sustaining life under conditions of modernity. Ethical consciousness makes me capable of critically sustaining normative discourse, on the one hand, without prescribing moral action, on the other. It is neither empty nor decisionistic. Conversely, Heideggerian authenticity is not only empty, in that it neither delivers me to ethical edification nor supplements moral discourse as a practical a priori, but it supplants altogether normative criteria for action.

Questions Concerning Symbolic Consciousness

I have belabored the point that Kierkegaard's existential thought offers a corrective to Heidegger's ontological view of situated subjectivity. Now let me pick up and weave back into this commentary the initial thread of Heidegger's potential advance over Kierkegaard. As previously noted, that advance consisted in the promise of a situated critical discourse characterized by the dual moments of methodological and existential authenticity. However, Heidegger's failure to interweave these two moments by no means rules out the desirability of the need for a critical relationship to our conceptual heritage. In isolating the deficiencies of Heidegger's thought, then, we should not ignore that he nonetheless provides his own limited conception of a critical "methodological consciousness."

Not only did Heidegger offer a philosophical critique of ahistorical and instrumental paradigms of rationality, his work paved the way toward the recognition that a crucial aspect of critical consciousness must include awareness of the way in which language, grammar, and the symbolic order function to restrict theory and praxis. Whereas Kierkegaard's authorship centers on cultivating a critical relation to my *personal motivational life*, Heidegger's ill-conceived revolution against metaphysics nonetheless points up the need to develop a *critical relation to the symbolic*. More broadly put, Heidegger calls into question the manner by which, in taking over our conceptual and linguistic heritage, we tend to reproduce elements of past structures of domination, mainstream discourses, outmoded ways of thinking.[37]

Here I wish to indicate programmatically why I think that Kierkegaard and Derrida offer two different, yet potentially complementary responses to Heidegger, whose later work continues to incline toward abstraction and ethical neutrality. In spite of the critical potential of his hermeneutics of suspicion, Kierkegaard nonetheless stops short of any critical interest in the symbolic world proper. His work is largely quietist on this front, whereas Heidegger's insistence on working out a transgression of Western tradition in and through a methodological destruction paved the way for Derrida's politics of symbolic representation. Precisely Heidegger's non-personalist turn away from questions of motive isolated the phenomena of language and meaning (being) as systems that determine individual and collective identities. While motivational and symbolic consciousness comprise two specific aspects of critical awareness, I believe each needs to be rounded out and corrected by the other, but in differing ways.

Let me suggest how this is so. Although antimetaphysical, Kierkegaard never undertakes an explicit genealogy of the origin of our symbolic matrices and linguistic practices. His own uncritical deployment of metaphors is far from consistent with the turn to language within contemporary philosophical discourses. This leaves his philosophy wanting, not only for what it does not do (e.g., flesh out a full social theory) but for what it does do (i.e., cultivate critical consciousness). Tamsin Lorraine makes this point forcibly when she argues that in *Fear and Trembling*, Johannes de Silentio can conceive of a transgression of universal categories (i.e., a feminine disruption of the masculine law of the symbolic in Lacan's sense) *only* in relation to God but not through relations with other humans, such as actual women.

> On the one hand, [de Silentio] wants to move away from the masculine position of appealing to fixed categories as the ultimate justification of meaning and action. On the other hand, he cannot allow the chaos that would result if those categories were permitted to crumble. He is thus caught in the dilemma of wanting to maintain both positions at once. He does this by maintaining a masculine position with respect to other human beings and positing the possibility of a feminine position with respect to God.[38]

Lorraine's demonstration of the limits of Kierkegaard's authorship is borne out by his extensive usage of traditional conceptions of male and female roles in interpersonal relationships for articulating the stages of inward growth. As Lorraine points out, "woman [in de Silentio's discourse] is the focal point for the man's agony," she is "more innocent than the man," she is "incapable of judging ethical boundaries."[39]

By implication, there is more than one way to concretize Heideggerian philosophy, though each incomplete in itself. While Kierkegaard introduces existential concretion through inwardness and a hermeneutics of suspicion, Derrida pins Heidegger's philosophical concerns down in a material conception of language. Against Heidegger's tendency to make being, language, and historicity abstract terms, Derrida roots language and the symbolic in the actual social practices of a culture.[40] Practitioners of Derridean deconstruction thus turn theory into a political and ethical activity. Theoretical strategies become interventions in the manner by which languages and concepts restrict possibilities for individual and collective identity. These strategies hold ethical import in that they strive to open up, as opposed to suppress, differences and counter the hegemonic and imperialist tendencies of mainstream discourses. And, finally, deconstruction engenders a capacity for critical sensitivity to the symbolic order, to the manner by which theory and thought invoke power hierarchies.[41]

Deconstructionist strategies, then, can be said to encourage the development of a specific reflexive capacity rooted in the awareness that thinking is inherently controlled by linguistic practices and not just in control over these practices. For reasons mentioned above, Kierkegaard's authorship needs to be situated or rewritten from the standpoint of this enhanced awareness, particularly with respect to his metaphor of woman. Nonetheless, given the ironic stance from which the authorship is generated, this type of revision does not appear to conflict with Kierkegaard's general philosophy, at least not on the reading given here. Since his metaphors are not bound or fixed (because ironic in some measure), the authorship lends itself to becoming a performative theory along the lines of French feminists, Luce Irigaray and Hélène Cixous. In other words, the authorship could critically instead of naively deploy the traditional metaphors surrounding masculine and feminine roles. Furthermore, there is no reason why Kierkegaard's model of situated but critical consciousness cannot incorporate metaphoric and symbolic awareness. Understood as disjunctive to social conventions, the theory of inwardness could articulate a transgression of the symbolic in a fashion analogous to the ethical suspension of normative paradigms. A teleological suspension of the symbolic—understood as the activity of cultivating personal awareness of gender (race, class) bias—would supply the existential prerequisite for transforming gender relations.

Turning now to postmodernism. In spite of the material and political concretion sought and to some degree won by deconstructionists, remnants of stoicism, decisionism (antinormativism), and even fatalism often reappear in various deconstructionist positions (though not as blatantly as in Heidegger). Given my argument throughout, that Kierkegaard offers a way to discuss rationality as situated without lapsing into antinormativism and that he furnishes a version of antifoundationalism that does not fall prey to decisionism, let me sketch three ways in which I think we could further explore Kierkegaardian correctives to these difficulties.

First, postmodern turns to language generally rely upon some version, weak or strong, of the thesis that the subject is a position in language.[42] This type of thesis, though often formulated independent of Heidegger, nonetheless is indebted to his work. Hence, it is instructive to note that Heidegger's later rejection of his early theory of situated agency was unnuanced. That is, Heidegger blamed his political actions on the excessive voluntarism in *Being and*

Time and this, in turn, on his failure to overcome modernity by retaining a theory of agency. Thus, he swaps out quietism for voluntarism and rejects theoretical paradigms of subjectivity and agency. But this shift from heroism to quietism, from agency to language, does nothing to address the twin problems of stoicism and decisionism. Hence, Heidegger overlooks both that not all versions of agency are voluntaristic and that the arbitrary adoption of non-violence does not overcome decisionism.[43]

Hence, even though Derridean deconstruction strives to counteract Heideggerian quietism by politicizing theory, this does not automatically alleviate the problems of stoicism and decisionism. Postmodernist conceptions of positionality offer at best weak versions of agency that repeat the Heideggerian turn away from motivational questions (since bound to paradigms of consciousness). The turn to positionality tends to lose the category of inwardness and its dialectical relation to the world (or to language) theorized by Kierkegaard.[44] Thus, although the notion of positionality offers fruitful insights into the situated character of theory and praxis, it cannot support a fully concrete understanding of how I come to critical awareness of my own positioning in power.

This occurs because these theories generally reduce the relation of identity and language to a one-dimensional or direct relation between two terms (identity-language). That is, they lack the third term thematized by Kierkegaard, viz., the activity of relating to both myself and my world. This third term links language to self-understanding in such a way that I retain a point of resistance to that which constructs me, without on that account abstracting from situatedness and finitude. Without this third term, the concept of positionality collapses personal identity into language. Identity winds up completely constructed by language and with this, agency and resistance are lost. The problem of something other than human being (e.g., language) dictating action reemerges (i.e., fatalism). Inasmuch as even weak versions of agency, e.g., paradigms of iteration or mimesis, lack the complexity of Kierkegaard's triadic view of situated subjectivity, they prove too weak to explain personal and political resistance. We need a way to articulate just how we are capable of reiteration, mimesis, and simple resistance to being located in a given position, as well as a way to assess our complicity in the power of those positions. Each could be addressed by the Kierkegaardian notion of a critical self-relation (inwardness).[45]

Second, the deconstructionist goal of forging a genuinely cohesive form of solidarity that recognizes diverse forms of oppression and, accordingly, a multiplicity of reasons for desiring the same practical objective requires, I believe, something like Kierkegaard's motivational theory in order to avoid stoicism. A genuine, non-stoic capacity to hear others whose experiences and identities are radically different than mine (i.e., to bond, empathize, and find a true ground of mutual commitment) requires more than a loose-fitting anarchism. Authentically letting others speak requires that I grapple with my own biases, not simply that I cognitively accept the legitimacy of others who appear different from me. We might look again to Kierkegaard's notion of inwardness to supply a more concrete basis for revisioning political solidarity. That basis, rooted in part in existential authenticity, if anarchist, would not be devoid of humanism. Though harnessing diverse groups in opposition to the same thing, it would cultivate in addition a capacity for solidarity based upon genuine understanding, conflict resolution, self-transformation. It would provide more cohesion than a simple formal or cognitive gesture toward others.[46]

Third, many deconstructionists cannot show how engendering a postmodern ethos will guarantee the production of individuals who can sustain a critical relationship to the very paradigms they recommend. Cultivating the value of hearing difference does not guarantee the continuation or protection of egalitarian society. As Benhabib points out, "The . . . defect of 'situated criticism' is to assume that the constitutive norms of a given culture, society, and tradition will be sufficient to enable one to exercise criticism in the name of a desirable future." Some might respond that postmodern interventions are conceived only as correctives to modernity, not its total displacement, which is an impossibility. That is, interventionist strategies presuppose that we already have institutions intact that offer procedural justice. Nonetheless, even this sidesteps the question of decisionism, or the need to link up one's vision of the good with normative discourse. Clearly justifications for turning to substantive modifications of community and culture rely upon negative analyses of modernity. Yet these critiques tend to reject the validity of discourses of legitimation, thereby collapsing strategies of intervention into substitutions for normative discourse. This conflation repeats the category mistake made by Heidegger, wherein he confuses altering our mode of existence (ethos) with jettisoning entirely the modern ideal of normative legitimation.[47]

In light of the generally unfruitful divide that obtains between critical modern and postmodern thinkers, we could look to Kierkegaard's existential thought as a middle term. Kierkegaard's corrective to stoicism and decisionism calls into question the postmodern tendency to do away with agency and normative theory, while retaining a strong version of situated rationality. Work remains to be done examining whether or not his concept of situated ethical agency can support the types of political praxis rightly desired by postmodernists. Indeed, Kierkegaard's uncritical usage of gendered metaphors exposes the importance of deconstructionist strategies. In seeking a pathway between antinormativism and a politics of symbolic representation, perhaps Kierkegaard and other existentialists can point the way toward bridging this divide.

Notes

1. Schrag offers the definitive comparison of Heidegger and Kierkegaard in English, *Existence and Freedom*.

2. See Brown, *Kierkegaard, Heidegger, Buber and Barth*, p. 80. Aspects of Heidegger's young personalism (1919-1926) certainly supported his inclusion in the category of existential philosophy; see Heidegger's comments to his students, quoted in Kisiel, "Heidegger's Apology," pp. 25-26; and Löwith, *Denker in Dürftiger Zeit*, pp. 20-21. However, van Buren's pioneering work on the young Heidegger reveals that *Being and Time* marked an "aberration" of Heidegger's personalist phase, "The Young Heidegger and Phenomenology," pp. 262, 246.

3. See Ballard, "Marxist Challenges," pp. 121-41; and Berthold-Bond, "A Kierkegaardian Critique," pp. 119-42.

4. See Harries, "Heidegger as Political Thinker," p. 648. On Kierkegaard, cf. Lukács, *Die Zerstörung der Vernuft*; Adorno, *Kierkegaard*; Westphal, "Kierkegaard and the Logic of Insanity"; Connell and Evans, Introduction; and Matuštík, this volume.

5. Heidegger, *Being and Time*, p. 12. I use the marginal pagination for this text which also appears in the *Gesamtausgabe* edition of *Sein und Zeit*.

6. Schrag, *Existence and Freedom*, p. 18, cf. xvi.

7. Heidegger, *Being and Time*, pp. 232, 326, 123, 126, 129, 268.

8. Caputo, "Hermeneutics as the Recovery of Man," p. 349.

9. On Heidegger's envisioned but never completed *Destruktion*, see *Being and Time*, pp. 20f., 35, 40.

10. Caputo, "Hermeneutics as the Recovery of Man," pp. 355-56.

11. Cf. Heidegger, *Metaphysical Foundations*, p. 158.

12. Heidegger's method of *Wiederholung* splits away from Kierkegaard's concept of repetition, since the latter delivers me to the life of inwardness, and not solely awareness of temporal finitude.

13. On Heidegger's correlative terms in parentheses, *Being and Time*, pp. 167-80.

14. See Harries's exemplary essay, "Heidegger as Political Thinker," p. 647.

15. See Westphal, "Inwardness and Ideology Critique," p. 106 *et passim*.

16. Heidegger, *Being and Time*, pp. 125, 251, cf. 130, 179-80, 298-300.

17. Berthold-Bond, "A Kierkegaardian Critique," p. 129, quoting Hegel's *Phenomenology*, p. 120.

18. Habermas, "Work and Weltanschauung," p. 449; Adorno, *Jargon*, pp. 93-95, 115 *et passim*; Kosík, *Dialectics*, p. 121 *et passim*; Lukács, "Existentialism or Marxism?" p. 139; Stern (Anders), "Pseudo-Concreteness"; and Ballard, "Marxist Challenges." During a presentation of this essay, Bill McBride noted ironically that Heidegger may not have been enough of a Stoic, to the extent that social conditions impeded the Stoics from realizing their social and political responsibility. This is correct insofar as Heidegger's concept of authenticity allows for rejecting responsibility to the public realm per se. By stoicism I mean the latter.

19. Habermas, "Post-Traditional Identity," pp. 261-62.

20. Heidegger, *An Introduction to Metaphysics*, pp. 38-39, 62-63.

21. See Schrag on the transmoral conscience, *Existence and Freedom*, p. 161.

22. Ibid., p. 155.

23. Heidegger, *Being and Time*, pp. 175-80, 269-80, 284.

24. Ibid., p. 284. See Zimmerman, "On Discriminating Everydayness," esp. pp. 120-27.

25. Heidegger, *Being and Time*, pp. 285-87.

26. Ibid., pp. 298–300, 308, 344–45. Cf. Berthold-Bond's extensive commentary, "A Kierkegaardian Critique," esp. pp. 125–130; and Harries, "Heidegger as Political Thinker," pp. 647–49, 652, 655.

27. Cf. Harries, "Heidegger as Political Thinker," pp. 659–63.

28. Cf. Harries, "Heidegger as Political Thinker," pp. 665–68.

29. Heidegger, *Being and Time*, p. 286.

30. See Wolin, *The Politics of Being*, pp. 32, 35, 63, 37–39; and *The Terms of Cultural Criticism*, pp. 88–89. See also Habermas, "Discourse Ethics," p. 170; and "Post-Traditional Identity," p. 262.

31. Here I key off Matuštík's argument that the charge of decisionism against Kierkegaard is a category mistake, *Postnational Identity*, chap. 5, sect. 2B. By extension, I argue that this charge is applicable to Heidegger.

32. Heidegger, *Metaphysical Foundations*, p. 158. Cf. Wolin, *Politics of Being*, p. 65; and Harries, "Heidegger as Political Thinker," p. 649.

33. On decisionism, see Wolin, *Politics of Being*, pp. 29–30, 32, 37–38. Cf. Habermas, "Discourse Ethics," p. 44 *et passim*.

34. Cf. Heidegger, *Being and Time*, pp. 383–87. See also Wolin, *Politics of Being*, pp. 55ff.

35. See Wolin, *Politics of Being*, p. 67.

36. See Matuštík, this volume.

37. See later Heidegger's critically reworked concept of destiny (*Geschick*), *The Principle of Reason*, p. 91 *et passim*; cf. *On the Way to Language*, p. 15.

38. Lorraine, *Gender*, pp. 118–19.

39. Ibid., p. 129.

40. This claim is controversial. Cf. Fraser, "Uses and Abuses," pp. 177–94; and Martin, *Matrix and Line*, pp. 110, 131ff.

41. See, for example, Martin, *Matrix and Line*, pp. 185ff.; and Butler, *Gender Trouble*, pp. 5–6.

42. See Flax, *Psychoanalysis, Feminism, and Postmodernism*, p. 32; cf. Benhabib, *Situating the Self*, p. 208.

43. Cf. Harries, "Heidegger as Political Thinker," pp. 668–69.

44. Kierkegaard demonstrates that Hegel never truly achieves a mediation of self-other. Hence, the notion of dialectic inwardness supplies this missing mediation (CUP 401ff.).

45. Weir initiates this type of critique against Butler's *Gender Trouble*, "Subversion of Solidarity?"

46. See Fraser on Butler, "False Antitheses," p. 175. Cf. Butler, *Gender Trouble*, pp. 14–15.

47. See Benhabib, "Feminism and Postmodernism," p. 145; and White, "Difficulties of a Postmodern Ethics and Politics."

4 | God, Anxiety, and Female Divinity
Alison Leigh Brown

Call yourself. Give, yourself, names.
—Luce Irigaray, *Elemental Passions*, p. 7

A COMMON UNDERSTANDING of anxiety is that anxiety is a psychological state of fragmentation, or, at the very least, of fracture. The individual is divided between her/his present and her/his future in ways that make her/him uneasy or not at home. Yet Haufniensis's argument that instead, anxiety begins in innocence is emotionally compelling. For Haufniensis, as innocence opens up into increasingly imaginable possibilities, anxiety likewise increases—hence the naïve and non-dialectical presupposition that anxiety derives from fragmentation. We notice anxiety in fragmentation but in order to notice the fracture one must first be *whole*, argues Kierkegaard's troubled pseudonym. Haufniensis's cure for anxiety is an education in significant actuality, that is, an education in the lessons of the Atonement. Anxiety dissolves only in a God relation, specifically in salvation. Turning the many into a higher unity is the only way to overcome anxiety—that "primal" state of humanity.

Irigaray, the other focus of this essay, does not specifically deal with the concept of anxiety. It would appear, however, that if she were to examine Haufniensis's conception of it, she would probably argue that such a conception was always already repressed. Irigaray's theme of reclaiming multiplicity from forced unity could force her to privilege, not try to overcome, what Haufniensis calls "anxiety." That is, she may well balk at yet another "solution" to multiplicity through unity. Still, Irigaray's focus on a reclaimed feminine divinity through an increased awareness of "mothering" in all its forms is not completely dissimilar to Kierkegaard's focus on re-finding an inner life through something transcendent. Woman, according to Irigaray, is forced to pretend a oneness when she is a multiplicity. The reclaiming of herself through the re-representation of her strongest images is necessary for woman's power to assert itself. For Irigaray, woman finds herself as grounded in possibility or in multiplicity only when women can reclaim their divinity in all its manifestations, or, when the metaphor of "mothering" is exploded into many kinds of female or feminine creativity. Irigaray writes, "And she has no need *once* to be a mother, *one* day to produce *one* child, to make her sex the place of unceasing birthing. To be a woman, she does not have to be mother, unless she wants to set a limit to her growth and her gift for life. Motherhood is only one specific way to fulfill the operation: giving birth. Which is never one, unique, and definitive. Except from the male standpoint" (Irigaray [1991] p. 86). Irigaray argues that female creativity, polymorphous "birthing," has been covered up over and over again but that that creativity reasserts itself in identifiable ways. The latent feminine can be seen in the texts of Plato, Freud, and Nietzsche, for example. Irigaray sees their inability to recognize anything "other" as partial evidence for their fear of "mothering" in all its forms. Her solution is for them to recognize and love "the other"—or even perhaps to return a love that is given them again, over and over again.

As we have seen, an aspect of Kierkegaard sees a fragmentation of representation expressing itself in a temporal/spatial psychological state that can only be dissipated (from actual to divine, from one to many, from dying-from to death, from finitude to infinity) through a special relationship. For this aspect, for Haufniensis, that relationship is with the God-man. Irigaray also calls for a resolution through a special relationship but for her it is with feminine divinity. Both writers act out such relationships through writing characters (both lovers and those beloved) to exposit their philosophical positions. Kierkegaard explains his voice-throwing as follows:

> Given the conditions in the world as it is, to be an author should be the extraordinary employment in life, an employment that escapes the dialectic of the universal (office and whatever pertains to that; a living and whatever pertains to that). Therefore, not only should the author's production be a testimony to the idea but the author's life should also correspond to the idea. But, alas, of all the categories, the category of actuality is the most mediocre. To be an author is to be in a fraternity and is just as cluttered up with finiteness as anything else. . . . By taking advantage of my pseudonymity, I have stayed completely clear of this. (COR 215)

In his fictive loving Kierkegaard loves both a completely alterior other, the unnameable God, and an unattainable but present other, Regina. Irigaray loves so much and so many more—and, one can imagine her being loved as well. She, but not Kierkegaard, can be beloved as well as lover. The fictive beloved leaves Irigaray a voice; Kierkegaard must throw his to his pseudonyms. This "poise," as he calls it, exacts no small psychic cost from Kierkegaard (COR 208). There is a dialectical flow between the fictive writings of Kierkegaard and Irigaray that helps throw light on reclaiming not unity, not divinity, but force and power in the world. The creative acts of writing out one's fears and fantasies allow a peace in disunity which fosters mutual recognition. In examining this dialectic we will be lead from anxiety through sacrifice to writing and finally to naming. On our way we must take Nietzsche up into this duplicitous dialectic.

1. *Anxiety.* Haufniensis argues that anxiety is ambiguous and derives from ambiguity. One is guilty for being anxious but one is anxious before one has any guilt (CA 43). Later, sin will bring its own anxiety but "when salvation is posited, anxiety, together with possibility, is left behind" (CA 53). In life, one does not ever get around anxiety, but one can deal with one's anxious states by choosing some psychological space which precludes every possibility.

Ultimately women and men dissolve their anxiety in the same manner through an education in the atonement. However, *pace* Haufniensis, woman's anxiety is greater than man's because she is the more sensuous. This is obvious because " . . . that woman is more sensuous than man appears at once in her physical structure" (CA 64). Women are more anxious than men but they may not be aware of this because sensuousness, not being sin, is on the innocent side of things. Sensuousness is "an unexplained riddle that causes anxiety. Hence the naïveté is accompanied by an inexplicable nothing, which is the nothing of anxiety" (CA 65). Before proceeding we should establish that Kierkegaard, not just his pseudonymous creation, holds this view. From a journal entry we read that

> . . . she is more sensate than man; for were she more spiritual she could never have her culmination point in another. Spirit is the true independent. Of course every religious view, like every more profound philosophical view, sees woman, despite this difference, as essentially identical with man; but it is not foolish enough to forget for that reason the truth of the difference, esthetically and ethically understood. (CA 189)

Curing anxiety through an education in the atonement is the solution offered for both sexes. It is important that every single person in the human race be accorded the possibility of atonement because otherwise, the entire notion of human race would be altered (CA 28). This universality allows sin to keep its nature as aberrant; sin is not purposeful: it just *is* (CA 58). Atonement brings us literally from death to life, for Haufniensis. It is a creative force—not unlike writing. To participate in the Atonement one must have faith in the fiction that repentance makes sense—when contemplation of it shows it to be the highest ethical contradiction (CA 117). To write, one must create a life where there was none and believe in the fiction that one's writing self could be reconciled with actuality. The atonement itself necessitates the erasing of anything other in humanity: in this case, the feminine. Writing, by contrast, creates more possibilities by allowing difference to persist.

A question arises: "Is a pseudonymous authorship a secular solution to anxiety?" Maybe Kierkegaard is actually inventing some fictive space through the creative act of writing/theorizing which act culminates in the creation of an other who is beloved? This love relation *saves* him from an unbearable anxiety. So far my discussion suggests that the act of fictive writing (writing fiction, writing to or from a pseudonym) is structurally the same as giving one-self over to the Atonement insofar as this throwing of oneself has to do with dispelling anxiety. There is faith, love, work in each case. In the equation, however, writing inches ahead because it has no exclusive end point. But couldn't I be found guilty of scientifically dissecting a pathology by making the comparison in this way? Isn't this just what Kierkegaard doesn't endorse? That Kierkegaard was unimpressed by the "science" of the mental is no secret. When Haufniensis describes what goes wrong in the scientific examination of what we have come to call psychopathologies, he says:

> To that end he imitates in himself every mood, every psychic state that he discovers in another. Thereupon, he sees whether he can delude the other by the imitation and carry him along into the subsequent development, which is his own creation by virtue of the idea. Thus, if someone wants to observe a passion, he must choose his individual. At that point, what counts is still-ness, quietness, and obscurity, so that he may discover the individual's secret. Then he must practice what he has learned until he is able to delude the individual. Thereupon he fictitiously invents the passion and appears before the individual in a preternatural magnitude of the passion. If it is done cor-rectly, the individual will feel an indescribable relief and satisfaction, such as an insane person will feel when someone has uncovered and poetically grasped his fixation and then proceeds to develop it further. If it does not succeed, it may be because of a defect in the operation, but it may also be because the individual is a poor example. (CA 55–56)

Haufniensis uses this passage to belittle scientific observation of emotion. Cataloging writing or anxiety dispelling action because they are structurally similar to a study of the Atonement is just being misguided by a *faux* psycho-analytic science. How could one ever abstain from such practice? one wants to ask. Look at Kierkegaard's de Silentio's psychological study of Abraham. Does not Kierkegaard find something he recognized, a madness he knows? Isn't there an indescribable relief in his exposition, as if, ah yes, I am home, no longer in my anxiety? Isn't it necessary to generalize at this point from the specific cases of covering up the fear of insanity? the fear of water? the fear of women? I think we can safely assume a doubly indirect message here. By here I mean the passage on the study of the mental with the intersection of Hauf-niensis, de Silentio, and Kierkegaard. First, there is the directly indirect manner of indirect communication, and, second, there is the real possibility that Kier-kegaard himself did not know what Haufniensis was getting at. The message is that the manner in which to dispel anxiety is to take a position of repetitive observation of an other in whom one's madness is confirmed as not quite so mad. In short, to create a character with whom one could be in love. To be in love is for one to help an other in a certain way. So we might create a fantasy with our own pathology (or sin) writ large. Kierkegaard's fantasy through

Haufniensis is that woman is more sensuous than man. Woman is more anxious than man. Anxiety must begin in innocence. Anxiety must begin in woman. Woman becomes the lack; sin the plenitude. Regina cannot exist for me, the seat of the pseudonyms sighs, therefore I must exist for myself in God. This fantasy that occurs through a frenzied writing allows Kierkegaard to resist madness. Because it does not go full force, that is, because it does not force him to an actual other, his position remains merely heuristic. But he has shown the way to apply the heuristic outward.

Slavoj Žižek suggests that one might see such a positioning in Kierkegaard if one teases out what it might mean to have man be less sensual than woman. It appears that such explanation (man less than woman) derives from a reaction formation to cover up the "lunatic" explanation. He says "The very masculine *activity* is already an escape from the abysmal dimension of the feminine *act*. The 'break with nature' is on the side of woman, and man's compulsive activity is ultimately nothing but a desperate attempt to repair the traumatic incision of this rupture" (Žižek, *Enjoy Your Symptom!*, p. 46). This covering up of the rupture may well be how the nothing of anxiety (sensuousness) becomes its something (sin) (CA 61) instead of the covering of possibility with unity as Irigaray suggests. So, the movement of repression is not the final dialectical step that Haufniensis thinks it is.[1] Instead, it is the covering of nothing (sensuousness) with something (sin). Irigaray uncovers something (the divine feminine, in this case) by exposing the fear of various philosophers. She makes us ask: Is Nietzsche afraid he will drown if he understands the Atonement? If he makes a stand with Salomé? That is, is Nietzsche using his Antichrist in the exact same manner as Kierkegaard uses his Christianity: to avoid saying yes to the feminine divine? If these questions can be answered "yes," then crucial other questions go a-begging, while something serious is sacrificed again and again and again. Nietzsche sacrifices the possibility of unstable rest; the possibility of communication with Salomé. Kierkegaard sacrifices the possibility of unstable rest; the possibility of communication with Regina. Writ large, momentary calm and women's voices are sacrificed to male fear.

2. *Sacrifice: Center of Atonement. Subject of the Pseudonymous Authorship*. Kierkegaard retells the story of his desire for, and subsequent sacrifice of, Regina as if it were the Abraham story. Arguably, all the roles are played by Kierkegaard. Some would say all the roles but one are so played. While later, de Silentio focuses on the inscrutability of Abraham's exterior, this is a minor part of the canonized version. In de Silentio's story Abraham is tired. He has done his best and although his son has been restored, he has misplaced something in a space so distant he despairs of remembering what it was. In the instant during which one realizes that one is capable of sacrifice one loses something the nature of which is also undefinable. Isaac is the issue. It is, after all, his body that could have been broken. His eyes are those that see the father

raising an arm. Isaac is he who had lived his life with the burden of being a miracle—whose mother's first thought of him was laughter. De Silentio sees what the original version contains only very obliquely: the sacrifice is Abraham as much as it is Isaac. Since Isaac is "saved," the only sacrifice is of the sacrificer.[2]

In the other version, the un-silenced, canonical one, it can be argued that Abraham symbolizes power in the world. Isaac is given the lines of the oppressed realizing that his difference is not miraculous but a marker of oppression. Because he is a miracle, he is singled out; his importance is negative and nothing to do with him. He asks: My father, behold the fire, and the wood: but where is the lamb for a burnt offering? The victim deserves what he gets: given the chance he would be over something less than himself, an oppressor. Isaac would have helped a different sacrifice. To sacrifice is to risk being sacrificed. To be sacrificed is to be in a context where sacrifices are made.

To then blame this victim for what he would have done, however, is to overlook the structure of struggle. Oppression is a tri-part relation: oppressor, oppressed, source of power. The source of power is strongest when abstract: one is powerful because of one's relationship with God, with a class, with a race, with a gender. One uses that power to create representational schemes with an eye to limitations, to exclusions. Abstraction is strongest because it cannot be located for concrete attack, but it is also most easily dissipated once it is located and the rails of habit are torn up. Isaac is the oppressed in this story; Abraham the oppressor; the power source is God. That there is no real agency involved is seen by Isaac's implicit willingness to perform the sacrifice of the lamb. (In that case the power source would have been Abraham.)

This version cannot be read in any reasonable manner such that no trace of authoritarianism remains. It is completely authoritarian. It is paradigmatic of power struggle: brutal, without definite end, forever. Kierkegaard, however, manages to personalize these forces, to subjectify Abraham. In doing so, de Silentio shows that individuation, to be worthy of the power source must, for some period of time or in some space, be independent from the power source. What is of importance to us is that de Silentio/Kierkegaard envisioned human consciousness untied from any power source and hence from the impetus to be either dominated or to dominate. This state appears to be a kind of madness in that believing in it presupposes an anterior belief that all ideologies come to an end in time. To use power is to gain the ability to sacrifice an other at the expense of something else. Writing this sacrifice itself dispels anxiety by making nothing something and by finding a repetition of altarity. Nietzsche repeats this moment over and over again as well. As Irigaray says:

> Sensing the impotence to come, Nietzsche declares he is the crucified one. And is crucified. But by himself.

Either Christ overwhelms that tragedy, or Nietzsche overcomes Christ. By repeating-parodying the Christian advent, what does he unmask in his gesture? That Christ is nothing that still deserves to live or that his age is yet to come? (Irigaray, *Marine Lover*, p. 188)

Men have painted themselves into a corner where love can know no other (Irigaray, *Marine Lover*, p. 189). The only solution is to become beloved in loving . . . the other. Both Nietzsche and Kierkegaard attempt this through or against God in their anxiety-dissolving parodies. Both fail to affirm anything but the infinite repetition of self-same-self.

Irigaray is not similarly (unconsciously) bound by images which direct power. Therefore she can make explicit the movement that Kierkegaard can only transfer upstairs or that Nietzsche can only transfer inward. Another way to put this is that writing the moment of possibility is something Kierkegaard does: through Haufniensis, through de Silentio, through others. It is not clear that Kierkegaard recognizes his actions, his creations as solutions to anxiety.

Irigaray, by contrast, creates possibility everywhere in her writing unleashing a power here and now. She draws pictures of structurally similar sacrifices—one version that is socio-politically motivated, another version, told as creative fiction, theory if you will, that repeats madness into sanity. Artemis, innocent, sacrifices her sexuality, her maternity. "Forever virgin, she will not threaten the reign of Zeus" (Irigaray, *Marine Lover*, p. 143). Zeus needs power, sole power. "But to achieve this, he needed to dominate women. . . . Those women he does not seduce, he makes divine—virgins in his suite. And his most beloved daughter, born of his voracious loves with Metis, woman of the sea, will have only passion—to be her Father's thought. Thus the all-fluid becomes the basis for the intelligence of the God of gods. She is born of him alone. Forgetting the passage into him and into her of all he assimilated of the mother" (Irigaray, *Marine Lover*, p. 150). As Zeus requires domination of the elements, that is, as he needs the control of all things which seem uncontrollable, which seem fluid, so too the philosopher needs control. Kierkegaard solves the anxiety of impotence, literally, the loss of possibilities, by creating the final possibility, by controlling the images that swim around him through his divine anchor. Nietzsche lashes out at this divine anchor. Irigaray tells both sides of such stories showing that the need for power necessitates sacrifices far greater than the philosopher has considered.[3]

3. *Writing.* If a pseudonymous writer prescribes a solution to anxiety, then Irigaray's fictive lovers and beloveds are an extension of the solution that is better defined and more powerful than that of Kierkegaard. The solution through Kierkegaard is too sacrificial. Reality is sacrificed for playing with pseudonyms that become the final product. Specifically, the possibility of being loved by Regina is sacrificed for the actuality of fantasizing loving her as others. The theoretical connection between Kierkegaard and Irigaray runs

through Nietzsche. The latter tells us over and over that he writes for those not yet born. He leads us to feel as if he were dead already. When we, those born after his death, read his yearning for a new world spirit, he sounds alive now, dead then. The marine lover of Nietzsche may well be Luce Irigaray. Writing missives to throw out on the water, to reply as connected, to broach his radical altarity. Irigaray's question "How I should love you if to speak to you were possible?" (Irigaray, *Marine Lover*, p. 3) does not call up just one possibility. The writing relationship is just one. Why does it matter that Kierkegaard in such a conceit can only be lover but never beloved? Precisely because Kierkegaard sees the horrors of a limited possibility for configurations, and seeing this, tries to break out of the confinement. However, he can only find a madness from which he is continuously running via repression. He protests too much: "Is the absence of inwardness also lunacy?" (CUP 194). Then, covering up the meaning, he flees:

> Even this is not true, however, because madness never has the inwardness of infinity. Its fixed idea is a kind of objective something, and the contradiction of madness lies in wanting to embrace it with passion. The decisive factor in madness is thus not the subjective, but the little finitude that becomes fixed, something that the infinite can never become. (CUP 194, note)

He can only be other because the colors of his pallet must connect with outer objects—he cannot go completely inward; and, because he runs from self, he cannot be beloved. There can be nothing there to love. The same claim can be made of de Silentio who can't even get to the point of introducing himself before the book is finished, run out. Problem after problem and no voice even hinting at a stable judgment on any of the problemata. Mark Taylor asks, in this connection: "What *can* Søren . . . say to Regina? . . . How can he describe the incurable wound opened by what he obliquely refers to as his 'thorn in the flesh?' How can he explain that he has *never* been the same but has always been 'different?' What can he tell her that she (or for that matter, he) could understand about difference? Almost nothing" (Taylor, *Altarity*, p. 306).

Climacus's fear is de Silentio's fear is Kierkegaard's fear. Irigaray pinpoints the fear of dispersion that the infinite induces. She says: "Your infinity? An uninterrupted sequence of projected points. With nothing linking them. Emptiness. There would seem to be nothing there but production, recalling nothing, anticipating nothing. Points programmed as such indefinitely on a background of absence" (Irigaray, *Elemental Passions*, p. 71). Some philosophers have shrunk with horror from positions such as these. One can solve this metaphysical horror at selflessness with a God-relation, or with an epistemology that makes of everything already a mask, or one can re-invent the infinity one fears as something to be affirmed, something actual, something with power. Irigaray's infinity in contrast to those who fear it is "movement, the mobility of place. Engendering time, yes. Always becoming. How can that future be brought to pass between your instants which are always already counted" (Irigaray, *Elemental Passions*, p. 71). Kierkegaard creates. Kierkegaard creates others and as such he is a middle term.[4] Nietzsche creates his real self as becoming, thereby creating material capable of being loved. Irigaray can be both lover and beloved because she creates both herself and others. So Kierkegaard is right: one needs to be out of the system—but he is wrong in supposing that this is any but a self-created conceit. No wonder, then, that his writing is a burden of an existential kind. "This existence is exhausting. I am convinced that not a single person understands me. The most that anyone, even an admirer, would concede is that I bear all this unpleasantness with a certain poise, but that I want it—of course no one dreams of that" (COR 208).[5] No one can understand Kierkegaard. There is no place for him in any representative scheme he values. Nietzsche cannot be understood until later, when someone else arises who actually creates herself. Irigaray is in the right time and with the right attitude (poise). She calls us to call ourselves—helping us along the way by freezing, then smashing exclusionary representations. She is never frozen within the rails of existing ideology. She does not need to command just because she finds a space where she is not commanded.

    4. *Naming the Creations.* Irigaray is particularly interested in the lack of representation of women in heavily value laden domains—like that of religion or the divine.

> The loss of divine representation has brought women to a state of dereliction, which is felt all the more because sensible representation is our primary method of figuration and communication. It has left us without a means of designating ourselves. It has also separated mothers from daughters, depriving them of mutually respectful mediums of exchange. It has subjected them to a reproductive order—natural and spiritual—that is governed symbolically by men. (Irigaray, *je, tu, nous*, p. 111)

The feeling women have when trying to assimilate and then accommodate their experiences remains at the innocent level because the accommodation cannot be forthcoming. Contrary Kierkegaard, this extra "anxiety" if you will, is not due to there being more of the sensuous in us. There just isn't sufficient representation to call . . . home. Even temporarily. But there is likewise no need to throw our voices to a place where sacrifice is the norm. Irigaray says,

> The fact that you no longer assert yourself as an absolute subject changes nothing. The inspiration which breathes life into you, the law or duty which guide you—are these not the very essence of your subjectivity? You feel you could abandon your 'I'? But your 'I' holds you fast, having flooded and covered the whole of everything it ever created. And it never stops breathing its

own emanations into you. With each new inspiration, do you not become more than ever that 'I'? Reduplicated within yourself. (Irigaray, *Elemental Passions*, p. 83)

Calling oneself, naming oneself means overcoming the representation that stands outside of us, without completely giving up the "I." Kierkegaard starts this coming out. His step has been crucially important. One re-creates others to voice a possibility of exiting systemic thought. But the self which is himself is not worked on. To fix on this projected interiority is to be mad. Nietzsche, Irigaray's deadly partner, works on self but seemingly at the exclusion of others. Irigaray alone sees that the process must be both a group and a solitary practice and that to do this one must re-create the others who might speak for us, but then realize that there are real others that we won't need or even desire to re-create. The fantasy, then, is necessary. We are capable of naming ourselves; that is, we are capable of fantasizing ourselves out of the fantasy that we needed to solve, in moments, to overcome, in moments, stages of anxiety.

Notes

1. "The hypochondriac is anxious about every insignificant thing, but when the significant appears he begins to breathe more easily. And why? Because the significant actuality is after all not so terrible as the possibility he himself had fashioned, and which he used his strength to fashion, whereas he can now use all his strength against actuality" (CA 162).

2. Cf. FT. Kierkegaard speaking for himself directly makes the connection between the ethical suspension and death. In FSE, Kierkegaard notes that death is much better than such a suspension. "In any case, when it is death, then it is definitely over, but dying to is not over in this way, because he does not die, indeed, perhaps a long life lies before him, the one who has died" (FSE 79).

3. In *Subjects of Desire*, Judith Butler gives a Nietzschean reading of Hegel, the latter of whom can scarcely be forgotten in this discussion of dialectic and sacrifice. Her analysis gives the *Phenomenology of Spirit* a healing status similar to that ascribed to Kierkegaard, Nietzsche, and Irigaray here. Butler, however, grants this status to the workings within the reader (p. 24).

4. How he would hate this expression applied to him!

5. He can only write but his ambivalence is never far from the surface. "But back to the manure pile! This manure pile represents literature, for just as the manure pile fertilizes the earth and makes it fruitful, so literature fertilizes and stimulates our immortal spirit" (COR 77). Notice in juxtaposition how calm Irigaray seems about the material aspects of writing: "I earn my living by writing. I am not a woman supported by a man or men; I have to meet my own material needs" (Irigaray, *je, te, nous*, p. 51).

Kierkegaard's View of
the Unconscious

C. Stephen Evans

No INFORMED OBSERVER of the twentieth century world of letters could fail
to notice the significance of the concept of the unconscious in psychology, psy-
chiatry, literature, and even in philosophy. We live in the age of depth psychology, an age in which the notion of the unconscious has passed over into
what is termed "common sense." Despite or because of the popularity of the
concept it is by no means evident that the unconscious is clearly understood.
Indeed, the very notion that there is such a thing as the concept of the unconscious is itself part of the confusion; a little reflection uncovers radically different concepts which are often confusedly rolled together.

Commentators have not been slow to notice the importance of the concept
of the unconscious in Kierkegaard's thought as well. The unconscious plays a
central role in *The Sickness unto Death* and *The Concept of Anxiety*, but is
nearly as prominent in *Either/Or*, and plays a significant role in quite a few of
Kierkegaard's published works. In this chapter I shall try to give a straightforward account of what I take to be Kierkegaard's view of the unconscious, focusing mainly on *The Sickness unto Death*.

It is of course impossible to discuss the unconscious without discussing a
host of significant concepts which are intricately linked to it: self-deception,
consciousness, and the nature of the self in general, to mention just a few. My
account will of necessity treat these related notions, but will just as necessarily
treat them briefly and schematically. My hope is that the sketchiness of my
comments will be redeemed somewhat by the ways in which these notions are
in turn illumined by closer attention to the unconscious.

I. Situating Kierkegaard's View of the Unconscious

In order to understand Kierkegaard's view, it will be helpful to situate it
with respect to some other major views of the unconscious. Two views stand
out as deserving special attention, that of Freud, because of its historical
importance, and the view of the school of psychoanalysis known as object-relations theory, because of the interesting parallels between this view and Kierkegaard's. Before looking at these views, we must first look briefly at Kier-

kegaard's Christian faith, which is surely the most significant factor in his perspective.

A. *Kierkegaard the Christian Clinician*

Though Kierkegaard was not a clinical psychologist in the contemporary sense, his primary aims as a psychologist must decidedly be viewed as therapeutic. Like Freud he is interested in the unconscious primarily in a clinical context. This is made quite explicit in SUD where the pseudonym Anti-Climacus grounds this therapeutic concern in Christianity: "Everything essentially Christian must have in its presentation a resemblance to the way a physician speaks at the sickbed; even if only medical experts understand it, it must never be forgotten that the situation is the bedside of a sick person" (SUD 5).[1]

It is hardly surprising, then, that Kierkegaard connects the unconscious with pathology. The ideal for human life is transparency. In part I of SUD this ideal is described simply like this: "In relating to itself and in willing to be itself, the self rests transparently in the power that established it" (SUD 14).

In putting forward this ideal of transparency, I do not think Kierkegaard is arguing that a person must constantly be aware of everything about himself. He certainly does not wish to claim that one must focus on one's own autonomic physical processes, and I see no reason to think that he wishes to deny that in a fully healthy person mental processes might occur which are not the focus of conscious attention. Hence Kierkegaard is not really denying that there are unconscious processes in the sense that the contemporary cognitive psychologist affirms, who thinks of the unconscious as "off-line information processing."[2]

The ideal of transparency is rather one of self-understanding, an ability to recognize and understand what needs to be understood about one's self. The unconscious which is relevant is not what I shall call the unnoticed unconscious, but the unconscious which I do not wish to notice, or have chosen to ignore, or perhaps have made myself unable to comprehend. That there are aspects of the self which are beyond one's conscious purview may be helpful in understanding how the development of the unconscious in Kierkegaard's sense is *possible*, but the unconscious in Kierkegaard's sense is clearly what Freud called the "dynamic unconscious," the part of myself which I actively resist confronting.

In linking his clinical analysis of the unconscious to Christianity, as Anti-Climacus does constantly in SUD, some might object that his view is thereby disqualified from comparison with genuinely scientific theories. If Kierkegaard's view of the unconscious is linked to his Christian faith, can it be genuinely scientific?

Anti-Climacus of course anticipates this objection to his work: "To many the form of this 'exposition' will seem strange; it will appear to them too rigorous to be edifying, and too edifying to be strictly scientific" (SUD 5, my translation). Though Anti-Climacus says he has "no opinion" as to the correctness of the latter opinion, this can hardly be because he accepts the assumption that scientific work must be completely objective and "value-free." Only a bit later he tells us that the kind of scientific learning which prides itself on being "indifferent," is from a Christian point of view "inhuman curiosity" rather than the "lofty heroism" it would like to make itself out to be (SUD 5).

Regardless of the merits of this view of Anti-Climacus in general with regard to science, it is eminently defensible with respect to theories of the dynamic unconscious. This unconscious is what I choose not to recognize, or intentionally fail to perceive. It is hardly possible for such an analysis not to impinge on our moral and religious concerns, since the motivation for such self-obscuring activity will surely relate to what we value and disvalue as persons, what we find admirable and noble, or base and ignoble. A theory of the dynamic unconscious which links the unconscious to pathology can hardly be a value-free affair, since the concept of pathology clearly presupposes a value-concept—that of mental health.

Some would argue that "mental health" is a value concern which can still be segregated from moral values. The therapist should deal with the former and leave the latter for the preacher and the moralist. But this distinction between mental health values and general moral values cannot withstand close scrutiny. It is true that people of different moral persuasions can agree on certain "minimal" characteristics of mentally healthy people. In general mentally healthy people are in touch with their environment, are not crippled by phobias, obsessions, or other neuroses, and so on. But though these characteristics may be generally desirable, there is certainly no agreement as to exactly what they are, and even less agreement that possession of such characteristics is enough to qualify someone as mentally healthy, or that their lack necessarily means someone is "sick." Most therapists would agree, in fact, that a facade of "normality" and being "well-adjusted" can hide a personality which is seriously damaged in a variety of ways.

It is true that in such matters it seems vain to hope for "objective proof" of a view, and if lack of such proof disqualifies a view from being scientific, Kierkegaard's view certainly is disqualified. But such a requirement presupposes a naive view of science and, in any case, its strict application would eliminate not only Kierkegaard's view, but those of such thinkers as Freud as well. Though Kierkegaard's view certainly is grounded in his Christian understanding, he has every right to present it in the marketplace of ideas and try to show its descriptive, explanatory, and therapeutic power. It may well be that the power of such a view will be opaque to non-Christians, though this is by no means certain, and in fact, the contrary is supported by the strong influence Kierkegaard has had on non-Christian psychologists. But the fact that one's ability to recognize the truth is conditioned by one's own subjectivity is hardly a thesis that Kierkegaard would want to shrink from.

I shall therefore take full account of the ways in which Kierkegaard's therapeutic analysis of the unconscious is rooted in his Christian vision. Both his analyses of sickness and health presuppose a Christian understanding of human beings as creatures of God who have rebelled against their creator.

B. *The Freudian View*

It is not possible to overestimate the significance of Freud's theory of the unconscious. Such Freudian concepts as repression and defense mechanisms have now penetrated deeply into ordinary modes of thought. Despite the influential character of Freud's view, and the centrality of the concept of the unconscious in his own thought, Freud's view of the unconscious is not altogether free of tension.

In Freud's original "topographical" theory of mind, the unconscious was one of three "systems": the unconscious (Ucs), conscious (Cs), and preconscious (Pcs).[3] The unconscious was closely associated with instinctual demands, which were blocked or repressed from consciousness. (Freud wavered back and forth between the view that the instincts themselves composed the unconscious, and the view that the unconscious was composed of "ideas" that represented the instincts.) The repression was attributed to a preconscious "censor."

The role of the censor in this theory is crucial. It is at this point that Sartre was later to concentrate his criticism of Freud in the famous section of *Being and Nothingness* which contains his critique of the unconscious.[4] Sartre argues that the person must in some way be aware of what he is repressing, since repression is a selective activity. (Note that I am here using the term "repression" as Sartre does, and as Freud himself sometimes does, to refer to the defense mechanisms in general, not to a specific mechanism.) Yet to be aware of the activity of repression would seem to make repression impossible, since a recognition that I am repressing X would seem to imply an awareness of X.

This problem is part of the motivation for Freud's revised "structural" theory of the mind, the well-known "id, ego, superego" view which he developed later in his career.[5] This theory emerged because Freud became aware that anxiety was not simply the result of the repression of instinctual material, but was often a signal or anticipation that instinctual material was not being adequately repressed. Anxiety here is not primarily a consequent of the damming up of instinctual material, but a consequence of the "leaking" of such material into consciousness. To deal with this phenomenon, Freud postulated the existence of unconscious elements in the ego, as well as in the superego, the moralistic element of the psyche which punishes the individual for forbidden instinctual desires.

The tension in Freud's view seems to me to be this: the unconscious appears to be both something primitive and something formed. On the one hand the unconscious is associated with biological instincts which are seen as givens in the psyche. On the other hand the unconscious is something which is formed as the individual confronts elements in the psyche which are unpalatable. This tension infects Freud's whole view of the self, even on the later "structural" model of the self. The id is the source of the psyche, the origin of all psychic energy. The ego and superego are simply aspects of the id which have developed special functions. It is this conviction that led Freud to borrow the term "Id" (it) from Groddeck, who had written, "We should not say 'I live' but 'I am lived by the It.' "[6] Such a view leads inevitably to seeing the self as a victim and the unconscious as a force which shapes the self.

Yet Freud also wants to see the unconscious as what is formed as a result of repression. Here the unconscious is not simply a force of which I am a victim; it is in some sense the result of my activity as my personality develops through interaction with others. This tension in Freud is part of his legacy, the reason that his successors include both biologically oriented thinkers such as Hartmann, as well as the object-relations theory, which we shall now discuss.

C. Object Relations Theory

Object relations theory is a form of psychoanalysis developed in England by W. D. Fairbairn and popularized by Harry Guntrip.[7] Recognizing the tension in Freud between the biological and distinctively psychological elements, which we alluded to above, object relations theory rejects the notion of the id altogether, and the theory of instincts closely associated with it. On this view, the infant is fundamentally an undifferentiated unity with "ego-potential." The unconscious is something which develops in the individual as a result of interaction with "objects," an odd choice of terminology since what is meant is primarily the significant persons in the infant's life.

The primary developmental task, in this view, is the passage from infantile dependence to the kind of mature dependence which is compatible with having an identity of one's own. This developmental task cannot be carried out properly unless the infant feels a strong sense of being loved unconditionally and an equally strong sense that the infant's love is accepted by the parent. The initial identity of the child is formed through "primary identification" with the care-giving parent. Without a basic sense of security, the child cannot develop an identity which is independent of this "internalized parent."

As Guntrip tells the story (relying heavily on Fairbairn), the unconscious is the product of interaction with this primary care-giver, which in most societies has historically been the mother. The mother is for the child both exciting and a source of frustration, since it is inevitable that not all of the infant's desires will be met. In the developing child a mental image of the mother is formed, which initially forms the core of the child's own identity. This introjected mother figure then is split or dissociated, as the child attempts to deal with the frustrating or "bad" mother by disowning those aspects.[8] The unconscious is formed as the child tries to deal with a part of himself which he wishes to regard as not really himself.

In people who are fortunate enough to have what Winnicott calls "good-enough mothering" the split or dissociation is not too severe, and people are able to function reasonably well despite the blow to their wholeness. In those who are not so fortunate, what Guntrip calls the "schizoid problem" descends with full force. All of us need what Guntrip terms a "basic security-giving relationship."[9] Those who lack this lose a sense of their true self. They become the victims of the "anti-libidinal ego," the internalized "saboteur" or "bad, sadistic mother," who does not allow them to discover who they are. Unless such withdrawn, dissociated people are able to find such a relationship later in life and repair the early damage, they have great difficulty in feeling or connecting with other people.

As we shall see, this object-relations theory of the unconscious is of great value in understanding Kierkegaard's own view. It consistently views the unconscious, however much power it may have over me and however difficult it may be for me to change it, as something I have formed, and therefore something for which I may be in some ways responsible. And it views the process of formation and the possibilities of transformation of the unconscious as closely linked to my relationships with others.

II. Kierkegaard's Relational View of the Self

It is not possible to describe Kierkegaard's view of the unconscious without briefly describing his view of selfhood. I believe that one of the best treatments of Kierkegaard's view of the self is found in Merold Westphal's paper, "Kierkegaard's Psychology and Unconscious Despair."[10] Westphal maintains that Kierkegaard's view of the self can be understood as involving Aristotelian, Cartesian, and Hegelian elements, in a creative, critical way, so that it is equally illuminating to understand his view as anti-Aristotelian, anti-Cartesian, and anti-Hegelian.[11]

Kierkegaard's view is broadly Aristotelian in that he wants to see the self as shaped by its activity, and the health of the self to be something which is dependent on what the self does, rather than what befalls it. It is anti-Aristotelian in that the health of the self is seen by Aristotle as happiness, and Kierkegaard insists that happiness is not an adequate understanding of the goal of human life once it is understood that human beings are spiritual creatures (SUD 25).

Kierkegaard's view can be understood as Cartesian in that it stresses the significance of the inner, self-conscious life of the individual, an emphasis which reflects the Cartesian focus on the interior life as the locus of selfhood. It is, however, anti-Cartesian in that the self is not merely seen by Kierkegaard as a mental substance, but as something to be achieved, a dynamic process rather than simply being a completed object.

Finally, Westphal characterizes the Kierkegaardian view of the self as Hegelian in that Kierkegaard, like Hegel, sees the self as fundamentally relational in character. (I shall postpone temporarily an account of how Kierkegaard's view is also anti-Hegelian.) The self-consciousness of the individual is not complete in itself but is mediated through the relationship to the other. Thus the "I" cannot be understood except in relationship.

This last characterization of Westphal's is controversial, yet it is of the utmost significance for an understanding of Kierkegaard's view of the unconscious. It is controversial because it seems to undermine the conception of Kierkegaard as a radical individualist, a conception firmly held by friend and foe alike. And it is controversial because many lovers of Kierkegaard have an inveterate dislike for admitting that Kierkegaard borrowed anything from his arch-foe, Hegel.

Even writers such as Sylvia Walsh and John Elrod, who would like to read Kierkegaard as putting forward a relational view of the self, have difficulty finding such a view there. Elrod, for example, says that Kierkegaard's pseudonymous works "pay no attention to the ontological and epistemological roles played by the other in the development of a concept of the self."[12] Elrod thinks this lack of a social perspective is remedied in Kierkegaard's later religious authorship, beginning with *Works of Love*, but oddly enough, he treats the crucial first section of SUD as belonging with the early, individualistic pseudonymous authorship.[13]

Sylvia Walsh (Perkins), in a fine paper, similarly bemoans the "absence of a relation to others in Kierkegaard's general description of the self" in the first part of SUD, especially given the clearly relational view in *Works of Love*.[14] Walsh says that one must either conclude that there is an inconsistency in the works or else one must interpret the social view of *Works of Love* as somehow implicit in SUD. She opts for the latter view, but still finds it distressing that Kierkegaard did not address more directly the relatedness of the self to others "in defining the structure of the self."[15]

These criticisms seem rather surprising in view of the explicit statement of Anti-Climacus that the human self is not an autonomous self whose being is self-contained: "The human self is such a derived, established relation, a relation that relates itself to itself and in relating itself to itself relates itself to another" (SUD 13-14). Elrod and Walsh are certainly familiar with this passage. Why then do they not think that part I of SUD contains a relational view of the self? The most plausible answer is that they interpret the "other" referred to in this passage as God, the "power" which "established" the relationship which constitutes the self. In claiming that Kierkegaard's view of the self here is not relational, they must mean that it does not include a relation to other human beings.

I find this objectionable. First, most obviously and most importantly, these critics seem to assume that God somehow doesn't count as a genuine "other person." But it is crucial for Kierkegaard's whole project of getting the individual to stand before God as an individual that God be construed as a genuine person to whom I can relate as an other. It is the fact that God can be the other to whom I relate, and must be that other if I am genuinely to be myself, that ultimately makes Kierkegaard's view anti-Hegelian.

Second, it is by no means clear that Kierkegaard thinks God is the only "other" who is significant in forming the self's identity. At this point we must take seriously the interesting differences between part I and part II of SUD. Although it has seemed obvious to most readers that the "power" in part I which constitutes the self must be God, several things make it necessary to go slowly in making such an identification, at least without qualification.

First, there is the fact that Anti-Climacus uses abstract, formal language. He talks about the "power" which established the self, and "another" to which the self is related. Given Anti-Climacus's strident Christianity and complete lack of reticence in using the name of God in other places, I think his choice of this abstract language is intentional and significant.

The second significant point is that Anti-Climacus describes the difference between parts I and II in a way that implies that the concept of God is somehow not fully operative in part I. In part II, the despair which was described in part I is redescribed as sin, and the difference is said to be this: sin is despair which is "before God" (SUD 77).

The odd thing about this is that the concept of God is by no means absent from part I. Those who wish to identify the "power" which established the self with God have abundant textual evidence to justify the equation, for Anti-Climacus frequently uses the word "God" in part I in ways which suggest that he is thinking of the other which forms the basis of the self (SUD 16, 27, 30, 32, 35, 38-42, 68-69, and 71).

To resolve this puzzle I believe we must recognize that Kierkegaard frequently intermixes ontological and ethical discourse in his descriptions of the self. He describes the self *both* as something I am *and* something I must become, *both* as a substance *and* as something to be achieved. This is not confusion on his part, because to understand the self it is imperative to see the self in both of these dimensions. But it is easy to become confused about the relationship of the individual to God and the relationship of part I and II of SUD if we do not distinguish the two contexts.

In Kierkegaard's view a relation to God is in one sense inescapable; in another sense it is a task. In a similar manner, a self is on the one hand something I simply am, something I cannot help being; the torment of the despairer who wills not to be a self is precisely that he has no choice in the matter. On the other hand, a self is precisely what no individual simply is as a matter of course. It is something that one must become.

Ontologically, the "other" to which the self must relate and cannot help relating to is God, who is indeed the creator of the self. However, God has created human persons as free and responsible creatures. As Anti-Climacus says, "God, who constituted man a relation, releases it from his hand, as it were" (SUD 16). Notice that there is no true independence from God. God does not really let the relationship go out of his hand ontologically, but he endows humans with the ethical freedom to define their own identity.

If humans misuse their freedom, they do not cease to be relational beings; that is part of their ontological structure. Nor do they cease to have a relation to God. They may, however, cease to relate *consciously* to God, consciously forming their selves in relation to what is less than God. One might say that individuals in this case attempt to ground their selves in a God-substitute. Their conscious identities are rooted in "powers" or "others" which are less than God.

Actually there is a sense in which the identity of the self is formed through relationships with others independently of the misuse of freedom. For Kierkegaard, genuine selfhood is a never-completed task of maturity which requires a consciousness of God, or, as we have claimed, a God-substitute. However, this mature self does not spring from nothing; individuals begin to form their identity in infancy. Thus, when an individual begins to be a self in the most profound sense, he or she already has a self of sorts, what one might call a "pre-self." This pre-self is certainly formed through early relationships. In the developing child, therefore, there is nothing inherently pathological in the grounding of one's identity in those significant others who shape the child's emerging self. Nor is there anything pathological in the adult's identity being partly rooted in relationships to other finite selves. The problem comes into being when the adult lacks a God-relationship and thus gives to the relations with other human selves (and with what is less than human) a priority and ultimacy such relations do not deserve. I am not here talking merely about a case of "arrested development," a case in which an individual does not discover God and fails to grow, but the case in which the individual chooses not to grow by suppressing the knowledge of God.

So Kierkegaard, as I read him, is very far from a non-relational view of the self. All selfhood depends ontologically on God, and genuine selfhood depends on a conscious relation to God, for which the individual may substitute a relation to what is less than God. All of this presupposes a developing "preself," which is formed through relations with other persons and which is a significant element in the identity of a mature, healthy self. That the self is constituted by relations with others, including those "others" other than God, is portrayed very clearly:

> And what infinite reality the self gains by being conscious of existing before God, by becoming a human self whose criterion is God! A cattleman who (if this were possible) is a self directly before his cattle is a very low self, and, similarly, a master who is a self directly before his slaves is actually no self— for in both cases a criterion is lacking. The child who previously has had only his parents as a criterion becomes a self as an adult by getting the state as a criterion, but what an infinite accent falls on the self by having God as the criterion! (SUD 79)

Here Anti-Climacus deepens our understanding of the relational character of the self by describing the self as a task. By a "criterion" he means that by which a self measures itself. To be a self is to be a being who is striving toward a certain ideal; that ideal provides the "measure" for the self. For human selves this measure is derived from the conscious relationships with others which have formed the self.

Human beings constantly define themselves through relations with others. A person who thinks of himself as a self through his superiority to the cattle he tends is actually not a self at all; one might say his standards are simply too low. Similarly, a person whose selfhood is grounded in his superiority to the slaves he owns fails to be a self. In this case it is not that he is not related to other selves; his slaves are persons. It is that in regarding the slaves as slaves, the owner does not regard them as genuine persons. Hence his measure is still a defective one, and this infects his own self-conception.

Kierkegaard therefore recognizes that actual human selves are formed relationally, but he thinks that a self which *only* has other human beings as its measure, even the "adult" who takes the "official" standards certified by the state as his measure, can never be secure. Genuine selfhood requires that the self stand consciously before God.

This means that though the ontological "power" which grounds the self is always God, insofar as the self is a task it is shaped by "powers" that are less than God. In the infant and the child this is not pathological, and even in the healthy adult relations to others continue to form part of one's identity. This is proper so long as those relations have an appropriate priority. Unfortunately, human beings are sinners, and hence do not maintain "an absolute relation to the absolute and a relative relation to the relative," as Johannes Climacus describes the task in *Postscript* (CUP 414). Other humans (and what is sub-human) do function as "God-substitutes."

III. Self-Deception and the Divided Self

In understanding the self as an achievement, Kierkegaard fundamentally divorces his view from the Cartesian conception of the self as a unified, self-transparent consciousness. What Descartes sees as the essence of the self, Kierkegaard views as the goal. The actual self God creates includes within it diverse possibilities, and with these are given the possibility of forming a unified self. These possibilities are not bare possibilities, but concrete potentialities of an actual bodily being. The self is not purely a set of possibilities, since there must be an actual being to contain the possibilities, as it were, and this actual being must be or contain an agent which has the power of choice. Otherwise freedom and responsibility would not exist. However, there is no reason to think that this agency is a transparent, unified Cartesian self. Rather, the self contains within itself "obscure powers," to use the telling phrase of Judge William (EO, II, 164).

Such a claim by itself only brings us to what we have called the unnoticed unconscious, and does not explain the reality of the dynamic unconscious. For that, will and choice must be brought into the story. The dissociation of consciousness is, however, part of the explanation of the *possibility* of the dynamic unconscious.

Many philosophers have, under the influence of a Cartesian picture of the self, denied that self-deception is really possible. Analyzing self-deception as a lie to oneself, they have argued that such a lie is impossible, since the person would have to be both deceiver and deceived, both the liar and the one lied to, and this requires that the person both know the truth and not know the truth. If the self were a unified, Cartesian, transparent mind, this would indeed be impossible.

It is not, however, impossible for the same person to be both deceiver and deceived if there is duality in the self. If my consciousness is dissociated, then this is completely possible, and in fact occurs frequently. Nothing is more common, in a case of self-deception, for the person to see in retrospect that he knew the truth all along, and yet failed to admit it to himself.

One might object at this point that such a view compromises the unity of the self, and still does not solve the problem of how self-deception is possible. For self-deception requires that it be the same self that both knows and does not know the truth. If the self's knowledge of itself is dissociated, so that the consciousness of the truth is divorced from the consciousness which obscures the truth, then have we not divided the self into two selves, innocent victim and guilty deceiver?

To answer this objection, we must explore the process by which the divided self comes into being. While it is a dissociated consciousness that makes self-deception possible, self-deception is a special kind of division in the self. In such a case the division in the self can be traced to the will of the self. In cases of self-deception the dissociation in consciousness is not simply a natural fact, but is grounded in the choices the person has made.

As we have noted, self-deception appears paradoxical and some have alleged that it is literally impossible. To deceive myself I must know the truth and intentionally obscure the truth. But how can I convince myself that what I know is true is not true? Such a project seems as difficult as trying not to think of a pink elephant. It might seem that the harder one tries to do it, the more difficult the task becomes. Kierkegaard's answer to this problem rests on the fact that human beings are temporal creatures and that the process of self-deception is therefore a temporal process.

The problem is treated by Anti-Climacus in at least a couple of passages, most notably in the course of analyzing the Socratic principle that sin is ignorance. Anti-Climacus agrees that from a Christian perspective this is in a sense correct. Sin is a kind of ignorance, or preferably, stupidity (SUD 88). What the Socratic view does not recognize is that it is a willed ignorance, an ignorance for which the individual is culpable. Obviously, however, to say that the ignorance is willed is to say that it involves self-deception, for to will to be ignorant of something, I must in some way be aware of the knowledge which I will to suppress.

Anti-Climacus wishes to trace evil back ultimately then to the will. But he recognizes that it is rare if not impossible for the individual simply to will what he knows to be evil. The normal process is for the will to corrupt one's knowledge; sin goes hand in hand with self-deception.

This process of corruption is a temporal one. When the will does not want to do what a person knows to be right, the usual response is not for the individual consciously to do what he knows to be wrong, but simply to delay doing anything. "Willing allows some time to elapse, an interim called 'We shall look at it tomorrow' " (SUD 94). This period of time allows the individual to carry out any number of strategies to subvert his understanding. "The lower nature's power lies in stretching things out" (SUD 94). Eventually, "little by little" (SUD 56), Anti-Climacus says, the understanding is changed so that knowing and willing can "understand each other," can "agree completely" (SUD 94).

What are some of these strategies? One is simply to *delay*, to wait for the knowledge to decay. Since we have seen that human beings are not Cartesian selves, and since they are temporal creatures, delay may result in some dissociation "naturally." As Anti-Climacus puts it, the knowledge simply "dims" or "becomes obscure." The fact that this is a natural process does not absolve the individual of responsibility, for it is the willed delay that makes this dimming possible, and the individual is guilty for the delay since it is motivated by the hope that just this dimming will occur. At particular moments the knowledge may come to consciousness, but over time these moments come more and more infrequently, and the consciousness involved becomes more and more dim.

A second strategy is distraction. Here the individual does not merely wait for nature to take its course, but actively intervenes. "He may try to keep himself in the dark about his state through diversions and in other ways, for example, through work and business as diversionary means, yet in such a way that he does not entirely realize why he is doing it, that it is to keep himself in the dark" (SUD 48).

Here Kierkegaard is helping us see that it *is* possible to intentionally avoid thinking of a pink elephant. Obviously one must think of a pink elephant at some time to have this intention, but the intention is nevertheless one that can be successfully carried out over time. Eventually one can put oneself into a state in which one is not thinking of a pink elephant. The trick is diversion. One must focus on something else. If the something else is engrossing enough for me to lose myself in it, I will eventually forget the elephant.

In the same way, if I plunge into various activities: useful work, committees, sports, games, or even religious work, I may eventually find that the disturbing insights into who I am no longer haunt my consciousness. The individual may even, Anti-Climacus says, do this with a certain shrewdness or insight into what is going on. That is, he may recognize in general terms that this process of diverting himself is a way of "sinking his soul in darkness" (SUD 48). This is psychologically possible so long as the individual does not clearly focus on the specific insights he wishes to avoid.

Such strategies could usefully be termed "defenses," to use Freudian language, since they are crucial not only in obscuring our self-knowledge originally, but also in keeping the troubling knowledge at bay. Kierkegaard does not systematically catalogue the various defenses available to human beings, but he does give interesting and insightful analyses of a variety of such strategies.

One of the most common and dangerous of such defenses might be termed "intellectualizing." The self-knowledge in question is existential knowledge, knowledge about how life should be lived. It is tempting for the individual to substitute for such knowledge a kind of intellectual knowledge. I convince myself that I am ethical because I know a lot about ethical theory. I convince myself that I am a Christian because I know a lot of theology. It is this kind of defense that Kierkegaard thinks the educated intellectual, "the professor," is particularly prone to, and it is one on which he pours unwithering scorn.

Even Socrates had recognized that there was a difference between "understanding and understanding." What Socrates had failed to see was that the intellectual understanding which in the genuine sense is no understanding at all is not simply ignorance. There is a difference between "not *being able* to understand and not *willing* to understand" (SUD 95). Intellectual understanding can be a defense against genuine understanding.

IV. Self-Deception and Sin

The paradoxicalness of self-deception and the difficulty of understanding it underlie one of the central problems of SUD, namely the paradoxical attitude of Anti-Climacus toward unconscious despair and toward paganism, the "despairing unconsciousness of God." On the one hand Anti-Climacus clearly wants to say that there can be unconscious despair. "Not being in despair, not being conscious of being in despair, is precisely a form of despair" (SUD 23). On the other hand, unconscious despair does not quite seem to be despair in a full-blooded sense; such despair one is tempted, humanly speaking, to describe as a kind of innocence. "It is almost a dialectical issue whether it is justifiable to call such a state despair" (SUD 42).

This ambivalence about unconscious despair is even more pronounced with respect to unconscious sin, as well it might be, since sin for Anti-Climacus is an intensified form of conscious despair. Sin is a spiritual disorder, and a spiritless being would seem to be incapable of sin. On the one hand Anti-Climacus seems to view paganism as a kind of innocence: "The sin of paganism was essentially despairing ignorance of god, . . . Therefore, from another point of view, it is true that in the strictest sense the pagan did not sin, for he did not sin before God, and all sin is before God" (SUD 81). Yet in the final analysis Anti-Climacus is loathe to give the pagan a blanket dispensation, and recognizes the strangeness of a view that absolves paganism of sin. "Christianity regards everything as under sin; we have tried to depict the Christian point of view as rigorously as possible—and then this strange outcome emerges, this strange conclusion that sin is not to be found at all in paganism but only in Judaism and Christendom, and there again very seldom" (SUD 101). So Anti-Climacus retreats from the general absolution of the pagan and insists that the lack of consciousness which forms the basis of the pagan's "innocence" is itself culpable, and must be seen therefore as grounded in self-deception. "Is it (being in a state of spiritlessness) something that happens to a person? No, it is his own fault. No one is born devoid of spirit, and no matter how many go to their death with this spiritlessness as the one and only outcome of their lives, it is not the fault of life" (SUD 102).

The problem is that this suggests that the ignorance cannot have been complete. One must have, or at least one must have had, spirit in order to have become spiritless. To be spiritless is to lack a consciousness of God. Kierkegaard's view here seems to lead to the conclusion that there is in all human beings an original knowledge of God, a knowledge which becomes obscured and repressed over time, but which is nonetheless enough to make the individual responsible.

V. Is There a Natural Awareness of God in All Humans?

This view that there is something like a universal, natural knowledge of God is puzzling and difficult to accept, but it seems implicit at many points in Kierkegaard's authorship and explicit at a few points. In the *Papirer*, in a draft version of *Philosophical Fragments*, it is said that there has never been a genuine atheist, only people who did not wish to "let what they knew, that God existed, get power over their minds" (JP 3:662). The hostility to the idea of proving God's existence in both *Postscript* and *Fragments* seems to be linked to the idea that such proofs are unnecessary because God is in some sense already present to human beings (CUP 545).

One may reasonably ask about such a universal knowledge of God, "In what does it consist?" On the surface many people do not seem to have any conscious awareness of God. This fact is quite compatible with Kierkegaard's view, of course, since the thesis is not that everyone is actually aware of God. The whole point of much of SUD is that this knowledge has become repressed, and that understanding this repression is the key to understanding the unconscious in humans. Still, in order to repress this knowledge, humans must once have had it, and one may reasonably ask whether such a view is in accord with what we know about human psychological development.

To make sense of Kierkegaard's position, I think we must distinguish between a conscious awareness of God, and a conscious awareness of God *as* God. It is implausible to claim that the latter kind of knowledge is universally present in human beings, even originally or as a kind of potential knowledge. It is not, however, absurd to maintain that human beings in fact have an awareness of God, even though they do not always understand that it is God whom they are aware of. Anti-Climacus explicitly claims that it is *conscience* which constitutes the relationship to God (SUD 124). This is consistent with the general Kierkegaardian view that the religious life, while never reducible to the ethical life, always arises out of a confrontation with ethical ideals.

Every child does not have a clear, explicit understanding of the nature of God. However, Kierkegaard thinks, every child does encounter ideals which are experienced as absolute in character, and in experiencing these ideals gains some sense of the "infinity" of the self. (A degree of cultural relativity in the content of the ideals does not matter, since it is their absolute form which is determinative.) In encountering such ideals I gain a sense of my self as more than a product of accidental circumstances. I am rather called to exercise responsible choice and become the ideal self I see it as my task to become.

Whether the child understands this or not, such an encounter is an encounter with the ontological "other" which is the "power" which constitutes the self.

VI. Conscience and the Self

That conscience is decisive in the development of the self is not a thesis unique to Kierkegaard. In a way this is Freud's view as well, since for Freud, the resolution of the Oedipus conflict and the development of the superego are also decisive in becoming an adult.

The differences with Freud are, however, more significant than the similarities. For Freud, the superego is simply the internalized parent; there is no question of the superego as in any sense the voice of God. It does not represent absolute truth but cultural relativity. For Kierkegaard, conscience, while certainly reflecting cultural norms, also reflects the coming into being in a human person of a sense of his own freedom and responsibility through an encounter with ideals that have absolute validity.

This difference makes one suspect that the Freudian superego and the Kierkegaardian conscience are simply not identical. I think this suspicion is correct, and that its correctness can be seen by looking at the crucial time period when each is formed. For the superego the crucial age is clearly around three. However, this cannot be the crucial age for the development of conscience in the significant sense for Kierkegaard. Once conscience is in place the capacity of the individual to despair and to sin is in place as well, but it is well known that Kierkegaard did not think children were capable of sin in any genuine sense. Anti-Climacus says plainly that children are not capable of despair, but only bad temper (SUD 49n.).

I think therefore that we must look to adolescence or at least pre-adolescence as the crucial period for the emergence of conscience in the Kierkegaardian sense. (The exact age surely differs from child to child.) It is in adolescence that the individual discovers that he or she must choose and affirm—or reject—what has been handed down to him or her by culture. Such a call to responsible choice is at the same time a discovery that choices matter—that one is called to choose responsibly. In Kierkegaard's language it is the discovery that human persons are spirit, and Kierkegaard interprets this encounter as God's call to individuals to become what God has created them to be.

One other significant difference between Freudian and Kierkegaardian views now comes into view, and that concerns the relation between conscience, pathology, and the unconscious. For Freud, the overactive superego is a source of pathology. It is the sadistic, internal saboteur which must be tamed and moderated for the sake of individual psychological health, even if we must retain it in some form for the sake of civilized society. Kierkegaard is hardly ignorant of the torments of the overly active conscience, but he is far from seeing this as the most significant source of human sickness.

Like Freud, he favors an approach to the child's development which avoids excessive guilt. The imposition of strict Christian concepts on the child is even characterized as a "rape, be it ever so well meant" (CUP 603). Children who are victims of such a rape have a struggle to go through, as they attempt to come to terms with the love and forgiveness of God.

Despite this apparent agreement with Freud and neo-Freudians who see the major problem of human life to be guilt-feelings caused by an overactive superego, Kierkegaard would by no means be enthusiastic about the banishment of guilt from contemporary life. The real problem is not that we have excessive guilt feelings, but that we avoid coming to terms with the fact that we are really guilty.

The development of the pathological unconscious must be seen in connection with just this point. The motivation for the development of the unconscious is our sensuousness, our failure to rise above the categories of what feels pleasant and unpleasant, for the experience of guilt is decidedly unpleasant. Most human beings do not have "the courage to venture out and to endure being spirit" (SUD 43).

When the call of conscience comes, humans therefore have a reason to ignore it. And once they have ignored it, they have a double reason for ignoring it, for to face conscience would be not only to face the unpleasantness of responsible decision-making, but the greater unpleasantness of having decided to shirk responsibility. Thus the dynamic unconscious emerges, the long process of deceiving oneself about oneself, employing the strategies outlined above, and a host of others.

Thus we see that Kierkegaard's view of the unconscious is as thoroughly relational as his view of the self. Object-relations theorists trace the emergence of the unconscious to the divided self which comes into being through relations with others. Kierkegaard recognizes the role of these relations in the formation of the self, especially with regard to what I have termed the pre-self, the identity the self already has when it becomes a self in a deeper sense. These early relations certainly will involve conflicts, and may lead to the development of dissociation and unconscious processes. So Kierkegaard does not have to reject the understanding of object-relations theorists about the significance of early relations.

Nevertheless Kierkegaard traces the emergence of the unconscious in the most significant sense to the divided self which emerges through a relation to *the* significant other which forms the basis for the true self. For Kierkegaard the really significant unconscious is the one that I form as an adolescent and as an adult, as I encounter God and deceive myself as I deal with the resultant moral failure and guilt. Of course this does not mean that Kierkegaard believes that the unconscious processes which result from early relations with others are unrelated to the deeper unconscious which is his primary concern. To the contrary, the psychological conflicts and predispositions which the child brings to adolescence are fraught with significance. I believe that these problems are understood by Kierkegaard as bound up with the nest of problems associated with original sin.

In *The Concept of Anxiety* Vigilius Haufniensis maintains that every individual "is both himself and the race" (CA 28). Original sin is not simply a physical, inherited malady. To the extent that I am a sinner, it is because I have chosen to be a sinner, just as Adam chose sin. Such a choice is scientifically inexplicable, but that simply shows that sin must be understood as the result of freedom (CA 32–33, 51, 92).

Qualitatively, therefore, the sin of every individual is the same. This does not mean, however, that sin does not have real consequences for the individual and for the race. The individual who is born to a sinful race does not begin life with a blank slate, but as possessing sinful inclinations, which he or she did not choose him or herself and which quantitatively differ from the innocence of Adamic Eden.

I believe that this provides the context for understanding early relations with others and the foundation of the personality for Kierkegaard. Though he will not hear of a "universal excuse," since individuals must recognize that they have become what they have chosen to become and take responsibility for what they are, it is nevertheless true that the child who is the product of a sinful race and a sinful upbringing bears heavy burdens. The self such a child will choose to be is a self "already bungled," a self already seriously distorted and misshapen by bad parental relationships and relations with others.

VII. Healing the Unconscious

To summarize, Kierkegaard's view of the unconscious is basically that the unconscious is something which I develop as I deceive myself about who and what I am. The process of forming and disguising my identity is in turn a process of relating to others, with God as the ultimate and intended other, but other persons playing a role in shaping what I have termed the pre-self and (later) playing the role of God-substitutes in the formation and maintenance of one's sinful identity. This view implies, as we have seen, some remarkable claims: that everyone has an unconscious relation to God and that every person has to some degree obscured this relation and thus divided the self.

On the surface such views may seem implausible, but we must recognize that if we are indeed self-deceivers, then such self-deception will not be obvious to us. Ultimately, I think Kierkegaard's view stands or falls with the Christianity to which it is so intimately linked, and it is well-known that Kierkegaard thought it crucial to maintain that Christianity could not be rationally demonstrated to be true. Rather, the possibility of offense must be safe-guarded, and we must therefore safeguard this possibility in his view of the unconscious as well. Kierkegaard's view of the unconscious contains an analysis of the condition of the "natural man" which that person can only hope to recognize as true with the help of divine revelation.

Nevertheless, it is important to see how Kierkegaard's views can be used to interpret contemporary psychological findings. Those findings cannot be demonstrative evidence of the correctness of Kierkegaard's views, but if Kierkegaard's perspective gives us no interpretive power, no ability to illuminate our situation, then the understanding it claims to offer must be illusory.

To this end I should like to draw attention to some interesting parallels between Kierkegaard's view and the object-relations theory which is, as we have seen, his closest neighbor on the contemporary psychological scene. The parallels are especially interesting with respect to possible cures for the problem of the divided self.

Kierkegaard's claim that the self-deception associated with sin and despair is a universal phenomenon closely parallels the claim of the object-relations theorist that the "schizoid self" is universal. W. D. Fairbairn, in his important paper, "Schizoid Factors in the Personality," recognizes that the universality of his claims will be disturbing to many. "The criticism for which I must now prepare myself is that, according to my way of thinking, everybody without exception must be regarded as schizoid."[16] Fairbairn's response to this criticism is simply that it is true that everyone is at bottom schizoid, and thus that the criticism is not a criticism. "The fundamental schizoid phenomenon is the presence of splits in the ego; and it would take a bold man to claim that his ego was so perfectly integrated as to be incapable of revealing any evidence of splitting at the deepest levels."[17]

If this is correct, Kierkegaard might well take this universal "splitting" to be confirmation of his claims about the universality of sin and despair. The object-relations theorist also agrees with Kierkegaard that this dissociation of the self from itself is fundamentally the result of faulty relationships with others. Of course the psychoanalytic thinker sees the faulty relationships to be primarily with the initial care-giver, while, as we have seen, Kierkegaard focuses attention on the relation to God. Once we recognize, however, that different ages are of concern here, there is no real contradiction between the two views. Object-relations theory is attempting to understand the initial formation of the psyche, and the focus is therefore on early childhood. Kierkegaard is analyzing the becoming of a self in the decisive sense, and thus his views center on adolescence and the early adult years. We have seen that Kierkegaard does not deny that significant psychological developments may occur in early childhood, developments that may, under the impact of original sin, predispose the self towards brokenness. Also, the psychoanalytic perspective of such thinkers as Guntrip and Fairbairn presupposes the possibility of a genuine self, which can continue to develop and assume responsibility for itself. So there is no objection from the psychological side toward seeing decisions later than early childhood as decisive in the formation of the self.

The significance of such later decisions and later relationships comes through clearly if we look at the views of Guntrip and Fairbairn on the healing of the broken self. Though Guntrip wants to affirm a genuinely "personal self," which can assume responsibility for itself and cannot see itself as the helpless victim of biological forces, he affirms in an equally emphatic way the need of the self for a healing relationship to become truly whole.

Guntrip sees the therapist as attempting to provide the client who was not fortunate enough to have had "good-enough mothering" a sense of identity and security which his parents failed to provide him originally. "At the deepest level, psychotherapy is replacement therapy, providing for the patient what the mother failed to provide at the beginning of life."[18] The therapist does not really use "techniques," but must simply be a real person for the client, a person who is accepting and non-judgmental, which allows the divided ego to accept all of itself.

From Kierkegaard's point of view, there is wisdom in Guntrip's view, but it fails to capture the depths of the self's situation in several ways. First, Guntrip, with his talk of "good-enough mothering," ignores the universality of the problem. If the divided self is as universal as he and Fairbairn maintain, one may well ask as to whether any parenting can be "good-enough" to produce the whole self being held forward as an ideal.

Even more significantly, Kierkegaard would, I think, while affirming the need for a "basic security giving personal relationship," question the adequacy of the therapist to play this role. However much the therapist may try to be a "real person" to the client, one must recognize that the therapeutic relationship is in the end an artificial one. The client and the therapist are engaged in a commercial transaction; the non-judgmental acceptance of the therapist can hardly be anything other than a therapeutic technique. Client and therapist do not interact outside the therapeutic session, and if by chance they do, one would hardly expect the therapist always to maintain an accepting attitude. Suppose, for example, that the client is having an affair with the spouse of the therapist?

But even if the therapist is a model of love and acceptance, the fundamental problem, from Kierkegaard's perspective, is that such a therapist would still provide an inadequate "criterion" of the self. The therapist would still be an inadequate substitute for the person whose love and acceptance can genuinely form the basis of selfhood.

This is not to say that therapy cannot be helpful for individuals who are psychologically crippled. Though I am not sure Kierkegaard has room for this idea, the therapist may indeed help a troubled individual move toward wholeness, much as a relationship with a good friend may help an individual. It may even be in some cases that therapy is part of what makes faith possible, since for some people the pre-self may be so broken that the idea of a loving, accepting God is literally unbelievable. "Perhaps there are times when the sick are too weak for the surgery that would cure them."[19]

In the final analysis, however, the ultimate cure is not human therapy but faith in God, at least as Kierkegaard sees it. My identity or non-identity cannot be rooted in the acceptance or non-acceptance of another self struggling towards wholeness. Only the absolute love of God can provide the security which allows the self to accept itself completely as it is, while recognizing the possibility and responsibility for becoming what it may fully be. The cure for the human condition is simply faith: "Faith is: that the self in being itself and in willing to be itself rests transparently in God" (SUD 82). Such a faith would mean that the unconscious as that part of myself which I cannot and will not recognize has been blotted out. I would know myself, even as I am known.

Notes

1. Though I cite the Hongs' pagination (SUD), where noted in the text I have preferred my own translation.

2. The typical cognitive psychologist views mental activity as information processing in the brain. The part of this activity that "gets noticed" is consciousness. See Winson, *Brain and Psyche*, for a lucid account of this perspective, which relates this view to Freudian theory.

3. This early account can be found in several of Freud's writings; for example, see his *An Outline of Psycho-Analysis*.

4. See chapter 2 of Sartre's *Being and Nothingness*.

5. See Freud's *The Ego and the Id*.

6. This account of Freud's relation to Groddeck is found in Guntrip, *Psychoanalytic Theory, Therapy, and the Self*, p. 105.

7. See the previous note for Guntrip. Fairbairn's most significant work is *Psychoanalytic Studies of the Personality*.

8. Guntrip credits Melanie Klein for the first account of how this takes place. See chapter 3 in Guntrip, *Psychoanalytic Theory*.

9. See Guntrip, *Psychoanalytic Theory*, p. 191.

10. Westphal, "Kierkegaard's Psychology and Unconscious Despair," in *International Kierkegaard Commentary: The Sickness unto Death* (henceforth IKC-SUD), ed. Perkins, pp. 39–66.

11. Westphal, "Kierkegaard's Psychology" in IKC-SUD, p. 49.

12. Elrod, "Kierkegaard on Self and Society," in Kierkegaardiana XI, pp. 178–96.

13. Elrod, *Kierkegaard and Christendom*, pp. 131–32.

14. Walsh, "On 'Feminine' and 'Masculine' Forms of Despair," in IKC-SUD, p. 125.

15. Walsh, "On 'Feminine' " in IKC-SUD, pp. 126–27.

16. Fairbairn, *Psychoanalytic Studies*, p. 7.

17. Fairbairn, *Psychoanalytic Studies*, p. 8.

18. Guntrip, *Psychoanalytic Theory*, p. 191.

19. This sentence comes from some comments by Merold Westphal on an earlier draft of this chapter. I am deeply in Westphal's debt for his suggestions.

6 | Amatory Cures for Material Dis-ease

A Kristevian Reading of The Sickness unto Death

Tamsin Lorraine

ONE PSYCHOANALYTIC PERSPECTIVE on the belief in God posits God as a kind of cosmic substitute for the all-powerful father of one's childhood. Thus, even after one has discovered that one's father is morally flawed and humanly limited, one still has a moral authority and infinite ideal to which to refer one's life and actions. Freud went so far as to suggest, in *Civilization and Its Discontents*, that religion forces people into a state of psychic infantilism by imposing on them but one path to happiness. According to Freud, every individual must work out her or his own way of reconciling libido with the constraints imposed by civilization. Religion's technique consists in "depressing the value of life and distorting the picture of the real world in a delusional manner"[1] and is not likely to do more than spare many people an individual neurosis at the cost of intellectual intimidation.

Yet we know that Freud practiced a kind of intimidation of his own and that the psychoanalytic scene is not free from encouraging psychic regression in the name of transference. Submission both to God and to the psychoanalytic process is supposed to effect some kind of cure for the spiritual ills of humanity. Does a comparison of the two merely trivialize the one or the other, or could something be learned from such a comparison?

In what follows, I give a reading of *The Sickness unto Death* that presents Kierkegaard's discourse of the God-relationship as an amatory discourse of self-transformation. Julia Kristeva, a Lacanian-influenced psychoanalyst, has suggested that it is due to the lack of such discourses (be they codes of love or religious discourse) that we are currently confronting a difficult situation.

> [W]e must live with different people while relying on our personal moral codes, without the assistance of a set that would include our particularities while transcending them.[2]

Psychoanalysis, as a discourse that could help fill in this lack, "through unraveling transference—the major dynamics of otherness, of love/hatred for the

other, of the foreign component of our psyche"[3] can be experienced as a journey toward an ethics of respect with political implications. Through the awak-
ening consciousness of the strangers within ourselves, "that 'improper' facet of
our impossible 'own and proper' "[4]—the unconscious—we can enable a more
cosmopolitan community in which differences among people can be respected.
Just as Kristeva's version of psychoanalysis represents an opportunity for self-
transformation in a space in which the analysand invites and confronts the
collapse of stable meaning that, it turns out, is always in some way present to
the self, so does Kierkegaard's God-relationship represent a passionate surren-
der to the collapse of meaning in the faith that meaning will be restored by
God. At the same time that both Kierkegaard and Kristeva perceive the paradoxical character of subjectivity, they refuse to relinquish the spiritual hope for
rebirth.

The comparison of these two discourses as codes that enable the transgression of the finite boundaries of the concrete self will suggest further possibilities for enabling a self-transformative transcendence that confronts the risk of
nihilistic self-dispersal. A Kristevian reading of *The Sickness unto Death* will
not only enable a less chauvinistic reading of the God-relationship than that
given by Kierkegaard himself, it will also suggest an alternative to the psychoanalytic nostalgia for the lost mother. Thus, together, these two discourses represent an opportunity for exploring that strange moment beyond all finite significance that, paradoxically enough, is also our only hope for meaningful
existence. This in turn will enable an approach toward rethinking social categories, such as those of gender, class, race, and ethnicity, as categories that can
never provide adequate descriptions of concrete individuals, but which must
always be existentially lived and radically reworked in our on-going struggles
to encounter that which we have labelled "other" both in ourselves and in others.

In section C of part I of *The Sickness unto Death*, Anti-Climacus states,

> The self is the conscious synthesis of infinitude and finitude that relates itself
> to itself, whose task is to become itself, which can be done only through the
> relationship to God. To become oneself is to become concrete. But to become
> concrete is neither to become finite nor to become infinite, for that which is
> to become concrete is indeed a synthesis. Consequently, the progress of the
> becoming must be an infinite moving away from itself in the infinitizing of
> the self, and an infinite coming back to itself in the finitizing process. But if
> the self does not become itself, it is in despair, whether it knows that or not.
> (SUD 29–30)

All despair can be traced to the will to be rid of oneself (SUD 20). Human
beings who become merely finite lose their selves. "To lack infinitude is de-

spairing reductionism, narrowness" (SUD 33). Such human beings absorb themselves in secular affairs and conform to the social status quo. They find it "far easier and safer to be like the others, to become a copy, a number, a mass man" (SUD 34). Human beings that dwell on the infinite get lost in the "fantastic"; they become so absorbed in imagining all the self's possibilities in the abstract that they lose the finite aspect of their selves. Thus, becoming conscious as self, which is for Anti-Climacus the only thing that can make one's life worth living (SUD 26–27), involves both imaginative reflection on one's possibilities, as well as recognition and acknowledgement of one's concrete situation in all its particularity.

A human being is a synthesis of the infinite and the finite, of the temporal and the eternal, of freedom and necessity, that relates itself to itself (SUD 13). But it is not enough for a human being to be a synthesis of these opposing aspects of life; a human being cannot be a self until in addition to relating itself to itself it also relates itself to another. The most important other to whom one can relate oneself as a synthesis is God. Thus, one can become oneself only through relating the synthesis of opposing aspects of oneself to a third party— God as irreducible other. Becoming oneself through the relationship to God involves gaining the impression that one's self exists before a God (SUD 27). The belief in God involves the belief that even in the face of one's inevitable downfall, God, for whom everything is possible, will provide a way out.

> The *believer* sees and understands his downfall, humanly speaking (in what has happened to him, or in what he has ventured), but he believes. For this reason he does not collapse. He leaves it entirely to God how he is to be helped, but he believes that for God everything is possible. To *believe* his downfall is impossible. To understand that humanly it is his downfall and nevertheless to believe in possibility is to believe. So God helps him also— perhaps by allowing him to avoid the horror, perhaps through the horror itself—and here, unexpectedly, miraculously, divinely, help does come. (SUD 39)

The believer faced with imminent calamity does not withdraw from the realm of the concrete; she or he is realistic about which options are socially meaningful and acceptable in the secular world. The believer is here in a situation in which every such option can lead only to disaster. But the believer is more than a number or a mass man—she or he can also imaginatively reflect on the situation in relationship to an other who is beyond all concrete situations. The believer has faith that unprecedented possibilities can emerge from the most unexpected places not only because for God everything is possible, but because God witnesses and cares about the believer's life in all its particularity. Thus, the believer synthesizes radically disparate aspects of the self in relationship to an omniscient and omnipotent other that lovingly witnesses that process from beyond.

A human being with anything like a "spirit" or "self" "has an essential interior consistency and a consistency in something higher" (SUD 107). The believer's consistency rests in the good. She or he therefore fears sin because it represents an infinite loss—the loss of one's consistency. But it is not just the loss of consistency that is feared, but the loss constituted by a rejection or denial of some aspect of oneself because it is deemed unacceptable. Thus, faith, rather than virtue, is the antithesis of sin, because faith is "that the self is being itself and in willing to be itself rests transparently in God" (SUD 82). That is, one knows that God in general "comprehends actuality itself, all its particulars" (SUD 121) and in particular comprehends every aspect of one's life as one struggles for synthesized consistency and yet still wills to be one's self. Sin is "after being taught by a revelation from God what sin is—before God in despair not to will to be oneself or in despair to will to be oneself" (SUD 96). That is, to sin is to know one has done wrong and to attempt to reject this act from one's synthesizing process or to let it define oneself as irredeemably sinful. To despair of forgiveness from God for one's sins is what Anti-Climacus calls "offense" (SUD 116).

> The person who does not take offense *worships* in faith. But to worship, which is the expression of faith, is to express that the infinite, chasmal, qualitative abyss between them is confirmed. (SUD 129)

The believer who worships in faith can thus not only believe that God will help in time of trouble against all odds, but that God will forgive one's wrongdoing thus enabling consistency despite the conflicting aspects of one's self-becoming. Just as the belief in unprecedented possibilities in a desperate situation speaks to God's limitlessness, so does faith in God's forgiving nature speak to God's infinitude. In both cases, the individual reconciles the disparate elements of her or his situation or self in relationship to a witness who neither rejects nor denies any of those elements, and who can enable their synthesis into unprecedented possibilities for happy solutions and consistent wholeness.

We know from *Fear and Trembling*[5] that the sin that is revealed to the faithful individual is not necessarily the same as what is considered to be unethical by the ethical community in which the individual abides as one among others. This is further borne out in the above description of the loss of self encountered by individuals who lack infinitude. Infinitude involves not merely having an intellectual conception of God as limitless, it also involves being able to reflect upon one's own possibilities before the one for whom all is possible. To merely do or be as one is told, to merely conform, is to lack imagination, and therefore to lose one's access to the eternal.

We also know from *Fear and Trembling* that faith involves a passionate encounter with the paradox presented by Christianity. It is only in refusing to "explain away" the paradox of God as man that one develops the inwardness of a person of faith. For the self described in *The Sickness unto Death*, inwardness also involves an individual's confrontation with the torment presented by the contradiction between one's wish to infinitize one's possibilities and one's inability to escape the limitations of one's self as it is. Recognition of one's despair deepens one's inwardness. Despair before God is sin. Faith is the antithesis of sin and the antidote for despair. In faith, one rests transparently in God both in being oneself and willing to be oneself. Taking God as one's criterion, existing before God, one is moved to infinitize one's possibilities without forgetting the qualitative abyss between God and human beings and the fact that it is humanity that sins and God who forgives the sinner. In accepting God's loving forgiveness, one both confronts one's finitude and accepts one's dependence on God.

> The child who previously has had only his parents as a criterion becomes a self as an adult by getting the state as a criterion, but what an infinite accent falls on the self by having God as the criterion! . . . [E]verything is qualitatively that by which it is measured, and that which is its qualitative criterion is ethically its goal. (SUD 79)

For Kristeva, too, human beings are in a paradoxical situation. They are signifying processes that operate in two modalities—the symbolic modality in which the subject posits itself as a unity in a certain relationship to the objects in its world, and the semiotic modality in which connections between the body in the process of constituting itself as a body proper and its world are governed by a preverbal functional state that Kristeva characterizes as "analogous only to vocal or kinetic rhythm."[6] The semiotic modality relates to the pre-oedipal state of symbiotic fusion with the mother from which the subject's initial body boundaries emerged. Since body boundaries can never be fixed and the subject's meaning never completed (until, perhaps, the ultimate dissolution of all body boundaries in death), the semiotic is a modality that is an on-going and integral aspect of all signifying activity. Human beings are thus not simply subjects whose consciousness changes in dialectical interaction with their world; they are also embodied subjects engaged in dialectical interaction between the body as already signified and the material excess of those significations.[7]

In *Black Sun*,[8] Kristeva suggests that melancholy and depression can involve a sort of vault of semiotic activity that has not been incorporated into the individual's symbolic activity.[9] Apparently, since primordial semiotic activity is linked to the maternal body, this means that one has not properly mourned or resolved one's loss of this body. Thus, we could give a Kristevian reading of Kierkegaard, relating despair and sin to an imbalance in the semiotic and symbolic modalities of subjectivity. Too much emphasis on the former and we have an emphasis on infinitude and the fantastic—the attempt to regain the lost Thing (one's rich and varied experiences of the maternal body in the mode of primary processes) through the imaginary.[10] Too much emphasis on the symbolic modality and we have an emphasis on finitude and the secular mentality of the conforming individual who refuses to question conventional meaning. Just as Kierkegaard concerns himself with the various forms of a lack of self and the possible collapse of self in the face of radical challenges to one's meaning, so Kristeva concerns herself with the despair of a subject reduced to a symbolic automaton with no access to the semiotic or the possible collapse of self precipitated by a flood of semiotic affect that overwhelms symbolicity.[11]

In *Desire in Language*, Kristeva cites avant-garde literature as a kind of language that can enable rejuvenating self-transformation. Experimental language evokes an extralinguistic response to instinctual drives and historical contradictions that the symbolic does not make explicit.[12] In the disorienting space created by this literature, the reader is moved to undermine conventional meaning and generate new meanings on the basis of her or his reactions to the text.[13] It is the reader's own biography, her or his own desire, that will allow the breakdown of old codes and the emergence of new formulations of desire as the semiotic motility that precedes and exceeds any constitution of the subject is activated, thus prompting new investments of instinctual drive.[14] These new formulations of desire involve more than a shift in perspective due to the further development of a rational progression of thought. They involve a shattering of language and of the body that negates any position of understanding and all previous articulations of experience, only to allow new articulations to emerge.

Kristeva clearly values what she calls the revolutionary potential of poetic language, yet she does not think that avant-garde literature will necessarily help us achieve the ethical communities that she would herself like to enable. In fact, in her later work she seems to suggest that amatory discourse, for example between lovers, or religious discourse, might be more appropriate or effective spaces in which to experience break-downs in subjectivity and the reconfiguration of desire.

> [I]n love "I" has been an *other*. That phrase, which leads us to poetry or raving hallucination, suggests a state of instability in which the individual is no longer indivisible and allows himself to become lost in the other, for the other. Within love, a risk that might otherwise be tragic is accepted, normalized, made fully reassuring.[15]

Kristeva claims that love, by enabling the connection of the psyche as one open system to another, can bring about renewal and rebirth. The individual in love abandons rigid fixation on a symbolic understanding of one's self in deference to one's beloved. "Libidinal auto-organization" (the semiotic modality) thus encounters "memory-consciousness" (the symbolic modality). The confusion caused by this encounter can become symbolized since the individual in love adapts to the situation in part through identification with the ideal presented by the beloved other.[16]

In psychoanalysis, transference love can elicit the same effect without the risk of loss of self that love (of the chaotic and fusional kind) can bring.

> By ensuring a loving Other to the patient, the analyst (temporarily) allows the Ego in the throes of drive to take shelter in the following fantasy: the analyst is not a dead Father but a living Father; this nondesiring but loving father reconciles the ideal Ego with the Ego Ideal and elaborates the psychic space where, possibly and subsequently, an analysis can take place.[17]

Thus, psychoanalysis can enable self-transformation by creating a space in which "fluctuations of primary processes and even bioenergetic transmissions" can be modified through a discourse that favors "a better integration of semiotic agitation within the symbolic fabric."[18]

Religious discourse can also perform this function. Just as the analyst ensures a loving space within which the patient may risk psychic instability, Christian discourse provides a narrative which represents Christ as a subject with fundamental and psychically necessary discontinuity. The story of Christ's relationship to his Father provides an image and narrative for the many separations that build up the psychic life of individuals. Birth, weaning, separation, frustration, castration, are all psychic cataclysms that can threaten an individual's balance.

> Their nonexecution or repudiation leads to psychotic confusion; their dramatization is, on the contrary, a source of exorbitant and destructive anguish. Because Christianity set that rupture at the very heart of the absolute subject—Christ; because it represented it as a Passion that was the solidary lining of his Resurrection, his glory, and his eternity, it brought to consciousness the essential dramas that are internal to the becoming of each and every subject. It thus endows itself with a tremendous cathartic power.[19]

In addition, the Christian story of God's relationship to humanity with his power to forgive represents a powerful possibility for healing psychic breaks.

> [F]orgiveness gathers on its way to the other a very human sorrow. Recognizing the lack and the wound that caused it, it fulfills them with an ideal gift—promise, project, artifice, thus fitting the humiliated, offended being into an order of perfection, and giving him the assurance that he belongs there.[20]

Kristeva suggests that it is important that this other be a father—not the prohibiting oedipal father, but the loving, forgiving father. According to Kristeva, the break with the pre-oedipal mother is enabled by primary identification with the "imaginary father." It is not just that the oedipal father who represents and upholds symbolic Law prohibits incest; the imaginary father is the father who lovingly receives one despite all one's flaws. Thus, it is this dual father who is the ideal with whom one can identify—taking on the position of a speaking subject without having to relinquish the affective meaning of prehistorical identifications.

> The supporting father of such symbolic triumph [over sadness] is not the oedipal father but truly that "imaginary father," "father in individual prehistory" according to Freud, who guarantees primary identification. Nevertheless, it is imperative that this father in individual prehistory be capable of playing his part as oedipal father in symbolic Law, for it is on the basis of that harmonious blending of the two facets of fatherhood that the abstract and arbitrary signs of communication may be fortunate enough to be tied to the affective meaning of prehistorical identifications, and the dead language of the potentially depressive person can arrive at a live meaning in the bond with others.[21]

On this reading, Kierkegaard's God-relationship would represent a rendering of a relationship to a fatherly other that could enable spiritual access to a realm beyond conventional social meaning, beyond language, beyond possibility. In the safety of transparency before God, one could acknowledge the disturbing indications of instabilities in one's self and open one's self to the profound disorientation that acknowledgement can cause, in faith that the loving father will both note and acknowledge one's transgressions as well as somehow enable one's return to meaning and community. Thus, Kierkegaard's God is not a rigid upholder of the Law, callously excluding those who don't abide by the Law upon which human community is founded; he is the Christian God who attends to each and every particular of each individual existence with loving care, sometimes enabling the miracle by which the excluded individual can be returned to ethical community.

Although Kristeva indicates a positive role for religious discourse, it is not clear whether she herself doesn't tend toward the anti-religious views with which I started this chapter. I would like to suggest that whatever problems Kristeva may have with Kierkegaard's God-relationship, it provides opportunities in self-transformation without some of the risks of her own preferred discourse of psychoanalysis. In particular, while the psychoanalytic discourse only serves to reinforce a highly gendered reading of self-transforming discourses, exploration of Kierkegaard's discourse, in light of Kristeva's emphasis on the body, could suggest other possibilities.

The psychoanalytic story emphasizes the originary moment of the self in the oedipal triangle. Kristeva is, of course, right to suggest that contemporary culture associates "woman" with the body and with deeper mysteries that may relate to the ultimate mystery of living an embodied existence. She seems to think, however, that this must be the case because it is, after all, from women that we are all born. In addition, since the psychoanalytic story is an originary one, the forward impulses of an individual's existence are explained with respect to conditional causes—in this case the biographical experiences of the individual in her or his relationship to the maternal body. The semiotic impulses of primary process as well as the form that the ideal other takes, are thus traced to the formative experiences of individuals (although both semiotic impulses and ego ideals are of course not unaffected by later events). The fatherly analyst can help the analysand construct a life-narrative and self-in-process with a more satisfying synthesis of the symbolic and semiotic. Such reconstructions are enabled and stabilized within the context of the oedipal triangle. This emphasis on personal reconstruction of one's own biography can affect the kind of liberating "cure" which concerns both Kristeva and Kierkegaard. Kierkegaard's story, however, depicts the God-relationship as predicated upon a genuine encounter with an infinite Other who is beyond not only all finite situation, but the oedipal situation and the paternal law. This Other for whom all is possible can, if the situation warrants, enable the emergence of possibilities inconceivable within the boundaries of the oedipal frame. Communication with others, for example, can bring not only new insights about our past along with re-organization of semiotic drive, it can also bring us into contact with symbolic systems and semiotic affects that are radically different from our own. In the attempt to make sense of such experiences, faith in an infinite Other could take us beyond the familiar positions constituted within the context of father/son, mother/daughter, and such relationships, to unprecedented configurations of self in relationship.

It has been suggested by more than one Kierkegaard commentator that Kierkegaard was more interested in spiritual inwardness than a spirituality that might wreak havoc with conventional ethical orders. Certainly his chauvinism vis-à-vis Christianity would seem to suggest a low tolerance toward alternative ethical systems. If we read the God-relationship in light of Kristeva's depiction of the contradictions presented by material existence, however, we may perceive healing possibilities for Kierkegaardian faith in a broader context. The religious notion of God as that which is always other to one's own synthesizing process (God attends to finitude and yet is unlimited), and yet witnessing it in all its particularity with loving (and yet discriminating) inclusiveness, suggests a possible solution to the contemporary problem of the alienated subject. Despite the singularity of an individual God-relationship, God witnesses all of life at once in its continual unfolding. Thus, embracing this

Other involves recognizing that it is not only oneself but everyone and everything in all their particularity that are witnessed by this Other. The infinite nature of such a witness both in terms of its all-inclusive attention to every detail no matter how "trivial" or nonsensical, as well as its limitless power and creativity in enabling meaningful solutions in the synthesis of that detail, encourages a responsibly creative response to postmodern confusion. Faith in such an infinite Other insures that we will neither deny the various and contradictory aspects of our lives, nor despair of becoming more deeply ourselves[22] despite our confusion.

Believers in postmodern society are often confronted not only with ineffable aspects of their own experience that take them beyond the secular, ethical realm, they are also confronted with the clash of one or more competing ethical systems. Kierkegaardian faith transposed to this context in light of our discussion of Kristeva, may involve belief that new syntheses and new meaning can emerge from ethical systems that seem in outright contradiction as well as from encounters with embodied others with desires that conflict with our own. Thus, the appeal to a loving Other that witnesses inter- as well as intra-subjective conflict, could involve both the refusal to reject or deny "unacceptable" persons or elements as well as the faith that meaningful connections and satisfying self-transformation in community with others could emerge from such conflict. The affective force for the emergence of new meaning would come not simply from the semiotic irruptions of specific individuals, but through the communication of subjective experience in both symbolic and semiotic modalities among individuals.[23] While a psychoanalytic appeal to attend to and incorporate disparate aspects of ourselves that hearken back to our corporeal origins is important and useful, the religious appeal to an Other for whom all is possible and who watches over each and every one of us without discounting any individual or any aspect of particular individuals, could provide a kind of transcendent ideal that would facilitate our attempts to build ethical community. Kristeva's psychoanalytic notion of a subject-in-process encourages an oedipal framework and an emphasis on personal biography. Kierkegaard's religious notion of a God-relationship could take us beyond the oedipal framework and shift emphasis to a self-in-world witnessed by an infinite Other without losing the materialist impetus of Kristeva's work. Whether the rifts at issue are within the subject or among subjects and worlds, it is through a faith that neither denies those rifts nor despairs because of them that ruptures in human significance and community can continue to emerge and be resolved or superseded in an on-going and highly paradoxical process of synthesizing activity. If, as Kristeva suggests, encounter with the stranger within as well as the encounter with human others, is an important part of a self-transformative process, and if we agree with Kierkegaard that such a process is the only thing that makes life worth living, then faith in the miraculous resolution of that moment beyond all meaning, beyond all possibility, is indeed a faith that may be needed to face the difficult problems of our own times without despair.

Notes

1. Freud, *Civilization and Its Discontents*, p. 34.
2. Kristeva, *Strangers to Ourselves*, p. 195.
3. Ibid., p. 182.
4. Ibid., p. 191.
5. I am here skirting the well-known problem of connecting the views put forth by Kierkegaard's various pseudonyms (Anti-Climacus "wrote" SUD and Johannes de Silentio "wrote" FT) because it is generally accepted that Anti-Climacus is relatively close to Kierkegaard's own position and I am here commenting on a resonance between Anti-Climacus and de Silentio, and because it is the conception of a God-relationship that comes out in these two texts (among others) rather than an argument about Kierkegaard's ultimate views on this matter that is at issue in this chapter.
6. Kristeva, *Revolution in Poetic Language*, p. 26.
7. "The heterogeneous element is a corporeal, physiological, and signifiable excitation which the symbolizing social structure—the family or some other structure—cannot grasp. On the other hand, heterogeneity is that part of the objective, material outer world which could not be grasped by the various symbolizing structures the subject already has at his disposal. Non-symbolized corporeal excitation and the new object of the non-symbolized material outer world are always already interacting: the newness of the object gives rise to drives that are not yet bound and prompts their investment" (ibid., 180).
8. Kristeva, *Black Sun*.
9. "Melancholy persons, with their despondent, secret insides, are potential exiles but also intellectuals capable of dazzling, albeit abstract, constructions. With depressive people, *denial of the negation* is the logical expression of omnipotence. Through their empty speech they assure themselves of an inaccessible (because it is 'semiotic' and not 'symbolic') ascendency over an archaic object that thus remains, for themselves and all others, an enigma and a secret" (ibid., 64).
10. "Thus the continuum of the body, which is in the process of becoming 'one's own and proper body,' is articulated as an organized discontinuity, exercising a precocious and primary mastery, flexible yet powerful, over the erotogenic zones, blended with the preobject, the maternal Thing. What appears on the psychological level as omnipotence *is the power of semiotic rhythms, which convey an intense presence of meaning in a presubject still incapable of signification.*

"What we call meaning is the ability of the *infans* to record the signifier of parental desire and include itself therein in his own fashion; he does so by displaying the semiotic abilities he is endowed with at that moment of his development and which allow him a mastery, on the level of primary processes, of a 'not yet other' (of the Thing) included in the erotogenic zones of such a semiotizing *infans*. Nevertheless, the omnipotent meaning remains a 'dead letter' if it is not invested in signification. It will be the task of analytic interpretation to search for depressive meaning in the vault where sadness has locked it up with the mother, and tie it to the signification of objects and desires" (ibid., 62–63).
11. "The excess of affect has thus no other means of coming to the fore than to produce new languages—strange concatenations, idiolects, poetics. Until the weight of the pri-

mal Thing prevails, and all translatability become impossible. Melancholia then ends up in asymbolia, in loss of meaning: if I am no longer capable of translating or metaphorizing, I become silent and die" (ibid., 42).

12. Kristeva, *Desire in Language*, p. 116.

13. "[T]his heterogeneousness to signification operates through, despite, and in excess of it and produces in poetic language 'musical' but also nonsense effects that destroy not only accepted beliefs and significations, but, in radical experiments, syntax itself, that guarantee of thetic consciousness (of the signified object and ego)" (ibid., 133).

14. "A reading, whose conceptual supports are muted, is the terrain of the reading subject's desire, his drives, sexuality, and attentiveness toward the phonematic network, the rhythm of the sentences, the particular semanteme bringing him back to a feeling, pleasure, laughter, an event or reading of the most 'empirical' kind, abounding, enveloping, multiple. The identity of the reading *I* loses itself there, atomizes itself; it is a time of jouissance, where one discovers one text under another, its other" (ibid., 119).

15. Kristeva, *Tales of Love*, p. 4.

16. "The effect of love is one of renewal, our rebirth. The new blossoms out and throws us into confusion when libidinal auto-organization encounters memory-consciousness, which is guaranteed by the Other, and becomes symbolized; conversely, it arises when the memory-consciousness system abandons its fixative systematicity (related to the superego) in order to adapt to the new risks of destabilized-stabilizable auto-organization. In Freudian terms, it would involve the desexualization of drive, deflecting it toward idealization and sublimation; and conversely, bringing together idealizing mechanisms with the processes of incorporation and of introjection of incorporated items" (ibid., 15–16).

17. Ibid., p. 30.

18. "There is perhaps a chance, then, for analysis to transform such subjectivation and endow discourse with a modifying power over the fluctuations of primary processes and even bioenergetic transmissions, by favoring a better integration of semiotic agitation within the symbolic fabric" (*Black Sun*, 66).

19. Ibid., p. 132.

20. Ibid., p. 216.

21. Ibid., pp. 23–24.

22. Here I am assuming a Kierkegaardian notion of a self that in a process of synthesizing finitude and infinitude strives both to will to be itself and to be consistently "good" in the eyes of an omniscient witness.

23. Brennan, in her book *The Interpretation of the Flesh*, develops a theory about the energetic connections that exist between people on the basis of Freudian theory. She argues that in making the Lacanian move to a linguistic rereading of Freud that we have lost the element of the physical in Freud's thought. The notion of a psychic imprint that occurs not only between mother and child, but in later relationships, has important implications that are relevant to the kind of "semiotic" communication I refer to here.

7 | Kierkegaard and Feminism
Apologetic, Repetition, and Dialogue
Wanda Warren Berry

1. Preliminary Expectoration: An Apologetic for Dialogue

HISTORIAN GERDA LERNER recently reminded us that one consequence of men's historical "power to define" was that "thinking women" were forced "to waste much time and energy on defensive arguments."[1] Lerner certainly is right that women have rarely been able to avoid the "brain drain" of needing to combat sexist definitions of themselves. It is tempting, therefore, to join radical feminist "freethinkers"[2] who reject on-going dialogue with male thinkers as well as patriarchally transmitted traditions, turning instead to the rich resources currently being re-discovered or newly-created as expressions of women's experience. Feminists who continue in dialogue with their male mentors in the Western[3] intellectual traditions sometimes are chided by others in the women's movement.[4] Such chiding encourages in them an apologetic approach, not only as they deal with manifest or hidden sexism in such authors, but also as they try to explain the very fact of their continuing dialogue with the giants of patriarchal traditions.

Kierkegaardian feminists feel these same needs for an initial apologetic, not only because of aspects of the writings which lead some influential interpreters to call Kierkegaard "bitterly misogynistic,"[5] but also because of the implications of the claim that, as Lerner says of the patriarchal past, "Every thinking woman had to argue with the 'great man' in her head, instead of being strengthened and encouraged by her foremothers."[6] A pathos-filled aspect of such an apologetic involves remembering that there simply were no women thinkers available, at least in print, to provide the existential maieutics needed in the formative years of previous generations. The silencing of our foremothers causes us to mourn; sometimes anger surges as we seek classical paradigms or historical examples which can bind time for ourselves or our students, only to find virtually all of them male-defined.

Nevertheless, respect for the historical resourcefulness and agency of women, which Lerner and other recent feminist theorists emphasize, suggests that each of us not simply turn away from "the great man in our head." Instead we should ask, "*Why did I let him into my head?*" For example, was I simply a victim, overpowered by Kierkegaard's influence? Or is it possible that I let Kierkegaard into my head because I *agreed* with him in some important respects? In that case, might not feminist thought be weakened if important steps in our own intellectual development are tossed out along with the bathwater of male dominance?

In the past I have emphasized the metaphor of "springboard," as it has been developed by Mary Daly,[7] to indicate one way in which feminism could reaffirm Kierkegaard: that is, I argued that aspects of his analyses provide optimal "jumping off places" for feminists to move into their own philosophical and/or theological process.[8] As I have gone forward with my feminist re-reading of Kierkegaard, I have decided that "springboard," like every useful metaphor, has limitations and needs to be supplemented by the metaphor of "dialogue," which keynotes the present volume of essays. There is nothing about "springboard" that implies on-goingness in relation to the diver's starting-point. "Dialogue," however, pictures a continuing conversation between two personal agents.

Dialogical imagery is important to the development of hermeneutical principles for feminist interaction with "the great men in our heads" since it presupposes the agency of both speakers. This allows for the possibility that one has let a "great man" into her head because she considers his fundamental orientation valid. Rather than assuming that one somehow was "carried away" or "seduced" by "the great man in one's head," the dialogical model for the relationship with one's intellectual mentor assumes that one had one's own reasons for choosing him/her rather than others.

A significant example is a memoir of her first encounter with Kierkegaard included in a recent essay by Dorothee Sölle,[9] an internationally influential German theologian who is identified with political, liberation, and feminist approaches. As Sölle recalls her first reading of Kierkegaard at age twenty, she speaks of "falling in love with Søren." However, we soon learn that her absorption with Kierkegaard was not due to infatuation, but to his communication of "a passion for the unconditional" which resonated with her own. This infinite caring delivered her from the existential nihilism which was so powerful in post–World War II Europe. While she says Kierkegaard "seduced her into religion," she also pictures herself arguing with his ideas of sexuality and women during an "intensive dialogue with Søren over a period of months."[10] Sölle therefore exemplifies the fact that Kierkegaard's authorship was engaged initially by at least some of those who later became self-conscious feminists without their naively accepting his directly or indirectly communicated views, especially of human sexuality.[11] Indeed, Sölle says of Vigilius Haufniensis, the pseudonymous author of *Concept of Anxiety*,

His phenomenological view of anxiety, its rediscovery, is more obscured than otherwise by the dogma of original sin and by his sexual psychology, which, with all affection for Søren, must be described as gloomy.[12]

Indeed, as a preliminary self-defense, I would say that at least three factors, in addition to his imagery and ideas (which will be discussed later), make Kierkegaard one of those rare authors who refuses to be read uncritically, especially by women: 1) his strategies of indirect communication, 2) his frequent disclaimers of authority in the signed works, and 3) the reader's constant awareness of the problematic of Kierkegaard's own renounced relationship with a woman. Some of these factors may be what Sölle means by the "inner humility of his style."[13]

Nevertheless, my awareness that there are deeply sexist and heterosexist passages in Kierkegaard's writings, some of which I critically address elsewhere,[14] intensifies the need for this apologetic for dialogue with Kierkegaard. In itself, this "preliminary expectoration" is deeply Kierkegaardian since it assumes that human existence is a temporal process grounded in ultimate concern and requiring on-going synthesis of freedom and necessity. In suggesting that we "take up again" our dialogues with the "great men in our heads," after we have experienced the break in our relationship to them through the recognition of sexist oppression of women, I am calling for something like a Kierkegaardian *"repetition"* [*Gjentagelsen* = "take again"]. The call for "repetition" in dialogue with Kierkegaard is of particular relevance to that generation of feminists which originally partook of Kierkegaardian perspectives *before* the massive raising of consciousness about women's existence which has taken place during the last quarter-century. For these thinkers, the "repetition" of a self-consciously feminist re-reading and re-interpreting of Kierkegaard affirms concrete existence, rather than rejecting it for the sake of the ideal eternality of what might have been "women's experience" apart from historical patriarchy. As Constantin Constantius says in *Repetition*: " . . . when one says that life is a repetition, one says: actuality, which has been, now comes into existence" (R 14).

"Repetition" involves consciously "re-taking" one's past; it requires both temporal concretion and existential freedom. As Gregor Malantshuk explains,

> . . . the content of the subject's previous experience is fully retained when a new factor enters or when a new stage begins, but each time the total content is seen in a new perspective.[15]

It is interesting that Malantshuk goes on to ground his interpretation of "repetition" in a passage from the *Journals* which resonates with the women's movement by stressing consciousness-raising. Here, however, Kierkegaard's musical metaphor ("key") illustrates a process in which such change is modulation of previous reality, instead of fragmenting discontinuity. Kierkegaard says, "The threshold of consciousness or, as it were, the key, is continually being raised, but within each key the same thing is repeated" (JP 4:3980).

Malantshuk's interpretation of the religious and psychological significance of repetition is particularly helpful:

> . . . Kierkegaard wishes to say that development in the individual life consists of a steadily deeper and more concrete knowledge of oneself. One is not to look at himself abstractly but "ought to use a special map" and thereby clearly recognize the numerous factors and motivations in his life. Kierkegaard believes that by taking this path a person can obtain, on the human level, an insight into his own inadequacy.[16]

Feminist "repetition" in re-reading the great men in our heads needs to differ in emphasis: it should seek awareness of our "adequacies," our past strengths in the midst of sexist oppression, as well as of our past failures.

In addition to thinkers like Sölle, who return to Kierkegaard for theological, philosophical, and/or existential reasons, there are male and female scholars whose focus has been on the study of Kierkegaard throughout their careers, who now are re-reading him with concern for women's issues. Here I am thinking particularly of Sylvia I. Walsh and Julia Watkin.[17] Whether their current attention to women's issues is a feminist "repetition" in the same sense as others, depends on there being existential as well as professional reasons for this "re-take." Probably such reasons can be assumed in scholars who have chosen to study Kierkegaard.

2. Springboard vs. Dialogue: Catherine Keller

A different kind of *direct*[18] use of Kierkegaard is found in feminists whose study of Kierkegaard did not antedate their self-conscious embrace of contemporary feminist perspectives and who, therefore, are not engaged in the same kind of *existential* "repetition." A representative and influential example is found in Catherine Keller's *From a Broken Web*.[19] Keller's book offers an excellent in-depth critique of the Western mythological, philosophical, psychological, and theological traditions as they express patriarchal psychological patterns. In her feminist response to these patterns, Keller argues for "the connective" psyche or "influent self" whose dynamics embrace the "other" rather than separating from it. Keller maintains that the psychological dyad characteristic of patriarchal conditioning, "separative selfhood" for men and "soluble selfhood" for women, obviates realization of such authentic selfhood for both sexes. She cites approvingly Kierkegaard's analysis of the two forms of despair as defiance and weakness as well as his correlation of them with masculinity and femininity (SUD 49). In addition, she sees as "perceptive" Kierkegaard's linking of "women's weakened sense of self to her self-loss in service to others, that is, to her devotion" (p. 12). Like other feminists[20] she sees Kierkegaard's "relapse into essentialism" as contradicting his own existentialism when he interprets devotion as woman's nature and destiny, thus confusing patriarchal acculturation with purportedly essential nature.

In spite of recognizing this patriarchal bias in Kierkegaard, Keller sees his treatment of sin as important to women since it holds sin not to be simply hubristic pride, which is so emphasized in the biblical traditions. She says:

> Rather than a matter of self-interest per se, or merely too much self, sin reveals itself as self-alienation and indeed too little self. A false sense of self shrinks subjectivity: a view that can support—if kept free of Kierkegaard's own sexism—woman's need for more rather than less self. (p. 34)

Keller also praises Kierkegaard's naming of self-denying devotion in women as "sin"; such a theological category indicates that a woman's tendency to be unable to will to be herself is *not* her created nature.

Keller seems to approve Kierkegaard's "classical theological view" in which the self finds itself only in self-transcendence, that is, in what Kierkegaard would identify as the God-relation. However, she also deeply disagrees with what she takes to be Kierkegaard's emphasis on God's "absolute self-sufficiency" (pp. 34–35) which she thinks draws deity in the image of the separative male ego, therefore sanctioning not only hierarchical power relations but also the perpetuation of non-relational, inauthentic selfhood in both men and women. Thus it becomes clear that, while Kierkegaard's analysis of the despair of weakness provides a "springboard" for Keller to develop more strongly her idea of the soluble self, he is only a convenient theological referent, rather than a source of her thought. Her constructive work in theology is developed primarily in dialogue with Alfred North Whitehead's process metaphysics, as well as with feminist theorists such as Mary Daly. Whitehead seems to be the "great man in her head," although she self-consciously rejects him as a necessary resource (p. 211). Her psychology also uses Jung's collective unconscious as a springboard for understanding human relationality, but develops that point primarily through Whitehead.

I want to suggest that Keller would benefit from a more thorough dialogue with Kierkegaard, both in her interpretation of Kierkegaard's theology and in her own psychological theory. While Keller is unusual on the current scene in that she recognizes Kierkegaard's fundamental religious insight into the ultimate relationality of the self,[21] her criticism of Kierkegaard's emphasis on the infinite transcendence of the love of God through attention only to *Concluding Unscientific Postscript* by Johannes Climacus reveals her lack of awareness of the complex irony of the pseudonymous works. She therefore fails to note the different character of *Sickness unto Death*, which Kierkegaard supports as "editor." A more thorough treatment of *Sickness unto Death* is needed; such a treatment might notice that its pseudonym, Anti-Climacus, holds that it is only as sinner needing forgiveness that the human being experiences the "chasmal qualitative abyss" between the self and God (SUD 122). Showing no awareness of the works published in Kierkegaard's own name, Keller has missed some fundamental congruences between her own concerns and Kierkegaard's. Attention to *Works of Love* would reinforce not only the relationality which she recognizes in *Sickness unto Death*'s definition of human existence; it also could reveal the intimacy of the God-relationship shown in his discussion of "the like-for-like" of "reduplication":

> Infinite love is this, that above all he wills to have to do with you and that no one, no one, so lovingly discovers the slightest love in you as God does. God's relationship to a human being is the infinitising at every moment of that which at every moment is in a man. (WL 352)

Keller's own religious psychology would have been clarified not only by dialogue with additional writings by Kierkegaard, but also by more thorough consideration of his view of the self in *Sickness unto Death* and *The Concept of Anxiety*. Kierkegaard's psychology could have illuminated the tensions between Keller's picture of the fluidity and plurality of the self/person and her own analyses of fundamental dialectics of human "selving" in her last chapter. Indeed, it might answer her rhetorical question about the "influent self":

> Everything, and most intimately my soul, flows in and out of the present occasion, which is my self. This is a light and loose sense of the unity of the person. Why would we need more? (p. 197)

Kierkegaard would answer that we need more than this influent self in order to live honestly and passionately the concrete lifetime which is ours. Keller probably would see Kierkegaard's imagination of the existential dialectic as "stages on life's way"[22] as expressing the "tight and heavy notion of personal identity" (p. 197) which she identifies with patriarchy. Keller interprets Whitehead through a postmodernist deconstruction of the self which rejects any "totalization" and argues that we should see ourselves as concrete and historically embedded, connective "superjects," rather than as separative or substantive *sub*jects. She adopts Whitehead's distinction between self and person, and emphasizes the multiplicity of "selves." "Self" is a "unique, immediate event" where "experience takes place and where the world is gathered as a unique composition," but which "in a moment . . . parts with its own selfness." On the other hand, she uses Whitehead's concept of "person" to point to the sense of time-binding continuity "from childhood to death" (pp. 195–96).

A more thorough dialogue with Kierkegaard's powerful analyses of aesthetical immediacy could challenge Keller to defend the existential validity of her "moment self." Recent psychological studies[23] call into question the postmodernist deconstruction of personal unity and support understanding "self" as precisely the concrete be-ing that one is "from childhood to death," which Keller distinguishes as "person." Kierkegaard also might encourage Keller to make more central the fact that this self is apprehended existentially *as* "person" by virtue of both freedom and consciousness (SUD 29). In one of the "upbuilding discourses" Kierkegaard formulates these emphases in terms of dialogue: "A person is not in an exclusively receptive relation; he is himself communicating . . . " (EUD 45). In Kierkegaard, time-binding personal continuity is a function of chosen commitments, one of which is to a personal relationship in which one "speaks *Du*" (FT 77) to the Ultimate; thus life's fundamental patterning is dialogical mutuality, rather than in the opaque separation which Keller recognizes in Sartre (pp. 29–33).

Keller's critique of our cultural heritage, which has elevated "separative selfhood" for men and "soluble selfhood" for women, is important. And it is strengthened by her dialogue with Kierkegaard's two forms of despair/sin. She herself also recognizes the importance to women of Kierkegaard's emphasis on self-transcendence (p. 41). She seems, however, to have stopped short in her dialogue with Kierkegaard, missing his emphasis on the fantastic unreality of any transcendence which is not synthesized with finitude/necessity (SUD 30–33). Much that she criticizes in the psychological and theological loss of immanence in the patriarchal traditions[24] is actually present in Kierkegaard's analysis of concrete existence.

It is to her credit that Keller recognizes existential complexities. She frequently moves dialectically, e.g., recognizing that women must not yield their recently-claimed "rooms of their own" too quickly for the sake of the value of relationality; she calls for the "private" as well as the "public," and "oneness" as well as "manyness" (see Keller, chap. 5). In the light of her own recognition of these dynamics, it would be better for Keller to frankly accept the reality of existential dialectics, as does Kierkegaard, rather than to celebrate prematurely the momentary, influent self in the interconnected flow of being. Such re-thinking might lead her to recognize that Kierkegaard's understanding of the self was not "substantive," but relational, dialectical, and dynamic.

3. The Promise of Dialogue

The above discussion of Catherine Keller has exemplified the possibility that even those from the new generation of feminist theologians, who are entering theology in the context of the wide contemporary influence of feminist and womanist religious thinkers, might benefit from an on-going dialogue with Kierkegaard, rather than only using him as a "springboard." Such a dialogue could be taken up as a *historical* "repetition," since orientations shaped by Kierkegaard's influence contributed importantly to the strength of the contemporary women's movement, at least in its manifestation in feminist theology. Religious existentialism, inspired by Kierkegaard, provided the framework for the development of both liberation theology and feminist theology. It is sufficient to note for the present argument that reception for Daly's groundbreaking *Beyond God the Father* twenty years ago was prepared by Kierkegaard (not only directly, but as he was mediated to American culture by Reinhold and H. Richard Niebuhr, Paul Tillich and Martin Buber). Daly's talk in that book of "nonbeing," "ultimate concern," "existential courage," "ontological hope," "self-naming," and a non-reified "Eternal Thou" was able to find an audience which had moved beyond the stifling frameworks of logical positivism and sheerly analytic philosophy, at least in part, because of the influence of Kierkegaard's sophisticated development of confidence that the criterion of truth was not objective verification alone but existential appropriation.

The aspects of Kierkegaard that are so influential in *Beyond God the Father* also tend to be emphasized by Dorothee Sölle in her re-reading of *The Concept of Anxiety*. The philosophical and theological orientations in Kierkegaard which Sölle, both in her youth and today, found important show that the non-authoritarian non-masculinist strategies of the authorship intersect with its central ideas to encourage female and male readers "to give birth to themselves" (EO, II, 206). For example, Sölle admires the arrogance with which Kierkegaard challenges the apparently happy securities of conventional society. She says she turned to Kierkegaard as a source figure for existentialism and found in him the "radical religion: transcendence of the factual situation; passion for the unconditional,"[25] which she still finds essential if we are to move toward justice and wholeness[26] rather than fatalistically acquiesce in the established systems of our societies. Sölle also clearly thinks dialogue with Kierkegaard can stimulate appropriation of authentic humanity beyond the paralysis of nihilism. She says: "What is at stake is a passion for the infinite, for that which surpasses all the possibilities I can now recognize."[27] The corollary of this ultimate concern, also Kierkegaardian, is "the way of freedom"; to see ourselves as free is the premise of the critique of cultural conditioning essential to all liberation movements.

In her recent essay on *The Concept of Anxiety*, Sölle only hints at the additional orientations in Kierkegaard which feminism would need to consider in order to understand why existential commitment and freedom can be especially well learned in dialogue with him. To appreciate Kierkegaard's value as a dialogue-partner one probably needs to share with the early Sölle and Daly a somewhat developed sense of the crisis of faith brought by modern skepticism and nihilism. At least in the field of feminist theology, a return to a more thorough dialogue with Kierkegaard might clarify and strengthen feminism's philosophical foundations through explicit apprehension of the existential truth criterion which many feminist theologians presuppose. Current feminist theory sometimes seems to assume that the only alternatives are, on the one hand, naive assumptions about objective truth or, on the other, nihilistic relativism.[28] In part because it unnecessarily associated existentialism with only privatistic individualism, feminist theology has failed to build strongly upon its own sources in the existentialist analysis of the meaning of truth, the self and freedom. As early as 1974, Sölle suggested that there could be a constructive development of existentialist theology through political theology, saying:

> Political theology reveals for the first time the truth of existentialist theology, because it enables and does not merely postulate an existential way of speaking, which also concerns the individual.[29]

It seems clear, then, that a thoroughgoing dialogue with Kierkegaard would challenge feminists to be much clearer about the concept of truth which they presuppose. Feminist theory tends to assume the standpoint of the engaged, concerned thinker, especially in theology. Dialogue with Kierkegaard can make it clear that this assumption is cognizant of the limits of human reasoning as well as the relational concern which ultimately grounds the human self. Few writers in the Western canon challenge thinkers on these matters as effectively as Kierkegaard.

For example, feminists could find in his philosophical pseudonym, Johannes Climacus, a stimulating foil within the philosophical canon for pointing out the irony of all claims to eternal or universal truth which do not acknowledge "a historical point of departure" (PF 1). From Sojourner Truth's famous, "Ain't I a woman?" to today, such irony is employed regularly by feminists when they deal with the essentialist claims characteristic of white, middle-class, racist, and/or patriarchal thinkers.

Contrary to common misunderstandings, Kierkegaard has Johannes Climacus develop the existential truth criterion, "Truth is subjectivity," in the *Concluding Unscientific Postscript*, not to deny the role of scientific objectivity within the realm created by knowledge of the natural world, but to insist that it cannot answer human questions for meaning and value. In addition, "Truth is subjectivity" was not intended to justify life in terms of sheer feeling or fantastic romanticism. For Kierkegaard, true subjectivity, i.e., authentic selfhood, is established by decisions, by commitments, by the chosen existence of the self. The criterion for existential truth is whether that which is claimed can be lived and *is* lived with infinite concern and without self-deception. Current analysis of the meaning of subjectivity in feminist theory could be strengthened by encounter with Kierkegaard's thorough development of the issues. Dialogue with Kierkegaard on the meaning of subjectivity might also offset stereotyped assumptions of sheer emotionality in women's thinking.

In its affirmation of personal and communal existence, Kierkegaard's religious existentialism transcends the nihilism and relativism which some contemporary feminists appear to embrace out of a sense of intellectual honesty. His authorship's emphasis on human freedom facilitates hope to change the world, avoiding the fatalistic determinism manifested in postmodernism's nihilistic turn. His truth criterion, "subjective appropriation" or "reduplication," urges us to choose the meanings which can be lived and then make them real by living them. Kierkegaard himself, of course, witnesses to faith as the orientation which can be lived. In its reliance on the transcendent "Power" which constitutes the self in its particularity (SUD), faith supports a renewed "striving born of gratitude" (JP 4:711). Kierkegaard speaks of faith as "jest" to highlight its dynamics. Knowing the finitude of all human achievement, faith trusts in the transcendent ground of being; at the same time, however, it earnestly works at life's tasks (FSE 183). All of these emphases are liberatory for women. As feminists passionately work for justice, they need an orientation which enables both hope and self-critical awareness of finitude. Such an orientation was to Kierkegaard the God-relationship, a "knotting of the thread" that establishes meaningfulness through orienting ultimate concern finally toward the Ultimate (SUD 93; PV 158).

Rather than joining in Keller's definition of selves as momentary pulses in the flow of being, the women's liberation movement encouraged women to appropriate themselves as personal centers of consciousness, freedom, and responsibility. Kierkegaard's emphasis upon the historically particular, relational self who consciously and passionately appropriates agential life can enable resistance to oppressive systems as well as affirmation of community in dialogue with other selves. In addition, Kierkegaard's psychology challenges conformisms and conventionalisms as means to self-definition. There is wide evidence that this challenge is particularly important to women.

A common criticism of Kierkegaard is that his individualism is antithetical to the communal methodologies needed for political change. Sölle has more thoroughly developed the liberatory political implications of existentialism's truth criterion than Kierkegaard himself, although possibilities for such a direction are implicit in *Works of Love* as well as in his polemical writings. Political/liberation theology is a needed corrective emphasis to Kierkegaard's stress on the individual; it explicates the systemic character of much that destroys intersubjectivity as well as the socio-political praxis needed to "enable" communal freedom. Nevertheless, feminism also needs approaches which, like many of Kierkegaard's works, aim to challenge the individual to emerge from the conventional conformity of mass culture. From Valerie Saiving to Catherine Keller, feminists have pointed out the special vulnerability to passive acquiescence or "solubility" which has characterized women's lives within patriarchy.[30] Both as individuals and as communities, women need to be challenged to choose that meaning which ought to be, rather than to acquiesce in systems which simply are. Human health is impossible without a dialectical emphasis on both individual responsibility and the need for systemic change together with communal belonging.

There are new dangers to the becoming of women which are best identified as new essentialisms. Much of the current talk of "the feminine" endangers the freedom of individual women; such talk is sometimes heard both from those who express what Susan Faludi[31] calls the contemporary "backlash" against feminism and from some feminists who slip into essentialist definitions of "woman." Dialogue with Kierkegaard can help us to avoid the oppression which persons experience when they are defined by predetermined essences or stereotypes which ignore their concrete individuality. We should embrace a consciously dialectical approach through which any generalization about women (for example, their "natural relationality") is challenged by an emphasis upon both cultural determinants and existential freedom. Perhaps the most important aspect of dialogue with Kierkegaard for women is his powerful presentation of concrete human existence as a synthesis of freedom and necessity, a view which supports historically realistic liberation. He stresses not only the importance of agency and possibility, but also the reality of finitude and necessity. This means that his view of the human being is pragmatically liberating in that it avoids "fantastic" (SUD 30) freedom and calls for a liberation which is lived in synthesis with concrete genetic and historical determinants. At the same time, Kierkegaard challenges all fatalistic determinisms with the call for choosing and willing to become the self one is potentially. Such a perspective supports historically realized liberation which can help women, whose development usually has been so profoundly limited by sexist systems that their liberation requires finding that next "small part of the work" (SUD 32) which freedom can realize in synthesis with necessity.

In addition to these philosophical orientations, other characteristics of Kierkegaard's life, thought, and authorship make him the kind of dialogue-partner whom a woman engages with less danger than most of the formative thinkers of inherited cultures. For example, Kierkegaard's extensive discussions of "woman" and issues of sexual/gender identity make the problematics of patriarchy manifest and invite women readers into a genuine dialogue, wherein they feel free to argue with opinions expressed both by the pseudonyms and by Kierkegaard himself. In many cultural giants, sexist presuppositions remain hidden and uncriticized, since they ignore women and gender analysis. By contrast, sexual identity and gender analysis are almost continuously central in Kierkegaard, both through imagery and explicit themes.

It is also the case that the authorship is unusually well-furnished with theological use of imagery associated with women's experience. A particularly interesting example is the weaning and mother imagery in the "Exordium" of

Fear and Trembling (FT 9–11); usually ignored is the poetic fact that "the mother" here represents God. Another example is the delicately humorous assertion of ultimate concern, alluded to above, when Kierkegaard says that trying to live without God is "like sewing without knotting the thread" (e.g., SUD 93; PV 158). While men have sometimes done sewing, this imagery would have communicated with women better than men during most of human history; it is interesting that the words "sister" and "sew" share an ancient root.[32]

There are also those shining moments in the authorship in which Kierkegaard clearly sees the test of religious truth in its recognition of the equality of women with men. A familiar example is from *Fear and Trembling*'s famous discussion of the radical choice of the knight of faith:

> If . . . the princess is similarly disposed, something beautiful will emerge. She will then introduce herself into the order of knighthood into which one is not taken by election but of which everyone is a member who has the courage to enroll oneself, the order of knighthood that proves its immortality by making no distinction between male and female. (FT 45)

Such moments surely encouraged some of us to let Kierkegaard into our heads. They must be "re-membered"[33] now, as indications that we were not simply bewitched by the enigmas of the authorship, but chose a thinker who often wrote what we needed to read.

At the same time, however, an on-going feminist dialogue with Kierkegaard must face honestly the times when our great man slipped back into patriarchally conditioned views. Examples abound in the selections organized under the topic "Woman/Man" in the *Journals and Papers* (JP 4:4987–5008). A more often ignored example is the passage in *For Self-Examination* supporting the silencing of women in the New Testament (FSE 46–51).[34] While we must respect our selves enough to re-member our good reasons for entering into dialogue with Kierkegaard, it is important at the same time to note his limitations. Since Kierkegaard participated in the privileges of male power, he must be read with hermeneutical suspicion, both watching for his subtle lapses into sexism and unflinchingly facing his blatantly patriarchal passages. Such reading requires concurrent attention to the many analyses now being developed out of women's experiences, in order to sharpen our skills for recognizing the romanticized paternalism to which his age made Kierkegaard vulnerable. While sometimes painful, this kind of reading also is that for which his own disclaimers of authority indicate that he would have hoped.

Finally, it is important to be very clear that the dialogue with Kierkegaard which I am defending and encouraging is *not essential*. Many women and men discover these same important life orientations in other traditions and dialogues. We must avoid any imperialistic suggestion that this terribly complex thinker, so immersed in Western intellectual history, is recommended as the only vehicle for religious and philosophical insight for feminists. For those of us who are involved in critical re-construction of the Western traditions, especially Christianity, dialogue with Kierkegaard can be strongly advocated as a conscious historical repetition which can lead us more deeply into our own concrete existence. At the same time, his emphasis on non-relativistic "infinite concern" as well as historical particularity could help establish philosophical foundations for affirming the other's difference at the same time as one is empowered by the passionate choice of one's own unique life, community, and/or tradition.

One of the ruling concerns of contemporary feminist theory is the need to avoid imperialistic denials of differences between women. As feminists, Kierkegaardians need to enter additional dialogues, listening not only for concurrence in such truths as they have learned from him, but also for the truths which his own "necessity" tended to obscure. For example, womanist theologians,[35] whose defining dialogues are with African American women, discover their own sources as emphasizing historical particularity, concrete embodiment, and freedom. Kierkegaardian feminists are tantalized into comparisons. This is especially true when womanists call for affirmation of the "dignity of the individual," "ontological freedom and equality,"[36] as well as for emphasis on the paradigmatic life of Jesus and on recovery of authentic Christianity.[37] The emergence of womanist theology exemplifies an additional kind of feminist dialogue with Kierkegaard which is needed, particularly by white feminists who find Kierkegaard "in their heads" or in their history. Such feminists might well test Kierkegaard's validity by the extent to which his perspectives resonate with the "Sister Outsider"[38] known through the womanist experience. In such a dialogue possibilities for being authentically human, many of which Kierkegaard's brilliant but culturally limited mind could not imagine, will call into question his cultural biases in terms of class, race, sexual orientation, sex, etc. While Kierkegaardians might well imagine a dialogue with him as strengthening any argument for "ontological freedom and equality" which aims to connect with on-going Western philosophical and theological debates, they also need to recognize that this may be irrelevant for those in different traditions. In other words, when Kierkegaard is neither in the history nor "in the head" of the other to whom one relates, to advocate dialogue with him as if he were absolutely essential completely misses the point of the authorship, which aimed "to find exactly where the other is and begin there . . . " (PV 29). On the other hand, since the "Power" which governs through all our existence is the educator (PV 88), both our direct and indirect communications with others can assume that they have learned in their individual and social histories some things in common with what we have learned. Our relations with feminists of other traditions need not be sheerly relativistic; we may seek some common understanding so long as we do not imperialistically suggest that our side of the dialogue is essential.

If one chooses one's own life and tradition out of a conviction that it can be lived with integrity and meaning, no denial of difference needs to be involved. Likewise with the choice of particular intellectual dialogue-partners. Only in terms of such a choice would Kierkegaard himself have wanted to get into our heads; only so would he have wanted us to "take him up again."

Notes

1. Lerner, *The Creation of Feminist Consciousness.*
2. Culpepper, "The Spiritual, Political Journey of a Feminist Freethinker."
3. The issues are not limited to Western culture, but I want to acknowledge a circumscription of my references since I am particularly aware of controversies surrounding feminist use of such Western cultural giants as Aristotle, Augustine, Aquinas, Nietzsche, Marx, Freud, Jung, Kierkegaard, etc.
4. See, e.g., Welch, "Ideology and Social Change," in Plaskow and Christ, eds., *Weaving the Visions*, p. 340. Welch cites Emily Culpepper, "New Tools for Theology and Ethics: Writings by Women of Color," *Journal of Feminist Studies in Religion* 4 (fall 1988).
5. Eagleton, *The Ideology of the Aesthetic*, p. 191.
6. Lerner, *The Creation of Feminist Consciousness*, p. 12.
7. Daly, *GYN/ECOLOGY*, p. 27, and *PURE LUST*, p. 198.
8. Wanda Warren Berry, "Finally Forgiveness."
9. Sölle, "Søren Kierkegaard and *The Concept of Anxiety*" in *The Window of Vulnerability*. Since this particular English edition transliterates "Sölle," I am following this usage.
10. Ibid., p. 117.
11. Ibid., p. 119.
12. Ibid.
13. Ibid., p. 118.
14. See, e.g., "The Heterosexual Imagination and Aesthetic Existence in Kierkegaard's *Either/Or, Part One*," *International Kierkegaard Commentary: Either/Or, Part One*, vol. 3 (Macon, GA: Mercer University Press, forthcoming 1995); and "Judge William Judging Woman: Essentialism and Existentialism in Kierkegaard's *Either/Or, Part Two*," *International Kierkegaard Commentary: Either/Or, Part Two*, vol. 4; also "Wresting and Jesting Silence: A Feminist Dialogue with *For Self-Examination*," presented to the Søren Kierkegaard Society, 1992.
15. Malantschuk, *Kierkegaard's Thought*, p. 136.
16. Ibid.
17. See, e.g., Walsh, "On 'Feminine' and 'Masculine' Forms of Despair" and Watkin, "Serious Jest? Kierkegaard as Young Polemicist in 'Defence' of Women." My own work may be closer to Sölle's kind of repetition than to Walsh and Watkin; however, Sölle's explicit attention to Kierkegaard is only occasional. Nevertheless, unlike Walsh, I began reading Kierkegaard only after theological school; many years later, my return to graduate school included study of Kierkegaard, but he was only one among many constructive sources of my doctoral dissertation. It was when doing feminist theology during the 1970s and '80s, that

I found Kierkegaard's analyses emerging as interpretive keys in my work and decided to "take him up again" in order to test his influence by my newly-explicit feminist concerns.

18. More or less *indirect* use is found in feminists who have done extensive work on thinkers such as Luther, Reinhold Niebuhr, and Paul Tillich. See, e.g., Hampson's treatments of Luther and Niebuhr, which lead her into direct treatment of Kierkegaard in "Luther on the Self" and *Theology and Feminism*. Also see Plaskow, *Sex, Sin and Grace*.

19. Page references to this text are in parentheses in this part.

20. See, e.g., W. W. Berry, "Images of Sin and Salvation in Feminist Theology" and Walsh, "On 'Feminine' and 'Masculine' Forms of Despair."

21. Hampson also recognizes the positive value of this aspect of Kierkegaard. See "Luther on the Self," p. 218.

22. See W. W. Berry, "Kierkegaard's Existential Dialectic."

23. An example recently reviewed in the *Chronicle of Higher Education* (June 30, 1993), A10: Glass, *Shattered Selves*. Based on studies revealing the suffering of women with personality disorders, Glass criticizes postmodernist "attacks on the 'unitary self.' "

24. Keller argues primarily with Reinhold Niebuhr on this point, see pp. 38–46; nevertheless, she uses a phrase from Kierkegaard to epitomize the issue: "the embarassment of God" (Keller, *From a Broken Web*, p. 35).

25. Sölle, *Window of Vulnerability*, p. 117.

26. Sölle, *Death by Bread Alone*, pp. 127–42.

27. Sölle, *Window of Vulnerability*, p. 120.

28. Davaney, "Problems with Feminist Theory."

29. Sölle, *Political Theology*, p. 92. See also p. 104, where Sölle speaks of "the necessary bridge from existentialist to political interpretation."

30. E.g., Saiving [Goldstein], "The Human Situation: A Feminine View" and Keller.

31. Faludi, *Backlash: The Undeclared War against American Women*.

32. Mills, "Sister," *Womanwords*, pp. 219–21.

33. This hyphenated usage recurs in feminists and womanists to indicate the recovery of the past which has been stolen from women. See, e.g., Toni Morrison, Mary Daly, and Nelle Morton.

34. See W. W. Berry, "Wresting and Jesting Silence."

35. The root definition of "womanist" was developed by Alice Walker as a "black feminist" or "feminist of color." See *In Search of Our Mothers' Gardens: Womanist Prose*.

36. Baker-Fletcher, "A Womanist Ontology of Freedom and Equality."

37. Grant, *White Women's Christ and Black Women's Jesus*.

38. Audre Lorde, *Sister Outsider*.

8 Paradoxes in Interpretation
Kierkegaard and Gadamer
Stephen N. Dunning

In his major work on philosophical hermeneutics, *Truth and Method*, Hans-Georg Gadamer mentions Søren Kierkegaard only a few times. Although those passages are significant, it would be an overstatement to suggest that Gadamer's debt to Kierkegaard is anything like that to his primary philosophical mentors: Plato, Aristotle, Kant, Hegel, Schleiermacher, Dilthey, Husserl, and Heidegger. However, there exists in both Kierkegaard and Gadamer an explicit affinity for ambiguity and especially paradox that is striking, and is relatively absent from those other thinkers (with the possible exception of Hegel). My purpose in this chapter is to show that Kierkegaard's thought, and particularly what I shall present as his "epistemology of the cross," reveals a level of meaning in Gadamer's hermeneutical position that is not normally discerned.

The only significant role that Kierkegaard is granted in *Truth and Method* is that of a precursor in the unmasking of the pretensions of romantic aestheticism. In his attack upon romantic notions of genius and aesthetic experience (*Erlebnisse*), Gadamer credits Kierkegaard with being the first to portray "how desperate and untenable is existence in pure immediacy and discontinuity," a "criticism of aesthetic consciousness that is of fundamental importance because he shows the inner contradictions of aesthetic existence, so that it is forced to go beyond itself."[1] Gadamer takes the point of Kierkegaard's criticism to be identical with one of the major points of *Truth and Method*: that aesthetic experience can be rightly understood only within "the hermeneutic continuity of human existence" (TM 96). He makes a correlative point in discussing the "contemporaneity" that belongs to a work of art. Rather than the "aesthetic simultaneity"[2] preached by some romantics, Gadamer attributes to Kierkegaard the notion of contemporaneity as a task to be achieved, namely, "to bring together two moments that are not concurrent, . . . and yet so totally to mediate them that the latter is experienced and taken seriously as present (and not as something in a distant past)."[3] Finally, Gadamer also applauds Kierkegaard's "brilliant" demonstration that modern subjectivism robs classical tragedy of its genuinely tragic element.[4] On the basis of these discussions in *Truth and Method*, it would appear that Kierkegaard and Gadamer share only the conviction that the aestheticism which has so dominated art and philosophy in the modern world is a flawed and even decadent posturing based upon a dogmatic negativism toward tradition and moral values.

I. The Crucifixion of Knowledge

Although much of Kierkegaard's most engaging writing appears in his portrayals and parodies of aesthetic self-consciousness, to be found in *Either/Or*, volume I, *Repetition*, and "In Vino Veritas," which is the first part of *Stages on Life's Way*, it can plausibly be argued that these texts about the aesthetic stage constitute only an introduction to the major literary task that he had set for himself. In *The Point of View for My Work as an Author*, Kierkegaard insists that his intention from the start was to use all his "aesthetic" (i.e., pseudonymous) works to direct readers to religious truth. Even if we are suitably cautious about accepting his testimony at face value,[5] there is also the fact that most interpreters of Kierkegaard's theory of stages have agreed that, as presented, the aesthetic stage leads to the ethical, and that ultimately both the aesthetic and the ethical are replaced by or taken up into the religious stage.[6] One result of this progression (or displacement) is that the knowledge achieved by both the aesthetic and the ethical is transcended in the religious. A closer look at this dialectic will show that it does, indeed, constitute an epistemology of the cross.

Let's start with the book that seems, at least in America, to be Kierkegaard's most widely read work, *Fear and Trembling*. Published under the pseudonym Johannes de Silentio, *Fear and Trembling* is ostensibly about Abraham's trial of faith as recorded in Genesis 22. Interpreters have argued instead that the book is really an encoded self-revelation, either by Kierkegaard-the-religious-writer, who has had to sacrifice his fiancée for the sake of his vocation;[7] or Kierkegaard-the-victimized-son, who had been sacrificed by his guilt-ridden father.[8] A reading that stays closer to the text would suggest that the focus of the book is not at all upon Isaac and only indirectly upon Abraham. Rather, the hero—or anti-hero—of *Fear and Trembling* is none other than Johannes de Silentio, the pseudonymous author who insists upon understanding both faith and the God who inspires it. Johannes reiterates that he can understand Abraham's willingness to obey God and kill Isaac, but he cannot grasp his ability to go on trusting in God and the divine promise (that he will become the father of nations through Isaac) in the face of such a demand. The problem posed by *Fear and Trembling* is not the spiritual issue of whether to obey a demanding God or even to trust an inscrutable God; the challenge is to believe in God "by virtue of the absurd" (FT 40), when all hope of understanding is shattered by the unintelligibility of God's demand. Abraham may be justified as an individual who is "higher than the universal" on the basis of his "absolute relation to the absolute," but it is a strange sort of justification, for it can neither be expressed in language nor mediated by any other means: it "remains for all eternity a paradox, impervious to thought" (FT 55–56).

The problematic relation of faith to knowledge is developed further in *Philosophical Fragments* under the pseudonym Johannes Climacus, who describes himself in *Concluding Unscientific Postscript* as an author and humorist who is decidedly not a Christian (CUP 1:466, 501, 617). But Climacus is more tolerant of paradox than is de Silentio:

> . . . one must not think ill of the paradox, for the paradox is the passion of thought, and the thinker without the paradox is like a lover without passion: a mediocre fellow. . . . This, then, is the ultimate paradox of thought: to want to discover something that thought itself cannot think. (PF 37)

Climacus then discusses the impossibility of trying to demonstrate or even to know the existence of the unknowable, particularly when that unknown is the god. This leads him to a more precise characterization of the paradox:

> The paradoxical passion of the understanding is, then, continually colliding with this unknown [the god], which certainly does exist but is also unknown and to that extent does not exist.[9] The understanding does not go beyond this; yet in its paradoxicality the understanding cannot stop reaching it and being engaged with it, . . . (PF 44)

Although the theme of paradox is mentioned in many of Kierkegaard's other pseudonymous works, it is in Johannes Climacus's *Concluding Unscientific Postscript* that it receives its fullest development. In its Socratic form, the paradox is the fact that eternal truth stands in a concrete relation to an existing person (CUP 1:208). Ever preoccupied with the difference between Greek and Christian thought, Climacus goes on to suggest that the latter presents an even more radical paradox than the former: "Let us now go further; let us assume that the eternal, essential truth is itself the paradox. . . . The eternal truth has come into existence in time. That is the paradox" (CUP 1:209). This paradox is even more unintelligible than the paradox of the faith of Abraham or the paradox of the understanding of the unknown:

> Instead of the objective uncertainty, there is here the certainty that, viewed objectively, it [faith] is the absurd, and this absurdity, held fast in the passion of inwardness, is faith. Compared with the earnestness of the absurd, the Socratic ignorance is like a witty jest, and compared with the strenuousness of faith, the Socratic existential inwardness resembles Greek nonchalance. (CUP 1:210)

The paradox of Christianity is manifested wherever the eternal enters the realm of existence. In addition to the incarnation, the event of redemption by which sins are forgiven is also an instance of the paradox, for it too depends upon "God's having existed in time" (CUP 1:224). There can be no explanation of this paradox; and any understanding of Christianity that claims to understand the paradox thereby demonstrates that it has "lost Christianity" (CUP 1:581; cf. 1:218–23).

All of this has often looked to critics a lot like an existentialist version of simple anti-intellectualism and irrationalism.[10] But Kierkegaard is not in any way calling for a sacrifice of intellect. As we saw in *Fragments*, his whole position is predicated upon the premise that becoming a Christian is precisely a matter of hard, passionate thought. In the terms developed in *Postscript*, one must become a subjective thinker *before* one can become a Christian.

It is in this sense that the embrace of paradox can be understood as an epistemological recapitulation of the theology of the cross. Just as the theological presupposition is a sinless son of God, the epistemic premise is that God is transcendent and unknowable. Both are equally beyond our experience and control. In both, however, the incarnation signifies that God has entered into the human condition in a radical way. As articulated by St. Paul in his praise of Christ: "though he was in the form of God, did not count equality with God a thing to be grasped, but emptied himself, taking the form of a servant, being born in the likeness of men" (Phil. 2:6–7 [RSV]). This theological kenosis or self-emptying has its epistemological counterpart in the paradox of the infinite and eternal god entering into the world of finitude and time.

That the theological and epistemological readings of the crucifixion can be correlated is also expressed by Paul in 1 Cor. 1:22–24: "For Jews demand signs and Greeks seek wisdom, but we preach Christ crucified, a stumbling block to Jews and folly to Gentiles, but to those who are called, both Jews and Greeks, Christ the power of God and the wisdom of God." The cross is an offense and a scandal. To Jewish piety, it is unthinkable that the majesty of God could be associated with sin or death, but the Christian claim is that the son of God took on the sins of the world and died to deliver from sin all those who believe in him. For Greeks, the cross offends not so much the glory of God as the rationality of humans; it is sheer foolishness to think that eternal truth might be bound up with a particular—and particularly inauspicious—moment in history. While the notion of a divine substitution offends theologically (and ethically), the paradox offends every bit as much epistemically. Climacus stresses that one who is offended at the paradox "does not speak according to his own nature but according to the nature of the paradox" (PF 51). Identifying the paradox with the moment, he continues: "The expression of offense is that the moment is foolishness, the paradox is foolishness—which is the paradox's claim that the understanding is absurd but which now resounds as an echo from the offense" (PF 52). This echo is an acoustic illusion, masking the fact that the paradox itself determines how the offended consciousness responds to it, just as God is the agent who wills the scandal of the cross, even though those who crucified Christ thought they did it by their own decision.

The obvious meaning of the cross is, of course, death. Theologically, Christ died to redeem the world from sin and thereby makes it possible for believers to "die" to the sin in their own lives. The epistemological death is to the need to know, the compulsion to understand God's revelation that is so clearly portrayed by Johannes de Silentio. This is the crucifixion of knowledge. It is not a sacrifice of the intellect, for it presupposes the passion for thought that leads to the collision with the paradox. But it does force the intellect to choose between its own claim to autonomy and sovereignty and that of God. And the result of such a dilemma is offense—or a yielding that is tantamount to death. Of course, even this death is not the last word. A final parallel emerges between the theological resurrection to a new identity and eternal life, on the one hand, and a new epistemic state of faith, a faith that is "by virtue of the absurd." Just as death has lost its sting (1 Cor. 15:55), so also the paradox is no longer an offense to one who believes.

The remainder of this paper will be devoted to exploring the extent to which Gadamer's thought, like Kierkegaard's, depends upon an embrace of paradox, an embrace that also requires—at least implicitly—a transforming death and resurrection of knowledge.

II. A Paradoxical Aesthetics

Although some readers dismiss the first part of *Truth and Method* as a philosophical attack upon earlier aesthetic theories that delays getting to the meat of Gadamer's own position,[11] in fact part I is crucial both in the structure of the total work and as an introduction to the fundamental paradox at the heart of Gadamer's hermeneutics. The structural point concerns the basic hermeneutical problematic, namely, how far "the ideal of scientific objectivity" has resulted in an "ontological prejudice" from which Gadamer wishes to "liberate" both aesthetic and historical consciousness, in order finally to contribute to a "universal hermeneutics . . . concerned with the general relationship of man to the world" (TM 476). This general relationship turns out to be grounded in the linguistic nature of all human consciousness. Thus he must begin with aesthetic and historical interpretation, for they demonstrate the problem we face. Language constitutes the culmination because it is only in language that we reach that fundamental, ontological unity out of which all the diversity and distinctions of aesthetic and historical consciousness arise.[12]

The extent to which Gadamer's aesthetic philosophy has a paradoxical character is demonstrated most clearly by his comments in part I on the nature of culture (*Bildung*) and picture (*Bild*). *Bildung*, as "the properly human way of developing one's natural talents and capacities" (TM 10), long competed with "formation" (*Formierung, Formation*) as the fundamental concept of human development. However,

> the victory of the word Bildung over "form" does not seem to be accidental [*zufällig*]. For in Bildung there is Bild. The idea of "form" lacks the mysterious ambiguity of Bild, which comprehends both Nachbild (image, copy) and Vorbild (model).[13]

Thus a picture is, in effect, a paradoxical unity of opposites, for it simultaneously unites ("comprehends") the model with the copy of it. This accounts for what Gadamer calls its "mysterious ambiguity."

A similar ambiguity and paradox characterize *Bildung*, which Gadamer describes as an all-embracing process. To develop a talent or to master a technique is merely a means toward an end. But in *Bildung* "that by which and through which one is formed becomes completely one's own" (TM 11). Here nothing is discarded as a mere means to an unrelated end. Everything is absorbed and preserved in the development of universal humanity. Alluding to the preface to the *Phenomenology* and Hegel's famous formula for Spirit as "pure self-recognition in absolute otherness,"[14] Gadamer argues that "the essence of Bildung is clearly not alienation as such, but the return [from the other, from alienation] to oneself" (TM 14). Moreover, in a later discussion Gadamer faults Hegel for adopting the romantic concept of *Bildung* as an aesthetic consciousness of "alienation from reality" that involves "rising to the universal, distancing from the particularity of immediate acceptance or rejection, respecting what does not correspond to one's own expectation or preference" (TM 84). Gadamer prefers to associate *Bildung* with Spirit to signify a reunion with and self-recognition in the alienated other.

Although Gadamer by no means unequivocally rejects all of the characteristics of aesthetic consciousness, he follows Kierkegaard in attacking the radical discontinuity that is idealized in such concepts as "aesthetic experience" (*Erlebnis*): "Every experience [*Erlebnis*] is taken out of the continuity of life and at the same time related to the whole of one's life" (TM 69). This aesthetic alienation is a complex phenomenon, for it sacrifices a meaningful relation to one's actual life and accumulated social and moral experience in order to enjoy an allegedly immediate experience of an infinity of meaning:

> Aesthetic experience is not just one kind of experience among others, but represents the essence of experience per se. As the work of art as such is a world for itself, so also what is experienced aesthetically is, as an Erlebnis, removed from all connections with actuality. . . . An aesthetic Erlebnis always contains the experience of an infinite whole. Precisely because it does not combine with other experiences to make one open experiential flow [*Er-*

fahrungsfortgangs], but immediately represents the whole, its significance is infinite. (TM 70)

One last characteristic of aesthetic consciousness—one that is especially familiar to those acquainted with Kierkegaard's portrayal of the aesthete—must be mentioned: aesthetic indifference. It matters not whether the objects and others with which the aesthete engages are real or fictional, for the only aesthetic requirement is that they be subject to the "unlimited sovereignty" of the aesthetic consciousness (TM 89; cf. 69).

The alienation created by the aesthetic consciousness affects not only itself but also the work of art, which is appreciated in abstraction from its context as a "pure work of art." Gadamer calls this phenomenon "aesthetic differentiation," and says that it distinguishes "the aesthetic quality of a work from all the elements of content that induce us to take up a moral or religious stance towards it, and presents it solely by itself in its aesthetic being" (TM 85). In other words, aesthetic alienation is as much an objective as a subjective phenomenon.

Gadamer's attack on the subjectivism of modern aestheticism now shifts to one of its major concepts—the notion of play. The importance of the "play impulse" as the goal of aesthetic education (according to Schiller) had been noted in an earlier discussion (TM 82). Like beauty, play is better understood in terms of the objective reality of "the mode of being of the work of art itself" than in terms of the subjective experience of the aesthetic consciousness (TM 101). Gadamer goes to great lengths to demonstrate that primacy in a game belongs not to the players but to the game itself: "play has its own essence, independent of the consciousness of those who play" (TM 102). Play relieves stress because it totally absorbs the players and puts them in a situation where, unlike actual life, they do not have to take the initiative (TM 105). Indeed, "all playing is a being-played. The attraction of a game, the fascination it exerts, consists precisely in the fact that the game masters the players. . . . The real subject of the game . . . is not the player but instead the game itself" (TM 106). In some games play becomes presentation, and then, like a religious rite or drama, it requires an audience. In such cases "play as such becomes a play," and "the difference between the player and the spectator is here superseded [*hebt . . . auf*]."[15]

It is in Gadamer's discussion of the "transformation into structure" of the play of art that the full ramifications of his critique of the aesthetic consciousness become clear. Only in this transformation "does play achieve ideality . . . [and] pure appearance, [for it becomes] repeatable and hence permanent" (TM 110). These qualifications show why the English translators have chosen "structure" for Gadamer's *Gebilde*, but it should be noted that *Gebilde* is normally translated as "creation," "work," or "image," all of which do a better job than "structure" of capturing its relation to the central themes of *Bild* and *Bildung*.

But the true surprise is the ease and ingenuousness with which Gadamer is now able to affirm the very characteristics that he had earlier rejected:

> Transformation is not alteration. . . . Alteration always means that what is altered also remains the same. . . . But transformation means that something is suddenly and as a whole something else, that this other transformed thing that it has become is its true being, in comparison with which its earlier being is nil. (TM 111)

Here the very discontinuity that Gadamer had criticized in aesthetic consciousness and the work of art is proclaimed as a defining characteristic of the transformation of play into art. Indeed, such play is said to have "an absolute autonomy" in relation to "the representing activity" or consciousness of the player or artist who has created it (TM 111).

Gadamer's real concern is now emerging. It is not that he opposes discontinuity or autonomy or any of the other concepts of modern aestheticism. Rather, he demonstrates that they have been usurped by human subjectivity in its determination to assert its own autonomy. By rights, however, they belong only to the work of art itself. It is "the presentation of the essence, [that] far from being a mere imitation, is necessarily revelatory" (TM 115). Gadamer is reversing the "subjective turn in aesthetics" in favor of a "return to the older tradition. If art is not the variety of changing experiences (*Erlebnisse*) whose object is filled subjectively with meaning like an empty mold, we must recognize that 'presentation' (*Darstellung*) is the mode of being of the work of art" (TM 115).

There is one remaining surprise as we explore what Gadamer means by a text or work of art. In a survey of various art forms, he discusses the manner in which they have their true being in presentation. This is obvious for plays and musical works, but Gadamer makes the same case for the plastic arts, even though paintings and sculpture seem to have a fixed identity that cannot vary according to context or "presentation." This would mean that a painting or a sculpture would be independent of and inferior to what it portrays—the "original" or *Urbild*—and would not participate in "the real being of the work" (TM 137). Here Gadamer appeals to yet another "mysterious ambiguity" in the word *Bild*, for his argument is essentially that an original becomes an original only by virtue of being presented in the work of art: "Paradoxical as it may sound, the original acquires an image only by being imaged, and yet the image is nothing but the appearance of the original" (TM 142). Art is no more the creation of the aesthetic consciousness than reality is the projection of the human mind. In the play of art, whether performances or pictures or texts or any other event of being, the world presents itself in its reality. And it is this real subject matter—*die Sache selbst*—that lies at the heart of aesthetic and hermeneutical truth.

III. Hermeneutical Paradoxes in History

Gadamer's concern about the content or subject matter that presents itself in works of art has already been manifest in his critical analyses of aesthetic differentiation and the alienation of aesthetic consciousness. In part II he turns from art to the human sciences, and focuses even more sharply on the question of the object of hermeneutical understanding. Just as he repudiates the detached "object" of aesthetic consciousness (TM 156, 158), Gadamer also observes that a modern reader of history would rather read Droyson or Mommsen, despite their sometimes outdated data, than a contemporary historian, for the simple reason that they are "properly" portraying the subject matter (*die Sache*), whereas recent history writing defines itself teleologically in terms of an " 'object in itself' " (*Gegenstand an sich*), following a model of detachment appropriate only to the natural sciences.[16]

This distinction between subject matter and object—*die Sache vs. der Gegenstand*—is related to a second that Gadamer also emphasizes and that is much more difficult to render in English. The concept of experience (*Erlebnis*) that he criticized in relation to aesthetic consciousness, is, it turns out, equally problematic when adopted by such historical thinkers as Dilthey (TM 222–23). But the common German word for experience (*Erfahrung*) carries a very different meaning. Whereas *Erlebnis* refers to experience without regard to contexts—whether that of the subject matter or that of the experiencing person—*Erfahrung* in a hermeneutical context implies a profound connection with the contexts and traditions that have influenced the person as well as those that have shaped the subject matter: "Real experience is that whereby man becomes aware of his finiteness. . . . Genuine experience is experience of one's own historicity" (TM 357); and "[h]ermeneutical experience is concerned with *tradition*. . . . But tradition . . . expresses itself like a Thou. A Thou is not simply an object; it relates itself to us" (TM 358). Thus the hermeneutical task is not to achieve explanatory knowledge of the other or even to understand the other as a moment within the reflexive dialectic of self-knowledge (as in Hegel's master-slave dialectic): "By understanding the other, by claiming to know him, one robs his claims of their legitimacy" (TM 360). The key to hermeneutical experience is an openness to the other and to tradition that is possible only by acknowledging one's own finitude. For "the dialectic of reciprocity that governs all I-Thou relationships is inevitably hidden from the consciousness of the individual" (TM 359–60).

The concept that Gadamer employs to express this I-Thou relation in action is application. Whereas the hermeneutical tradition rooted in Schleiermacher ignores application as well as explanation in favor of attempting to understand a text in its own terms,[17] Gadamer argues that legal and theological hermeneutics demonstrate that understanding occurs only when the meaning of the text can be applied to a concrete, present situation (TM 329, 332). When Schleiermacher attempts to "divine" the mind of the original author and audience, he "actually skips the task of mediating between then and now, between the Thou and the I" (TM 333). In other words, it is in the act of applying the meaning of the Thou to the world of the I that the hermeneutical experience of genuine interpretation takes place:

> Application does not mean first understanding a given universal in itself and then afterward applying it to a concrete case. It is the very understanding of the universal—the text—itself. Understanding proves to be a kind of effect and knows itself as such. (TM 341)

Within this context, Gadamer's central hermeneutical concepts can easily be grasped. At the heart of his program are the notions of the history of effect (*Wirkungsgeschichte*) and the fusion of horizons (*Horizonverschmelzung*). The history of effect refers to the hermeneutical experience of standing within history while trying to understand a subject matter: "A hermeneutics adequate to the subject matter would have to demonstrate the reality and efficacy of history within understanding itself. I shall refer to this as 'history of effect.' *Understanding is, essentially, a historically effected event*" (TM 299–300).

The historically effected person who understands is not, however, a merely passive knower of the content of a tradition. Although Gadamer affirms that "history does not belong to us; we belong to it" (TM 276), it is a misunderstanding to portray him as an authoritarian apologist for tradition. Authority, he insists, must always be earned; it is an "acknowledgement of superiority" rather than a subjection based upon intimidation (TM 279). This is where the history of effect must be grasped in its intimate relation to the fusion of horizons. The metaphor of horizon connotes for Gadamer both "finite determinacy" and the fact that "one's range of vision is gradually expanded" (TM 302). Although it is always necessary for the interpreter to try to identify with the situation of the historical other, the goal must remain mutual agreement with the other about the subject matter. Simply to understand the other in the other's own terms ignores the truth question and "makes an end of what is only a means" (TM 303). This means that the interpreter is just as active an agent in the pursuit of the truth of the matter as the voices from the past that speak through tradition. The result is a dialogue between interpreter and subject matter, between present and past, in which a new reality is created:

> When our historical consciousness transposes itself into historical horizons, this does not entail passing into alien worlds unconnected in any way with our own; instead, they together constitute the one great horizon that moves from within and that, beyond the frontiers of the present, embraces the his-

torical depths of our self-consciousness. Everything contained in historical consciousness is in fact embraced in a single historical horizon. (TM 304)

There are two revealing phrases in this passage. First is the notion of transposing oneself into an alien horizon. Gadamer explicitly denies that this requires some sort of disregard for oneself: "Transposing ourselves [*sichverset-zen*] consists neither in the empathy of one individual for another nor in subordinating another person to our own standards; rather, it always involves rising to a higher universality that overcomes not only our own particularity but also that of the other" (TM 305). This higher universality helps to clarify the other key phrase, "the one great horizon that moves from within." What happens in "the miracle of understanding" (TM 292) is that two previously independent horizons are fused in a new horizon that embraces them both but is (ideally) dominated by neither. It is a horizon that moves *from within*, neither from the weight of the past horizon nor the urgency of the present horizon but *from the inner nature of the subject matter*. Gadamer's argument is that "the task of what we call historically effected consciousness" is to "bring about this fusion in a regulated way" (TM 307). This is the hermeneutical enterprise, a "circle" (TM 293–94) that unites part with whole, past with present, strangeness with familiarity, and the subject matter with our understanding of it.

Gadamer's hermeneutical conclusion—that questions have priority over answers—shows how fully his program involves the paradoxical sort of death and resurrection of knowledge that emerged in Kierkegaard's writings. Having insisted that we must bring our question about the truth to the text, he now asserts that the "most important thing is the question that the text puts to us" (TM 373). Indeed, the universal horizon that moves from within now emerges as "the *horizon of the question* within which the sense of the text is determined" (TM 370). This question is not one that can easily be answered. On the contrary, it calls us to recognize our own finitude and to confess our own ignorance. It is, in effect, a death of knowledge: "It is the historically effected consciousness that, by renouncing the chimera of perfect enlightenment, is open to the experience of history" (TM 377–78). Only in the dialogue of questioning and being questioned do we seek to reach agreement or understanding with the historical other about the subject matter: "To reach an understanding in a dialogue is not merely a matter of putting oneself forward and successfully asserting one's own point of view, but being transformed into a communion in which we do not remain what we were" (TM 378–79).

IV. Language as Paradox

The transformation that occurs in hermeneutical understanding is made possible, according to Gadamer, by language. The thrust of the third and final part of *Truth and Method* is that all understanding is linguistic in nature, and that language is nothing less than the medium by and in which the world presents itself to us.

Gadamer begins explicating his theory of language with the observation that "language is the medium in which substantive understanding and agreement take place between two people" (TM 384). To know that we are in accord with another person about a particular subject, it is necessary to discuss that subject together. If there are any obstacles that impede such discussion, a work of translation is necessary for the conversation to occur. The process of interpretation begins with the first statement in the conversation, and pervades every aspect of the dialogue and any necessary translation (TM 384). Indeed, the best translation is one that "brings into language the subject matter that the text points to" (TM 387). Contrary to the common view, "understanding does not precede interpretation, but occurs in it" (TM 389).

Gadamer indicates the central role of language by referring frequently to "the linguisticality [*Sprachlichkeit*] of understanding." (*Sprachlichkeit* is also translated, in its various forms, as "language," "linguistic," and "verbal.") The idea here is that, in the tradition of German romanticism (Hamann, Herder, and even Hegel), all thought is linguistic in nature, and cannot occur apart from language. Gadamer extends this qualification to include historically effected consciousness and tradition, which both "exist in the medium of language" (TM 389).

This position has two particularly significant ramifications. First, Gadamer accords to verbal tradition a "special priority over all other tradition" (TM 389). Monuments and other mute artefacts just cannot communicate without the aid of language. Second, written texts offer "the highest task of understanding," since "writing is self-alienation" (TM 390), a detachment from the emotional and psychological elements of the spoken context and thus also from their influences. This allows the reader relative freedom from the persuasive power of the speaker and from the speech as one more "unfamiliar opinion," so that the text can be encountered as an "always possible truth" (TM 394).

Given his view that language is the universal that embraces all other forms of expression and can therefore never be objictified (TM 404), Gadamer is suitably critical of both the Sophists' claim that a word is only a name and Plato's belief that a word can be assigned only after the being in question is already known (TM 405–407). He prefers to refine the older theory that words are somehow similar to the things for which they stand, not in the primitive sense of a magical participation of the one in the other, but in the sense of a word as that which "brings the thing to presentation (Darstellung)" (TM 410). In short, words are not merely artificial signs, and language does not reach its acme in the enlightenment ideal of "unambiguously defined symbols" (TM 414). Words are the medium through which the experience of the subject matter seeks to express itself (TM 417).

Gadamer credits Christianity with undermining the goal of an ideal language by affirming the incarnation of divine truth in a very real, historical, body. This was consistent with the equally un-Greek idea of the creation of the world through the medium of language (TM 418–19). Most important, the notion of the incarnation "prepares the way for a new philosophy of man, which mediates in a new way between the mind of man in its finitude and the divine infinity. Here what we have called the hermeneutical experience finds its own, special ground" (TM 428). Just as the incarnation paradoxically unites the divine nature with human nature in one person—Christ—hermeneutical experience proves to be that place within human consciousness where the infinite and the finite meet in one mediating reality—language.

This brings us to the second and more radical claim that Gadamer makes in part III of *Truth and Method*, a reinterpretation of Humboldt's view that every language constitutes a worldview:

> Language is not just one of the endowments that come to a person who is in the world; rather, the fact that we have a *world* at all depends upon it and presents itself in it. The world as world exists for man as for no other creature in the world. But this existence of the world is linguistically constituted.[18]

Paradoxically, it is precisely this linguistic nature of the world as it presents itself to us that frees us from the world as "objective" environment (TM 444). Although there can be no consciousness of a pre-linguistic world-in-itself for Gadamer, his primary concern is to defend not a Kantian agnosticism but the capacity of language to reveal being to us: "The particular linguistic world in which we live is not a barrier that prevents knowledge of being-in-itself; rather, it fundamentally embraces everything with respect to which our insight can be enlarged and deepened."[19]

In language the divine infinity of meaning is united with a finite expression or presentation. Thus every word implies a totality even though it can say only a fraction of that totality (TM 458). This higher, paradoxical unity of infinite and finite definitely follows the Christological model. In the same way, the subject and object of understanding belong together, rather than in the bipolar relation of Cartesian objectivity (TM 461):

> To say what one means, on the other hand—to make oneself understood—means to hold what is said together with an infinity of what is not said in one unified meaning and to ensure that it is understood in this way. (TM 469)

In the end, Gadamer returns to the concept of presentation (*Darstellung*). Just as a game is primarily a self-presentation of the players within the self-presentation of the game (TM 108); just as a picture (*Bild*) can be a presentation only by virtue of its "essential relation to its original [*Urbild*]" (TM 137); and just as presentation is the concept that embraces all other aesthetic concepts because it alone expresses how the world "comes into its own in the picture" (TM 151, 153); so also language is the presentation of being that can be understood in the same paradoxical sense that Christ is the presentation (incarnation) of the divine. But in neither case does this imply an Arian dualism:

> That which can be understood is language. This means that it is of such a nature that of itself it presents itself to be understood. Here too is confirmed the speculative nature of language. To come into language does not mean that a second being is acquired. Rather, what something presents itself as belongs to its own being. Thus everything that is language has a speculative unity: it contains a distinction, that between its being and its presentations of itself, but this is a distinction that is really not a distinction at all.[20]

V. Conclusion

It is tempting to suggest that Gadamer is a covert Christian who may even be aware of the extent to which his philosophy requires an affirmation of Christian belief in the incarnation and the cross. But the most that can be demonstrated from *Truth and Method* is that Gadamer, like Hegel before him, is fully aware of the extent to which all products of any tradition must stand within that tradition even if they do not fully accept it. Gadamer affirms the historical role that Christian thought has played in the developing tradition of Western philosophy, and his own dependence upon that tradition. But nowhere in *Truth and Method* does he imply that the revealed and confessional claims of faith are prerequisites for philosophy's pursuit of universal truth.

Be that as it may, we may conclude by noting that, just as Kierkegaard's epistemology of the cross has afforded us insight into Gadamer's philosophical hermeneutics, Gadamer's thought sheds light upon Christian beliefs central to Kierkegaard. This is especially true with regard to the question of power, which, although marginal to Kierkegaard's writing, is often the focus of Gadamer's text. Indeed, it could be argued that his major goal is to subvert modern assumptions about who controls whom in hermeneutical situations (that is to say, in all occasions of human communication and understanding).

Gadamer's political hermeneutic has appeared often in the foregoing analysis of *Truth and Method*. In a game it is not the players who are in control, but the game itself that plays itself out through the players. In artistic presentation it is not the artist but the subject matter that legislates meaning. In order to achieve understanding, an interpreter must give up striving to know the mind of the author or artist and instead enter into dialogue about the truth of that subject matter. Even then, as we take our question to the text, we discover another level of our own ignorance and must yield the initiative to the text, which puts its own questions to us as readers who seek the truth. This implies a virtual death of our previous knowledge and an undermining of that sense of power and autonomy with which modern interpreters approach their task. The aesthetic consciousness that differentiates itself from its world and seeks through an experience (*Erlebnis*) of immediate yet transcendent meaning to understand a work of art is displaced by a more humbling experience (*Erfahrung*) of the autonomy and truth of the subject matter itself.

This political hermeneutic develops in detail a point made quite briefly by Johannes Climacus in *Philosophical Fragments* on the subject of attempting to understand the Christian paradox. Climacus employs the terms "acoustical illusion" and "echo" (PF 51, 52) to express the false sense of ownership that interpreters often have over their responses to the paradox. In fact, the discernment of the paradox as such is created by and dependent upon the paradox itself, which is "the originator who hands over all the splendor to understanding" (PF 53). Gadamer's political hermeneutic traces that transfer in reverse, for it shows how no claim to truth can be validated by any power other than the truth—the subject matter—itself.

Second, Gadamer's hermeneutical circle, in which the interpreter forsakes individual autonomy, constancy, and certainty in order to be changed and empowered to discern a higher universal that unites new horizons with old ones, demonstrates the epistemological implications of this spiritual rebirth. That Kierkegaard's epistemology of the cross requires a death to knowledge and a rebirth in faith has already been shown. What Gadamer adds is a fuller description of the sort of epistemological humility that will follow from this sort of hermeneutical awareness. This, again, makes fully explicit something that remains for the most part only implicit in Kierkegaard's texts, particularly those works assigned to pseudonyms.

The re-centering of truth away from an individual subject (whether as author or as interpreter) and onto the subject matter is accomplished only through language, which is another concept by which Gadamer illuminates Christian belief. Language can free us from one-sidedly subjective or objective perspectives because, as the sole medium by which anything that can be understood presents itself to us, language actually constitutes our understanding as a historically effected fusion of many horizons—all of which together make up a tradition. This presentation of being in language, which Gadamer likens to the incarnation of God in Christ, is the paradoxical unity of the infinity of meaning with its finite expression.

The incarnational and paradoxical power of language stands as a challenge to the claim made in *Fear and Trembling* that Abraham cannot speak about his ordeal, for it defies "[t]he relief provided by speaking [which] is that it translates me into the universal" (FT 113). If, as Gadamer has shown, language is the unity of infinite and finite, then it can just as well convey the unity of universal and particular. For all the limitations of language, it can and does express being, even the being of paradox. No one has shown better than Kierkegaard that language can communicate the reality and character of those very paradoxes that it declares to be beyond language and understanding! As the human incarnates the divine, so also language is the body of spirit. By language God created the world; as linguistic beings humans are created in God's image; and it is presumably through language that—even in heaven—God is to be praised. The Christian understanding of life and truth is thoroughly grounded in language. Although Gadamer provides no hermeneutical rules or methods for the interpretation of sacred scripture, he does show that Christian language is the speculative unity of infinite and finite that must be the presupposition as well as the Christological content of all Christian interpretation.

Notes

1. Hans-Georg Gadamer, *Truth and Method*, pp. 95–96. Hereafter references will be to TM and included in parentheses.
2. Gadamer, "Afterword," TM 572.
3. TM 127–28. The reference to the fourth chapter "and elsewhere" in PF is so vague that it is hard to know just where Gadamer got the idea of contemporaneity as a task. In PF what we find is less a discussion of "task" than a sustained critique of the notion of "immediate contemporaneity" (PF 69, 106, etc.).
4. TM 132. Cf., EO, I, 137–64.
5. See Fenger, *Kierkegaard: The Myths and Their Origins*, for a compelling warning against reading Kierkegaard uncritically.
6. For a sampling of such analyses, see Clair, *Pseudonymie et paradoxe: Le pensée dialectique de Kierkegaard*; Elrod, *Being and Existence in Kierkegaard's Pseudonymous Works*; Sponheim, *Kierkegaard on Christ and Christian Coherence*; and M. C. Taylor, *Kierkegaard's Pseudonymous Authorship*. My own contribution to this genre is *Kierkegaard's Dialectic of Inwardness*.
7. This is virtually the standard interpretation. See, for example, Lowrie, *Kierkegaard*, p. 256.
8. See Hohlenberg, *Kierkegaard*, pp. 118–19; Malantschuk, *Kierkegaard's Thought*, pp. 236–43; and Green, "Deciphering *Fear and Trembling*'s Secret Message," 1986, pp. 95–111; and Green, *Kant and Kierkegaard: The Hidden Debt*.
9. Climacus's reasoning here has been spelled out in the preceding pages, where he argues in Anselmian fashion that, since existence is presupposed by essence, then we must reason from the existence of something to its nature and works, not the other way around (PF 39–41).
10. See Gill, "Faith Is as Faith Does," p. 204; Crites, Introduction to *The Crisis [and a Crisis] in the Life of an Actress*, p. 38n; McKinnon, "Kierkegaard: Paradox and Irrationalism"; and N. H. Søe, "Kierkegaard's Doctrine of the Paradox."

11. It must be admitted that Gadamer encourages this impression with comments such as the following: "The intention of the present conceptual analysis, however, has to do not with theory of art but with ontology. Its first task, the criticism of traditional aesthetics, is only a stage on the way to acquiring a horizon that embraces both art and history" (TM 137).

12. Although this observation presupposes much of the analysis that follows, it is worth remarking at this point that there is also an implicit dialectic in the three parts of the book: part I deals with the claim of the modern aesthetic consciousness that art is experienced as immediate to the self but discontinuous from the historical contexts of either the artwork or the self; part II treats the contrary effort of the historical consciousness to grasp the continuity of historical subjects while remaining discontinuous from it as a historical self; and part III proclaims that the fundamental continuity of all artworks and all subjects of any kind, with both their own contexts and with those who understand them, is established by and in the fundamental linguisticality of all human consciousness.

13. TM 11. Translation altered (see Gadamer, *Wahrheit und Methode*, p. 8).

14. Hegel, *Phenomenology of Spirit*, p. 14 (par. 26). Cf. TM 13.

15. TM 110. Cf. *Wahrheit und Methode*, p. 105.

16. TM 284-85. Cf. *Wahrheit und Methode*, pp. 268-69. Despite his insistence upon the importance of contextuality, Gadamer gives very few concrete examples of "subject matter." One of those is the ideal of bravery (TM 320).

17. TM 184-85. Gadamer uses the Latin rubrics here: *subtilitas intelligendi* for understanding a text in its own terms; *subtilitas explicandi* for explanation of a text; and *applicatio* for application.

18. TM 443. Translation altered (see *Wahrheit und Methode*, p. 419).

19. TM 447. Translation altered (see *Wahrheit und Methode*, p. 423). Dostal has clarified the meaning of Gadamer's cryptic maxim, "Being that can be understood is language" (TM 474) as follows: "[It] does not deny that there is non-linguistic Being but only that insofar as such non-linguistic Being cannot be brought to language it cannot be understood. It does exclude any non-linguistic intuitive grasp of things." See "The World Never Lost," p. 427. I am grateful to Professor Dostal for his helpful comments on an earlier draft of this chapter.

20. TM 475. Translation altered (see *Wahrheit und Methode*, p. 450).

9 | Kierkegaard, Wittgenstein, and a Method of "Virtue Ethics"[1]

Robert C. Roberts

> But when we listen to [Socrates], or to someone else repeating what [Socrates has] said, even if he puts it ever so badly, . . . we're absolutely staggered and bewitched. . . . Yes, I've heard Pericles and all the other great orators, and very eloquent I thought they were, but they never . . . turned my whole soul upside down and left me feeling as if I were the lowest of the low. But this latter-day Marsyas, here, has often left me in such a state of mind that I've felt I simply couldn't go on living the way I did. . . . He makes me admit that while I'm spending my time on politics I am neglecting all the things that are crying for attention in myself. So I just refuse to listen to him. . . . I've been bitten by something much more poisonous than a snake; in fact, mine is the most painful kind of bite there is. I've been bitten in the heart, or the mind, or whatever you like to call it, by Socrates' philosophy. . . . He talks about pack asses and blacksmiths and shoemakers and tanners, and he always seems to be saying the same old thing in just the same old way. . . . But if you open up his arguments, and really get into the skin of them, you'll find that . . . nobody else's are so godlike, so rich in images of virtue, or so . . . entirely pertinent to those inquiries that help the seeker on his way to the goal of true nobility.
>
> —*Symposium* 215d–216a, 218a, 221e–222a

LIKE MANY AN ambitious student looking for a career in philosophy, I applied for admission to the Harvard Ph.D. program. The application required an essay telling how I conceived philosophy and why I wanted to go into it in a big way. I suppose it would have been more effectual to write that I was puzzled by the Kantian idea of the thing in itself, or that I wanted to explore the prospects of a new social contract theory for our time, or that the problem of indeterminacy in translation had captivated me. Instead I told the truth, vaguely though it wafted in my mind. I said I thought philosophy should make people better, and that my purpose in going into it was to warm and uplift my future students' hearts. The philosophy of the warm heart was not prevalent at Harvard in 1970, and I received no invitation. But I have continued to think that philosophy ought to be healthy for the heart, however far short of this ideal my own performances in the classroom, in conversation, and in print may have fallen. That sentiment largely accounts for my interest in the writings of Kierkegaard and Wittgenstein, and in that amorphous newcomer to professional philosophy that is sometimes called "virtue ethics." I offer here some reflections that bring these three areas of inquiry together.

Philosophical Ethics as Wisdom

The work of the recent virtue ethicists has many, sometimes conflicting, facets. Some inquirers seek a new foundation for ethics, want to find somehow in virtue an improvement on Kant's categorical imperative or the utilitarian greatest happiness principle.[2] Some only think that normative ethics in the twentieth century has been one-sidedly concerned with actions, and needs supplementing with an account of the character of the moral agent.[3] Some are not much interested in developing a theory at all, but use a character-rich concept of the agent to highlight shortcomings in the ethical theories.[4] Alasdair MacIntyre seemed once to think that returning to a focus on the virtues in the dominant Aristotelian style held the key to overcoming the basic ethical disagreements that dog liberal societies.[5] Some inquirers have pursued basic questions in moral psychology, such as "What sort of thing is a virtue?"[6] and "How do emotions intersect with the virtues?"[7] People sometimes reflect metaphilosophically about how the virtues should be studied, as this chapter does.[8] And some philosophers have attempted to trace the conceptual and psychological contours of particular virtues.[9]

This last activity strikes me as having the most potential to fulfill the conception of philosophy as wisdom, a kind of discourse that can improve persons by speaking to their hearts. It is also at the very center of that family of inquiries known as virtue ethics. The first and most fundamental thing the character ethicist will want to do is to become acquainted with the virtues! "Acquainted," for a philosopher, means conversant with the inner structure of the virtues, their logic, their "meaning." But if this understanding is to count as wisdom, it must include personal appreciation, by the philosopher, of the good things she describes. She must be more than a conceptual technician. Such knowledge is driven and oriented by love, by an enthusiasm for those goods, a participant's concern that they should be realized in human lives. So the philosopher's language will be careful and analytical, while at the same time expressive, "lyrical," engaged, concerned—the language of love, the natural eloquence of the serious speaker. Analytical lyricism speaks as much to and from the heart as to and from the mind, like the language of Socrates about which Alcibiades groans in our epigraph. Alcibiades is a man for whom the concept of virtue has been "clarified" with the force of a perception.

By the standard of wisdom so articulated, I'm afraid that not much in the recent virtue ethics literature will count as wisdom; and if not, then little of it represents the center of virtue ethics. It tends, instead, to skirt the central issues, to mention virtues without much articulating them and for other purposes than that of understanding them. It speaks in a mood foreign to that of ethics and especially an ethics of character. It is, from an ethical point of view, largely language idling, to use Wittgenstein's expression; it is a language, much like that of the ethical theory that preceded it, that has little ethical traction (attraction).

Among philosophers whose conceptual analysis is informed by personal concern for the goods they describe, Socrates of course comes to mind, as do Nietzsche and Wittgenstein. I hope to convince you that Kierkegaard, with a little hermeneutical help from Wittgenstein, is a source to which character ethicists should be looking, a model we should be following, so as to begin filling in the lacuna in our enterprise. "Modern" philosophers—partisans of the project of finding a morality to which all rational comers must subscribe— have tended to think Kierkegaard uninteresting insofar as he is spiritually parochial, committed as he is to the understanding and promotion of a Christian outlook. He is interesting, to such philosophers, only to the extent that his insights can be detached from what is distinctively Christian in them. But it is becoming increasingly clear that the idea of a single, rationally compelling rationality is either the idea of a rationality too thin to entail any moral outlook (perhaps formal logic is such a rationality), or it is a chimaera. If so, then we have only particular and rival moralities, and their particular versions of courage, love, patience, truthfulness, generosity, etc., to look at as we develop philosophically a clarification of the ethical life. Among ethicists of character our preferred examples will be thinkers strongly committed to and deeply imbued with some *distinctive* moral outlook. Kierkegaard qualifies on that account. Being self-consciously both a "dialectician" and a "poet," he also qualifies as one who holds in balance the two qualifications essential to any ethicist of character.

Let us begin by looking at Wittgenstein's notion of philosophical grammar, for I shall be arguing that Kierkegaard too is a grammarian of sorts: in his grammatical analysis of virtue concepts he finds a way to be properly philosophical and at the same time to speak to the heart of his reader.

Wittgenstein: Wisdom as Corrective Grammar

To speak of grammar is to speak of order, tradition, and human practice. The grammar of English is constituted of the ordered or ruled ways in which English is spoken and written. When we speak grammatically we are following the rules of English grammar even if we cannot articulate any formulae for the rules we are following. (It follows that following a rule doesn't entail consulting it.) Most of us know immediately if one of the rules of English grammar is violated; we "hear" the violation even if we cannot identify it in the formal way a grammarian would. The grammarian's role is humble. She does not invent rules (at most she may tidy some up); her ingenuity is used to *discover* regularities already there in the practices of the human tradition we call the English language, and to find neat ways of formulating these regularities.

To apply the notion of wisdom here, we might say that her wisdom derives almost entirely from a collective wisdom that is already embedded, though for the most part inarticulately, in the practices of innumerable generations of English speakers. People who learn standard English, especially as a native language, absorb this tradition as they do their mothers' milk; it is in their bones. If, on the other hand, one grew up on the outskirts of standard English, in some dialectical ghetto, then one's grammar may be accounted corrupt by the standard of the tradition's mainstream, and may have to be "corrected." One of the ways it may be corrected—as often happens in school—is by help of the sorts of "rules" one finds in grammar books. (Another way is simply by associating with good English speakers and trying—or perhaps not trying—to imitate their practice.)

The kind of grammar with which grammarians of English work is the ordered ways in which *words* are combined in sentences. When Wittgenstein speaks of 'grammar'—at least of "depth grammar"—he is not talking about the grammar of words, but about the grammar of the *concepts* that are carried by the words. (But we get access to these concepts through considering how the words are used, and we might say, for certain purposes, that the concept just *is* how the word is used—but now we do not mean by 'used' just how it is placed with respect to other words, but how it functions *in our lives*.) The philosophical grammarian, like the grammarian of English, is beholden to something traditional, that is OK as it stands. And this tradition is a body of concepts embedded in our ordinary thought, speech, and practices—ordinary concepts carried by such ordinary words as 'exact,' 'simple,' 'same,' 'mean' ('meaning'), 'understand' ('understanding'), 'number,' 'time,' 'true,' 'read,' 'proposition,' 'pain,' 'think,' 'name,' 'see,' 'color,' 'act,' 'because,' 'believe,' 'know,' 'mind,' 'point,' and many others. The interconnected uses that we make of these and other words help constitute the fabric of distinctively human life. We use them quite fluently in our everyday activities and experiences, without being able to describe the regularities of those uses and interconnections, any more than we can describe the regularities in the surface-grammar of the language that we speak fluently.

Wittgenstein thinks that much of philosophy, as practiced by such notables as Plato and Kant, is a kind of mental disorder due to losing touch with the rich adequacy of the conceptual "tradition" referred to in the above paragraph. If we are insufficiently sensitive to the depth-grammar of such philosophically crucial words as I mentioned above, we are likely to be misled by the surface-grammar of our language to perform unnatural acts with them. In the opening paragraphs of *Philosophical Investigations* he discusses the tendency of philosophers to suppose that every word has a meaning and that the meaning of a word is what it refers to and that reference is essentially a kind of naming. Connected with the idea that the meaning of a word is what it names are a number of other knots in our understanding, such as the idea that common nouns refer to real but atemporal, non-spatial, non-physical, and non-sense perceptible entities called "universals"; that when a person uses a word meaningfully, or understands a word used by someone else, a mental representation of the referent (meaning) comes into his mind; and that the most fundamental way of establishing the meaning of a word is by pointing at whatever the word refers to and uttering or "thinking" the word. This nest of philosophical "problems" comes from our being misled by certain surface-features of our language, for example the fact that 'two' and 'also' don't look or sound essentially different from names; and that for any word we can ask "What does it signify (mean, refer to)?" Such surface facts of our language invite us to see false analogies between words, and obscure from us the enormous variety of ways in which words are used and indeed the fact that it is how we use words that determines their meaning. In *Philosophical Investigations* Wittgenstein offers, not an alternative theory of language, but a set of exercises designed to help us see the variety of ways in which our language works. These exercises, including what he calls "language-games," constitute a conceptual therapy in which we are provided, not answers to our philosophical questions, but relief from asking them. While it would be odd to call Wittgenstein's activity "virtue ethics," it is a kind of philosophical discourse that aims to improve us as persons, to liberate us from debilitating compulsions, to help us find our way back to a *human* life, after having wandered in the far country of conceptual vanity and illusion.

Kierkegaard as Moral Grammarian

Wittgenstein's intentions parallel those of Kierkegaard, who also addresses himself to people he regards as conceptually confused, to the detriment of the quality of their lives, and calls himself a dialectician—something similar to a depth-grammarian—and a "corrective." And what Kierkegaard wishes to draw his readership back into is, like Wittgenstein's "everyday use" of words, something traditional, something that in itself needs no improvement. As he says of his pseudonyms,

> . . . their importance . . . absolutely does not consist in making any new proposal, any unheard of discovery, . . . but, precisely on the contrary, consists in wanting . . . to read solo the original text of the individual, human existence-relationship, the old text, well known, handed down from the fa-

thers—to read it through yet once more, if possible in a more heartfelt way. (Following CUP, unpaginated)

But it is not just the more general concepts in terms of which good lives are to be lived—concepts like duty, constancy, honesty, courage, the eternal, friendship, loyalty, the individual—that Kierkegaard wishes to revive in the minds and hearts of his readers. He has a well-delineated, historically distinct tradition that he wants dialectically to "reintroduce to Christendom"—Christianity.

> If . . . the language of Christian concepts has become in a volatilized sense the conversational language of the whole of Europe, it follows quite simply that the holiest and most decisive definitions are used again and again without being united with the decisive thought. One hears indeed often enough Christian predicates used by Christian priests where the names of God and of Christ constantly appear and passages of Scripture, etc., in discourses which nevertheless as a whole contain pagan views of life without either the priest or the hearers being aware of it. (OAR 166)

We must hold fast the decisively Christian thoughts, and not just the Christian vocabulary, because it is these thoughts that shape people's *experience*. Kierkegaard wrote the book from which I last quoted about a contemporary of his, one Adolph Peter Adler, who held the equivalent of our Ph.D. in theology and was a pastor in the Danish Lutheran Church. While active as a pastor, Adler had an experience of being spiritually moved, and wrote some books in which he claimed to have had a revelation from Jesus Christ. Later he wrote some other books in which he gradually became less an "apostle" and more "an amateur lyrical genius," as Kierkegaard puts it. He showed, by this change and by other indications, that he had little personal grasp of the Christian concepts, despite his Ph.D. in theology. However intense his religious experience, it did not have the Christian grammar—was not the Christian version of, say, contrition, or joy, hope, gratitude, or peace. But in his confusion, Adler mistook this emotion for something Christian:

> . . . the experience of being shaken, of being deeply moved, the coming into being of subjectivity in the inwardness of emotion, the pious pagan and the pious Jew have in common with the Christian . . . to express oneself Christianly there is required, besides the more universal language of the heart, also skill and schooling in the definition of Christian concepts, while at the same time it is of course assumed that the emotion is of a specific, qualitative sort, the Christian emotion. . . . The fault or irregularity [of indiscriminately using the Christian vocabulary for the more universal emotion] is then a double one: that a person thus moved begins to talk in a language which stands in no relation to his emotion, since the language is specifically, qualitatively concrete, and his emotion is more universal; and that he naturally speaks this language in a confusing way. For when one is not in a

stricter sense seized by a Christian emotion, and on the other hand is . . . not strictly disciplined in the language of the concepts in which he expresses his emotion—then he is like one who talks too fast and does not articulate clearly . . . it is twaddle. (OAR 163, 164, 165)

Adler not only fails to understand the logic of the Christian emotions; he is equally and connectedly inept with the Christian concept of revelation if he thinks that to be deeply moved is to have a revelation from God.[10] In response, Kierkegaard remarks that a revelation from God, in the Christian sense, is not primarily experience, but something that God does in history, an action that would be done even if nobody noticed it. "No, even if no one had perceived that God had revealed himself in a human form in Christ, he nevertheless has revealed himself" (OAR 169). This remark, which identifies a facet of the Christian concept of revelation, thus correcting possible abuse of the word, is what Wittgenstein would call a grammatical remark.

Adler's confusions concerning the grammar of faith are more than "theoretical":[11] they affect the very practical matter of how he lives the Christian life and how, as a pastor, he leads his flock. So Kierkegaard's use of grammatical analysis and remarks, like Wittgenstein's, is in the service of the good life. But I am arguing something a bit more definite than that in this paper, namely that Kierkegaard is pre-eminently a "virtue ethicist," and that in his grammatical analysis of various virtues we find a model for the central method of virtue ethics, a method largely neglected by present-day practitioners of the discipline. I want to demonstrate Kierkegaard's use of the grammatical method in his account of the virtue of Christian love in *Works of Love*, but before I go on to that, let me do two things: first, dispel a doubt that may be percolating in the reader's mind regarding my interpretation of Kierkegaard; and second, make a few observations about grammar and virtues, preparatory to discussing the grammar of love.

Kierkegaard and Virtues

Kierkegaard used to be regarded as a sort of proto-existentialist, and thus as a thinker strongly opposed to the Aristotelian notion of settled dispositions (e.g., character traits, including virtues). Existentialists tend to think we betray ourselves unless we are living on the very knife-edge of decision, reconstituting ourselves ever anew by acts of sheer contextless and dispositionless will. It is our nature always to be ahead of ourselves, living into the "future," so as soon as we live in terms of the established selfhood created by our upbringing or our past actions and decisions, or in terms of a tradition that is given to us independently of our decision, we are betraying our individuality and being "inauthentic." This Sartrean Kierkegaard is the anti-hero of Alasdair MacIntyre's saga of the Enlightenment project of finding a rational foundation for morality. According to MacIntyre, Kierkegaard's real worry, at least early in his authorship, is not the reintroduction of Christianity to Christendom, as he retrospectively rationalized it to be in *The Point of View for My Work as an Author*; it is rather the worry that drives MacIntyre's work—worry about how moral debates can be resolved and agreement achieved in a morally pluralistic social context. Kierkegaard's brilliance was to see the impossibility of establishing morality in the way Kant and his Enlightenment colleagues tried to do it—by finding in Reason, independent of any historical tradition, an unrefusable foundation. Seeing that pure reason couldn't bear the building's weight, MacIntyre argues, Kierkegaard offered in *Either/Or* an alternative solution to Kant's problem that has turned out to be

> the distinctively modern standpoint . . . which envisages moral debate in terms of a confrontation between incompatible and incommensurable moral premises and moral commitment as the expression of a criterionless choice between such premises, a type of choice for which no rational justification can be given.[12]

Thus the name of the book—*Either/Or*—and the fact that it is written by pseudonym within pseudonym, with Kierkegaard winking in the background, not advocating any of the alternative life-views because he knows that none is to be rationally preferred over the others. MacIntyre admits that his reading flies in the face of the best Kierkegaard scholarship and that it renders *Either/Or* incoherent: The ethical life, as depicted in volume II, requires the acknowledgment of values that in principle could not be brought into existence or validated by an individual's choice. But MacIntyre is undeterred.

Kierkegaard regards the ethical life as vastly superior to the esthetic life, without denying that the latter can be chosen and carried to term. And this is the impression that a reading of *Either/Or* is supposed to give. The esthetic life, as depicted in volume I, and even more as interpreted in volume II, is a psychological disaster. When carried to term it results in despair, some aspects of which are noticeable by the esthete himself, and become even more so when pointed out by the ethical Judge William of volume II. *Either/Or* assumes throughout that the esthete and the ethical individual can understand one another—though the ethical person understands the esthete better than the esthete understands the ethical person or even himself. An Aristotelian assumption operates throughout Kierkegaard's authorship, to the effect that human nature has fixed parameters that can be developmentally violated, all right, but to do so means, to one degree or another, failure as a person, and more or less obvious dysfunction. A theme that comes up in work after work, pseudonymous and otherwise, is that the human self is a synthesis of the temporal and the eternal. In Kierkegaard's view this is a basic fact about human nature that any adequate developmental scheme or conception of personality fulfilment (any projected set of virtues) must accommodate. Kierkegaard's accounts of the grammar of faith in *Fear and Trembling*, and of Christian love in *Works of Love*, conform to this condition.

Since the virtues are for the most part gradual accretions of personality for which the foundations are mostly laid in childhood, regarding ethics as centrally concerned with the virtues goes hand in hand with the idea of moral education. Kierkegaard complains,

> In former times men set a high value upon the significance of bringing up, understanding by this a harmonious development of that which was to support the various gifts and talents and peculiarities of personality ethically in the direction of character. In our times one seems to want to do away impatiently with this upbringing and therewith emphasizes instruction. One wants the young to learn quickly and as early as possible much and all sorts of things, to learn what one almost palpably can ascertain is knowledge and is something. Formal culture, the ethical culture of character, is not such a something, and yet it requires much time and much diligence. In our time one seems to think that if only one takes pains in all ways to see that the child learns something, learns languages, mathematics, religion, etc., then for the rest the child can pretty much bring himself up. (OAR 180)

Furthermore, intellectual moral instruction, of the sort one acquires in the university, plays a secondary role. In explaining how Adler can have a Ph.D. in theology and yet be as spiritually addlepated as he is, Kierkegaard comments,

> alas, the knowledge acquired for the theological examination—if one does not bring along to the university what purely religiously must be held in infinite esteem, a deep veneration for the Christian faith instilled in childhood and by upbringing, so that in [a] later moment of decision he will resolutely and frankheartedly stand up for the choice he had made, rather forego everything else than to alter the least tittle of the Christian faith—alas, the knowledge acquired for the theological examination, though it might be worth ever so much regarded as knowledge, avails but little for standing fast in time of battle. (OAR 166)[13]

Kierkegaard here gives us some insight into how he conceives the relationship between character and decision, and it differs from that of the Sartrean Kierkegaard of the freshman philosophy textbooks, for whom authentic decision is always a movement *away from* what is fixed in one's personality and given to one by others. Here decision is motivated by the veneration, the esteem, we might say the love of the good that has been instilled in one through one's upbringing. No doubt, despite the veneration the decision will sometimes be difficult. It will involve foregoing pleasures, opposing immediate inclinations, subjecting oneself to discomforts emotional and physical. In the actions deliberately taken out of veneration for Christ, and for the things of Christ, one takes the role of master with respect to those immediate inclinations that need to be denied to give full expression to the veneration, and thus one comes to own that veneration in a way one did not own it before. Through significant decisions, what was before merely an inheritance from others becomes gradually more deeply integrated into one's self as agent. If Kierkegaard had a use for the word 'authenticity' this, and not the existentialist version, is what authenticity would be.

What, then, does Kierkegaard have in mind when he says, "the opposite of sin is not virtue, but faith" (SUD 82)? Is he suggesting that faith is not a virtue? This is a grammatical remark about sin, that employs the word 'virtue' differently than it is used in this chapter. He has in mind a conception of virtue as unaided human accomplishment, perhaps something like Aristotle's picture of the magnanimous man who takes great pleasure in thinking himself glorious because of his courage, his generosity, his temperance, etc. If the Christian thinks of himself as glorious, it is in the humility of acknowledging God his creator and giving him credit for the human glory (Psalm 8). But the Aristotelian, or the corrupt "Christian," is proud in the contemplation of the glory that distinguishes him from his less glorious fellows; he demands attention for it and takes "credit" for it himself. If this is virtue, then by Christian lights virtue *is* sin, and not its opposite, for it arrogates to oneself honor that belongs properly to God. But pagan virtue is not the only kind there is, and we have seen that Kierkegaard insists on the importance of Christian character. Once we acknowledge that different virtues, belonging to different traditions, have different grammars it is quite natural to grant, with the broad Christian tradition, that the *virtue* of faith—the disposition to acknowledge, trust, and love God— is the opposite of sin.

Some Observations about Grammar and Virtues

When I speak about the grammar of a virtue or of some virtue-term, I am not talking about what the analytical philosophers of thirty to sixty years ago had in mind when, lumpingly, they talked about "the logic of science" or "die logische Aufbau der Welt" or "the logic of ethical (or religious) statements." People who talked that way were offering philosophical theories in a way quite foreign to the central work of Wittgenstein. They were given to extravagant and dubious generalizations, such as that all scientific statements could be analyzed in terms of empirical protocol sentences and logical form, or that the logic of ethical statements was that they all expressed approval or disapproval that was logically independent of facts. When I speak of the grammar of the virtues, I am speaking not of any *general* traits these concepts may have, but of the particular features of particular virtue concepts like honesty and courage. I am speaking in large part of what distinguishes one virtue from another, or what distinguishes a virtue, such as courage, as it exists in one tradition, from its counterpart in another tradition.

What makes a remark grammatical, in our present sense, as opposed to psychological, stipulative, historical, methodological, etc.? I especially raise the question of psychological remarks, since they are so close at hand when one speaks of the virtues. Initially we can say that psychological remarks are about *people*, while grammatical remarks are about *concepts*, even if the concepts in question are psychological ones—ones in terms of which people are understood, explained, and formed. (The concept of love is in this broad sense a psychological concept.) Psychological remarks make some claim about what motivates people, what causes people to behave or experience as they do, how the psyche is structured, what is easy or hard for people to do and why, how most people act under some given conditions, etc.

In the discourse "Love Believes All Things" one of Kierkegaard's chief grammatical points is that *the Christian lover cannot be deceived*. In forms of love that are essentially reciprocal, such as erotic love and friendship, one may venture to love the other, thinking one is being loved in return, and then discover that one has only been "used"—and so be deceived. But if one loves the other in the Christian way, one loves her "in God," makes no demand of reciprocity, finding satisfaction in the love itself. Such love cannot be deceived. The remark that the Christian lover cannot be deceived is thus a grammatical remark, one that makes a purely conceptual point about Christian love, defining it in distinction from most other loves. But in the same discourse Kierkegaard notes how difficult it is to hold on to this concept of love in the course of life, and thus how difficult it is to embody it in one's attitudes and actions:

> . . . the lower level of conception and the pact between earthly passions and illusion are very difficult to shake loose. Just when a man has understood the truth best of all, the old ideas suddenly pop up again. The infinite, the eternal, and therefore the true are so foreign to a man by nature that it is with him as with the dog which can indeed learn to walk upright but still always prefers to walk on all-fours. (WL 229)

These remarks, about what is difficult for us, about what usually happens to people on a spiritual quest, and about our human nature, are psychological remarks.

Being conceptual, a grammatical remark "locates" a concept like love in its position vis-à-vis other concepts. To give just a sampling: In *Works of Love*, Kierkegaard makes comments locating love with respect to the concepts of consolation (75f.), envy and arrogance (81–83), self-renunciation (187–90), upbuilding (200ff.), mistrust (214–21), judging others (220), courage (229), hope (231ff.), honor and shame (243–46), justice (248ff.), domineering (252f.), small-mindedness (253–55), reduplication (261f.), discovery of sins

(262–68), and forgiveness (273ff.). One might say that the concept of love just *is* the way in which the use of 'love' (in a given tradition, of course) intersects the uses of these and many other words. We can see from this that a grammatical remark supplies part of the "definition" of the word involved, with respect to some concept that the word carries. But it differs from a dictionary definition in that it makes no attempt to specify the entire "meaning" (presumably the totality of its patterns of usage) of the term in a short formula, but only displays an aspect of its usage, notably some connection or disconnection of the concept in question with some other concept. Grammatical remarks are often contrastive: some feature of the concept is brought out by noting a way in which the usage of the word diverges from a counterpart usage. Thus Kierkegaard notes that we say of erotic love that it "blossoms," but no one would say this of Christian love.

Stipulative remarks are, like grammatical ones, "definitional" and about some concept, but to the extent that they stipulate they do not describe traditional usage, but notify the reader of a usage that will *not* follow tradition. It is one of the biddings of the grammar metaphor that grammatical remarks identify and remind us of features of concepts that are already embodied, perhaps inarticulately, in our ways of life and speech. Often in theology a remark that is intended to be about how a tradition uses a particular word—say, love—may be revisionary of the tradition and thus inadvertently a stipulation as to how the word should be used in the future. Under pressure from some philosopher or psychologist—a Kant, a Hegel, a Heidegger, a Whitehead, a Jung—virtue concepts undergo changes which only a person with unusual moral intensity and conceptual sophistication may detect. Kierkegaard is particularly alert to changes of this sort emanating from the philosophy of Hegel, and exposing them is part of his program of reintroducing Christianity to Christendom. A question the reader may wish to ask when reading conceptual-grammatical discourse is whether the remarks made there are truly grammatical or are a covert proposal of a *new* usage.

This last observation leads us to notice a difference between Kierkegaard and Wittgenstein. I have said that both of them are "traditional" in attempting to return us to a forgotten wisdom, to remind us sensibly of the riches of a way of life we have turned our backs on. But the traditions to which they would reintroduce us are not just different, but different *kinds* of tradition. Wittgenstein's program is a therapy in which people afflicted with philosophy can find their way out of the pointless frustrations and bruises of life in the conceptual fly bottle, out into the real world where peace is found in the everyday language that has traction in the activities of ordinary life. The tradition to which he returns us is something with which we are imbued from infancy. True, Kierkegaard thinks we have forgotten what it means to "exist," something to which we ought to have automatic access, but his point in reintroducing us to our existence is to reintroduce us to Christianity, a shocking and in some ways unnatural, even "paradoxical" tradition. One cannot fail to be properly instructed in concepts like *equal, same, understand,* and *mean.* Our grasp of these concepts can be loosened by following miscues in the surface grammar of our language, but that is parasitical on our being able to use the corresponding words properly. By contrast, we not only may be, but probably have been, misinstructed or underinstructed in Christianity. We may all have been trained from earliest childhood in a Christian vocabulary that has "passed over into a volatilized traditional use" that has become "the conversational language of the whole of Europe" (OAR 164f., 166).

In most such situations *some* "memory" of the authentic use of the Christian vocabulary will persist, but it will take an individual of unusual learning and deep Christian character to plumb the riches of the tradition: knowing the ins and outs of Christian personality is a different sort of knowledge from that of Christian "doctrine" and depends more on personal appropriation of Christianity. The language of faith will need to be *taught* in a way that Wittgenstein does not need to teach us our everyday language. This is perhaps why Wittgenstein's grammatical remarks only bear on particular confusions, never giving us anything like a "complete" account of *understanding, meaning,* or whatever. Kierkegaard, by contrast, must teach us what Christian love is, and so needs to give a fuller grammatical-lyrical-psychological account of it, one that does not assume that the basic understanding of the concepts is already in place. In the case of the Christian concepts we are not only confused; we are very often also ignorant.

The grammar of a virtue, as displayed in grammatical remarks that display its essence,[14] is some kind of internal conceptual order that the virtue possesses; it is the rules for any trait to qualify as the virtue in question. Just as the grammar of English orders various parts of speech to one another, internal to proper English sentences, there must be kinds of things that are ordered internal to the virtues, the ordering of which the grammatical remarks pick out. What might some of these things be?

Early in the recent revival of interest in the virtues, some philosophers who had always thought ethics to be chiefly about actions and the identification and justification of the rules that prescribe, proscribe, or license them, thought that virtues must be simply dispositions to perform actions that follow the ethical rules. If this were true there would be little to say about such a virtue as honesty, except to remark that truth-telling and truth-seeking are the kinds of actions that honesty is a disposition to perform.[15] But this restriction makes us miss or greatly underrate the fact that honesty is primarily an attribute of persons, and only derivatively an attribute of actions. It is to miss the grammatical fact that an honest person rejoices in truth and truth-telling (other people's as well as his own) and is angered, disgusted, sad, contrite (as the case may be) in the face of hypocrisy and falsehood. Thus his honesty may be manifested without his *doing* anything at all. To think honesty is just a disposition to act is also to miss the complex "psychology" of honesty, the ways in which this virtue requires patience, perseverance, and hope to counteract discouragement, courage to resist fear, and self-control to withstand the appeal of easy answers. It is to miss how honesty needs to be tempered by other virtues like gentleness and compassion, and how it takes wisdom to judge when and how the truth is to be told.

Besides laying out the ways in which types of emotion and other virtues intersect with the virtue in question, the grammar of a virtue identifies in a general way how the possessor of the virtue understands himself and his situation. It displays the concepts that shape the virtue, and indicates how they shape it. Virtues are not just "habits" in our contemporary English sense of the word (to do something out of habit is to do it mechanically and without thought) though virtues certainly involve some habits of thought and behavior. To say that a virtue has a grammar is to suggest that even to know *what* a person is doing, when in acting he exemplifies the virtue, requires us to know what concepts are operating in his understanding of what he does, of why he is doing it, of whom he is acting toward, of what the context of his action is, etc. After remarking that Christian love differs qualitatively from the love that is celebrated in poetry (such as Shakespeare's Sonnets), Kierkegaard remarks,

> Neither is it required of a Christian that he, in blind and unwise zeal, should go so far that he could no longer bear to read a poet—any more than it is required that a Christian should not eat ordinary food with others or that he should live apart from others in seclusion's hermitage. No, but the Christian must *understand* everything differently from the non-Christian. . . . Therefore simply let the poet be, let the individual poet be admired as he deserves, if he really is a poet, but also let the single one in Christendom try his Christian convictions by the help of this test: how does he relate himself to the poet, what does he *think* of him, *how does he read* him, how does he *admire* him? Such things are hardly ever discussed these days. (WL 6of., my italics)

But these are precisely the topics that come up in grammatical remarks about the virtues. The grammar of faith or love, in Kierkegaard's hands, brings out those distinctive concepts in terms of which an exemplifier of these virtues "sees the world," and by the assimilation of which his personality has been transformed.

Let us turn now to a more detailed look at Kierkegaard's grammatical account of the virtue of Christian love.

The Grammar of Christian Love

I am suggesting that *Works of Love* be read as a grammar book, a collection of rules for the use of the word 'love' in the context of the Christian way of life, and thus of rules governing the Christian concept of love, specifying what does and does not count as Christian love. To make this manifest I will focus on a few of Kierkegaard's remarks about this concept. But the book is more than a *bare* grammar of love. One can imagine a grammar of love that is in the coldest way a mere listing of the logical properties of Christian love, a technical accounting without lyric and using minimal examples from life. Perhaps such a course would be useful for seminarians in much the way that a course of technical grammar would be useful as a background discipline for aspiring writers of English prose: a helpful skeleton of the living thing. But Kierkegaard's writings are not technical in that sense. He called himself not only a dialectician but also a poet. He was preoccupied not only with "logical problems" (to use the words with which he once intended to title what became the *Concluding Unscientific Postscript*), but also, throughout his life, with questions about how to *reach* people, speak to the heart, move people to live in the Christian categories. He firmly believed that "true up-building consists in rigorous speaking," but also characteristically remarks at the beginning of one of his discourses that "We shall, with the powers we have, seek to make this as enlightening as possible, as alluring as possible, to bring as close as possible to the poor the consolation he has in being able to be merciful" (WL 56, 293). And so the grammar of love emerges, in *Works of Love*, in a lyrical body rich in metaphors, analogies, illustrations from life, irony, humor, and thought experiments. I warn my reader that in what follows I am discussing a *dimension* of Kierkegaard's work in virtue ethics, and by no means the whole living thing—and of that dimension I select only a few examples.

The Concept of Neighbor

A constant theme in *Works of Love* is that Christian love is non-"preferential." This feature marks off Christian love from two other kinds, the erotic love into which one "falls" with a member of the opposite sex, and intense friendship. In each of these cases the lover "prefers" her partner; her attitude is determined by the particular identity of the one she is "attached" to. By contrast, Christian love is not motivated by what distinguishes the beloved from others, but by something common to all human beings. Thus we get a family of other remarks, that elaborate on this theme: You can think somebody is your friend when she isn't (say, when some of the grounds for your preferring her cease to hold, such as her preferring you), but you can never err in taking somebody to be your neighbor. And you will always err in thinking somebody is *not* your neighbor (see WL 64f.). Neighbors cannot be "lost": "The beloved can treat you in such a way that he is lost to you, and you can lose a friend, but whatever a neighbour does to you, you can never lose him" (WL 76). "He who in truth loves his neighbour loves also his enemy" (WL 79).

What is the Christian rationale for cutting through all the obvious distinctions between potential objects of love, distinctions of intelligence, beauty, talent, education, age, race, nationality, social position, and particular relationship to the "lover"? The Christian lover perceives the neighbor as kin to himself and all others, says Kierkegaard, "because kinship of all men is secured by every individual's equal kinship with and relationship to God in Christ . . . " (WL 80). Thus the grammar of Christian love has a historical character, and depends on the particular narrative of the redemption of humankind in Jesus of Nazareth. We have become equal and thus we have been shown to be equal through this historical act of God. We can imagine substitute rationales for non-preferential love—say, Immanuel Kant's idea that we all have equal "dignity" in virtue of being rational creatures—but that would not be the grammar of Christian love, in which the neighbor is defined as one for whom Christ died.[16] Another fact about the concept of Christian love follows from this "dogmatic" determination of the concept of equality: " . . . the likeness of everyone's sharing the same temporal distinction is by no means Christian equality . . . the likeness which is obtained by the mighty climbing down and the poor climbing up is not Christian equality; this is worldly likeness" (WL 82f.). Note, however, that Kierkegaard does not deny that a worldly "climbing down" could be a most fitting way for the mighty to *express* their recognition that the poor are their neighbors—that is, that before God the poor are equal to the mighty.

Love as Obedience

Friendship and erotic love, at least as "the poet" celebrates them,[17] are not responses to any command, nor does the lover see them as an ethical task. Instead they "blossom," happening or not happening as they will, and if they happen it is a matter of good fortune (WL 64). I found an especially graphic example of this life-view in *Time* magazine recently. Woody Allen, in an interview in which he defended his behavior in having a sexual affair with an adopted daughter of the mother (Mia Farrow) of one of his own children, commented, "The heart wants what it wants. There's no logic to those things. You meet someone and you fall in love and that's that."[18] In contrast, notes Kierkegaard, "No one, if he understands himself, would think of saying of Christian love that it blossoms" (WL 26).

But we should not conclude from the above considerations what we so often hear about Christian love, namely that it is "not a feeling." It would be easy to slide from noting that Christian love is an ethical task rather than an immediate inclination, to thinking that it is no inclination at all, but just a sort of teeth-gritting doing of one's duty, such that it is only the behavior that counts, or at most the commandment-respecting attitude. Christian love is a warmth of affection for the neighbor just because the individual with this virtue sees the neighbor as his or her kin in God. From the perspective of Christian love, a banquet feast to which were invited the halt, the blind, cripples, and beggars is properly called a *feast* and not "a charitable gesture, . . . so scrupulous is Christian equality and its use of language that it demands not only that you shall feed the poor—it requires that you shall call it a feast" (WL 19). That Kierkegaard is talking not just about correct action, but about a qualification of the lover's heart, is evident in a comment in the following paragraph, where he says,

> Does it seem to you, my reader, that the preceding paragraphs are only an argument over the use of the word *feast*? Or do you perceive that the issue concerns loving one's neighbour? He who feeds the poor but yet is not victorious over his own mind in such a way that he calls this feeding a feast sees in the poor and unimportant only the poor and unimportant. He who gives a feast sees in the poor and unimportant his neighbours—however ridiculous this may seem in the eyes of the world. (WL 92)

Kierkegaard the grammarian of the moral life knows that an attitude does not qualify as Christian love if it is not tenderhearted and enthusiastic, but Kierkegaard the psychologist knows how difficult this kind of vision is, and that it requires a victory over one's own mind. And he accepts the implication, so often denied, that affections are subject to command:

> I do not have the right to harden myself against the pains of life, for I *ought* to sorrow; but neither have I the right to despair, for I *ought* to sorrow; furthermore, neither do I have the right to stop sorrowing, for I *ought* to sorrow.[19] You have no right to harden yourself against this emotion, for you *ought* to love; but neither do you have the right to love despairingly, for you *ought* to love; just as little do you have the right to misuse this emotion in you, for you *ought* to love. (WL 57)

God as the "Middle Term"

The grammar of a virtue reflects a conception of our situation in the universe. Thus Stoic απαθεια reflects a situation in which nothing of importance is subject to human control other than the individual's attitudes; the Nietzschean virtues reflect a situation in which there are no standards of value other than the ones we devise for ourselves. Situations to which Christian love pertains are conceived to involve essentially three characters: the human lover, the human beloved, and God. Both beloved and God are loved, but in very different ways:

> There is only one whom a man can with the truth of the eternal love above himself—that is God. Therefore it is not said: "Thou shalt love God as thyself," but rather, "Thou shalt love the Lord thy God with all thy heart, with all thy soul, and all thy mind." (WL 36)

Kierkegaard comments, "In love and friendship preference is the middle term; in love to one's neighbour God is the middle term" (WL 70). In logic, a middle term links two other terms in such a way that a new proposition follows from two others. For example, in "Caius is a man, men are mortal, therefore Caius is mortal," 'man' is the middle term linking 'Caius' and 'mortal' from the first two propositions to form the third, "Caius is mortal." To say that preference is the middle term in friendship is to say that it is what links the beloved to the lover; it is the lover's reason for his love. If asked, Why are you so attached to Malcolm?, Malcolm's friend will mention something about Malcolm that makes Malcolm preferable above many, if not all, others. (Maybe it's just that "Malcolm is Malcolm"; but that is enough to exclude all the others!) By contrast, if a Christian is asked why he loves this or that person whom he loves as his neighbor, the Christian mentions nothing that would distinguish the neighbor from anyone else, but instead he mentions God, to whom he and the neighbor bear a common relationship. It is because of God, in particular God's love to the lover and to his neighbor, that the lover loves his neighbor. As Kierkegaard remarks, " . . . it is really only in [God's] company that one discovers his neighbour, for God is the middle term" (WL 87). This is not a psychological comment, but a remark about the concept of neighbor, and thus about the concept of loving one's neighbor.

Grammar, Incommensurability, and Truth

If we lean hard on the metaphor of grammar, we may seem to deprive ourselves of an important application of the concept of truth. Spanish, Hebrew, and Mandarin have different grammars, but the differences are only to be noted, not adjudicated. Similarly, Nietzsche's ethics, Stoicism, and Christianity have different concepts, with different depth grammars, in terms of which human beings are understood and formed in their self-understanding. But these ways of understanding and living seem, on the face of it, to be in competition with one another in a way that Spanish, Hebrew, and Mandarin are not. Stoics *disagree* with Nietzscheans, and Nietzscheans *reject* Christianity. These ethical ways of life seem to invite not just noting, but adjudication. We can imagine a grammarian of ethics who was concerned only to note the differences among the concepts of person that occur in these various life-views, but it would seem to follow from such an attitude that the grammarian herself was neither a Stoic, a Christian, nor a Nietzschean. But if she is not a participant in *any* analogous way of life and self-understanding, then it seems to me she does not live a human life. Perhaps she is a god or an angel—more likely, a computer. On the other hand it is not anomalous for a Hebrew-speaking grammarian of Mandarin complacently to describe the differences between the two languages without ever raising the question of which one is right.

Someone might speak Mandarin, Hebrew, and Spanish off and on throughout the day. But a person who switched back and forth, at short intervals, among Christianity, Stoicism, and Nietzscheanism, is impossible because such a "person" would be involved in existential contradictions that would undermine the unity of his personality. Have we identified a fault in the metaphor of grammar as applied to ethics? We have certainly identified a limit of the metaphor, but not a fault; metaphors naturally have limits. Indeed, it seems to be *part* of the grammar of concepts internal to ethical ways of life to be contentious in some ways against their counterparts in other ways of life. The truth of their claims seems to be an issue that is built into the conceptual grammar of many, if not all, ethical ways of life.

Some philosophers infer from Wittgenstein's notions of grammar and related ideas that rival ethical and religious practices and ways of thinking and speaking are "incommensurable." This is to say that, because the concepts hook up with one another in different ways in the different systems, and because a concept just *is* the ways in which the usage of one word hooks up with the usages of other words within an integrated way of thinking and speaking about life, there is really no commonality of concepts between the ways of life. But absent such commonality, the two sets of concepts cannot be mapped onto each other, or compared with each other in such a way as to generate disagreement between ethical and religious views. For example, Nietzsche, Stoicism, and Christianity may *seem* to be disagreeing about the nature of persons, but since they do not mean the same thing by "person" they cannot really make polemical "contact" with each other. They are just talking past one another.

Such philosophers infer from the doctrine of incommensurability that while the grammar of Christian love (for example) *differs* from the grammars of Aristotelian friendship or Romantic erotic love, or the grammar of Christian faith differs from that of Nietzsche's ethics, it is illegitimate to say that one of these is *superior* to the other, or that one is "true" and the other "false," or that one leads to genuine human flourishing and the other only to ersatz flourishing, etc. Such a claim is illegitimate, according to these philosophers, because it falsely supposes a standard or measure of truth or human flourishing that is above or independent of these ways of living and their grammars. Since it is only within a way of life that criteria for flourishing can be set up, there can be no criteria by which disagreements among traditions about what flourishing is can be adjudicated. If we try to decide whether Aristotelian friendship or Christian love is more fulfilling by appeal to the human nature that is to be fulfilled, where will we find our concept of human nature? If we take it from Christianity or Aristotelian theory, we beg the question in favor of the one or the other. If we take it from elsewhere, then we are just appealing to *another* life-view.

D. Z. Phillips chides Paul Holmer for being inconsistently Wittgensteinian when Holmer claims that Christianity covers the hard cases as other ways of living do not, that the richness and joy and peace of the life of a saint and the coming to rest in God and the fulfillment in loving one's neighbor are reasons to prefer Christianity to other ways of life:

> Holmer suggests that the way one's life develops as a believer will be different from the way it will develop if one is not a believer, and that this difference in development can serve as an external check on the faithfulness of Faith's promises and their superiority over the alternatives.[20]

In perusing the book to which Phillips addresses his criticism[21] I have not found any place where Holmer calls such a criterion "an external check." It seems clear that anyone who judges Christianity superior to alternative ways of life judges *as a Christian*, or at least as a very serious inquirer. Phillips is right to say that the full-blooded notion of success in life by which Christianity is here judged superior depends on accepting some Christian beliefs. One can hardly regard being at peace with God as a mark of success in life if one thinks there is no God, or think it a mark of fulfillment to see every person as one's equal, if one thinks, with Aristotle or Nietzsche, that there is no important way in which all people are equal. But Christianity might appeal to a non-Christian in ways that do not presuppose the full panoply of Christian beliefs, but only some more generically human sensitivities.

Holmer seems right to suppose it part of the grammar of Christian faith that people who deny the articles of the faith, or regard erotic love as the highest form of love, have missed something fundamental and important in life, and that they believe falsehoods. The grammar of faith has a place for concepts of truth and error and genuine versus ersatz flourishing, as applied to whole ways of life. Imagine a Christian saying, "It is the goal of my life to be at peace with God and to love my neighbor as myself, but having read Phillips on the great Wittgenstein I realize that I can't say that Nietzsche is *wrong* when he says that Christianity is nothing but a rationalization of the will to power. Since Nietzsche's way of life is a completely different game than the one I'm playing, we can't be contradicting one another." It is clear that such a "Christian" is violating the grammar of faith, and in a way that is especially demoralizing to faith.[22]

A distinction between philosophy and theology runs through Phillips's text, such that one might say, *as a theologian*, that Christianity is superior to its rivals (this being just one of the things that Christians "say"), while one would, *as a philosopher*, respect the incommensurability of ways of living and eschew any comparative evaluations. But a theologian/philosopher like Holmer or Kierkegaard—a passionate thinker of the sort whose activity I am advocating in this chapter—would not be able to bifurcate his activities and sayings in this way. To violate the grammar of his faith because at the moment he is wearing his philosophical hat can only be moral treason. Wittgensteinian theologians prefer to speak of the grammar of faith rather than its metaphysics so as to free Christian life and thought from alien philosophies that threaten to distort Christianity in various ways. Grammar is supposed to be purely descriptive, thus leaving Christianity just as it is actually practiced and spoken by its best representatives. But an incommensurability doctrine that prohibits Christians from thinking Christianity superior to Marxism or ethical egoism imposes a philosophical framework at least as distorting to Christian thought as Whiteheadian or Heideggerian metaphysics. The concept of incommensurability, as Phillips uses it, is a theory (or part of a theory) of just the sort that Wittgenstein intended his philosophical work to discourage.[23]

Shall we conclude that Christian faith is incompatible with Wittgenstein's philosophy? I have called the belief in the incommensurability of rival ways of life a "theory," and this will irritate Wittgensteinians, who think their philosophical assertions are only grammatical remarks, not hypotheses or theories or doctrines. My reason for thinking incommensurability to be a theory is that adhering to it requires the believer to abandon a crucial grammatical feature of his own way of life and speech, namely the claim that the Christian life is better than its rivals (John 14:6). The incommensurability doctrine is itself incompatible with a policy of merely displaying the grammar of faith. But Wittgenstein is more careful than the Wittgensteinians to refrain from philosophical theorizing, and I think a case can be made that he does not hold the despotic incommensurability thesis.

He seems to suggest that some facts are not merely a function of our concept of them, and that we can imagine states of affairs so different from certain general facts of our world, that if these states of affairs obtained our concepts would differ from what they presently are:

> If anyone believes that certain concepts are absolutely the correct ones, and that having different ones would mean not realizing something that we realize—then let him imagine certain very general facts of nature to be different from what we are used to, and the formation of concepts different from the usual ones will become intelligible to him.[24]

No doubt, in doing Wittgenstein's exercise we utilize concepts that we already have, and thus do not access an imagined reality that would be *completely* "external" (to use Phillips's word) to the concepts that we use in daily life. But the point of the exercise is to get us outside those concepts that we falsely believe to be "the absolutely correct ones," and so it shows the possibility of a *partially* "external" check on our concepts, and it shows the capacity of our minds to utilize such a check. Wittgenstein gives an example of imagining a very general fact of nature to be different when he says, "The procedure of putting a lump of cheese on a balance and fixing the price by the turn of the scale would lose its point if it frequently happened for such lumps suddenly to grow or shrink for no obvious reason."[25] To do this exercise, we employ our concepts of *lump* and *grow* and *shrink*, but we use them to imagine a nature which is very different from our own, and in which our concept of *weighing* would no longer have a place. It seems, then, that Wittgenstein does not hold that the conceptual scheme and practices to which our concept of weighing belongs are necessarily incommensurable with a scheme from which our weighing would be excluded. Our concepts of lump and grow, for example, supply a bridge between the two schemes (I am of course not saying that the concept of lump would be *exactly* the same in the two schemes). We can imagine a denizen of our world visiting in the world Wittgenstein imagines, and resisting, at first, the idea that he has to give up weighing things. Gradually, however, the facts of the world he is visiting become irresistible to him, and he undergoes a conversion in his concepts and practices: he quits talking about weighing things, and he quits weighing them, stops insisting that other people weigh them, etc. His conversion includes the judgment that, given the nature of the world he is visiting, the conceptual scheme that lacks the concept of weighing is superior to his old scheme, is "truer" to reality.

Rival ethical and religious practices and ways of speaking are analogous to the above example. They differ, but not so much as to be incommensurable. With a bit of empathic imagination a practitioner of one can understand the language and practices of another, and may even see that the other way of life speaks to some of his needs, or some facts of his nature, in a way more satisfactory than his own. This fact about the dialectic of ways of living is presupposed by Kierkegaard's strategy in *Either/Or*, where Judge William, the ethical individual, attempts to convert an esthete by describing what the ethical life is like (in large part by exploring the grammar of its concepts), comparing the ethical life with the esthetic, and criticizing the esthete's way of life. Both his ability to describe the esthete's way of living, and his hope that the esthete may find something attractive, indeed superior to his own way of life, in this description,[26] bespeak the commensurability of the esthetic and ethical "stages." We have also seen that one of Kierkegaard's important strategies for displaying the grammar of Christian love is to contrast it with that of erotic love and pagan friendship; it is hard to see how such a comparison would be possible if the incommensurability doctrine were true.

A final example is supplied by Epictetus, who counsels a disciple what to do when he meets a man weeping for grief (we can take the advice as reflecting the grammar of Stoic compassion):

> As far as conversation goes . . . do not disdain to accommodate yourself to him and, if need be, to groan with him. Take heed, however, not to groan inwardly, too.[27]

Confronted with an authentic case of Christian compassion, one in which the compassionate person does groan inwardly, weeping with him who weeps, the

Stoic may come to think that the self-protection of the Stoic strategy is bought at too high a price. Despite the pain involved in Christian compassion, he may come to feel that the human solidarity embodied in the emotion fulfills human nature better than the detachment characteristic of Stoicism. The example of Christian compassion may speak to something in him that Stoicism discouraged him from seeing, but which, once he has seen it, he must admit does not come as complete "news." He may come to see his need for "fellowship," and admit something that before he only dimly recognized—that the Stoic way of life was oppressively lonely. Again, in judging Christianity to be better, or truer, than Stoicism, this convert does not take up a standpoint external to and transcendent of all the rival ways of living. He judges on the basis of sensitivities some of which may be traceable to Stoicism, though he may have others *despite* his nurture in Stoicism, in virtue of some "very general facts of [human] nature."

The kind of "virtue ethics" that I am advocating describes the virtues of a tradition by tracing their grammar, but in doing so it may also function as an "apologetic" for that tradition. For if it is well done it displays the depth, the humanity, the human adequacy, the spiritual and ethical riches and beauty of the tradition, and so provides reasons for living a certain kind of life, within a certain language of existence, reasons which are not entirely inaccessible to people outside the tradition or on its edges. Such an apologetic does not absolutely compel all rational persons in the way that some more ambitious Christian thinkers have tried to make their apologetics do. As Wittgenstein's and Kierkegaard's labors suggest, rationality is gentler and more variegated than such apologists suppose. Rationality does come in a variety of rival and incompatible forms. But the overlap between those forms is no accident. It is often traceable to our common humanity. And it is enough to enable the grammarian of some deeply human way of life and thought to speak fetchingly to people outside his or her tradition.

Conclusion

I have argued that Kierkegaard combines some of the most important virtues of a "virtue ethicist." He gives us sustained grammatical analyses of several virtues (something we rarely see among contemporary character ethicists). Close attention to such writings as *Works of Love*, a work to which I have given only the scantest attention in this chapter, could be very instructive for ethicists, regardless of their tradition. Kierkegaard has a healthy understanding of the relativity of the virtues and their grammars to the life understandings and the ways of living in which they are at home. He writes as a practitioner of one of these ways of life and thus with the passion and insight characteristic of a person who loves the good things he describes, and is striving to get more and more inside them himself. In addition to dialectical skill and personal pathos, Kierkegaard, like Wittgenstein, has a wonderful sense of "rhetoric," that is, of how to write about concepts in such a way as to encourage the *inculcation* of what is proposed, and not merely to convey it in an abstracted academic dialect—in such a way as to speak, that is, to the reader's heart.[28]

Notes

1. It is not usual to dedicate a chapter, but I want the publication of this one to be in honor of my teacher Paul L. Holmer, to whom I owe so much in the life of thought. It is especially fitting to dedicate this one to him, since it reflects the character of my debt more clearly than anything else I have written.

2. Elizabeth Anscombe's "Modern Moral Philosophy" is an example: Because an ethics of moral law is essentially tied to the concept of a divine Lawgiver, belief in whom can no longer be assumed, philosophers should turn to an analysis of the virtues. James Wallace says he undertook the study of virtues in the hope of dispensing with moral rules and thus with "the familiar problems about the origin, nature, and authority of such rules," but concluded that the program would not work since virtues like honesty, fairness, and being a person of one's word "are essentially attitudes toward moral requirements or rules" (*Virtues and Vices*, p. 9).

3. See Joel Kupperman, "Character and Ethical Theory," and Robert B. Louden, *Morality and Moral Theory*.

4. See Michael Stocker, "The Schizophrenia of Modern Ethical Theories," and Charles Taylor, *Sources of the Self*, pp. 3–107, 495–521. On Utilitarianism in particular, see Bernard Williams, "A Critique of Utilitarianism," especially pp. 108–18.

5. MacIntyre, *After Virtue*.

6. See Richard B. Brandt, "Traits of Character: A Conceptual Analysis" and "The Structure of Virtue"; and Amélie Rorty, "Virtues and Their Vicissitudes."

7. See Justin Oakley, *Morality and the Emotions*, and R. C. Roberts, "Aristotle on Emotions and Virtues."

8. See also my "Virtues and Rules."

9. See the articles by John Benson, Lester Hunt, Alasdair MacIntyre, and Lawrence Blum in Kruschwitz and Roberts, *The Virtues*; the articles by Leslie Farber, Thomas E. Hill, Jr., and Mark Jefferson, on particular vices, represent a related sort of undertaking. See also Annette Baier, "Why Honesty Is a Hard Virtue."

10. We hear this confusion expressed quite a bit today too, especially in the mouths of Christians who have been influenced by Carl Jung or New Age religion.

11. In fact Adler may not be confused at the purely "theoretical" level. He passed his theological examination, which may have included questions about the nature of revelation and the distinctiveness of the Christian emotions. It is an odd fact of human nature that a person's ability to *talk* logically does not predict very reliably his ability to *live* in the categories he "understands." Academic life seems to widen the gulf between the two.

12. *After Virtue*, p. 39.

13. We are reminded of Aristotle's comment that the study of ethics will be useless for the morally immature, since "an immature person, like an incontinent person, gets no benefit from his knowledge" (*Nicomachean Ethics*, 1095a9).

14. "*Essence* is expressed by grammar." *Philosophical Investigations,* part I, §371 (Wittgenstein's italics).

15. We would no doubt find plenty to talk about in the way of casuistry: rules for correlating kinds of actions with kinds of situations, that is, rules for the application of the original rules in the complexly varying situations of life. The philosopher of character wants to understand the disposition—to discern how the moral subject "sees" such situations and what "moves" her to take virtuous actions, that is, how the "rules" are lodged in the personality.

16. In *Works of Love* Kierkegaard does not strongly emphasize this "dogmatic" and historical basis of Christian love. Sometimes he may even sound in these pages as though the love of neighbor he is expounding is an ahistorical universal human potential. But his pseudonym Johannes Climacus insists on the distinction between "Socratic" religiousness and Christianity (see CUP, 493–97), and Kierkegaard explicitly calls the present set of discourses "Christian." On the place of historical beliefs in Christian faith, see *Philosophical Fragments,* and for discussion of the views expressed in that book, see C. Stephen Evans, *Passionate Reason: Making Sense of Kierkegaard's* Philosophical Fragments and Robert C. Roberts, *Faith, Reason, and History: Rethinking Kierkegaard's* Philosophical Fragments.

17. Kierkegaard does not deny the existence of ethical friendship and ethical erotic love; an extended description of the latter can be found in the second volume of *Either/Or.*

18. *Time,* August 31, 1992, p. 61.

19. But it seems that sorrow and love are disanalogous in this respect: that whereas it is *always* one's duty to love the neighbor, in only *some* circumstances is sorrow prescribed.

20. D. Z. Phillips, *Faith After Foundationalism,* p. 241.

21. Paul L. Holmer, *The Grammar of Faith.*

22. To assert that the grammar of Christian faith requires one to affirm that Christianity is superior to alternative ways of life is of course to make no judgment about the frequency with which an individual Christian makes this judgment, or the propriety of the Christian's dwelling on this truth or expressing it to others. Christians may well learn things from other ways of life, and Christianity itself, when it is really assimilated by a person, engenders a humility, non-defensiveness, and affection toward individuals of other persuasions, that make the Christian especially teachable by other ways of life.

23. I owe this point to Richard Olmsted, in conversations long ago.

24. *Philosophical Investigations,* part II, §xii.

25. Ibid., part I, §142.

26. Not to speak of Kierkegaard's ability to describe both these ways of life from "inside," in such a way as to display both their strengths and weaknesses, while himself occupying yet another perspective, which he regards as higher than they, and which has reasons unknown to them for approving and disapproving aspects of the lower ways of living.

27. Epictetus, *Enchiridion,* XVI.

28. I thank Steve Evans, Richard Olmsted, Mark Talbot, Merold Westphal, and Jay Wood for helpful comments on earlier drafts of this chapter.

10 | The Politics of Existence
Buber and Kierkegaard
Robert L. Perkins

Buber thought, and a lot of other people still do think, that Kierkegaard had little or no responsible understanding of the social and political aspects of existence.[1] On the contrary, I wish to argue that in spite of their many differences they have strikingly similar views about some issues of politics and society. In this chapter I shall show that both hold a conception of politics that connects it closely with ethics and religion. It should be stressed at the outset that both Buber and Kierkegaard have a different understanding of social and political relations from those who claim politics to be empirical, "value-free," or a statistical social science. Neither Buber nor Kierkegaard is "objective," in that numerical sense, for they are concerned with values, human relations, and the concrete way we organize our lives together. Both are also concerned with more existential issues than the constitution of the state, the nature of the law, punishment, regulation, interests, "the general welfare," or "the common defence," important as these are. They are not so much political or social scientists as interpreters and critics in these domains.

Politics and Society

Both Buber and Kierkegaard are fundamentally concerned with how we organize ourselves into communities and societies in a sense that includes but is not limited to the narrower concepts of everyday politics. Buber presents the narrower sense in "The Validity and Limitation of the Political Principle" where he distinguishes between the social and the political principles.[2] By the expression "social principle" Buber means the forms of local association such as labor unions, clubs, and natural communities such as the family. The "political principle" serves to subordinate the associations and communities to the state, which is the protective and unifying element of the society as a whole. Buber finds the communities to be humane and upbuilding while the state, at best, is neutral if not negative. Some Buber scholars argue that there is also a wider understanding of the political in Buber based upon the dialogical principle of *I and Thou*. They claim that the dialogical principle is *sui generis* political, and as a result, Buber's thought is political through and through.[3] I agree with that reading of *I and Thou*, but wish to stress that if one starts with this broad an understanding of political activity, Kierkegaard's polemic against the spirit of the modern age is as political as Buber's masterpiece.

Brief references to things to be discussed in more depth later show that both the narrow and the broader understanding of the political are present in Kierkegaard. The constitution of 1848 and the National Liberals provoked Kierkegaard's commentary on the political in the narrow sense. However, Kierkegaard's most famous analytic tool, the doctrine of the stages on life's way, is broadly and fundamentally social and political in the same sense that Buber's dialogical principle is. This wider sense of the political would include—to appeal to an instance Kierkegaard emphasizes—sexual and gender relations that reach down into the person and enable the person to fulfill or to flaw his or her humanity. Kierkegaard implicitly suggests that if the flawing kinds of personal choices and social relations are generalized, governing is near impossible. Kierkegaard constantly engages and criticizes the strengths and limits of the various forms of life precisely as providing or undermining the bases of society and politics.

It may appear that the comparison of Buber's and Kierkegaard's political principles is a comparison of apples and oranges because of the different levels of political activities in which Buber and Kierkegaard engaged. Buber was involved in the political arena as a youth when he was an activist in a despised and frequently persecuted East European minority; as a journalist and educator; as a theorist of Zionism in Europe, where he attempted to frustrate the effort to make Zionism a mere expression of nationalism, and in Palestine and later Israel, where he urged an accommodation with the Arabs and their nationalistic aspirations; as a communitarian socialist and founder of the kibbutz movement; and as an advocate of international peace in the early days of the Cold War. There is no question that Buber was involved in politics both actively and theoretically all his life.

By contrast it could be claimed that Kierkegaard was not politically inclined, that he was not politically engaged, and that moreover, it was not necessary for him to be involved politically because he was a complacent member of the dominant class in a conservative society and political order. Such criticisms, which go far beyond Buber's criticism of Kierkegaard may in part be true, but they are also oversimplifications. They assume the narrow meaning of the political principle and political activity. Such an understanding of political activity leaves the intellectual and social critic outside the sphere of political activity. To be sure, historical circumstance, and perhaps inclination, forced Buber into political activity. However, a brief mention of Kierkegaard's more explicit political activities at the beginning and the end of his authorship will indicate that he was not a Robinson Crusoe in the midst of Golden Age Denmark.

Kierkegaard's very first publication was a satiric newspaper article on female emancipation. This article is aesthetic and conservative, and it shows that at the age of twenty-one, Kierkegaard had little sympathy for the modern emancipation movement. However, the treatment of this topic, whatever its merit, indicates that Kierkegaard had decided political opinions. This article was soon followed by a series of articles in which he engages the emerging Danish liberals. About one major political issue of the times, the freedom of the press, Kierkegaard sides with the liberals against the king: that press restrictions are wrong. The liberals never acknowledged his agreement on this issue, but another issue did provoke their attention. Kierkegaard poked a lot of ironic fun at the liberals' frequently revised history of Denmark. What concerned him was, first, that the original physiocratic agricultural reforms of the king were not noted by the liberals as a significant beginning of liberal reform, and, second, that since the liberal intellectuals offered a different account of the origins of liberal reforms in each rendition, it was obvious that they practiced ideological history, a point they never grasped.

Kierkegaard's last entry into politics was through the (in)famous attack on the People's Church (*Folk kirke*) in the last year and a half of his life. Although it is not as commonly recognized, this attack was as much against the social arrangements of the previous absolutist state as the new constitutional form of government. The attack shows that Kierkegaard had decisively broken with his conservative background. Neither is it commonly recognized that the structures of economic privilege that underlay Danish society are also rejected in those fiery pamphlets. This brief mention of Kierkegaard's more explicit political activity at the beginning and at the end of his writing career suggests that though apples are different from oranges, they are both fruit, even if the apple is very large and the orange small.

The Politics of *I and Thou* and the "Stages on Life's Way"

Having established both a narrow and a broad concept of the political in Buber and Kierkegaard and briefly characterized their political activities, I shall now examine their respective major analytic tools or concepts in order to show that they had many of the same political aspirations and concerns in spite of the great differences between their methods of analysis.

Buber's fundamental analytical tool, the distinction between "I-Thou" and "I-It," was introduced in his famous book, *I and Thou*.[4] Buber's views of the political principle are not derived from this distinction; rather it penetrated all of his thinking "from [his] youth" as if by anticipation (I-T 171). After the publication of *I and Thou* all of his writings and activities bear the explicit impress of this distinction. This suggests that he has no concept of individual existence apart from the social context within which the person exists.

Buber allows some blurring of the relation of "I-Thou" and "I-It." The I can and sometimes does reduce a Thou to the status of a thing. In addition, we can, in a qualified sense, transcend the "I-It" relation to things (I-T 172–73). Thus, the same objects, works of art (I-T 60–61), trees (I-T 58), horses,[5] and other items, can legitimately be treated either as Thous or as Its (I-T 54–55).

By contrast, Kierkegaard's analytic tool, the doctrine of the stages on life's way, is concerned only with relations between humans, the interhuman. Although Kierkegaard recognizes the power of works of art, particularly literature and music, to move and educate us, it would never occur to him to regard trees, horses, or even works of art under the same category of relation with humans as did Buber.[6] Certainly, today there is a politics of trees (i.e., environmental politics), of horses (i.e., animal rights), and works of art (i.e., NEA funding disputes), and some of these issues could, only in the loosest sense possible, compare with Buber's treatment of these objects. The work of art is more ambiguous and may have a stronger claim to the I-Thou relation than the natural object. It has a dual status, being both an object with which we may deeply communicate and a human product expressing creative effort. By contrast, horses and trees exist apart from human creativity and are one-sidedly invested with "I-Thou" significance and relation by a human act (I-T 12–13). Kierkegaard's single-minded focus on the interhuman expresses a conceptual and axiological simplicity that eludes Buber.

The common emphasis upon persons and interhuman relations may be one reason why both Buber and Kierkegaard express much of their thought through literature. That Kierkegaard's thought on human relations is shown through a philosophically rich literature no more lessens its political import than the poetic and aphoristic form of *I and Thou* reduces the political import of Buber's thought.[7] Moreover, the fact that Kierkegaard's understanding and appreciation of the interhuman is finally theological only enforces the sense of the ultimate significance to which he assigns human relations and no more lessens the political import of his thought than Buber's theology of the Eternal Thou renders his thought apolitical or asocial. The literary, the political, and the theological come together seamlessly in both writers.

In addition to the concern for everyday political issues such as those mentioned above, Kierkegaard also reflected upon the political dimension of human existence throughout his adult life. In his dissertation, *The Concept of Irony with Continual Reference to Socrates*, he is almost completely overcome by the Hegelian distinction between morality and concrete ethical life, a subservience that he later criticized (CI 234–35; JP 4:4281). The dissertation was written in 1841, and the journal entry in which he confesses that he had been a "Hegelian fool" in his youth was written in 1850. Thus, Kierkegaard meditated upon the categories of Hegel's *Philosophy of Right* throughout most of his productive career. In addition, after 1848 Kierkegaard concentrated on the nature of politics and consciously rejected the easy relation he had previously enjoyed with the monarchy, and began serious reflection on the nature of the political and the social, but more of this below.

Thus, throughout his life Kierkegaard thought about the nature of the political, but he began to involve himself directly in political debate only after 1848. These political disputes expose the deep political content of his literature and its central analytical tool, the stages of life.

Kierkegaard began the pseudonymous literature in which he presents the stages on life's way immediately after the defense of his dissertation. According to his analysis there are three stages: the aesthetic, the ethical, and the religious forms of life; the last being subdivided into the religion of Socratic subjectivity (Religiousness A) and Christianity (Religiousness B). Each stage is judged and interpreted by the one or ones following it, with the result that the religious stage, and ultimately Christianity, interprets and judges both the aesthetic and the ethical forms of life. Kierkegaard discusses these forms of life and offers a sustained reflection on the relations of power, domination, manipulation, status, and the legitimation of these relations through art, ideology, custom, law, rhetoric, religious practices and institutions, and philosophy from the standpoint of his ultimate ethical ideal, neighbor love (WL), which is based squarely on Christian theology (PC; JFY; FSE).

Although his rhetorical devices are utterly different, Buber also maintains the logical connections of the social and the religious. In each encounter with a finite entity one can find the Eternal Thou who can never become an It (I-T 123). If one attempts to reduce this Thou to the status of an It (say, through magic), one may destroy the foundation of the I-Thou relation. Thus both authors lead us from the interhuman through the religious to the political.

I shall now discuss the political import of each of Kierkegaard's stages and comment on Buber's analogous positions. When one examines Kierkegaard's presentation of the aesthetic mode of life one finds two levels of criticism. First, there are the writings under the pseudonym Judge William, who has his own critique of aestheticism from the standpoint of the ethical (EO II; SLW 87–191). Second, it is clear that Kierkegaard's own critique of the aesthetic mode of life is that it fails to conform to the Christian commandment that a person must unconditionally love the neighbor as one loves oneself (WL). The appropriation of the command is, unfortunately, limited by the clarity of one's thought and by one's unconscious appropriation of the prejudices of the culture.[8] But even with these qualifications, the unconditionality of the command remains.

Among the large number of aesthetic characters presented in Kierkegaard's pseudonymous writings, the inherent immorality and duplicity of the aesthetic mode of life is perhaps best manifest in the character of Johannes the Seducer, who shows egoistic hedonism at its worst in "The Seducer's Diary" (EO, I, 301–445) and in his speech in "In Vino Veritas" in *Stages on Life's Way* (SLW 71–80). The Seducer manipulates, controls, deceives, and ultimately destroys the inner ethical coherence of his victim. Buber's category of the "capricious man" (I-T 107–109) is similar to Kierkegaard's ideal aesthetic type.[9] There is, however, a concreteness and exhaustiveness in Kierkegaard's presentation and critique of modern aestheticism lacking in Buber. In addition to the two long volumes that comprise *Either/Or* and a second volume, *Stages on Life's Way*, Kierkegaard offered many other critiques of the aesthetic mode of existence by other pseudonyms from other points of view. In addition to Johannes the Seducer, there are several other rather unsavory characters who bring out other socially destabilizing aspects of egoistic hedonism. One can only conclude that Kierkegaard paid vastly more attention to the pitfalls and dangers of the capricious or aesthetic person than did Buber. This contrast is, however, primarily a matter of emphasis.

Buber spells out his assessment of modern egoism (in Buber's German, *Eigenwesen*, "one's-own-being") by showing how the egoist turns in on himself or herself and attempts to hide an empty ego with glib self-assurance and talkativeness. Opposed to the egoist is the "person" who is able to relate to other persons and who, together, share a world (I-T 110–12).[10] Buber's critique is then primarily psychological, for he shows how the egoist is less authentic and happy (a word emphasized by neither Buber nor Kierkegaard) than the person. Although there are marked differences in the emphasis, detail, and mode of presentation, both Buber and Kierkegaard reject modern egoism in favor of a view of persons in mutual relation. The aesthetic mode of life makes social life and politics impossible, because egoism, manipulation, deception, and the disrespect for the person that characterize aestheticism undercut the common assumptions and absolute necessities of political existence. It is also important to note in passing that both make their primary critique of modern hedonism on the basis of its inherent anti-humanism and social destructiveness rather than on the basis of their appeals to the theological categories of neighbor love or the Eternal Thou.

Kierkegaard calls his positive view of human relations the ethical stage of life. The ethical mode of life has three levels in Kierkegaard. The first is the bourgeois ethical life which he presents primarily in *Either/Or* (EO II) and *Stages on Life's Way*, although, as in the case of the aesthetic form of life, there are other discussions of concrete ethical life by other pseudonyms who set the issues in other contexts. Through Judge William, the complex persona who presents the ethical mode of life, Kierkegaard attempts to develop a character who expresses the unity of the aesthetic and the ethical in the institution of marriage. Marriage is the paradigm of ethical relations for Judge William, who urges the seducer to despair over his past, to choose himself in his ethical and eternal validity, and to marry (EO, II, 5–154). Judge William subjects each of these terms—despair, choice, eternal validity, and marriage—to a philosophical analysis, and in so doing lays out his view of society, choice, action, duty, love, ethics, the self, and the nature of an ethical religion that emphasizes more of Luther than of Kant and Hegel. Still, Kierkegaard attempts to honor as worldly an ethic as he can concede in the ruminations of Judge William. His ethic also has a religious dimension, but it is always limited by the insights and assumptions of the bourgeois form of life as, for instance, when the Judge criticizes the religious exception (SLW 176–81) and the monastery (EO, II, 337–38).

Judge William does not present or argue a politics. Though a civil servant, he exemplifies the ethical at the level of marriage, the immediate level of Hegelian *Sittlichkeit*. There is, moreover, an ethical optimism in Judge William that we can do our duties, that "ought" implies "can." This optimism carries over into the Judge's understanding of the state, for his utter silence on the political dimension indicates that he is, like the bourgeois generally, largely apolitical and unconsciously compliant with the order and necessities of a bourgeois state. Judge William never suggests that there are duties over and above what is owed to the wife, son, the persons with whom he associates, and his vocation. That is, there are no duties owed specifically to God over and above the duties owed other persons (EO, II, 269–72; FT 54–55, 68–69). The upper reaches of Hegelian *Sittlichkeit* are implicit in Judge William, for he is essentially apolitical like most of the bourgeois. His discussion of the "civic self" is concerned with the mutuality of the personal and civic life, but there is no discussion of the other forms of *Sittlichkeit*, the civil society and the state. His life is complete within the bourgeois expression of the ethical, political, and religious, as the latter confirms the first two.

Kierkegaard, by contrast, presents two other dimensions of the ethical, both of which are related to the religious interpretations of existence. He calls them, for brevity's sake, Religion A and Religion B. Using the pseudonym Johannes Climacus, Kierkegaard develops his second mode of understanding the ethical. It is the ethic of religious subjectivity (Religion A) based on an original reading of Socrates, who views personal evil as a result of ignorance (SUD 87–96), that is even more deeply radicalized (CUP 204–10) into an ethico-religious subjectivity characterized by resignation (CUP 387–430), suffering (CUP 431–524) and guilt (CUP 525–54). The political content of the ethics of religious inwardness in Climacus's work is threefold. First, Climacus thinks of the tasks of ethical subjectivity as universally human for which each and every human being has the requisite capacities (CUP 356–57). The ethical and religious requirement of a human life is *sui generis* and different from intellectual capacity or achievement and social status. There is then a radical ethical and religious egalitarianism in the task of becoming subjective (CUP 228). It has been argued that religious and ethical equality have no political consequence; rather the case is that without the religious and ethical ideal of equality, there can be no moral challenge to unjust political and social inequalities. Climacus articulates a basis for just such challenges. It should also be emphasized that Climacus's view of subjectivity is not erratic, whimsical, arbitrary, or subjective; rather, ethical subjectivity is the expression of the universally human and is a ethico-religious requirement for every human being. Subjectivity is a ruled concept (CUP 73, 358–59). Second, the striving for religious inwardness that unites the individual and the universal is the model for the relation of the individual to the social and political unit in the politics of the liberal state. "In thinking [the subjective person] thinks the universal" (CUP 73), but as existing the person appropriates the universal into life policies. Liberal politics, that is, nonauthoritarian politics, is based upon the same model, for the state, being the universal, is coherent with the life policies of the individual who thinks the universal. Third, by appeal to universal principles the subjective existing thinker can resist the limitations and necessities of history, including those an authoritarian state would impose.

This complex understanding of the implications of ethico-religious subjectivity necessitates a vital revision of the way Kierkegaard was perceived during the hegemony of the existentialist reading of his thought. These insights show that the ethics of religious inwardness is laden with political consequences and insights. In fact, Kierkegaard's appeal to the ideal places him on the side of those for whom the universal would provide an ideal model of the state and who demand and expect a humane and rational politics. Such a conclusion no doubt would come as a surprise to Kierkegaard, for there is absolutely no indication that he drew this conclusion. Moreover, his radical attention to existence protected him from speculating over such matters. Nevertheless, his later conflict with the church is based, in part, on the implications of ethical subjectivity.

Works of Love, Kierkegaard's most important non-pseudonymous book on ethical relations, is a thorough analysis of the third mode of the ethical in his writings, the Christian concept of neighbor love. It contains the ethics of Religion B. This "new" or "second ethics" (CA 20–21) is more straightforwardly political than the ethical in Religion A. Here Kierkegaard argues that "*it* [Christianity] *has made every relation between human beings a relationship of conscience*" (WL 137, my italics). Thus in Religion B even the political is a matter of conscience. All aesthetic and ethical relations must finally be interpreted and judged by religious categories, and not just religious categories in general or of whatever happens to suit one, or even by the universally ruled categories of human subjectivity (Religion A), but by the Christian commandment to love one's neighbor as one loves oneself (Religion B). Kierkegaard, at least implicitly, contends that the Christian ethic cannot unqualifiedly support a state based on egoism even if Christians must live in and support such a state.

Buber does not distinguish three levels of the ethical as did Kierkegaard, but he is no less insistent than Kierkegaard upon the inclusiveness of love as the ultimate basis of ethics; and he just as completely draws the political under the judgment of ethics. Buber expressly rejects the simple dichotomy of "friend-enemy," a false dichotomy that is the source of massive moral and political evil. In a passage that inversely suggests the normative unity of politics and ethics Buber claims that, "when the party has specified who the enemy is . . . people day after day, with peaceful and untroubled conscience, lie, slander, betray, steal, torment, torture, murder. In the factories of party doctrine good conscience is being dependably fashioned and refashioned."[11] Love, on the other hand, is the primary relationship, and persons are complete only when they dwell in their love. Buber does not define love sentimentally; rather it is the responsibility one feels for the other and that they each feel reciprocally (I-T 66–67).

It is apparent that Kierkegaard's and Buber's analyses of the ethical situation share many characteristics, the most important of which must surely be the intimacy of ethics and politics. One notes the great detail and exhaustiveness of Kierkegaard's presentation of the ethical mode of life and that at each level there is a clear political dimension. The view that his thought is apolitical and/or asocial is a serious misunderstanding, a misunderstanding for which Buber is in part responsible.

The differences between Buber's and Kierkegaard's ethics are more matters of expression, philosophic sources, and history than substance. The fundamental similarity between them is that their final mode of judgment in understanding the political is religious.

Kierkegaard also appears to be the better analyst and offers a more deeply nuanced view of the variety of ethical stances and the relation of ethics to politics. One suspects that Buber makes fewer analytic distinctions than Kierkegaard because Buber stresses the mystical reading of Judaism, especially Hasidism, with its pressure toward the unity of creation and the divine. Kierkegaard, by contrast, was more influenced by the modern analytic movement initiated in the late Middle Ages and early Renaissance and its program of making distinctions. Still, their politics is set within the broad perimeters of an ethical and theological view that promotes a psychological and moral wholeness within the terms of our finitude. Both could find reasons to condemn specific political modes from purely ethical (i.e., universal) as well as theological viewpoints.

Kierkegaard, Buber, and the Politics of the Everyday World

I shall now consider a few specific political issues in the very different common lives of Buber and Kierkegaard to indicate how they came to terms with their everyday political actuality within the terms of their different views of the religious.

As noted above, Kierkegaard began to add a rather uncharacteristic activism to his philosophic view of politics after the revolution of 1848, even though that was a very quiet affair in Copenhagen. The revolution swept away the form of political organization he had known throughout his life and with which he was comfortable. The change in the locus of power from a monarch to a prime minister and parliament (*Folketing*) challenged him to think about politics more carefully than he ever had before. He did not develop a new set of categories nor did he read the classical or the modern sources of political thought when he began to think about the new political situation. Rather, he used the categories of the aesthetic, the ethical, and the religious forms of life that he had honed throughout his authorship in order to understand both the absolute monarchy that had been swept away and the new constitution.

He questioned the more idealistic views of the state, both Platonic and Hegelian, as well as his own previous complacency, in favor of a more Hobbesian[12] view of the state as a lesser of evil. The basic flaw of everyday politics is that it is based upon egoism, the hallmark of the aesthetic mode of existence. Kierkegaard urges that

> The state is of the evil rather than the good, a necessary evil, in a certain sense a useful, expedient evil, rather than a good. The state is human egoism in great dimensions, very expediently and cunningly composed so that the egotisms intersect each other correctly. But this, after all, is anything but the moral abandoning of egotism. (JP 4:4238)

Since the state is founded upon the egoism of the aesthetic mode of existence, it cannot serve religious purposes no matter how many priests are hired to preach the legitimacy of the political arrangements. The religious prostitutes itself to the aesthetic if it legitimizes the political in any way (JP 4:4242).

This pessimistic view of the state was based on his own observation of the last years of the monarchy, which he considered "demoralized" (JP 4:4180), and the beginning of the modern constitutional state, which he thought incapable of governing (JP 4:4181).

Kierkegaard's extensive analysis of the aesthetic mode of life provides the basis of his critique of the monarchy and the modern state. First, the monarchy. In his text, *Works of Love*, which is a "Christian reflection in the form of a discourse," Kierkegaard attempted to "fetch [persons] out of the cellar, call to them, turn their comfortable way of thinking topsy-turvy with the dialectic of truth" (JP 1:641). Although there is no theological critique of the details of Danish politics in the text, it shows Kierkegaard thinking through human relations in the public domain. He attempts to lay the foundation for such a critique of politics in the treatment of the monarch. This text is about the ideal conception of kingship "in a secular sense," and just as the aesthetic stage of life is judged by ethical and religious categories, just so here—the king is judged by the religious category of conscience. Most of us, like the scrubwomen to whom Kierkegaard compares the king, have to answer to others *and* our conscience. The absolute monarch, relieved of answering to others, still must answer to his conscience (WL 137). Ironically, Kierkegaard's most positive view of the monarch states that the monarch is not absolute in any moral or political sense, but rather that he must square his acts with his conscience "and thereby [with] a relationship of love" (WL 138).[13] The implication is that if ruling does not conform to love, then it is not conscientious, and as a result the king falls entirely into the category of the aesthetic. This is such an astounding limitation on the absoluteness of absolute monarchy that one can only wonder if Kierkegaard was ever the conservative and absolute monarchist he is generally thought to have been.

Kierkegaard was just as critical of the new constitution that restricted the powers of the king (and instituted the form of government that Denmark still has). Kierkegaard did not long for the restoration of the absolute monarchy. Kierkegaard considered such thought of restoration to be "humbug." He is not an escapist.[14] Neither did he bemoan the passing of the "Christian state," for he thought such talk to be nonsense (JP 4:4168). Rather, he came to terms with the strange new situation that required a complete revision of his previous political thinking. However, it would be a mistake to think that he had originally been uncritical of the monarchy and only became critical in his later years. In his earliest book, *From the Papers of One Still Living* (1838), Kierkegaard had suggested that the age for the formation of political granite and limestone was past and that the present age was the time for the formation of peat (FPOSL 63–64). This frosty evaluation of the last years of the monarchy suggests that Kierkegaard was less of an unqualified supporter of the monarchy than is commonly thought, for it, at best, is only limestone, not granite. But an icier dislike for contemporary politics is suggested by the reference to "peat," and the same disdain for contemporary politics is also present in the late journal entries, beginning about 1848. Thus the absolute monarchy was, and the new constitutionalism will be, less than an ideal form of government. Perhaps there had been in the geological past an age of granite formation, but Kierkegaard avoids entering into that mythology.

The transition in Kierkegaard's views is that in his early years his lack of enthusiasm for political change was based on the lack of political vision and direction among the liberals (FPOSL 63–64); after 1848 he attributes political change to the demoralization of the older leadership, a demoralization based entirely upon aesthetic indecisiveness and self-indulgence (JP 4:4180). He also rejects any claim for the adequacy, much less the superiority of the present political situation, because of its dependence upon egotism and lack of ethical and moral principle (JP 4:4182). This is congruent with his criticism of the present social situation because of its lack of regard for the individual (TA 86–96).[15]

Kierkegaard's attack on the People's Church was based on what he took to be the imposition of aesthetic categories into the realm of the religious. The aesthetic and historic concept of nationality, for instance, had become confused with being a Christian, a critique of Christendom's intellectual apparatus that goes back to the *Postscript* (CUP 51; KAUC 157–58, 166–67). Because of this imposition of the aesthetic into the religious, the category of "Christianity" had become confused and corrupt, and both church and state had been deflected from their proper roles in the common life (KAUC 97). Kierkegaard's term for this corrupted state of affairs is "Christendom." The attack on Christendom was not an attack upon the political principle as such, any more than it was an attack on the religious as such, but it was concerned with the proper marks or boundaries of the political and the religious.

Though their historic circumstances are entirely different, Buber's conception of modern politics is scarcely more enthusiastic than Kierkegaard's.[16] Buber has a dim expectation of the political based on the experience of the Jews in Europe and the failure of the new state of Israel to come to terms with the Arabs. On both of these issues Buber's thought flows directly out of his concept of "I-Thou," for in both instances the failure to recognize the personhood of the other and to enter into dialogical relations resulted in the failure of politics. Perhaps Buber's most dramatic statement of the failure of politics in Germany, dramatic because of its terseness, penetration, and stark truth, is a remark regarding the arch-antisemite, Hitler. After hearing Hitler speak, Buber "recognized [his own] dialogical powerlessness," for Hitler was "incapable of addressing one and incapable of really listening to one."[17] From the standpoint of Buber, that summarizes as briefly and as well as possible the nature of European anti-semitism; it was, in its deepest nature, monological rather than dialogical.

The major response to anti-semitism was the emergence of Zionism under the leadership of Theodor Herzl in the late nineteenth century. Buber joined the movement in 1898, a year after the first Zionist Congress, but almost from the very first was in conflict with its founder over the nature of Zionism. Whereas Herzl foresaw the emergence of a new Israel in the form of a liberal, industrial, and secular state, Buber and his associates saw the task of Israel to be the reintroduction of Jewish culture and religion in the region and in the hearts and minds of his fellow secularized and assimilated Jews. Those who agreed with Buber about the cultural and religious nature of Zionism considered Herzl's vision to be un-Jewish. This problem of defining Zionism remained the major dialogue within the movement.

This same kind of dispute within the ranks lasted throughout Buber's life. He urged a new and spiritual Zionism, arguably even a Judaism without a God.[18] He was a non-practicing Jew and had to discuss his highly personalized reading of Judaism many times during his life. Such an attitude was not entirely welcomed by the institutional Judaism represented by the chief rabbinate in Jerusalem.[19] His political dispute with the founders of Israel focused on the relation of Jews and Arabs in the new state. Before the war for independence, Buber urged the principle of equal political treatment of the two religions and defended the principle of a binational state with the two religious and cultural groups in constant and open political dialogue. Binationalism became impossible after the war for independence, but he continued to work for cooperation and dialogue between the two peoples. These positions led him into deep conflict with the Israeli government when he urged, for instance, equal civil rights for the Arabs and attention to the refugee problems both inside and outside of Israel.

The conflict over the religious significance of Israel, despite all the differences, is in many ways analogous to Kierkegaard's struggle with the official Christianity and politics of Denmark. One wonders what insight unites them in this common and loyal dissent from everyday politics.

Conclusion

Buber and Kierkegaard are united against aspects of society that, though they appear to be quite different, are fundamentally the same. Buber understood Hitler as monological, that is, unable to communicate as a Thou to other Thous. The same phenomenon appears in the reduction of the idea of Zion to a modern, secular, and industrialized state. It is the staple of Marxist, Nietzschean, and Kierkegaardian critique of modern societies that language and human relations dry up and are smothered in modern societies. Likewise, the Israeli government's refusal to talk to the Arabs as Thous is also monological, that is, it talks to itself when it does not address the Arabs as co-human. It is then arguable that monologicality is the object of Buber's critique in these different controversies.

Kierkegaard, to adopt Buber's contrast, can also be understood as resisting the monologicality of some aspects of modern society. The aesthete manipulates, controls, lies to, and deceives his victim. That is, he speaks to control the situation, but this speech produces no change in the relationship. The dialogue of the aesthetes indicates that they do not listen to the speech of humans in the sense that they are willing to change, but rather to impose their will in every situation (SLW 7–86). By contrast, Judge William speaks to his friend, writes him letters, they discuss issues during visits, but his young seducer-friend still proves incapable of changing, for he cannot hear. Language is focused again when we see Judge William and his wife in intimate conversation drinking breakfast coffee in a secluded bower (SLW 82–85). The subjective thinker lives with other individuals and is decisively interested in the dynamics of communication (CUP 72–126). The believer in Religion B hears and responds to a teacher (PF). Kierkegaard's thought is pervaded with the risk and opportunity of dialogue.

Both thinkers are philosophers of the word, of dialogue, of the dynamics of communication, and understand that one's life and will can be changed when one hears the word of the other. Thus they affirm the politics of existence while at the same time they critique much of the malpractice of politics as a violation of existence.

Notes

1. Regarding what was available to Buber about Kierkegaard's social thought see, Janik, "Haecker, Kierkegaard and the Early Brenner," pp. 189–222. For an examination of each of Buber's texts about Kierkegaard, see Perkins, "Buber and Kierkegaard," in Gordon and Bloch, eds., *Martin Buber*, pp. 275–304.

2. Buber, *Pointing the Way*, pp. 208–19. See Gordon, "Existential Guilt," in Gordon and Bloch, pp. 215–31. Also, Sausser, *Existence and Utopia*.

3. Woocher, "Martin Buber's Politics of Dialogue," *Thought*, 241–57. Weltsch, "Buber's Political Philosophy," in Schilpp and Friedman, eds., *The Philosophy of Martin Buber*, pp. 435–50.

4. Buber, *I and Thou*, part One, esp. p. 53. I will use the sigla "I-T" for interlinear references to *I and Thou*.

5. Buber, "Autobiographical Fragments," in Schilpp and Friedman, p. 10.

6. For an interesting defence of Buber's extended sense of "Thou," see Berry's *Mutuality*, chap. 1.

7. On Buber's loose and frequently obscure writing, see Kaufmann, "Buber's Failures and Triumph," in Gordon and Bloch, pp. 3–18, esp. pp. 8–10.

8. In this sentence I refer to the compromises in neighbor love permitted or demanded by the prejudices of our culture and which we unconsciously appropriate. It does not befit any of us, for instance, to be self-righteously harsh on Monica for her purchase of a concubine for the sexual relief of her passionate son, Augustine.

9. For an extended discussion of these parallels, see Perkins, "Buber and Kierkegaard," in Gordon and Bloch, pp. 275–78.

10. Buber, of course, uses the word "person" here in a normative sense, for an egoist is still a person. Buber's rejection of the term "ego" is included in a note in Kaufmann's translation of *I and Thou*, pp. 111–12. However, "ego," which Buber preferred and which Kaufmann used, is too bland and does not indicate the admonition against the egotist voiced by Buber in these sections. See also, Wood, *Martin Buber's Ontology*, pp. 81–82.

11. "Validity and Limitation of the Political Principle," in Buber, *Pointing the Way,* p. 217. Weltsch, "Buber's Political Philosophy," in Schillp and Freidman, p. 442.

12. Kierkegaard's single reference to Hobbes (from 1842–1843) is to the problem of evil and was suggested by Leibniz. See Kierkegaard, JP 1:894.

13. I shall not analyze the argument that conscience is a relation of love (WL 136–52).

14. See Mannheim's critique of the escapist and his misleading remark on Kierkegaard in *Ideology and Utopia,* pp. 259–60. Such inane remarks do less harm to the reputation of Kierkegaard today than to that of Mannheim, but they constitute a sad chapter in the history of Kierkegaard's reception in the "learned" disciplines.

15. For details about Kierkegaard's adjustment to the modern state, see especially, Perkins, "Kierkegaard's Critique of the Modern State," *Inquiry* 27 (1984):207–18. On Kierkegaard's politics, see Westphal, *Kierkegaard's Critique of Reason and Society.* On Kierkegaard's relation to the broad cultural and political movements of the age, see Kirmmse, *Kierkegaard in Golden Age Denmark.* See also Perkins, ed., *International Kierkegaard Commentary: Two Ages.*

16. See the distinction between the social and political principles elaborated at the beginning of this chapter and note 2.

17. Buber, "Reply to My Critics," in Schilpp and Friedman, p. 725.

18. Kaufmann argues that "As long as we fail to see Buber's central attempt to create a humanistic religion, we do not understand him." Kaufmann, in Gordon and Bloch, p. 17.

19. Buber's relation to official Judaism is not widely discussed. See Gordon, "The Sheltered Aesthete" in Gordon and Bloch, pp. 37–39, where Gordon recounts the pettiness surrounding Buber's appointment at the Hebrew University. On the relation of Buber and the law, see Friedman, ed., *Martin Buber's Life and Work,* discussion with Rosenzweig, vol. 2, pp. 40–49; with Prinz, pp. 230–32; on *For the Sake of Heaven,* pp. 321–25.

11 | Communicative Freedom and Negative Theology

Jürgen Habermas[a]
Translated with Notes by Martin J. Matuštík
and Patricia J. Huntington

MICHAEL THEUNISSEN owes the measured, yet radical character of his thought to the fact that he was equally receptive to Kierkegaard and Marx, i.e., to those two thinkers who in their own way confronted Hegel's thought more radically than others did. Thus, the two philosophical theories that brought Kierkegaard and Marx back to philosophical life for the first time in our century, namely, existential ontology and Hegelian Marxism, attract Theunissen's particular interest. Theunissen engages in critical exchange with both traditions in order to retrieve their original inspirations: From his point of view, the authentic Kierkegaard and the critically appropriated Marx are not shown wrong by either Heidegger and Sartre or Horkheimer and Adorno.[1] In this Theunissen can find support in the results of an earlier enacted communications-theoretic turn. This turn brings out [zur Geltung bringt] the relevance of the second person attitude (of the other in the role of a thou) in contrast to the subject-object relationship determined by the attitudes of the first and the third person.

The dialogical encounter with the addressed other, whose response eludes one's control, first opens to the individual the intersubjective space for his or her authentic selfhood.[b] Theunissen developed his philosophy of dialogue in confrontation with the theories of transcendental intersubjectivity from Husserl to Sartre. His philosophy not only received some suggestions from Buber's "theology of the between" [Theologie des Zwischen], but is itself derived from theological themes. In effect, Theunissen understands that "center" of the intersubjective space, which is opened by the dialogical encounter and in turn enables the dialogical self-becoming of the self and the other, as the "Kingdom of God" that precedes and underlies the sphere of this subjectivity. Referring to Luke 17:21 — "the Kingdom of God is *in the midst of you,*" Theunissen explains: "It [the Kingdom of God] exists as a present future *between* those human beings who are called to it." Throughout his life Theunissen attempted to capture *philosophically* the content of this one central saying. For,

[p]resumably, the reality that the dialogic of the between shows itself to be from a theological viewpoint is *the* [only] side of the kingdom of God that philosophy can grasp at all: this is not the side of "grace," but that of the

"will." The will to dialogical self-becoming belongs thus to the "striving" after the kingdom of God in such a way that its future is promised in the present love of human beings for one another.[2]

Later Theunissen attempted to link this theological subject matter with critical social theory in order to make Kierkegaard compatible with Marx by using the help of the concept "communicative freedom." To be sure, he did not avoid the option that finally presented itself: the choice between the theological and the materialistic reading of reconciliation. Instead of a rationally *encouraged* transcendence from within, he always preferred the proleptic prefiguration [*Vorschein*] of the eschaton that can instill *trusting faith* [Zuversicht] in the present.[c] Still, one should be able to ground this option philosophically as well. That is the claim that I wish to examine in what follows. Theunissen finds such grounds above all in Kierkegaard; and he seems to find them especially in a Fichtean form of thought that was renewed by Kierkegaard. Naturally Theunissen does not wish to hide behind the authority of the author of the *Sickness unto Death*. Kierkegaard's arguments, however, give Theunissen the impetus for a negativistic grounding of authentic selfhood.

First, I would like to delineate the character of the claim that the essential contents of the Christian expectation of salvation can be justified under the conditions of postmetaphysical thinking.[d] Next I discuss the arguments with which Theunissen attempts to redeem this strong claim for those "paths of philosophical thinking that can still be traversed" today. My critical inquiries do not touch my solidarity with an admirable undertaking whose practical incentives and intentions are close to mine.

I.

Throughout the history of Western thought since Augustine, Christianity entered into numerous symbiotic relations with the metaphysical traditions of Platonic origin. In concurrence with such theologians as Jürgen Moltmann and Johann Baptist Metz,[3] Theunissen strives to restore the original eschatological content of Christianity, freed from its Hellenistic wrappings. Its core is a form of radically historical thinking that is incompatible with essentialist concepts: "The power of the past over the future first originates the constraining character of the reality that is in need of salvation. This reality, which stands in need of salvation, forms a universal connection of constraints because in it the future is constantly overpowered by the past."[4] This sentence has a distinct theological meaning in Theunissen that stretches beyond Adorno's *Negative Dialectic*: "If it is the power of the past that makes humans sink into the powerlessness of not being able to act, they awaken from this powerlessness through the liberating hand of God. Temporal existence, negatively viewed in Plato's metaphysics as that which changes, receives the positive character of that which *can* be changed."[5] What separates Theunissen's position from similar theologians is especially his claim that he carries out their shared intention of dehellenizing Christianity by non-theological means. Theunissen derives these means from the fundamental metaphysical principles of the very Platonism that he seeks to overcome. In doing so, he abandons that careful distinction between the aspects of "grace" and "will," that allows the kingdom of God to reveal itself only to theologians or to the theologians and philosophers.[e] Meanwhile he appears to believe that, with arguments, he can close the gap that stands between the appeal to the reality experienced in faith, on the one hand, and the persuasiveness of philosophical grounds on the other.

The Benjaminian intuition that the bad continuum of all previous history must be broken up—the scream of the pained creature that all "must become otherwise"—certainly holds more than the mere power of suggestion after the catastrophes of our century. Today we are plagued by the regressions that were triggered by the fall of the Soviet empire. Furthermore, in light of these phenomena, neither the impulse to *rebel* against the power that the past exercises over the future[6] nor the imperative to break the shackles of the fatal return of the same are in need of extensive justification: "Benjamin has described the inexpressible sadness evoked by the sight of history fossilized into nature. Only if time were to become different would there be real history."[7] In which sense, however, can we understand such an expectation? Should we understand it as an expectation of an imminent event, as trusting faith [*Zuversicht*] in a promised turn, as hope for the success of a favored or even blessed undertaking? Or should the semantic potential of the expectation of salvation only keep open a *dimension* from which, even in profane times, we can obtain a measure that allows us to find direction in that which is better at *any given time*, and from which we can draw courage?

By means of more or less adequate reasons, we can wrest from pessimism and even from doubt the hope that our actions are not *a fortiori* meaningless. Such rationally motivated encouragement, however, should not be confused with existential faith [*existentielle Zuversicht*], which emerges from a fully completed skepticism that originates from a despair that is turned against oneself. *Hope* that "all will change in time" differs from the *belief* [*Glauben*] "that time itself will change." The ambiguity of the formulation of the "change of time" occludes the difference between confidence [*Vertrauen*] in an eschatological change of the world and the profane expectation that our praxis in the world can, in spite of all, promote a turn towards the better. On this side of *spes fidei*,[f] which thrives on a Kierkegaardian dialectic of despair, a space remains for fallible hope that has been taught by a skeptical, yet not defeatist reason. This *docta spes* is not contemptible, but it is not indestructible either. Theunissen would probably not want to deny this distinction, but would hold fast to the task of anchoring with philosophical reasons the profane hope in the eschatological one.

In his most recent publication Theunissen names three paths of philosophical thinking that appear still traversable to him today. First, philosophy should be able to give a critical appropriation of the history of metaphysics in its entirety. Second, philosophy can contribute to reflection on the special disciplines. And third, from its postmetaphysical position, philosophy can even salvage the metaphysical contents of tradition that elude scientific objectification. According to this program of historical self-reflection, philosophy assures itself of the ideas that it developed as much in the passage through the sciences as by systematically going beyond them.[8] So both themes, which Theunissen treats historically, already betray a systematic purpose. Going through Hegel's *Logic*, Theunissen analyzes the relationship of subjectivity and intersubjectivity under the heading of *communicative freedom*. And having in view the *proleptic future* of the Christian promise that reaches into the present, he analyzes those metaphysical concepts from Parmenides to Hegel that are forgetful of time [*zeitvergessene Begriffe*]. In both cases Theunissen ontologizes theology, i.e., he hellenizes Christianity, and thus covers up the soteriological content of radically historical thinking. Like Heidegger, Theunissen strives for a deconstruction of the history of metaphysics. He does not, however, entertain the "archeological" concern to take a leap that would return him from modernity to the time before Jesus and Socrates. Rather, Theunissen aims at a philosophically grounded negative theology whose goal is to call back an alienated modernity from its dispersion and to make intelligible yet again the message of salvation that has become incomprehensible.

II.

Theunissen brings a hypothesis derived from the post-Hegelian philosophy of dialogue into Hegel's *Logic*, which in its way summarizes the history of Western metaphysics: "Hegel grounds the entire logic on the hypothesis that all that is can be itself only in relation, indeed exists only as this relation to 'its other.' "[9] Theunissen contrasts this self-relation that is actualized in the intersubjective relation to the other with the being-for-itself of subjectivity. Genuine selfhood expresses itself through communicative freedom, i.e., as to-be-in-the-other-as-in-one's-*self*. Love, i.e., to-be-in-one's-self-as-*in another*, is the complement of communicative freedom. The connection, or even the coincidence, between freedom and love characterizes the intact [*unversehrte*] intersubjectivity of a relation of symmetrical and reciprocal recognition. In this interrelation the one is not a barrier to the other's freedom but rather a condition for the other's self-realization. And the communicative freedom of the one cannot be complete without the realized freedom of all others. With the concept of solidarity-based and noncoercive individualization through socialization, Theunissen places the concrete universal into a dialogic setting which he can turn critically against Hegel himself: "Abstraction" means then "indifference towards what is different," an indifference which neutralizes "the relation to the other." This indifference in turn amounts to domination because it distorts communicative freedom. Therefore, if we read Hegel's dialectic from the point of view of a theory of communication, we find that it contains a *critique of domination.*

Theunissen argues with Hegel against Hegel. He emphasizes those passages in which Hegel deviates from the path of dialectically investigating the "praxis of speaking with one another" and fails to pay attention to the dimension of a linguistic pragmatics that is within reach, turning instead to the logical analysis of "mere judgment or proposition."[10] Hegel's undue narrowing of communication to the logical-semantic perspective exaggerates the importance of the reflexive model. In this fashion, he privileges the being-in-itself of the epistemic self-relation over against the relation to the other. Where communicative freedom would demand the reciprocal recognition of difference and otherness, the reflexive model enforces unity and totalization.[11]

Theunissen also resists the affirmative dimension of a theodicy concealed in the dialectical logic for which the real is the rational. The difference between that which is without content and that which is simply undeveloped vanishes in Hegel's concept of the untrue [*der Begriff des Unwahren*]. Theunissen wants to restore this difference with the help of Marx's distinction between representation and critique. The dissolution of objective appearance does not always bring to light the truth of a new positivity; it quite often retains the destructive meaning of unveiling the hidden truth about something.[12] Interestingly, we can see already at this juncture what, for all his criticism of Hegel, Theunissen exempts from critique, namely, the concept of the absolute.

Indeed, Hegel's conception of determinate negation presupposes a unity between critique and representation [*Darstellung*], and this does remove the critical sting from representation. Yet Theunissen reduces this supposition to a merely methodological question, even though Hegel's claim to the unity of critique and representation relies upon the substantive assumption that the world process as a whole is logically constituted. Theunissen does not touch upon the metaphysical core of the problem that no pathogenesis of history can arise from the orthogenesis of nature, if the procession of history follows the same logical forms as natural processes. He stops short of criticizing Hegel for *totalizing* the being-in-oneself-in-another into a communicative constitution of the world *as a whole.* The idea of the unity between one's self-relation and the relation to the other dominates the movement of Hegel's *entire* logic and extends to reality as a whole conceived as intersubjectivity. This idea of unity is not at all limited to the sphere of interhuman relations. Theunissen agrees to that, even if he believes that Hegel's *Logic,* grasped as a universal communication theory, "must reveal a structure that finds its appropriate reality in the relations that human subjects have to one another."[13] Theunissen does not, however, reject Hegel's metaphysical assumption that the basic structure of the being-in-oneself-in-another, read off from dialogical understanding,[g] reaches beyond the horizon of the life-world to the world as a whole.

Theunissen is indeed convinced that every interpersonal relation is embedded in the relation to a wholly other that precedes the relation to the concrete other. This wholly other embodies an absolute freedom which we must presuppose in order to explain how our communicative freedom is possible at all: "the absolute can only be that which releases the other from itself in such a way that the other's freedom is at the same time its own freedom from and to the absolute."[14] This way of thinking goes back to Jewish and Protestant mysticism, mediated by Schwäbian Pietism: God confirms himself [*sic*] in his freedom in that he sets an equally free alter ego apart from himself. By releasing humans into their freedom, so that they can lose [*verfehlen*] and achieve their selfhood by themselves, God moves from the world back into Godhood. In the history of human communication, God remains present only as the enabling and at the same time orienting structure of reconciliation.[h] God is present as the promise as well as the existing presence of a fulfilled future.[15]

As one can see, the systematic appropriation of the history of metaphysics can make contemporary problems that are perhaps not yet passe. But can this appropriation eliminate the distance by which we are removed from the solutions that are proposed in the language of metaphysics? Reading speculative logic in terms of communications theory at best *familiarizes* us with the idea that the communicative freedom of [the] being-in-itself-in-another presupposes the absolute freedom of the wholly other. In the end it remains undecided how we are to understand the possibility admitted in the structure of undistorted [*unverzerrter*] intersubjectivity. Should we understand it as an idealized surplus that demands from the participants in communicative action that they engage in acts of transcending *all by themselves,* or as the breakthrough of an occurring event [*vorgängiges Geschehen*] of communicative liberation that requires *self-abandon* from those who have been emancipated into freedom? If God, who is said to have withdrawn once into the surplus [*über-schießende*] structure of mutual linguistic understanding, had given history over to creatures who are condemned to communicative freedom, then this myth of the self-limiting God would ultimately also have to fall victim to their labor of profanization. If, however, God *remains* the only guarantor in history who keeps open the possibility that one can escape from the natural cycle and continuity of history ruled by the past, then the concept of the absolute—already presupposed in every act of successful mutual understanding—stands in need of an adequate philosophical explanation. This task cannot be solved by following the path of the destruction of the history of metaphysics.

III.

For this reason Theunissen attempts to achieve a postmetaphysical grounding for the metaphysical contents of communicative freedom. He develops his argument in connection with Kierkegaard's *Sickness unto Death*.

a) First, Theunissen demarcates his "negative" mode of proceeding from a "normative" one. The architectonic of reason supplanted objective teleology in modernity after the substantive and essentialist concepts of metaphysics that anchored what ought to be[i] in the very order of things were discharged. Ever since, we can no longer win normative contents ontologically from being itself, but rather must obtain them reconstructively from the necessary subjective conditions of the objective validity of our experiences and judgments. Admittedly, the pragmatic-linguistic turn from the paradigm of consciousness to that of mutual understanding has once more imparted a new direction to this investigation of the transcendental and normatively rich conditions. Now it is necessary to explain how this fact of successful intersubjective understanding is possible. In the general and unavoidable pragmatic presuppositions of communicative action we confront the counterfactual content of those idealizations that all subjects must assume insofar as they orient their action at all towards claims to validity. We can ascertain the nonarbitrary character of normative contents *in the broader sense*, viz., as unavoidable presuppositions of communication, neither ontologically through the goal-oriented constitution of being nor epistemologically through the rational constitution of subjectivity. The nonarbitrary character is confirmed only by the lack of an alternative to the praxis in which communicatively socialized subjects always already find themselves. Using this formal pragmatic approach I myself have tried to locate a rational potential in the validating basis of an action oriented to reaching mutual understanding [*die Geltungsbasis verständigungsorientierten Handelns*] to which critical social theory can refer as its normative ground.[16]

Theunissen rejects this "normativism." Yet he does so not because he worries that there are metaphysical traces of essential determinations and objective teleology in this normative approach.[17] Rather, the "negativism" that is to guide Theunissen's own account introduces once again normative content into the ontic, although it does so by way of an inversion of the ought inherent in being. While the logical operation of negation refers to an affirmatively raised validity claim made by the second person [hearer], the "ontic negativity" is supposed to belong to the thing itself that we evaluate negatively: "By the 'negative' we understand that with which we do not agree or that which we do not want (are incapable of wanting) to exist. In this (ontological) sense the negative should not be."[18] Admittedly, for Theunissen the negativity of that which should not be, or of that which is the objectively untrue, no longer refers, as does an objective teleology of being, to entities in the world or to the universe of being as a whole. From the point of view of an inverted philosophy of history, the constitution of the historical world in which humans live and suffer is negative. The negativity of the constitution of being is the negativity that we or I *experience* in the life world and in life history. Therefore, the investigation must start from "the negative of the existing world" and first recover from it a criterion for critique. Theunissen justifies this "negativistic" procedure by claiming that the complete pathology of the ruling global condition long ago corrupted the criteria for a *nonsuspicious* differentiation between health and sickness, truth and untruth, and idea and appearance. Once we have unmasked the sickness of the healthy, every diagnosis carried out in light of an unquestioned and presupposed normality falls prey to a hermeneutics of suspicion.

b) Following Marx and Kierkegaard, there appear to be two points of departure for attempting to justify negatively the potential contained in communicative freedom for reconciliation and improvement: the social *alienation* of societies characterized by capitalistic rationalization and the existential *despair* of the individual particularized in secularized modernity.¹ To a large extent Theunissen left the first approach to his followers.[19] He himself concentrates on working out Kierkegaard's argument for the identity of religious faith and selfhood.[20] Theunissen's reconstruction of this train of thought characterizes the phenomenon of despair in terms of ontic negativity. Despair radicalizes the negativity of a difficult or oppressive condition—as experienced in boredom, care, anxiety and melancholy—by rendering it a deficient mode of human existence itself. Despair manifests the failure of human life as a whole. Yet as that which per se ought not to be, despair also betrays something about its failed opposite: successful "selfhood." Therefore, the entirety of the phenomenon of despair can offer Kierkegaard the initial subject matter from which he can begin his analysis by considering the sickness of the self, even before he determines a normative concept of self.

After this methodological clarification, Theunissen turns his transcendental questioning to the phenomenon of despair: "how must human beings be constituted and how is the human self to be thought, if despair, which humans experience as their reality, is to be possible?"[21] This question immediately implies a further question: How is that selfhood possible that must be presupposed in the very process of emancipation from the ever present undertow of despair. What makes selfhood as a process of "permanent annihilation of the possibility of despair" possible? Kierkegaard gives the following answer: the self can succeed in being its own self only insofar as in its self-positing it relates to another through which it has itself been posited. One escapes despair only to the extent that one rests one's self "transparently in the power that has established it."[k] This thesis is grounded by an existential dialectic concerning two basic modalities of despair.[l] In the despair of not willing to be oneself, we experience that we cannot escape ourselves, that we are condemned to freedom, and that we must posit ourselves. But in the next stage of in despair willing to be oneself, we experience the futility of our self-willed striving to posit ourselves as a self by our own power. In the end, we can wrest the despair of *defiant* self-grounding from ourselves only by becoming aware of the finitude of our freedom and in that fashion become cognizant of our dependence on an infinite power: "The conditions of not being in despair are at the same time those of successful selfhood. That in positing oneself one must presuppose the other, who posited one in this very self-positing, thus defines one's selfhood."[22]

c) Theunissen considers this proof of the foundation of one's selfhood in faith by existential dialectic as "an argument that is difficult to refute." However, even from his point of view the argument needs to be supplemented with regard to the communicative constitution of the potentiality for one's selfhood.[m] As an explication of the fundamental structure of being-in-oneself-in-another, this explanation implies only this much: One can only be oneself in one's finite freedom to the extent that, in recognizing God's absolute freedom, one frees oneself from a narcissistic, self-enclosed selfhood and returns to one's own selfhood from the infinite distanciation of faith-inspired communication with the wholly other. The explanation remains, however, incomplete with regard to that trivial this-worldly aspect of being-in-oneself-in-another in terms of which we encounter communicative freedom first and foremost. Theunissen criticizes the peculiar worldless character of selfhood that Kierkegaard's negative procedure posited against despair: "No doubt Kierkegaard, like Hegel, conceives selfhood or freedom as being-in-oneself-in-another, yet in his understanding the other is ultimately God and no longer the world."[23] We must still bring the mere *reflexivity* of facing one's self-relation into the *intersubjectivity* of letting oneself get involved with the other: "Accordingly, the original dimension of becoming free from oneself is revealed by love. This has also been represented to us in faith."[24]

Thus, Theunissen takes a reconstructed Kierkegaard and turns back to a Hegel whom he read previously through a theory of communication.[n] He does so in order to ground the complementary relationship between communicative freedom and love in the absolute freedom and love of God. But then "all true love of other humans [is] love of God."

IV.

Even when we follow this communication theoretical expansion of existential dialectic, the question remains whether or not Theunissen's judiciously reconstructed Kierkegaardian argument that must carry the real burden of proof achieves what it must achieve. The question is whether or not it succeeds in proving that, in order to be wholly oneself, one must presuppose the empowerment of one's own communicative freedom through the absolute freedom of God. My reservations are directed as much at the negative method as at the application of transcendental questioning to anthropological facts.[25]

To be sure, we prefer not to be in despair. But rejecting the negatively valued phenomenon of despair does not issue in any positive significance for the bare absence of the phenomenon—namely, of not being in despair.° This state of affairs may well represent a necessary condition for one's authentic selfhood, but it is not by itself a sufficient condition. Only when, utilizing clinical concepts such as spiritual health, we make *from the outset* a strong internal link between the phenomenon of despair and the mode of willing to be oneself, can the *conquering* of despair indicate the *successful* achievement of selfhood from one's own self. But then it is only the normatively substantive hermeneutical preunderstanding that discloses despair as a symptom of sickness. Such an interpretation can no longer be considered as entirely negativistic.

Furthermore, we may only apply transcendental questions concerning the conditions of the potentiality for being oneself to existential mood, such as despairingly willing to be oneself, if we assume the universality and irreplacability of this "fundamental state of mind."ᴾ The transcendental analysis of conditions is meaningful only with regard to achievements of a general nature for which there are, thus, no functional equivalents. Making the factual states of affairs or personal existential experiences transcendental has the awkward consequence that we must make something that occurs in the world into a category that is constitutive of the world itself. If the transcendental grounding of selfhood is to function as the state of non-despair, then the act of despairingly willing to be oneself would have to belong to the human condition and so would have to represent something like a general anthropological fact. In addition, we would have to be able to rule out other phenomena of undespairingly willing to be oneself as candidates for an analogical grounding of selfhood.

This is not all. The real difficulty arises from the circumstance that the fact that is in need of explanation somehow must already be a proven result; but the question concerning the conditions of its possibility can only begin with this fact. We must pose the transcendental question with regard to *validated* products that fulfill the relevant conditions of validity: true statements, grammatical sentences, valid speech acts, rightful norms, plausible theories, successful works of literature and art, etc. From Theunissen's reconstructed view, Kierkegaard also inquires about the conditions of the possibility. Even though Kierkegaard is not concerned with the conditions of the possibility of a successful product, he still raises the questions of the process of successful selfhood: How is selfhood possible as a *process* of overcoming an ever increasing despair? However, the Kantian question of how objective experience is possible concerns making transparent the genesis of an achievement that has already been accepted as valid. We *encounter* it as a fact in need of an explanation, and we can reproduce it in any number of examples. Kierkegaard, however, begins from a fact of quite another kind—from the despair of *willing* to be oneself in which success remains an open question. Validation is still outstanding for that which Kierkegaard wants to make transparent in its genesis. For the normal is the sickness that provides the contrasting background against which a "healthy" form of human existence first becomes apparent. The mode of successful selfhood can be posited only *hypothetically* for the purposes of a transcendental elucidation of the conditions of its own possibility. From these premises one can justify faith at most functionally, namely as a suitable means for reaching the goal that is implied by willing to be oneself. The functional grounding of faith, however, is insufficient for what Theunissen would like to ground by Kierkegaard's argument, namely the following thesis: "The becoming of freedom *for* oneself out of freedom *from* oneself occurs at the core of faith itself as the communicative genesis of selfhood."[26] A faith that is functionally grounded destroys itself.[q]

Theunissen overestimated the significance of his reconstructed Kierkegaardian argument. Even the attempt to supplement the vertical communicative relation to God with the horizontal axis of interpersonal relation in the philosophy of dialogue does not supply the expected result.[r] To be sure, from the perspective of formal pragmatic analysis, communicative actors who orient their action towards context-transcending validity claims are in every successful act of mutual understanding challenged to achieve a transcendence from within. But Theunissen does not rest content with this thin [*spröden*] truth. He would like to see in successful acts of mutual understanding a transcendence that breaks into history and constitutes the promising presence of an absolute power that first makes possible our finite freedom. Thus he constantly adduces new arguments aimed at transforming the Kierkegaardian "leap" into a rationally comprehensible movement.[27] For Theunissen is too much of a philosopher to accept Dostoyevsky's claim: "If someone were to prove to me that Christ existed outside of truth, and were it truly so that the truth existed outside of Christ, then I would rather remain with Christ than with the truth" (from a letter to Natalja Vonwisin of February 20, 1854). Theunissen believes that he has *philosophical grounds* which justify and reinforce him in holding onto a dehellenized conception of the eschaton. I may not recognize these reasons, or indeed recognize the rational motives behind the conviction for even having such reasons.[s]

V.

I gather that one motive for this certainty issues from the harsh polemic that Theunissen carries out against the formalism of duty-based ethics [*Sollens-*

ethiken], following in the footsteps of Hegel's critique of Kant.[28] Freedom understood in the moral sense of self-determination manifests itself in a free will; and Kant calls free only the will that is committed to moral insights and which acts in the equal interest of all. The task of moral theory consists in clarifying how correct moral judgments are possible. In principle, we think that we are already capable of making a rational decision in practical matters. However, given that the ideas of justice and solidarity are interwoven with forms of communicative socialization, discourse ethics is an attempt to explain this fact in terms of the general pragmatic presuppositions of communicative action and argumentation. Against this weak moral conception, Theunissen renews Hegel's critique of the powerlessness of abstract duty. Indeed, in order to attain practical effectiveness, moral insights must take into account concrete forms of life.[29] For moral insights appeal only to *forces in need of encouragement* in autonomous human beings who are able to know that, even though they are dependent upon the luck of circumstances, they can only count on themselves.

This is different with freedom understood in the ethical sense of self-realization. Ethical freedom manifests itself in a consciously led life whose success cannot be expected exclusively from the autonomy of a finite being. Theunissen seems to proceed from the view that the task of ethics is to clarify successful selfhood, in a manner analogical to the way moral theory explains the fact that we always trust that we are capable of correct moral judgments. However, ethics must then be in a position to name something that guarantees for everybody the same possibility of a life that does not fail' so that we may categorize the *potentiality* for being oneself as a transcendental fact in a similar manner as we do the competence to pass correct moral judgments. But achieving a successful life does not lie in the same way in our power as do correct moral judgements and moral action. When we attempt to find the transcendental condition of the possibility of a successful life in the same way, the inaccessibility of the condition of a successful life shows why some *other* power must guarantee the success of being oneself. This problem shows why already for Theunissen argumentative strategy cannot succeed without having recourse to absolute freedom. Yet Kant saw that the logic of *this* type of questioning warrants at best positing God as a practical postulate. Our need not to be in despair and to keep open a prospect for happiness even under the domination of time constitutes an insufficient ground for holding that philosophy can give *confident* information [*zuversichtliche* Auskunft].

These reflections at least make clear the point of contention: Under the conditions of postmetaphysical thinking, can we reply to the classical question of the good life (in its modern rendition as a question of successful selfhood) not merely formally but in such a fashion that, for example, we draw a philosophical silhouette of the evangelical message?

I suspect that one additional motive for Theunissen's affirmative answer to this question lies in his selective description of communication. That is to say, instead of making use of the entire system of personal pronouns, the philosophy of dialogue replaces the subject-object relation (or the relationship between the third and first person found in the philosophy of consciousness) with the relationship between the first and second person. The epistemic self-relation is first conceptualized according to a model of self-observation; then, a communicatively mediated self-relation, structured after the ideal of an I-Thou relationship, takes the place of this reflexive model. The communicative self-relation is conceived as a practical self-relation. Accordingly, it accentuates either the second person (in the relation of love, viz., that to be in oneself is to be in *another*) or the first person (in communicatively mediated freedom, viz., that to be in another is to be in one's *self*). However, in doing this, a special case—namely reaching a reciprocal ethical self-understanding concerning who one is and wants to be—is transformed into the prototype for processes of mutual understanding in general. The philosophy of dialogue de-emphasizes the structure of mutual understanding itself and shifts attention onto the existential self-experience of the participants in dialogue which occurs *as a consequence* of successful communication.[u] In the structure of coming-to-an-understanding-with-one-another-about-something, the philosophy of dialogue overemphasizes intersubjectivity, thereby neglecting the relation to the objective world or to that *about which* we communicate. In this fashion the dimension of truth claims is closed off in favor of authenticity. And even this truth dimension can only be held open, against the narcissistic undertow of a worldless discourse of self-understanding, by invoking a universality that is established, so to speak, behind our backs but which ought to first make communication as such possible.

For this reason, Theunissen pressed already in 1969 for a recovery of an "absolute objectivity" that "stretches beyond intersubjectivity and grounds the subject as such."[30] In a later study dedicated to the "obscure" relation between universality and intersubjectivity, he repeated the thesis, "that we must realize universality in our self-realization."[31] Theunissen does not believe that we may give up the reference to a foundational moment that guarantees objectivity and truth because otherwise "intersubjectivity . . . is only an expanded subjectivity."[32] Such a corrective, however, is no longer necessary if we free the structure of coming-to-an-understanding-with-one-another-about-something from its unduly narrow reference to "the other" established by the philosophy of dialogue. If we *integrate* the third person attitude toward something in the objective world with the performative attitude that the first and second person participants in discourse take towards one another, then the complementarity, which Theunissen claims for the relation between freedom and love, also crumbles. Communicative freedom thus assumes the profane but not contemptible form of a competence for responsibility ascribed to communicatively acting subjects. This freedom consists in the following: That the participants are able to orient their actions toward validity claims and, in doing so, they raise validity claims, adopt a "yes" or "no" position toward other validity claims, and enter into illocutionary obligations.

In the interplay of communicative freedom among finite subjects, a horizon opens in which we experience *even* the domination of the past over the future as a stigma; this stigma permeates the social as much as the living historical reality. Whether we cynically adapt to this reality or submit to it with melancholy, whether or not we despair of it and ourselves, we get information about this from those phenomena in which Theunissen rightly takes a burning interest. The philosopher, however, will have to give *another* description of these phenomena than the theologian, even if it is not at all a discouraging description. Reflections from the damaged life are the subject matter equally for the one discourse as for the other, but they are different according to their status and claim once the theological and philosophical discourses are distinguished [*entmischt*].³³ We recognize philosophical discourses by the fact that they remain on this side of the rhetoric of fate and promise.ᵛ

If, as Theunissen takes for granted, anomalies themselves become a norm, then admittedly the above phenomena can no longer be kept separate. Still, in order to recognize these relevant phenomena at all, we may have to conduct philosophy in the fashion, but no more than *in the fashion* of a negative theology.

Author's Notes

1. On Heidegger, cf. Theunissen, *Negative Theologie der Zeit*, 343ff.; on Horkheimer, see Theunissen, "Gesellschaft und Geschichte," 1ff.
2. Theunissen, *The Other*, 383 / *Der Andere*, 506. (Translator's note: We have altered the published English translation; italics are in Theunissen's German original.)
3. Metz, "Anamnetische Vernunft," 733ff.
4. Theunissen, *Negative Theologie der Zeit*, 370.
5. Ibid., 370f.
6. Habermas, *Vergangenheit als Zukunft*.
7. Theunissen, *Negative Theologie der Zeit*, 65.
8. Theunissen, "Möglichkeiten des Philosophierens heute," in *Negative Theologie der Zeit*, 13–36. (Translator's note: On the three ways, see also n. 27 below.)
9. Theunissen, *Sein und Schein*, 29.
10. Ibid., 468ff.
11. Ibid., 455ff.
12. Ibid., 70ff., 88f.
13. Ibid., 463.
14. Ibid., 326f.
15. This explains Theunissen's interest in an additional theme of the forgetfulness of time in metaphysics. He wants to find an appropriate concept for the future presence of the "time of eternity." Theunissen, "Zeit des Lebens," in *Negative Theologie der Zeit*, 299–320;

also Theunissen, "Die Zeitvergessenheit der Metaphysik. Zum Streit um Parmenides, fn. 8, 5–6a," in Honneth, et al., *Zwischenbetrachtungen*, 262–304.

16. Habermas, "Handlungen, Sprechakte, sprachlich vermittelte Interaktion und Lebenswelt," in *Nachmetaphysiches Denken*, 63–104. (Translator's note: This essay is not translated in *Postmetaphysical Thinking*.)

17. Theunissen, "Zwangszusammenhang und Kommunikation," in *Kritische Gesellschaftstheorie*, 41ff., esp. 53f.

18. Theunissen, "Negativität bei Adorno," in Friedeburg and Habermas, eds., *Adorno-Konferenz*, 41f. Additions in parentheses are mine.

19. Cf. the interesting work by Lohmann, *Indifferenz und Gesellschaft*.

20. Theunissen, *Das Selbst auf dem Grund der Verzweiflung*; cf. also the introduction and Theunissen's contribution to Theunissen and Greve, eds., *Materialien*.

21. Theunissen, *Das Selbst*, 25.

22. Theunissen, *Negative Theologie der Zeit*, 354. In this treatment of the prayer-based faith of Jesus ["den Gebetsglauben Jesu"], Theunissen summarizes his reconstruction of a Kierkegaardian argument that he thoroughly developed elsewhere (345ff.).

23. Theunissen, *Negative Theologie der Zeit*, 359.

24. Ibid., 360.

25. I am thankful to Lutz Wingert for his critical suggestions. (Translator's note: Lutz Wingert has worked as Habermas's assistant professor in Frankfurt since 1991.)

26. Theunissen, *Negative Theologie der Zeit*, 360.

27. Here we can also note the interesting studies on how psychiatric patients experience time: "Können wir in der Zeit glücklich sein?" and "Melancholisches Leiden unter der Herrschaft der Zeit," in Theunissen, *Negative Theologie der Zeit*, 37–88 and 218–84. I understand these philosophical attempts to appropriate psychological findings (mainly from the school of Binswanger), as steps toward the second of the three pathways of philosophical thinking that are still possible. (Translator's note: see n. 8 above.)

28. Theunissen, *Negative Theologie der Zeit*, 29–32.

29. Habermas, "Was macht eine Lebensform 'rational'?" in *Erläuterungen*, 31–48.

30. Theunissen, *Kritische Gesellschaftstheorie*, 30.

31. Theunissen, *Selbstverwirklichung und Allgemeinheit*, 8.

32. Theunissen, *Kritische Gesellschaftstheorie*, 31 and *Selbstverwirklichung und Allgemeinheit*, 27.

33. Habermas, "Transzendenz"/"Transcendence."

Translators' Notes

a. "Kommunikative Freiheit und Negative Theologie," copyright 1992 by Suhrkamp Verlag, is translated for this collection by permission from Jürgen Habermas and Suhrkamp Verlag. This essay was published in Emil Angehrn, Hinrich Fink-Eitel, Christian Iber and Georg Lohmann, eds., *Dialektischer Negativismus: Michael Theunissen zum 60. Geburtstag* (Frankfurt a/M: Suhrkamp, 1992), pp. 15–34. We are very grateful to Manfred Kuehn for helpful suggestions, though we bear sole responsibility for the final English text.

b. We find it more felicitous to express Habermas's active concern with one's inability to control or possess the other, rather than the passive or formal expression of "not being at one's own disposal" that unfortunately plays Habermas's existential sensibility down. Habermas's "eigentliches" ("authentic," "actual," or "genuine") "Selbstsein" ("being one's self," "being-oneself," "selfhood," "being of the self") is a frequently used term by Heidegger as well as by Theunissen in his *Der Andere / The Other*, which records the latter's commentary on Heidegger. Heidegger transcribes Kierkegaard's ontic categories of radical self-choice into formal categories of existential ontology. Habermas's own usage of this terminology discloses that he wants to retrieve for this and similar terms their Kierkegaardian ontic context, i.e., their performatively existential sense. For Heidegger's usage and translation, see the Glossary and Index for German and English expressions in Heidegger's *Being and Time*, and Feick, ed., *Index zu Heideggers "Sein und Zeit,"* 76.

c. Habermas utilizes this expression (found throughout this essay) first in the title of his earlier paper "Transcendenz von innen, Transcendenz ins Diesseits"/"Transcendence from Within, Transcendence in this World," where he thinks with Kierkegaard's performative-existential identity claim *against* some readings of Kierkegaard (and of communication theory) in new metaphysical justifications of theodicy and in theological dogmatic. Instead of the transcendence beyond this world, and consequently instead of any theological uses of communicative ethics, Habermas holds for the possibility of discursive transcendence towards the other in the world. This latter move provides a key to a linguistification of Kierkegaard's self-reflexive attitude. Habermas employs this linguistified existential posture in the service of critical social theory and of procedural justice in deliberative democracy.

d. See Habermas, *Nachmetaphysisches Denken / Postmetaphysical Thinking*.

e. The last two paragraphs of this essay clarify this formulation.

f. See translator's n. c above.

g. "Verständigung" in Habermas means mutual or intersubjective understanding. Note the related terms: "die Struktur des Sich-miteinander-über-etwas-Veständigens" = the structure of coming-to-an-understanding-with-another-about-something; and "Verständigungsparadigma" = the paradigm of mutual understanding. In order to be consistent with the previously published translations of Habermas's *Postmetaphysical Thinking* and *Justification and Application* we have rendered "ethische Selbstverständigung" as ethical self-understanding. But the reader should keep in mind that Habermas envisions this as a mutual or intersubjective act among individuals who come to their self-understanding in a dialogical setting of ethical-existential discourse. Below he will criticize the philosophy of dialogue for disregarding the third person perspective (the cognitive relationship to the objective world) in overemphasizing the first and second person perspectives (the reciprocal ethical self-understanding of the I-Thou relationship).

h. This sentence leaves open whether the structure of reconciliation is identical with God or whether God enables humans to achieve reconciliation. Habermas takes up this issue in the next paragraph where he speaks about the undecidability and inconclusiveness of the mystical model of absolute freedom.

i. "Das Seinsollende" = what ought to be, the necessity of being.

j. Habermas already links Marx and Kierkegaard in this fashion in his 1987 Copenhagen lecture; see his "Geschichtsbewußtsein," 172f. / "Historical Consciousness," 260f.

k. For Habermas's paraphrase of Kierkegaard's answer and for the last text cited by Habermas from Theunissen, see the first two pages of Kierkegaard's SUD (part 1, sect. A, a). This same portion of Kierkegaard's SUD is cited and discussed by Habermas in *Nachmetaphysisches Denken*, 203 / *Postmetaphysical Thinking*, 164.

l. For these two modalities, see the major divisions of Kierkegaard's SUD, part 1, as announced in the title for section A, a.

m. "Selbstseinkönnen" (potentiality for being one's self) or "Seinkönnen" (ownmost potentiality for being) are terms used by Heidegger in order to transpose Kierkegaard's ontic or performatively existential terminology of willing to be or not to be oneself into ontological or formally structural categories of the question of Being. See the German and English Indices in Heidegger's *Being and Time*; Feick, ed., *Index zu Heideggers "Sein Und Zeit,"* 75f. and translator's n. b above.

n. It is correct to say that Habermas's characterization of Theunissen's move fits equally well with Habermas's own (to be sure, profanized) communicative reconstruction of Kierkegaard's existential attitude. See Habermas, *Nachmetaphysisches Denken*, 33, 47, 155, 169f., 183, 191, 197, 200, 203f., 206, 208f., 268 / *Postmetaphysical Thinking*, 39, 24f., 117, 131, 143, 152, 159, 162, 164–67, 169f.

o. See Kierkegaard's observation that one's ignorance of one's being in despair is itself a form of despair (SUD, part 1, B).

p. Here Habermas uses a number of Heideggerian expressions: "Befindlichkeit" is usually rendered as "state-of-mind." This is related to the concepts of "Selbstseinkönnen" (see translator's n. m) and "Stimmung" ("mood"). For this usage and translation, see the Glossary and Indices for German and English expressions in Heidegger's *Being and Time* and Feick, ed., *Index zu Heideggers "Sein und Zeit,"* 7f.

q. Compare Habermas's functional reading of faith with Max Horkheimer, "Theismus und Atheismus" (1963), and "Zur Zukunft der kritischen Theorie" (1971), both in *Gesammelten Schriften*, 182–86 and 429–34; on Horkheimer, see Habermas, *Texte und Kontexte*, 91–126. See also Habermas's "Transcendenz von innen, Transcendenz ins Diesseits" / "Transcendence from Within, Transcendence in this World," for his debate with the theologians. See also translator's n. c above.

r. The notions of vertical axis (Kierkegaard's existential mode) and horizontal axis (Habermas's linguistification of Peirce's theological model of the ideal speech community to radicalize Theunissen's as well as Buber's philosophy of dialogue) appear for the first time in Habermas, *Nachmetaphysisches Denken*, 206 / *Postmetaphysical Thinking*, 167. See also Habermas's Kierkegaardian attack on "the leveling force of a universalism propelling itself inferentially from within reality itself" and his defense of the individual ("the moment of Secondness") in a critique of Peirce's emphatic Hegelianism, in Habermas's "Peirce and Communication," 109ff., an essay added only to the English translation of *Postmetaphysical Thinking*, 88–112.

s. On rationally redeeming one's claims and entertaining rational motives for having one's convictions, see also Habermas, *Nachmetaphysisches Denken*, 60, cf. 23, 34, 185 / *Postmetaphysical Thinking*, 51, cf. 15, 25, 145; and the concluding two paragraphs of this essay.

t. "Ein nicht-verfehltes Leben" = successful life, a life that does not fail, a life that is not misspent.

u. On Habermas's category of "ethical-existential" discourse that the last two sentences describe and that the following text distinguishes from moral discourse, see Habermas, *Die nachholende Revolution*, 118–26, 141, 144; and "Vom pragmatischen, ethischen und moralischen Gebrauch der praktischen Vernunft," 103ff., 109, 111–12/4–6, 9, 11–12.

v. To the extent that Heidegger can be said to translate Kierkegaard's self-choice into a beyond of the rhetoric of fate and deliverance, Habermas considers Heidegger's discourse and any other "postmodern" radicalization of this move not as philosophical but as quasi-theological. Against this rhetoric, Habermas translates radical self-choice, to be distinguished from Christian contents of choosing, into a performative-existential transcendence that speakers effect ontically towards one another about something on this side of the world.

12 | Kierkegaard and Critical Theory
James L. Marsh

A FEW YEARS ago an essay on this topic would have seemed unnecessary and implausible. For at that time one could have plausibly asked what Kierkegaard and critical theory possibly have to do with one another? Do not Marxism and critical theory take their bearing primarily from a social stance that is critical of all spiritual inwardness, indeed is suspicious of such inwardness as a form of bourgeois ideology? And is not Kierkegaard interested in the existentially and ethically committed religious individual who wishes to flee inauthentic mass society?

Yet in recent years these positions have gradually softened, and both have gradually moved toward one another. Forms of existential and phenomenological Marxism have themselves argued for a critical, reflective consciousness and selfhood as essential to social critique. And a spate of thinkers such as Westphal, Kirmmse, and Hall have argued that Kierkegaard is a social thinker engaged in his own kind of ethical and religiously inspired critique of society.[1]

Thoughts of complementarity, therefore, suggest themselves. Can a form of ideology critique be argued for that integrates both perspectives, that brings the social and individual, outer and inner, economic and religious together? This question will be the theme of this chapter. The full purview of social critique, I will argue, includes economic, political, social, and religious levels. Critical theory in its fullest manifestation embraces both secular and religious ideology critique. The secular critique fleshes out and renders incarnate the ideals and aspirations of religious critique, and guards against and criticizes the ideological abuses of religious belief. Religion can be and often is an opiate, but does not have to be. In its own fundamental core it is prophetic and critical.

The religious dimension of critical theory, on the other hand, prevents a merely secular critique from absolutizing itself epistemologically and ethically—there is more in heaven and earth, Marx and Habermas, than is dreamt of in your philosophies. The religiously inspired person asks whether there is not a form of pathology more fundamental than class or group domination, a pathological, demoniacal flight from intelligence and freedom into the aesthetic, a flight which class or group domination encourages and twists and uses for its own purposes. Finally we ask whether existential and religious self-appropriation is not necessary for an adequate social critique. If the individual is not living in reflexive integrity before God and others, how can s/he carry out an adequate social critique and praxis? If such critique and praxis express and incarnate the authentic individual, is not s/he necessarily at the same time the ground of such critique and praxis?[2]

This chapter, therefore, will be divided into four parts: economic, political, social-cultural, and religious. As we move through these parts, Marxism-critical theory will play less of a role and Kierkegaard more; both, however, play a role in all stages. By "Marxism-critical theory" I understand a tradition of Western Marxism extending from Marx through Hegelian Marxists in the 1920s such as Bloch, Gramsci, Korsch, and Lukács, to the Frankfurt School theory of such thinkers as Marcuse, Adorno, Horkheimer, Benjamin, and Habermas. Such theory is distinguished from "vulgar Marxism" or "Soviet Marxism" in its emphasis on dialectic as opposed to merely positive science, the necessity of normative social critique, the importance of the political and social-cultural domains, and the significance of the free, reflective subject. Already obvious, therefore, should be the affinity between such social theory and Kierkegaard's thought, which in its own way, as I will show later on, is dialectical, normative, culturally aware, and emphasizing the subject—truth is subjectivity.[3] As I will use the terms in this paper, "Marx," "Marxism," and "critical theory" are roughly synonymous.

The Economy

In Marx's theory the basic root of alienation in modern society is capitalist social relations. Because of capitalist ownership and control of the means of production, labor is alienated from the object produced, the process of work, its consciousness of itself as labor, and other people. Because labor in capitalist society is initially divorced both from means of subsistence and means of production, labor has to work on capital's terms, and capital has a right to appropriate the product produced and profit for itself. Labor, because it is in an unequal relationship of power with capital, has to be content with wages that remain at a subsistence level.[4]

Because the capitalist is animated by a "vampire thirst" for profit, he tries to make work as efficient as possible by divorcing the worker from organization and control of the process of work and transferring the mind of the work to the capitalist manager and machine. Division of labor is progressively introduced as the laborer becomes an automaton, more and more just an appendage of the machine.[5]

Because profit measured by money is the goal of capitalist investment, labor becomes a mere means to such profit. The enjoyment of the worker and the worker's consciousness of herself, her species life, are sacrificed on the altar of profit, and she becomes alienated from herself. Such alienation from oneself is accompanied by alienation from other people, the capitalist, and other people with whom she is competing for a job. In an individualistic society with little or no community, money becomes the real mind and community of all things, and others become either obstacles or means on my way to Wall Street or Greenwich. Capitalist society becomes a "pursuit of loneliness" in which wealth is the goal and general human misery is the result.[6]

Capitalism as Marx defines and articulates it has a certain logic: expansionary, quantitative, exploitative, and inverted. If making some money is good, then making more money is better and making the most money is best. Capital as a process of self-expanding value (abstract labor time measured in money) tends to extend its sway over more and more areas of human life. If consumer demand is a problem, then advertising emerges as a way of solving this problem. If market instability is a difficulty creating the possibility of depressions and recessions, then state investment in the economy becomes legitimate and necessary. If inadequate national demand or shortage of raw materials or excessively expensive labor is a problem, then capital expands into areas with more consumers, more raw materials, and cheaper labor. Imperialism is rooted in and is a natural consequence of capital logic. Imperialism is simply unjust capitalist social relations transplanted abroad.[7]

Because the goal of expansion is surplus value or profit, surplus, unpaid labor time measured in money, quantity reigns over quality in capitalism. Commodities have to have a real or imagined use value in order to be salable to the consumer, but this use value ultimately serves profitability. The subordination of real human need to profit is itself a perversion manifested in such phenomena as planned obsolescence, creation of artificial or unnecessary needs, and spending for relatively useless but very profitable items such as weapons rather than education or health care or housing for the poor.[8]

Capitalism is exploitative because, as our account of alienation already shows, people are used as mere means for the sake of profit. Surplus labor time is stolen from the laborer in a way that contradicts the bourgeois justification for private property that people should have the right to appropriate the objects containing their own labor. Capitalism turns this right into the legal right to appropriate the fruits of other people's labor.[9]

Because capital logic is expansionary, quantitative, and exploitative, it is also inverted, means are turned into ends and ends into means, the lowest into the highest and the highest into the lowest, the intrinsically valuable into the instrumental and vice versa. Because of the thirst for surplus value, capital extends its sway into more and more areas of human life; nothing is sacred, everything becomes salable, everyone becomes a commodity.

> Money is the hangman of all things, the moloch to which everything must be sacrificed, the despot of commodities. . . . Universal prostitution appears as a necessary phase in the development of the social character of personal talents, capacities, abilities, activities. More politely expressed, the universal relation of utility and use.[10]

What happens as a result of all the above is the minimizing or denying of real individuality. Capitalism creates the conditions for full individuality, but because of the lopsided distribution of wealth and income, these are not shared with most of the population. Because of the division of labor and the dehumanizing conditions of work, the laborer becomes a mutilated monstrosity and a deformed human being. Because of the domination of exchange value over use value, a quantitative sameness is forced on the population. Individualism is substituted for individuality, a deep, qualitative awareness of myself and other. I think that I am being an individual when I purchase the same perfume, watch the same program, or read the same magazine as everyone else. "The really with-it, fashion-conscious man reads *Playboy*."[11]

Capitalism creates the conditions for a rich, many-sided individuality, but is unable to realize it because of the alienated, class-based exploitative nature of capitalist social relations. One of the little known aspects of Marx and critical theory is their passion for genuine individuality, which passion they share with Kierkegaard. Unlike Kierkegaard, they stress the socio-economic conditions for the emergence of such individuality, which is full economic, social, and political democracy. This is the so-called "communism" of Marx, which has little to do with the Soviet version. Communism as Marx envisions it is simply the creation of the socio-economic framework for the emergence of the rich, many-sided, social individual. How this solution relates to Kierkegaard's religious faith, the primary focus for him of the emergence of the genuine individual, is one of the central issues of the chapter. What I will be arguing is that both are necessary. Full individuality requires both the transformation of capitalism into full democracy and religious belief. Neither critical theory nor Kierkegaard are adequately dialectical in that they have not synthesized adequately the opposites of radical social practice and religious belief.[12]

In this way communism is a dialectical solution to the alienation of capitalism, bringing the conditions for the fulfillment of individuality into relationship with those individuals themselves. Human history will have moved from a stage of one-sided immediacy of workers to land and to each other in pre-capitalist societies, through a stage of one-sided capitalist mediation, dualistic, alienated, individualistic, to a stage of mediated immediacy. Community is restored but now in a context where expression of individuality is given full play.[13]

Kierkegaard does not place the same emphasis on the economy as Marx; the economy for him is an instance of and manifestation of the public, which I will discuss later. Since both Marx and Kierkegaard, however, refuse to reduce the economic to the social or vice versa, we can note an approximation of their positions to each other. One of the ways in which the economy expresses the public is the dominance of money in our lives. "What is a woman's loveliness if it is for sale of money? and what is a bit of talent if it is in service of vile profit?" (COR 159)

In Kierkegaard's encounter with *The Corsair*, which he criticized for being a form of journalism that was extremely commercial, meretricious and degrading, he also encountered the universal, leveling, quantifying, expansionary power of money.

> But, alas, when passion and commercial interest determine the issue, when there is no ear for the harmony of spheres of category relations but only for the rattle of money in the cash box, and when passion is propelled to the extreme that every subscriber buys along with the paper the right contemptibly to dispatch what is written—this is another matter. (COR 171–72)

Kierkegaard indicates here the way money corrupts and degrades authorship by way of turning it into a kind of prostitution, and the way money plays a role by covering up or obliterating differences between categories. Publications such as *The Corsair* arouse a superficial, commodified passion that allows people to think that they can dismiss significant, profound authors who resist any reduction to a least common denominator. For this reason there is no middle ground between publishing significant material and being condemned for earning money by writing for and editing *The Corsair*. For this reason Kierkegaard does not wish to waste the time of businessmen (COR 28).[14]

Because the capital-public possesses a quantifying, expansionary, exploitative logic, it is also inverted. Both critical theory and Kierkegaard develop this point in different ways. Enterprises such as *The Corsair*, Kierkegaard argues, turn relationships upside down. Because of such inversion, the non-essential, Kierkegaard's trousers, is substituted for the essential, inwardness. Cowardice in *The Corsair* appears as inwardness, false comedy as true comedy, irresponsibility as responsibility. People reading *The Corsair* find his critique of it dull and pedestrian, its critique of him funny and satirical (COR 170, 179, 189).

In the face of such an expansionary, quantifying, homogenizing power, genuine individuality is more and more eclipsed. Because all human beings are simply numerical units of a quantitative mass, quantity has driven out quality, mediocrity has eclipsed excellence, and fashion has triumphed over originality.

No person makes his own decisions. Like Marx's worker, Kierkegaard's citizen is passive, "distracted from distraction by distraction," easily manipulated by the media, willingly seduced by the latest entertainment fad. The public becomes a fetish supplying the community, thought, security, and authority that human beings are unable to supply for themselves. Public opinion invades interiority more and more. If I am unable or unwilling to come up with my own opinions, convictions, and commitments, I can always have recourse to Tom Brokaw or Dan Rather or David Letterman (TA 90-104).[15]

Like paper money, ideas, opinions, and witticisms circulate at second hand, divorced from passion, thought, and responsibility. Abstract, inauthentic reflection buys everything at second-hand prices. Because thought has become a commodity, a dog the public keeps for its own amusement, and a technique that anyone can learn, the only way thought can be redeemed is through the leap of religious faith (TA 74-76, 88-89, 94-95, 104-105).

In the leap of faith the individual her/himself is able to establish links with other human beings.

> But through the leap out into the depths one learns to help himself, learns to love all others as much as himself even though he is accused of arrogance and pride—or of selfishness—for being unwilling to deceive others by helping them, that is, by helping them miss what is highest of all. (TA 89-90)

Kierkegaard's approach here is dialectical insofar as contemporary mass society, which is alienated and one-sidedly mediated, points back to antiquity, in which there was an immediate relation of human beings to one another; and points forward to faith, in which alienation is overcome and there is true reconciliation between such opposites as silence and speech, inwardness and revelation, individual and community. In contrast to the present age's false reconciliation of opposites, creating the public and crushing the individual, the religious individual is no longer isolated and reaches out to other human beings (TA 84-91).

The Ethico-Political

In the history of Marxism there is a developing awareness of the importance of the ethico-political level. Under-emphasized and undeveloped in Marx himself, the political in thinkers such as Gramsci and Habermas comes more into prominence in itself as a reality and category distinct and yet related to the economic. In this part of the essay I will focus on Habermas himself as the most fully developed account of the ethico-political within Western Marxism. His is the most thoroughgoing rethinking within this tradition of the relationship between the economic and the political.[16]

This rethinking occurs on a number of distinct, but related categorical levels, moving from abstract to concrete. 1) On the level of a theory of historical materialism, Habermas argues that moral learning is a pace-setter for historical change, and the institutionalizing of such learning allows a society to respond to crises arising on an economic level. 2) On a descriptive-phenomenological level, Habermas distinguishes between a communicative praxis governed by qualitative norms and a purposive rational action oriented to quantitative prediction and control, and among moral, scientific, and aesthetic forms of communication, each with its own telos, norms, and logic. 3) On the level of a theory of modernity, Habermas argues that moral, scientific, and aesthetic forms of rationality have been differentiated, and that these forms of cultural rationalization are distinct from social rationalization, the institutionalization of purposive rational action in the economy and state. 4) On the level of a synchronic account of modern capitalist society, Habermas argues that there are not only economic and rationality crises (economic crises mediated by the state) but also legitimation and motivational crises. The latter two have their roots in capitalist society's inability to meet the legitimate ethical and political expectations of its participants. Can modern capitalist society be adequately democratic if the state and economy must serve the preservation of capitalist profit over the interests of the polity as a whole? He questions whether there is not an inevitable contradiction between democratic legitimation and capitalist accumulation, universal and particular, capitalism and democracy. Is not American capitalism, for example, ostensibly "of, by, and for the people," ultimately of, by, and for capital? Are not such tendencies manifest in the way we prefer military spending, very profitable for corporations, to spending for other human needs such as housing or food or rapid transit, the way money influences disproportionately the formation of state policy, and the way other voices, such as those of the poor, the unemployed, and the homeless, are shunted to the side? Communicative action is oriented to the universal claims of truth, sincerity, rightness, and clarity and to the universal good of the whole society, but is ultimately contradicted by and, too often, overridden by particular capitalist class interest.[17]

For Habermas the critique of society has a moral-political component as well as an economic component. The moral-political component manifests itself in early Habermas's critique of science-technology as ideology shoving to the side the claims of ethical reason and making politics merely the art of selling the president according to an economic model of rationality, and late Habermas's account of the different kinds of crisis and his critique of a capitalist colonization of the life-world, in which domains normally governed by communicative action are subject to economic imperatives. Universities become primarily launching pads for Wall Street, television programs become primarily ways of making money for the sponsor, and politics becomes the art of "manufacturing consent," in which a manipulative strategic action (purposive rational action used against people) prevails over communicative action.[18]

In its growing awareness of the importance of the ethico-political, critical theory approximates Kierkegaard. Fundamental to his whole project is the notion of ethical self-choice leading to and implying commitment to the human or Divine other. The movement from the aesthetic to the ethical level of existence is a move from a life of rootless floating and experimenting to a life of existential commitment, from sensuous particular to ethical universal, from selfishness to selfhood. The highest religious level, in which the ethical is brought out of its conflict with the aesthetic, completes this process of self-becoming. We will discuss this level more in the section of the chapter, Religious Belief (SLW).

Suffice it to say that Kierkegaard speaks to the necessity of a series of conversions or leaps, from the aesthetic to the ethical and from ethical to the religious, in which the inwardness or interiority of the self manifests itself. I find fruitful complementarity here with Western Marxism's emphasis on individuality but which, compared to Kierkegaard, remains undeveloped. Crucial to individuality according to Kierkegaard is inwardness, the reflective, free consciousness of the individual as a self choosing itself in relation to a human and Divine other. Even Habermas, whose own interpretations of Mead and Durkheim point to such interiority, finally does not take the full turn into it, for reasons I have developed elsewhere. As I will show later, this refusal has atheistic consequences.[19]

I find complementarity and not contradiction for two reasons. First, such interior, existential conversion to selfhood can strengthen and enhance communicative praxis, whereas this formalizes, expresses, and externalizes inwardness. I commit myself firmly and habitually to an ethical form of life, from which communicative praxis springs and without which it remains fitful, inconstant, and vacillating. The existential and the political, inwardness and communicative praxis, self-awareness and ideology critique complement one another; no adequate communicative praxis without full choice of myself as existentially and historically ethical, no adequate selfhood without communicative praxis.

Kierkegaard thinks and lives this reciprocity in his participation in the *Corsair* affair in which he allows himself to be pilloried by the *Corsair* as a way of revealing its cultural bankruptcy, and in his later critique of Christendom. Even the social expression of his critique has more of the private, inward, and individual in it than the forms of public, political action and protest favored by Marxism. Against the corrupt *Corsair* and corrupt Christendom, he manifests the full resources of an authentic inwardness, reminding Marxism and critical theory that within the heaven of critique, there are many mansions (COR; KAUC).

Adorno, who perhaps has a more developed idea of inwardness than

Habermas, recognizes the above claims in a way that approximates Kierkegaard.

> In the face of the totalitarian unison which the eradication of difference is proclaimed as a principle in itself, even part of the social force of liberation may have temporarily withdrawn to the individual sphere. If critical theory lingers there, it is not only with a bad conscience.[20]

In the face of a commodified, exploitative, one-dimensional society, the struggle for individual enlightenment and authenticity can be the beginning of political resistance and have at least an indirect political resonance.

Culture

It is perhaps on the level of culture, a public domain where exchange of information, ideas, and values occurs, that critical theory and Kierkegaard are closest. For Marxism, culture produces ideology that expresses, legitimates, and covers up class and group domination: racist, sexist, heterosexist, classist. For this reason the leading ideas of an epoch are those of its ruling class. The individualism, for example, so rampant during the Reagan era expresses and legitimizes the private ownership of the means of production, the orientation to private profit, and the reluctance to use the state for public spending that helps the poor, the unemployed, and the homeless.[21]

As capitalism develops and economic and legitimation crises emerge more frequently, ideology becomes more of an issue. If depression is to be avoided, people need to be persuaded to buy goods that they might otherwise not buy. If revolution is to be avoided, a population whose interests the economy and the state generally do not adequately serve needs to be convinced that its interests are served. As a result, in the twentieth century a "consciousness industry" emerged that is in most respects the same as and a development of Kierkegaard's "public." The economy and consciousness industry require one another and lock into one another. Indeed media such as radio, television, newspapers, and movies not only sell money-making as a way of life but are themselves committed to making a profit. General Electric buying NBC during the 1980s and newscasts praising its military weapons used during the Gulf War are typical examples. The very Patriot missiles you see being deployed are produced by GE; "GE brings good things to life."[22]

Within the consciousness industry are at least two main functions: reporting and interpreting the news in a propagandistic manner and the creation of "phantasmagoria." Both of these functions have as their ultimate goal the subjugation of the viewing, consuming public to the imperatives of capital. Reporting of the news occurs in a way that is selective, biased, one-sided, and false. For example, the press understates the number of protesters going to Washington to protest the Gulf War, or fails to mention crimes of client regimes supported by the United States, or mentions such crimes on the back page, or describes as "democratic" what are actually repressive, undemocratic client regimes in Brazil, Argentina, and Guatemala. An "economic miracle" of free trade is proclaimed in Central and Latin America, which actually leaves most people in those countries worse off, more hungry, more illiterate, and more repressed than they were ten or fifteen years ago.[23]

Another function of the media, however, is to create "phantasmagoria," images functioning as commodities and commodities functioning as images. Phantasmagoria are a cultural expression of the fetishization of commodities described by Marx, in which relations between people take the fantastic form of relations between things. The commodity becomes fantastic, seeming to have properties it does not have and having properties that are not apparent. In the consciousness industry images become commodities as sports figures are used to sell basketball shoes, sexy models to sell clothes, and movie stars to sell deodorant. Michael Jordan, Cindy Crawford, and Clint Eastwood become reified, fetishized gods and goddesses, expressing the reign of the gods capital and money. At the same time commodities like basketball shoes become images, seeming to possess magical qualities. If you buy Nike, then you too can "be like Mike."[24]

Like postmodernists such as Baudrillard, Marx and critical theory recognize the fantastic, fictional, "simulative" character of the commodity. Unlike Baudrillard, however, they relate this simulation to the real capitalist world of production and consumption; in this way they do more justice than does postmodernism both to the fiction and reality of the late capitalist consciousness industry. Benjamin's account is that these phantasmagoria "express," not simply reflect, this real economic world, the way a dream expresses the interplay between id and superego. Ideology critique consists in showing the relationship between such expression and economic-political processes and in criticizing both as false and unjust. Late capitalism promises what it really cannot deliver, happiness, and claims to practice what it really violates and frustrates, namely justice. Because of the gap between promise and reality, the consciousness industry has to intervene in order to prevent people from seeing what would be otherwise obvious, that the American dream is a nightmare. Indeed, the function of the consciousness industry is to create a mass, collective dream, from which critical theory tries to awaken us.[25]

Kierkegaard's notion of the "public" also recognizes the unreal, fantastic dimension of the consciousness industry. He describes the public as "an evasion, a dissipation, and an illusion. . . . The public may take a year and day to assemble and when it is assembled it does not exist." Further the public is "an abstract void and vacuum that is all and nothing" and "reflection's mirage . . . the fairy tale of an age of prudence" (TA 91, 93, 106). Like Marx and critical theory, Kierkegaard relates the public to its basis in real social life, criticizes it normatively in the light of criteria proceeding from ethical selfhood, evaluates it dialectically in the light of an ontology of the self, synthesizing such opposites as necessity and possibility, finitude and infinitude, and points towards its overcoming in a more just society. Like Marx and critical theory, Kierkegaard's conception of self, normativity, rationality, and critique is fundamentally modernist, or at least has significant modernist strains, not simply postmodernist as some are wont to argue.[26]

What is the public? It is a collection of inauthentic individuals living amorally as a mass or crowd and expressing itself anonymously, abstractly, passionlessly, and irresponsibly. The public is the expression of a conformist society in which individuality has lost all depth and social life all ethically defensible mediation. Nothing is sacred, everything is for sale and no one is willing to take seriously anything besides her own pleasure or profit (TA 94).

As we have already shown in the first section of the chapter, the press for Kierkegaard is an instance of the public, consuming everything in its path, turning everything into grist for its mill, making everyone a celebrity for fifteen minutes. The genius of Kierkegaard lies in his understanding so early the quantitative, homogenizing, infinitizing, inverted, exploitative logic of the public or capital-public; twentieth century capitalism has turned emergent tendencies in Kierkegaard's Denmark into an art form. The later critical theory of Adorno, Benjamin, and others develops these insights of Marx and Kierkegaard and shows how their claims are even truer today. Merely emerging tendencies have turned into a system of "totalitarian" or "quasi-totalitarian" control.[27]

Such claims may strike the reader as overstated and one-sided. Do not we in the United States have a real set of freedoms and rights unlike those of the formerly brainwashed Russians and the currently brainwashed Chinese? Critical theory's response is to admit that such freedoms and rights are institutionalized and even operative in a minimal sense, but are significantly compromised and violated in practice. Indeed, that we are legally and formally free makes ours a more efficient system of brainwashing. When people in Russia, prior to 1989, sat down for the evening news, they knew they were just receiving propaganda, the party line. When we hear Dan Rather or Tom Brokaw, we think we are getting the unvarnished truth. Because propaganda comes bearing gifts, ideology under the guise of truth or fantasy in the guise of fact, the brainwashing is even more effective. For this reason as well as others, an ideology critique inviting us to rediscover the socio-economic roots of such ideology and our own authentic individuality is necessary.

Religious Belief

Here on this level is affinity and difference, agreement and disagreement between Kierkegaard and critical theory. For critical theory, religion is something to be criticized and transcended, because it represents an alienation of the human being from his own essential powers and because it often functions as an ideological prop for a corrupt, unjust social status quo. Critique of religious belief as such a prop, therefore, functions as an element of ideology critique.[28]

Kierkegaard argues against Marx and critical theory that authentic religious belief helps the human being overcome alienation and that such belief can function as ideology critique. Inauthentic religious belief, such as operated in Kierkegaard's Christendom, can and does function in the way that Marxists describe it. Coming down to the present, we can see that this process continues. We have only to note the way organized religion celebrated and supported the Gulf War, ringing its church bells all over the country on a day designated by Bush to celebrate the great triumph, or the way an individualistic interpretation of religious belief mirrors individualistic capitalist society, an individualism Reagan and Bush raised to an art form. For the religious believer, therefore, such critique can purify her notion of God. God is not, and should not, be conceived as simply the God of the ruling classes. If this is all God is, then s/he is dead and deserves to be dead. Rather God is identified with the poor and exploited and suffering; we can find in Kierkegaard beginnings of a "preferential option for the poor."

> In order to invite them to come to one in this way, one must live in the very same manner, poor as the poorest, poorly regarded as the lowly man among people, experienced in life's sorrow as anguish, sharing the very same condition as those one invites to come to one, those who labor and are burdened. (KAUC; PC 12-15, 33; quotation from PC 13)

The only kind of God worth talking about is God as liberator, as partner and companion in the project of overcoming racist, sexist, classist, heterosexist injustice. Such a conception of God, I would argue, is necessary if critical theory is to achieve its full range and effectiveness. Critical theory can and should include a religious component. The first strand in this critique is the negative critique of religious belief undertaken both by Marxism and Kierkegaard.

A second is that religious belief has positive resources upon which one can and must draw in order to make his critique. If, as I have already argued in this chapter, interiority and critique dig into one another, and if interiority in its full aspiration and range implies religious belief, then critique and liberation in their full range imply religious belief. Kierkegaard argues that human subjectivity is a passion for the infinite, for that in which I can believe and entrust myself unreservedly as an unrestricted source of intelligibility and love. Short of such an adequate "object" for one's belief, she is in danger of committing herself unreservedly to a finite object, of divinizing it. If a contradiction emerges between the infinite passion and finite object, this contradiction can be adequately resolved only by making the full-fledged commitment to God and to Jesus Christ as the most adequate historical revelation of God (CUP 30–31, 387–94).

Marx and critical theory, because they fail to take the full turn into interiority, miss the positive reality and importance of religious belief and thus shortchange themselves. Interiority becomes a crucial middle term mediating political critique and religious belief.[29]

The argument up to this point may seem abstract and this is not necessarily a bad thing, since any good philosophical argument will have an element of abstractness about it. A third step, however, that is more concrete is to show hermeneutically how Kierkegaard's Christianity has positive resources for making such a critique. Here it is important to note how he insists, in the *Corsair* affair and in the critique of Christendom, that Christianity most comprehensively and deeply interpreted not only resists being incorporated into an unjust status quo, but can function as a critique of that status quo. In identifying reason with a corrupt public sphere mediated by the Danish state and economy, one makes reason irrational by uncritically deifying it and by ignoring the authenticity of the individual.

In making Christianity merely an affair of the educated middle and upper classes, a person does violence to the universality of Christianity as it extends to the poor and oppressed. If Christianity is genuinely universal and it extends to the poor, oppressed, and suffering, then as Christ and any Christian who follows him seriously, one must wish not merely to aid these people from on high but to be with them, suffer with them, identify with them. Here is a religiously motivated identification with the oppressed similar to Marxism's identification with labor and other victims of capital. Identification with the poor and oppressed becomes the epistemic and ethico-religious vantage point from which I make my critique and engage in praxis; short of such identification my critique is not fully true nor my praxis fully ethical. Also, in making religion state-supported and financed, one does violence both to the secular character of the state and to the transcendent character of religious belief. One divinizes the state and renders immanent religious belief. In doing so one also misses the legitimate modern differentiation between secular and religious. Once again Kierkegaard's modernist roots are apparent. Like Habermas, he insists on legitimate differentiation occurring in modern society (TA, COR, PC, KAUC).

Kierkegaard, then, undertakes from the perspective of a vantage point outside of reason itself, the level of freedom and commitment oriented to a transcendent God, a critique of reason. Such a critique, however, benefits reason by allowing it to become fully self-critical and not to divinize itself; in so doing it becomes uncritical and therefore irrational. Similarly a right-wing Hegelian reason, or in the twentieth century a liberal, scientific reason that divinizes the status quo, sacrifices its ethical, critical substance and becomes irrational. To the extent that such a reason invites the individual to identify herself with the social whole and ignore her own individuality, such a reason becomes inauthentic, and, therefore, irrational. Reason in order to fully realize itself must become fully self-critical by transcending itself. Short of such self-transcendence reason remains partial, limited, truncated, and in danger of divinizing itself. The benefits of such an approach for a Marxism always in danger of divinizing itself in the dialectic, the party, and the state should be obvious. Only God is God.

Finally, the life of Kierkegaard himself most concretely expresses and conforms to his thought. Fact proves the genuine possibility of a religious belief that is genuinely, prophetically resistant to and critical of a corrupt, unjust society in his time and our time. In the presence of God the "single one" recovers his sense of self, uniqueness, and integrity. In the face of the conformity encouraged by mass culture, the single one becomes an original creative self. In the face of the leveling tendencies of consumer culture, the single one develops capacities for self-transcendence toward God and other human beings. In the face of the mindless togetherness of such a society, the single one learns to choose and cherish a life-giving solitude. Through such solitude the person develops a critical distance enabling him to see through the myths of such a society: consumerism, militarism, rugged individualism, imperialism, "the new world order," technocracy, sexism, and hedonism. Kierkegaard's life and thought manifest the possibility of a prophetic philosophical and religious critique that can be wedded fruitfully to critical theory. Such possibilities continue to be expressed in our own time by such people as Martin Luther King, Malcolm X, and Daniel Berrigan. Each in his own way testifies to the falsity of a religious belief that identifies with and refuses to question an unjust status quo, the necessity to join faith with justice, the importance of linking peace with justice, the identification with the poor and oppressed, and the truth of a prophetic religious critique and transcendence.

Conclusion

We have noted here many affinities between critical theory and Kierkegaard: the importance of the individual, the significance of ideology critique, the relationship between capital and the public, the necessity of praxis, a pathological logic in capital and the public that is inverted, quantitative, exploitative, and expansionary, the importance of the ethical-political, a use of dialectic moving from one-sided immediacy to one-sided, contradictory mediation to integrative individualism and social transformation, and the critique of fetishism.

At the same time at each stage in our inquiry we have noted differences and disagreements: the relative weight each gives to capital and the public, the different importance each gives to interiority, the different weights given to public, collective action versus a resistance and critique that is more on the individual level, and the differing evaluations one gives to religious belief. I think that most of the differences are complementary rather than contradictory. If one realizes, for example, that for both Marxism and Kierkegaard the relationship between economy and the public is reciprocal, dialectical, and non-reductionistic, then the only question remaining concerns priority, importance, and dominance. I have indicated elsewhere why I think the Marxist answer is preferable. Again, as I have already shown, existential inwardness complements the public and communicative, and vice versa, and individual, religious, and ethically motivated resistance can complement a Marxist emphasis on public mass action.[30]

Where the differences are less easily resolved is on the religious question itself. Is religious belief merely ideology or is it also a positive component essential to ideology critique? I have briefly argued why I think the latter is true. An approach integrating both the negative and positive evaluations of religious belief is, therefore, more comprehensive hermeneutically than one that emphasizes simply the negative or the positive.

The formal result of my essay is, then, a conception of critical theory as having at least four different levels, economic, political, cultural, and religious, which interrelate in different ways. One way in which they interrelate is that we can affirm the necessity of radical political conversion as a basis for doing critical theory. Such a conversion establishes a habitually lived horizon within which I as theorist and human agent operate rationally, ethically, politically, and religiously. The movement from aesthetic to ethical to religious, which Kierkegaard describes as a series of leaps, has a social, political component to it, an identification with the oppressed, a preferential option for the poor, and a commitment to work for justice. Such radical political conversion has at least four components. The first is a commitment to rational, communicative praxis, in which I habitually am oriented to affirming and living out the implications of the better argument.[31]

A second level is ethical, in which I move from mere self-centered aesthetic enjoyment to ethical commitment to the other as an end in herself. A third level is social, in which I opt and live and theorize from the perspective of a preferential option for the poor, marginalized, and oppressed. A fourth level is religious, in which I commit myself to a God inviting me to share in the work of liberating the oppressed. Radical political conversion, therefore, wedding an existential, reflective component and a critical, political component, is the final fruit, and, at the same time, the basis of the marriage between critical theory and Kierkegaard that I present here.

Notes

1. For existential and phenomenological Marxism, see Sartre, *Critique of Dialectical Reason*; Kosik, *Dialectics of the Concrete*; Paci, *The Function of the Sciences and the Meaning of Man*; and Marsh, *Post-Cartesian Meditations*. For interpretations of Kierkegaard as social theory, see Westphal, *Kierkegaard's Critique of Reason and Society*; Hall, *Word & Spirit: A Kierkegaardian Critique of the Modern Age*; and Kirmmse, *Kierkegaard in Golden Age Denmark*.

2. Doran, *Theology and the Dialectics of History*, pp. 387–417. Hall, *Word & Spirit*, pp. 1–14.

3. Jay, *Marxism and Totality*. Strictly speaking, Western Marxism also includes thinkers such as Merleau-Ponty, Sartre, Williams, and Althusser, but I am stressing the resources of critical theory here.

4. Marx, *Economic and Philosophic Manuscripts*, pp. 106–10.

5. Ibid., pp. 110–12. *Capital*, pp. 492–639, quotation from p. 367.

6. Marx, *Economic and Philosophic Manuscripts*, pp. 112–19.

7. Marx, *Capital*, pp. 247–57. See Dussel, *Ethics and Community*, pp. 113–69, for a development of the imperialistic implications of capitalism.

8. Marx, *Capital*, pp. 125–77, 283–306. *Grundrisse*, pp. 401–16. Marcuse, *One-Dimensional Man*, pp. 1–54.

9. Marx, *Capital*, pp. 725–34.

10. Marx, *Grundrisse*, p. 163.

11. Ibid., pp. 161–62. Ewen, *Captains of Consciousness*.

12. Marx, *Economical and Philosophic Manuscripts*, pp. 132–46.

13. Marx, *Grundrisse*, pp. 161–62.

14. For a fuller development of these ideas, see Marsh, "The *Corsair* Affair: Kierkegaard and Critical Social Theory," pp. 63–83.

15. The quotation is from T. S. Eliot, "The Four Quartets," p. 120.

16. See Gramsci's *Prison Notebooks*, and Habermas's *Communication and the Evolution of Society* for their own rendering of the ethico-political.

17. Habermas, *Communication and the Evolution of Society*, pp. 95–176; *Toward a Rational Society*, pp. 81–122; *Reason and the Rationalization of Society*, pp. 1–42, 216–42, 273–37; *Lifeworld and System*, pp. 343–56. Lindbloom, *Politics and Markets*.

18. Habermas, *Toward a Rational Society*, pp. 81–122; *Lifeworld and System*, pp. 332–73. Chomsky, *Manufacturing Consent*, pp. 1–35.

19. Marsh, "The Religious Significance of Habermas." Habermas, *Lifeworld and System*, pp. 1–111.

20. Adorno, *Minima Moralis*, p. 18.

21. Wills, *Reagan's America: Innocents at Home*.

22. Adorno and Horkheimer, *The Dialectic of Enlightenment*, pp. 120–67. Kellner, *The Persian Gulf TV War*, pp. 11, 59–60, 115–16, 177–78.

23. Chomsky, *Year 501*, pp. 155–95; *Manufacturing Consent*, pp. 37–142. Parenti, *Inventing Reality*. Benjamin, *Passagen-Werk*, I, pp. 60–61, 63–64, 76–77.

24. Marx, *Capital*, pp. 163–77. Benjamin, *Passagen-Werk*, I, pp. 435–36. Ewen, *Captains of Consciousness*. Parenti, *Make-Believe Media*.

25. Baudrillard, *Selected Writings*, pp. 119–47. Kellner, *Jean Baudrillard*, pp. 60–121. Benjamin, *Passagen-Werk*, I, pp. 495–96, 573–74.

26. See Caputo, *Radical Hermeneutics*, pp. 11–25, for a reading of Kierkegaard as postmodernist. See Taylor, *Kierkegaard's Pseudonymous Authorship*; Elrod, *Being and Existence*; Dunning, *Kierkegaard's Dialectic of Inwardness* for his stances on the self, normativity, dialectical rationality, and critique.

27. See Marcuse, *One-Dimensional Man*, p. 3, for a critique of American capitalist society as totalitarian.

28. Marx, *Manuscripts*, pp. 143–46. *Selected Writings*, pp. 39–74, 159–91.

29. Marsh, "The Religious Significance of Habermas."

30. Marsh, *Post-Cartesian Meditations*, pp. 200–58.

31. See Marsh, "Praxis and Ultimate Reality," for a fuller development of this idea of radical political conversion.

13 | Instants, Secrets, and Singularities

Dealing Death in Kierkegaard and Derrida

John D. Caputo

Jacques the Seducer

THE "officials of anti-deconstruction"[1] have long indulged themselves in the reassuring illusion that Derrida's work is a form of aestheticism, that, on a Kierkegaardian register, deconstruction is to be fitted in as a version of the "rotation method," as a kind of endless playing that entertains itself from moment to moment with the merely "interesting." These "knights of good conscience"[2] would be scandalized to hear that the right Kierkegaardian analogy is not to the aestheticism of Johannes—read: Jacques—the Seducer, nor to the moralism of the sanctimonious Judge William, but to the religion of the parson on the Jutland heaths. They would be chagrinned to learn that the seduction is on them, that they have failed to recognize the comic as the incognito of the religious, that Derrida is one more child of father Abraham, defending the claims of singularity and of the incommensurability of the individual against the universal.

Reb Derrisa: an ironical rabbi from the Jutland heaths, a scarce commodity in a world where everyone is a Christian!

The defenders of the Good and the True, who have appointed themselves to make the world safe from deconstruction, would be surprised to find that undecidability does not mean aesthetic indecision but supplies instead the condition of possibility of deciding, i.e., of taking a risk. They would be stung by the suggestion that, if *différance* spells trouble for ethics, it is rather the sort of trouble that Johannes de Silentio makes for ethics in *Fear and Trembling*, not the sort made by Johannes/Jacques the Seducer. They would turn away in a huff, incensed at the very idea that Kierkegaard and Derrida have a common nemesis—the infinite appetite of Hegel's totalizing dialectic—and a common affection for everything singular and fragment-like.

In the past Mark Taylor, Louis Mackey, Sylvia Agacinski, and many others, I among them, have had to laboriously construct this argument based upon multiple clues in Derrida's texts that any attentive reader of Derrida who has also read Kierkegaard—in particular *Fear and Trembling*—will readily recognize.[3] But with the recent appearance of *"Donner la mort"* (1992), which contains a sustained and striking interpretation of *Fear and Trembling*, I would be tempted to say that the argument is over and the case closed—were it not for the fact that everything in deconstruction resists closure. In this text, Derrida makes it plain for those of little faith that deconstruction is a philosophy of singularity and of responsibility to the singular, that Derrida himself is a "supplementary clerk"[4] of singularity, picking up the shards and fragments left behind by philosophy's search for universality.

One hopes that, with the publication of this text, Derrida's critics will learn a little bit about fear and trembling, both about the book and the concept—particularly when it comes to passing judgment on Derrida. At the least, one would hope that hereafter the moralizing and self-approving critics of Derrida, who are too given to praying in public, will find other means to display their love of the Good and the True. Perhaps they will take up giving alms to the poor and feeding the hungry, in public of course, as proof positive of their superior moral character, while leaving the interpretation of Derrida's text to those who actually read them. In any case, as Johannes de Silentio said of the defenders of the Hegelian omnibus (FT 8), I wish them all well in their good works, both public and secret.

Death Dealing

The French expression *"donner la mort,"* literally "giving death," means in English something like causing or bringing about the death of someone or something, dealing death to someone, including oneself (suicide). "Giving" seems like altogether the wrong word in any language inasmuch as visiting death upon a living thing is usually not a gift but rather its utter destruction; such giving takes everything away. Derrida is interested precisely in this "economic question," the question of giving and taking, in the economics of giving death, in whether giving can be reduced to an economic issue at all, in whether and when giving death is a good deal, a solid investment that promises a good return.

In fact, the positive and productive power of death, of giving death, has long been recognized, not only in religion, where the contemplation of mortality and ascetic practices—exercises in "self-mortification"—have long been basic stock in trade, but also in philosophy as well. One of the inaugural moments of philosophy is Plato's definition of philosophy as the practice or exercise of death (*melete thanatou, Phaedo,* 80e), philosophy as the mortification of bodily desire, of the life of sensual pleasure, of sentient life generally. The business of making death important is no less present in our own time, as witnessed by Heidegger's now classic analysis—which wants a footnote or two to Kierkegaard—of "being-toward-death" in *Being and Time* (§§46–53). Dasein is or becomes authentically itself only inasmuch as it makes its death its own, projecting itself upon its own death. Death alone strips Dasein down to its ownmost singularity, ready and free for death. Levinas—and Gabriel Marcel—have likewise insisted upon the importance of mortality, not upon my mortality but rather, in a mirror-like reversal of Heidegger, upon the death and mortality of the "other."

In each of these cases, from Plato to Levinas, dealing in death is ultimately taken as a good investment, whether as the only way to purify the soul, or to break the grip of everyday fallenness in the world, or to achieve that transcendence which releases the hold of the *conatus essendi* and makes one a subject of responsibility, a substitution for the other. Philosophy has long looked upon dealing in death as a good deal. The views of Plato, Heidegger, and Levinas are discussed by Derrida in the course of an analysis of Patočka's *Heretical Essays on the Philosophy of History*, which is the focal text and point of departure for the first two sections of "*Donner la mort.*"

But it is against the backdrop of the Hegelian way to give death that Derrida's interpretation of Kierkegaard, which is to be found in the final two sections of the essay, can be best understood. In Hegelian terms, the very life of the dialectic turns on its capacity for giving death, for exposing the life of the individual or the community, of spirit or nature, of the concept or the physical force, to its opposing, negating, death-dealing opponent. Hegel recognized the power of negativity, the necessity of the way of the cross, the need for the Golgotha and Good Friday of the Spirit. For Hegel this all makes good sense; indeed it is the very definition of sense, of reason itself; it is the way that reason makes itself real and that reality makes itself rational. For the loss, the expenditure, the negation, the destruction are—this is what dialectics means—always recouped and preserved in a higher unity in which whatever dies to itself is reborn and resurrected in the famous *Aufhebung*, which destroys and preserves by lifting up. Death dealing is a good investment, the very essence of *rationem reddere* and good economics.

What interests Derrida about *Fear and Trembling* is that it is an exercise in "mad economics,"[5] in the madness of the instant, which tears up the circular unity of dialectical time. Kierkegaard thought that the doleful influence of Hegelianism on Christianity had been to depress the price of faith, to drop it so low that anyone could afford it—millions of Europeans all over Christendom could come up with the price—with almost no effort. Hegelianism cheapens Christianity to the point that it was to be had at a "bargain price," *ein wirklicher Ausverkauf*, a real steal (FT 5). The point of *Fear and Trembling*, accordingly, indeed of much of what Kierkegaard wrote, was to raise the price of faith, like the merchants in Holland who threw their spices into the harbor to drive up the price (FT 121). Faith had become a "counterfeit coin" (*la fausse monnaie*)—to invoke the story of Baudelaire that constitutes the point of departure for Derrida's *Given Time* (*Donner le temps*), an important cognate work to *Donner la mort*.[6] In Baudelaire's story, a man gives a beggar a generous donation, a two-franc silver piece, only to confess to the narrator that the coin was in truth counterfeit. This elicits the disapproval of the narrator who condemns his friend for the stupidity of thinking that he can "win paradise economically." Hegelianism is just such a counterfeit coin for Johannes de Silentio, because it attempts to purchase faith on the cheap, without the fear and trembling, with a minimum of expense and difficulty, by removing the paradox and the terror, the instant of madness. In Hegel's attempt to win the Christian faith economically, the Word seems to have become flesh in order to read about himself in German philosophy, while providing the theologians with the opportunity to earn a good living off the crucifixion. The whole thing was a good bargain, a real steal.

It is in order to raise the price of faith, to persuade European Christendom that it was trading in false coin, that it had not begun to come to grips with the death dealing character of faith, with the *mysterium tremendum*, that Kierkegaard retells the story of Abraham to his contemporaries. This is the terrifying story of the *akedah*, the binding of Isaac, in which the father of faith, the father of us all—of Jew and Christian and Muslim, as Derrida likes to insist (DM 65, 70)—is told to deal death to his son, Isaac, and so seemingly to his hope of being the father of many generations, which is the deal he had cut with the Lord. This is a story of madness, of a mad economics, a radical and literal case of death dealing in an economy of sacrifice. Abraham was willing to make a gift of the life of Isaac. Were a man later this week to take his son and head up to the top of the World Trade Center, with the intention of offering his son in sacrifice, we would send a SWAT team in to seize the man and put him under arrest for attempted murder, for defying the most elemental command of ethics, which is not to deal in death. To see this story thus in all its contemporaneity, to imagine it repeated right here in the midst of us, today, is the effect that Johannes de Silentio wants to produce. For that is the paradox by which he himself is arrested and silenced, the fearfully high price of faith before which he trembles. Abraham deals in death; he courts death without flinching. When death calls—or God, God or death—Abraham does not blink.

That is what interests Derrida—in Abraham and in Kierkegaard's very Pauline reading of the story of Abraham.

The Secret

If "*Donner la mort*" is an essay on giving and death, it is no less an essay on the "secret."[7] The *mysterium tremendum* is a secret that makes us shudder. *Tremendum* means what is to be feared, something fearful that is to come, something that I cannot see or foresee. I know that there is something that I do not know and that causes me to tremble. Paul, who in prison has received a gift from the church in Phillipi, the first church he established and one for which he always retained a heartfelt and special love, is sending the Philippians a thank you note, a letter from a (*Roman*) jail. "Therefore, my dear friends (*agapetoi*), as you have always obeyed—not only in my presence (*parousia*) but now much more in my absence (*apousia*)—continue to work out your salvation with fear and trembling (*meta phobou kai tromou*" (Phil., 2:12). Why with fear and trembling? "For it is God who works in you to will and to act according to his good purpose (*eudokias*)" (Phil., 2:13).[8] Minimally, Paul may be understood to say that we can do nothing without God's help. Taken more rigorously—and this is Derrida's reading—Paul means that God does not have to give reasons (*rationem reddere*); God can give or take away salvation without giving an explanation. We are in the hands of God and we do not know what God wants, what is God's pleasure, which is a secret (DM 59–60) shrouded in silence. We do not see (*voir*) or know (*savoir*) what God wants, otherwise God would not be God, i.e., Wholly Other (DM 59). God does not share his reasons with us; we cannot have a conversation with God; we cannot establish the homogeneity with God that having a conversation, and so a common language, would imply. The word of God is the word of the Wholly Other, and the word of the Wholly Other is wholly other than a word, otherwise than what we mean by a word. His word reduces us to silence, is received in silence, cannot be understood, and cannot be repeated to anyone else.

When God speaks his word, when God calls, Abraham obeys, *me voici*,[9] but he cannot understand. He is rendered incommunicado, cut off from the consolation of consensus and community, from the common sense of the *sensus communis*, stripped down to the madness of solitude, to fear and the trembling before an unutterable secret. The word of God cuts us off from all *Sittlichkeit*, from the reassuring community of practices that shape communal life, from family, society, nation. The deal Abraham cuts with God cuts Abraham off from Sarah. Sacrifice is strictly men's business, between God and him—and Isaac. Sarah is being sacrificed as well as Isaac; the whole family, the most immediate sphere of *Sittlichkeit*, will be sacrificed by this secret. So there are two levels of secrecy at work in the story: the secret that God keeps from Abraham, who does not know what God's pleasure is; and the secret that Abraham keeps from Isaac and Sarah, from the servants who accompany him to Moriah, from family and friends, from anyone who would ask what he is doing, who do not know what the patriarch is up to, because he does not know himself (DM 60). The secret severs the whole sphere of *Sittlichkeit*. Abraham is singularized, alone before God and alone before death (DM 61). He has left the sphere of public language, of publically shared reasons, and entered upon the solitude and silence of the secret. That is why, when Isaac asks where the lamb is, Abraham answers without saying anything, answers without truly responding. He has left or suspended ethics and consensus, the concrescence of concrete ethical and historical subsistence, and ethics abhors this secret.

Derrida is thus sensitive to the fact that in *Fear and Trembling* the "ethical" refers, not only to Kantian *Moralität*, the universalizability of the law, but also to Hegelian *Sittlichkeit*, the concrete ethical community, so that the religious transcends both Kantian and Hegelian ethics, both the pure law and the *polis*, both deontology and eudaimonism.[10]

Abraham's responsibility is absolute, ab-solved from the universal, both abstract and concrete. That is why ethics is a temptation for Abraham, why ethics would make Abraham irresponsible. Were he to give a reason (*rationem reddere*) for what he is doing, were he to respond to Sarah, to the human community, which is the ethical—the responsible—thing to do, he would betray his absolute responsibility to God. In the name of his responsibility to God, he cannot be responsible to his family and friends. He is in a bind, a double bind, and he can't win, although in virtue of the madness of his faith he believes that he can't lose (DM 62–63).

The question posed by this story, according to Johannes de Silentio, is whether one admits a sphere of the interior secret, which is justified by the fact that the individual is higher than the universal; otherwise Abraham is lost (FT 82, 120). Hegelianism is consistent in denying the secret and demanding public disclosure and manifestation while also denying the incommensurability of the individual. The only inconsistency of Hegelianism is to tip its hat in public whenever it is mentioned that Abraham is the father of faith. Hegelianism is counterfeit coin; it wants to win heaven economically. The sphere of absolute responsibility is beyond duty, because in doing one's duty one is related to the universal, not to God. So Abraham is beyond ethics, beyond duty *qua* duty, transcending Kantianism in favor of the religious, which is absolute duty, which means to be related to God.

Kierkegaard wants to keep the cost of faith high. If you want to build a tower, Jesus said, will you not first estimate the cost (*dapanen*)? (Luke 14:28). If you want to be a disciple, then you must be willing to meet the cost, which is very high. "If anyone comes to me and does not hate (*misei*) his father and his mother, his wife and children, his brothers and sisters—yes even his own life—he cannot be my disciple" (Luke 14:26). Abraham is the father of faith because he is willing to pay the cost, because he shows a hatred for ethics and for his family. Of course there is no great merit in dealing death to those whom one hates; the greatness of father Abraham is to hate what he loves, to deal death to his beloved son, by undertaking what ethics calls hatred. To "sacrifice" is to deal death to what one loves; it is the sacrifice of love to love (DM 65).[11]

In making this sacrifice to God, Abraham makes a gift of the death of

Isaac. He gives death in an instant of madness. He does not make a present (*présent*) in the present. The present belongs to the time of economics and to the economics of philosophical time: to the rational give and take of investment and return, protention and retention (Husserl), negation and preservation (Hegel), forgetting and recalling (Plato), oblivion and memorial thinking (Heidegger). The gift (*don*), on the other hand, is an expenditure without return, occuring in the madness of the "instant." The instant is not a graspable moment in a unitary flow; it is nothing we can seize or understand or stabilize. The instant tears up the circular unity of time. In the instant everything is spent, an infinite, an absurdly high cost is paid, and one loses everything. In giving (*donner*) death to Isaac, his beloved son, and in giving this death to God, Abraham breaks the circle of the present and representation in a moment of paradox and madness. Abraham must love Isaac, he must love Sarah and the whole ethical order, and at the very instant he loves them he must sacrifice them (DM 66).

The story of the sacrifice of Isaac, Derrida comments, is not only a story for believers in a biblical faith. On the contrary, this story—and I think, we must insist, the specific version of this story presented in *Fear and Trembling*, which Derrida does not question—is a narrative version of:

> . . . the paradox which inhabits the concept of duty or of absolute responsibility. This concept puts us into relation (without relation, and in the double secret) with the absolute other, with the absolute singularity of the other, of which God is here the name. (DM 66)

The name of God, of the biblical God of Abraham and Isaac, need not mean God for us; it is enough for "God" to be the name of the absolutely other, of the absolute secret which is nestled within the heart of every individual. The *alter ego*, as Husserl shows, is never present to my consciousness. God's mind is wholly other to Abraham, as is the mind of every other, my friends and my family, who are as transcendent to me as Yahweh (DM 76). The story of Abraham, this story of the absolute incommensurability of the individual with the general, Derrida thinks, makes a general point, one of use in any religion or outside religion. What Kierkegaard calls the "religious" is not confined to religion, and that is because it establishes the "logic" of absolute responsibility, which is the logic of a double bind. Whether one has faith or not, "there is a morality . . . in this story," a morality which is "morality itself," one might say the very "morality of morality," the bind that descends upon every morality, the delimination or deconstruction of morality. The (general) point made by this story is that the notion of absolute responsbility, responsibility to the absolutely singular, which means the absolutely other, requires that "at the same time one denounce, take exception to, and transcend every duty, every responsibility and every human law" (DM 67). Absolute duty requires us to betray the order of universality and generality, of being and essence and manifestation. "In a word, ethics ought to be sacrificed in the name of duty. It is a duty that one not respect, through duty, ethical duty." In the name of absolute and infinite duty, one ought not to be ethical.

The story of Abraham is the story of the sacrifice of ethics. "And this name which ought always to be singular is nothing other than the name of God as the wholly other, the name without name of God, the unpronounceable name of God as the other to which I am bound by an absolute, unconditional obligation, by an incomparable, non-negotiable duty" (DM 67). The story of Abraham is the story of obligation without ethics, without the reassurance and consolation of ethics. It is written, as I have argued elsewhere, "against ethics," and as a "contribution to a poetics of obligation."[12] Derrida writes:

> We insist here, in the name of the morality of morality, on something which the moralizing moralists and the good consciences often forget, those who every morning or every week, in the newspapers, the weeklies, on radio and on television, recall the sense of ethical and political responsibilities. Philosophers who do not write an ethics fail in their duty, one often hears, and the first duty of the philosopher is to think the ethical, to add a chapter on ethics to each of his books and thereby, as often as possible, to return to Kant. What the knights of good conscience do not recognize is that the "sacrifice of Isaac" illustrates, if one is able to speak in this case of such a nocturnal mystery, the most daily and most common experience of responsibility. (DM 67)

But how does this extraordinary story—of a father given an incomprehensible command from the wholly other to sacrifice his son—illustrate ordinary moral life? How can the paradox of Abraham become a paradigm for the rest of us? Because responsibility is in the first place responsibility to the other, and the name of God is the name of the absolute other, so the story tells of my obligation, in my singularity, to the absolute singularity of the other, which "casts me immediately in the space or the risk of absolute sacrifice" (DM 68):

> I am not able to respond to the call, to the request, to the obligation, nor even to the love of an other without sacrificing to him the other other, the other others. *Every other is wholly other.* (DM 68)

Obligation is thus caught in a scandal, an aporia, a paradox, but a paradigmatic paradox, which constitutes the sacrifice and spells the death and the limit of thinking obligation through conceptually:

> From the moment that I am in relation with the other, with the look, the request, the love, the order, the call of the other, I know that I am able to respond to it only by sacrificing ethics, that is to say, that which obliges me to respond also and in the same way, in the same instant, to all the others. I deal death, I perjure, I do not need to raise the dagger over my son on the

top of Mount Moriah to do this. Day and night, in each instant, on all the Mount Moriahs of the world, I am doing this, raising the dagger over what I love and ought to love, over the other, such or such an other to whom I owe absolute fidelity, incommensurably. (DM 68–69)

Isaac thus occupies the place of all the others, of the ethical community, of the *oikos* and *Sittlichkeit*, of the bonds I have to everyone else whose needs I do not address when I respond to the singular other who claims me in this instant, every instant, day in and day out. If I help to feed and clothe *this* other, I abandon the other others to their nakedness and starvation. If I attend to my children, I sacrifice the children of other men. Ours is a world built on the sacrifice of others, the faces of whom we daily see on the evening news.

One remarkable thing about Derrida's gloss of *Fear and Trembling* is its relationship to Levinas. His interpretation draws upon Levinas's transition from "substitution"—my absolute, singular obligation to the other who comes to me from on high—to "justice," my general obligation to everyone else. Justice for Levinas intervenes in order to limit, to calculate—by dividing and multiplying—my obligation among the entire community. Justice for Levinas is a way of stopping me from spending everything on one account. For Derrida, this moment of "calculation," this moment of the *rationem reddere*, represents a moment of sacrifice or loss of the unique demands of singularity, of an always imperfect reconciliation, one might even say a tragic conflict of duties, whereas Levinas himself does not appear to regard the possibility of the reconciling calculation of justice as inherently troubled.

What is furthermore interesting is the way in which Derrida's gloss opens up a Levinasian interpretation of Kierkegaard that is missed by Levinas himself. Levinas, who admires many things about Kierkegaard, is a critic of *Fear and Trembling*, but certainly not of the story of father Abraham. Levinas writes:

> Kierkegaard has a predilection for the biblical story of the sacrifice of Isaac. He describes thus the encounter with God by a subjectivity that is raised up to the religious level, to God beyond the ethical order! His interpretation of this story can be doubtlessly taken up in an other sense. Perhaps the ear that Abraham had for hearing the voice that leads him back to the ethical order has been the highest moment of the drama.[13]

The wonderful thing about *Genesis* 22 is its endless reinterpretability, which is testified to by the staggering literature surrounding it (in which it is endlessly reinterpreted).[14] Levinas has every right to see the story differently, as a story of the *end* of sacrifice, of the sacrifice of sacrifice, at least of human sacrifice, which is precisely how it is seen by a great deal of biblical scholarship. Levinas rightly criticizes Kierkegaard for his love of violence, something I have also criticized under the name of the *Kampfsphilosophie* of Kierkegaard and

Heidegger.[15] Derrida himself remarks upon the "absence of women from the story," and he wonders whether the intervention of a woman might not alter the "implacable universality of the law, of his law, the logic of sacrificial responsibility" (DM 75). Kierkegaard's reading follows St. Paul's, whose concern was to delimit the law in the interest of faith. This Pauline-Kierkegaardian reading is not questioned by Derrida, who shares Paul's and Kierkegaard's interest in the deconstruction of the law—not in the name of faith, to be sure, but in the name of the justice due to a singular other, for the name of God is the name of the wholly other.

By siding with Kierkegaard (and Paul), Derrida opens up a distinction between obligation (*devoir, obligation*) and ethics. Derrida makes it plain that what Kierkegaard calls the "religious," *re-ligare*, is *structurally* the obligation, *ob-ligare*, the being bound over, the responsibility, of the subject to the wholly other, which is precisely what Levinas calls the "ethical." Derrida's difference with Levinas, his Kierkegaardianism, lies in his willingness to sacrifice "ethics," both the word and the concept, which for Derrida and Kierkegaard (and Heidegger[16])—means the *calculability of obligation*, allowing the power of the *rationem reddere* to hold sway over the question of obligation. We should notice that when Kierkegaard says "ethics" he means the universal or general which cannot bind me in an unconditional way; when Levinas says "ethics" he means the unconditional which does not bind me in a general way, although general obligations can be derived from it, or follow along after it. Like Kierkegaard, Derrida subscribes to the notion of an unconditional obligation—but without ethics, or beyond ethics—which is what he calls a "hyper-ethical sacrifice" (DM 70). This means a responsibility to singularity which at one and the same time, "in the same instant," transcends or sacrifices my generalizable obligations to the community. In meeting my obligation to the one I sacrifice my obligation to the others.

Seen in terms of this distinction between obligation and ethics, what Levinas calls "ethics" is nothing more than the obligation that ethics seeks to shelter with language and universality. Derrida and Kierkegaard advocate an obligation laid bare, unprotected, a naked obligation, which lacks the reassurance, the shelter, the comfort, the consolation of ethics, i.e., of universality. Levinas leads us to believe that the transition from substitution (singularity) to justice (universality) can be made without sacrifice, without conflict and loss, that it is possible to formulate a wisdom of love (ethics) without a loss of wisdom (about individuals). Kierkegaard and Derrida, on the other hand, are willing to make the sacrifice of ethics; they think that obligation is an abyss, that any attempt to formulate such a wisdom of love, or of obligation, is caught up in aporia, scandal and paradox, that our duties clash in irreconcilable conflicts, awash in incommensurability. The disagreement comes down to an old debate about the unity of virtue, about whether our duties as a whole form a unity.

What then does Derrida make of the moment in which God stays the patriarch's hand, the instant when the angel calls off the (human) sacrifice, which is the highest moment in the story according to Levinas, representing the return to the ethical, a teleological suspension of the religious, as it were, in the name of the ethical? Hearing the voice of Elohim speak once again, Abraham responds, *me voici*. He has shown that he understands what an absolute obligation means; he is prepared to meet its demands, to embrace its unconditionality, to deal in death (to deal death to Isaac, to the other others, in order to keep the deal with the wholly other). He is prepared to act in an instant where reasons can neither be demanded nor rendered, in an instant where "there is no more time, where time is no longer given" (DM 72), a time in which having been ready to act is as good as having already acted. This no-more-time is the given time (*donner le temps*) of absolute obligation, which is not the present of ordinary time.

The essential thing, Derrida says, is the secret that he will not share. He will not give reasons. There is no language common to him and the wholly other in which he could negotiate,[17] no ethics in which his case could be stated and defended. He cannot explain what is going to happen because he does not understand it himself; the secret he keeps from Isaac is a secret to him as well. The tragic hero can explain himself, but Abraham is reduced to silence by the secret.

But if Abraham cannot share his absolute secret with us, and if we—let us say, we philosophers *qua* philosophers, who must put faith out of action, in *epoche*—do not share his faith, what do we share with Abraham?

> . . . what *Fear and Trembling* says of the sacrifice of Isaac is the truth. Translated into an extraordinary story, it shows the structure of the quotidian. It expresses in its paradox the responsibility in each instant for every man and every woman. In fact, there is no ethical generality that does not already fall prey to the paradox of Abraham. At the moment of every decision and in the relationship with *every other as wholly other*, every other asks us at each instant to act like the knight of faith. (DM 77)

Derrida thus wants to make a paradigm of this paradox, an exemplar of this knight of the extraordinary, to universalize this exception, to say that we are always already caught up in exceptionality, caught up in a singular secret that we cannot communicate to others. The religious exception, the singularity of the religious situation in which ethical generality is suspended, is always upon us. Such exceptionality is the daily business of life—which implies that the unexceptional regularities found in the ethics books are highly unusual.

We share with Abraham the secret—the incommunicable command from the wholly other—that we cannot pass on to the other others. This secret cannot be taught and passed on in a historical tradition from one generation to another. It is encountered in the instant, each time for the first time; each time is an absolute beginning, history being nothing more than the incessant repetition of absolute beginnings.

Kierkegaard has inscribed this story within the Christian Gospel, even though it is the common legacy of the Jewish, the Muslim, and the Christian religions—these very names being the names of the most fierce and bloody combatants over the centuries, and no less in our own day. It is to this Christian inscription that Derrida next turns.

Tout autre est tout autre

The paradigmatic character of the story of the binding of Isaac is a function of Derrida's elliptical formula "every other is wholly other"; all others, not just God, are wholly other.[18] The otherness of God is paradigmatic of all otherness, of the otherness of all others. In the *Cartesian Meditations*, Husserl pointed out that the intentional acts (*Erlebnisse*) that make up the flow of the other's conscious stream are inaccessible to me; they cannot be known to me without becoming mine, without destroying the alterity of the other. Levinas gave what had been for Husserl a primarily epistemic conception—the constitution of our knowledge of other persons—an ethical force. For Levinas the alterity of the other had to do with the irreducible ethical claim that the other makes upon the responsible subject, the demand made upon me by the other who is not me or mine, but the stranger.

This seeming tautology (in French) thus stands at the core of a radical heterology, the effect of which is to attribute the radical and infinite alterity of God to everyone, something that can be seen in Levinas, who does not confine *l'infini* to God. The infinite one means, first of all (in the order of experience), the other person, the one who comes to me from "on high," and then, in and through the other person, the "seal" that marks ethical experience, the trace of infinity of *il*, of the illeity of God which seals and stamps and warrants the infinity of the other person.[19] Levinas's thought moves about in the space or "difference" between the face of my neighbor and the face of God, between other persons and God, between "two, but unique 'wholly others' " (DM 84). This difference is not conceived in the traditional way, as a difference between the finitude of other persons and the infinity of God, but rather as the difference between two infinities, the infinity of other persons visited upon us in ethical experience and the infinity of God as a fainter trace left behind on others.

Is there then not a certain "analogy" between these infinities, which are no longer separated by an infinity but rather likened to each on that account, for being "wholly other" is what "all others" share (*partager*)? But is not analogy a trace of paganism for Levinas? However that question is answered by

Levinas or for Levinas, Derrida argues that the effect of this formula, which weakens the distinction between *the* "wholly other" (God) and "every other," is to weaken the distinction between the generality of ethics and the singularity of the religious, and hence to weaken the distinction between Kierkegaard and Levinas (and Derrida himself). Neither Kierkegaard nor Levinas can make an assured distinction between these two orders; accordingly the disagreement between them tends to wither. For if every other is infinitely other it would not be possible to distinguish the ethical as an order of generality that would then have to be sacrificed to the religious as an order of singularity. The positions of Kierkegaard and Levinas would then begin to drift towards each other:

> Kierkegaard would have to admit, as Levinas recalls, that the ethical is also the order of and the respect of absolute singularity, and not only that of generality or repetition of the same. But on his side, taking into account absolute singularity, that is to say, absolute alterity in relation to the other man, Levinas is no longer able to distinguish between the absolute infinity of God and that of each man: his ethics is already religion. (DM 81; cf. 108n.8)

What is true of the generality of ethics would hold *a fortiori* of the generality of the law and politics—and here Derrida is alluding to his recent work on the philosophy of law—in which the problematic effects of singularity invade the decisions which the legal system, the "justice" system, is required to render about each individual "case."[20]

It is to raise the level of our responsibility to singularity, to heighten our sense of the idiosyncratic claims of singularity, that deconstruction, if there is such a thing, does its work. Like Kierkegaard, Derrida's interests turn on the incommensurability of the individual, the philosophically problematic notion that the individual is higher than the general, and on the undecidability that disturbs all decision-making. The difficult thing to do—shall we say, the responsible thing?—is to grope with the undecidability of the concept, or the quasi-concept, of responsibility. The easy thing—shall we say, the irresponsible thing?—is to follow the lead of the knights of good conscience, who castigate as nihilists anyone who enters the troubled waters of undecidability:

> It suffices to deny the aporia or the antinomy indefatigably, and to treat all those who continue to be disturbed in the face of so much good conscience as irresponsible people, nihilists, relativists, indeed post-structuralists or, worse, deconstructionists. (DM 81–82)

Winning the Kingdom of Heaven Economically

Derrida now returns to the question of the secret (DM 85ff.). At the end of *Fear and Trembling* (FT 120), Johannes de Silentio praises the greatness of the patriarch for his ability to go it on his own, without human approval or human understanding of his actions, for the solitude and secrecy in which he is able to act. De Silentio alludes to Matthew 6:6, in which Jesus instructs the disciples on how to pray and is about to tell them the "Lord's Prayer." Jesus warns them not to make a great show of themselves, praying like hypocrites on street corners, for such people already have their reward. "But when you pray, go into your room, close the door and pray to your Father who is unseen. Then your Father, who sees what is done in secret (*videre in secreto, en to krypto blepein*) will reward you." God knows everything I am doing—and he knows whatever I need before I even ask for it; he can count our tears—although I do not know a thing about God. The relation is completely asymmetric: he sees me but I do not see a thing of him. This is what Derrida calls the "denegation" of the secret: I know there is a secret but I do not know what the secret is.[21] I do not know what God knows (*secretum*, negation) but I know that God knows what he is doing (denegation). As Patočka has pointed out, the Platonic "Good," the invisible source and medium of intelligibility and knowing, becomes in Christian Neoplatonism someone who sees us while remaining himself unseen, more a "look" or "eye" than a "sun," and indeed a divine eye that we cannot see (DM 89).

Blinded from seeing what he is doing, Abraham does what God asks, sacrificing his own love in sacrificing his beloved Isaac (a very Kantian gesture of doing violence to self-love). Abraham acted "without calculation, without investment, without the perspective of reappropriation," sacrificing every economic consideration, every consideration of an "economy of sacrifice" (DM 90). And *in that instant*, when the dagger is raised and Abraham has every intention of going through with the bloody deed, "God returns his son to him and decides sovereignly, by an absolute gift (*don*), to reinscribe the sacrifice in an economy which hereafter resembles a compensation" (DM 91). In the instant that Abraham makes a sacrifice of economy, God on His side—this is none of Abraham's doing—turns his act into an economy of sacrifice.

God returns Isaac *only* in the instant when He is assured that Abraham has made a *don*, a pure gift (not an exchange), without hope of return, a gift to the death, a gift of death, of Isaac who has no price. Abraham does not enter into negotiations with God (as he had haggled over the price of Sodom and Gomorrah in Genesis 18); he just says *me voici*. God gives a return in the instant when it is clear that Abraham gives a pure gift, without hope or expectation of a return, in an un-calculating an-economy. When "dissemination" was defined as "that which does not return to the father," Derrida remarks, it well described the moment of "Abrahamic renunciation" (DM 91).

That is the story of Abraham; but *Matthew* is a different story. Matthew, around whom the anonymous author of *Matthew* has organized this gospel, was a tax collector (Matthew 9:9), who was interested in keeping balanced books and accounting for every dime. Now in Matthew 6, the expression

"And your father who sees in secret will reward (*rendra, reddere*) you" is repeated three times (4, 6, 18). It is as if it were the formula to be learned "by heart," that is, by an economy of the heart, which is itself an economic principle: where your treasure is, there is your heart (6:21). In *Matthew* Jesus is portrayed as the author of a more sublime, secret, invisible, celestial economy which trades in higher, heavenly profits. If you make a public display of your prayer, you already have your reward (*misthon*); but if you pray in secret, then your reward will be from the Father. Store up invisible treasures in heaven, where things do not rust or get stolen, and not perishable earthly goods. The kingdom of heaven is a return promised to those who are poor in spirit, merciful, and persecuted for justice's sake. The poor in spirit will be compensated (*merces*) in heaven for their sacrifices on earth, as opposed to the pharisees who shortsightedly succumb to earthly profit-taking, thus forfeiting long-term heavenly returns. To be sure, the poor in spirit do not enter into finite, visible transactions, but secret, invisible, heavenly ones, and they are on that account much shrewder investors than the pharisees. If you love those who love you, what good is that? Do not even the tax collectors do the same? The truly "meritorious" thing is to love those who hate and persecute you. Do not return an eye for an eye, but repay hatred with love and turn the other cheek. That will have a real and everlasting payback, for the Father who sees in secret is keeping invisible books on all these transactions and is entering these finite losses into an infinite calculus.

The Matthean economy is neither Jewish (hypocritical and pharisaical) nor pagan (*ethnikoi, gentiles, goyim*), but specifically Christian; not Judeo-Christian but Christian *versus* Jewish (DM 100). Do not seek to be just or to give alms or to pray before men, or even, were it possible, before yourself: do not let your left hand know what your right is doing, lest your heavenly reward be forfeited by this exposure to the light of the day. Pray, fast, and give alms— but in secret; don't walk around looking half dead from your good works, not if you are in the business of storing up heavenly treasure.

This does not mean, Derrida adds, that God is some kind of high-powered satellite circling the earth who maintains perfect surveillance on everything down below. It means rather, in Augustine's formula, that God is something interior and more intimate to me than I am to myself. If we step outside the framework of specific religious beliefs—Jewish, Christian, or Islamic—Derrida remarks, we can say that "God" here is the name of "the possibility for me to keep a secret which is inwardly visible but outwardly invisible." "God" constitutes the invisible sphere of conscience, of *l'être avec soi* (DM 101). What I call God, God in me, calls me to be me, the interior I, which Kierkegaard calls "subjectivity" (DM 102). It is getting difficult to distinguish God, the secret, and the structure of the subject: God is what calls up—what is called(?)—subjectivity. Derrida here sketches a deeply Pauline, Augustinian,

Lutheran, Kierkegaardian interiority. The subject confesses to God what God already knows, for God already sees in secret everything there is to confess, so that the confessor is confessing to himself:[22]

> This is the history of God and of the name of God as a history of the secret, which is a history at the same time secret and without secret. This history is also an economy. (DM 102)

The Matthean—as opposed to the Abrahamic—sacrifice is thus quite equivocal. It begins by renouncing earthly rewards, by denouncing all visible, earthly calculation as pharaseeism, so that on the outside it looks like perfect renunciation. But this renunciation is undertaken only in order to capitalize on a secret, infinite, invisible, heavenly return, so that on the inside it seeks a reward, which means that it reproduces the essential structure of the pharisaical. Hardly the pure gift, such alms giving reminds us of Baudelaire's *Counterfeit Money* and the narrator's friend, who seeks to win heaven economically—this time by a higher level counterfeit of the gift which is really a long-term investment in an invisible, heavenly economy. By drawing the gift back into a calculus, *Matthew* reproduces a second, more sublime phariseeism, a higher, holier, heavenly hypocrisy.

To guard against this subversion of giving, one would have to give without knowing that one gives, without cognition (by oneself) or recognition (by others). In *Given Time* a "pure gift" is possible only in a giving that gives without any intention or intentionality at all, a giving that is guarded both from the generous intentionality of the donor and the grateful intentionality of the donee, because it is guarded from all intentionality, a gift (*don*) in which the donor-subject, the donee-subject, and the gift as "present" (*présent, cadeau*) are all disseminated.[23] For Derrida, the only way to break the circle of self-aggrandizement and wage-labor—earthly or heavenly—in which the gift is inevitably trapped is the dissemination of intentional subjects and identifiable objects. A celestial economy is economy still, however heavenly, reproducing the hypocrisy on a higher level by seeming to give with the one hand even while secretly storing up treasure for oneself with the other.

In the Matthean economy, the left hand inevitably catches a glimpse of what the right(eous) hand is doing. For as soon as anybody knows anything, as soon as there are subjects, as soon as either hand knows what it is doing, the secret is out. The pure gift demands an absolute structural secret, below the level of conscious agency, of knowledge and recognition.

In *The Genealogy of Morals*, Nietzsche showed the consequences of such economic thinking when it is carried to its conclusion. Nietzsche criticizes the Pauline "economy of salvation" as a system of exchange, of paying off debt/guilt (*Schuld*) with the coin of sacrifice, suffering, and cruelty. This system finally self-destructs, or auto-deconstructs, at that point of particular madness which Nietzsche calls Christianity's "stroke of genius" (*Geniestreich*),[24] viz., the Pauline theology of a sin/debt/guilt so infinite, so bottomless, that only God himself can pay it off, and all this under the cover of the beautiful name of "gift," *gratia*. The Pauline-Christian economy culminates in the idea of an infinite, unpayable debt, of a state of guilt/indebtedness (*Schuldigkeit*) that is so vast and deep that only God Himself can pay Himself back. Only the Creditor has the resources to pay off the debt! Nietzsche's critique, Derrida comments, has the effect of suspending faith (*foi*), of letting it twist in the wind, between belief (*croyance*) and credit (*créance*). Growth in faith is capital growth, an infinite extension of a (very) long-term credit line. And how can we believe in that, Nietzsche is asking? Is that merely a rhetorical question? Does not something resonate in rhetorical questions that makes the established, questioned order tremble? (DM 107).

Counterfeit Kingdoms

It is important to see that Derrida is not saying that *The Genealogy of Morals* is the final word on Christianity, or the only way to gloss *Fear and Trembling*. It is not as if Christianity means—contrary to everything that deconstruction labors to show—just one thing. The point of this analysis is deconstructive, "demystifying." That is why, Derrida adds, " 'The stroke of genius,' *if there is such a thing*" that one would "*attribute* . . . to someone or something that *one calls* 'Christianity' " (DM 106; emphasis mine), would be enveloped in another secret, the secret connection between faith and credit. That is to say, there are many strokes of genius, and many Christianities, depending on the reading, some of which are nothing more than the religion of *The Genealogy of Morals*.

Derrida's discourse on the pure gift delimits and demystifies the economy of sacrifice by showing where the logic of exchange and sacrifice, of giving and taking, of giving up and getting back, can lead; by showing, in short, how such a logic deconstructs or auto-deconstructs. Deconstruction shows what happens when the divine madness of the faith of Father Abraham becomes an economy pure and simple, when faith deteriorates into a credit system. The analysis shows the difficulty of keeping the true coin of faith separate from the counterfeit coin of a credit system, that there is nothing to guarantee that the one will not become the other, nothing that says it cannot reverse itself and turn into its opposite, that it does not already contain its opposite.

Even Abraham's sacrifice—and this is what deconstruction shows—is not absolutely safe, absolutely removed, absolutely safeguarded from hidden, subterranean, unconscious, unwanted, unwilled motivations that would turn it into the reverse of what it means to be (*vouloir*). Who knows what wills (*qui veut?*) here? "God knows what's going on!" we say with exasperation, by which we mean, who knows? it's a secret.[25] The "merit" of deconstruction—for which I think it should be rewarded—is to put us on the alert to the way things can pass into their opposite, the way they can turn around and reverse themselves, by a secret operation, so that they produce effects diametrically opposed to what they intend (*vouloir dire*). Derrida's deconstructionist vigilance about reversibility, like a certain hermeneutic of suspicion, is a salutary admonition.

But Derrida's analysis, deconstruction itself, makes possible another Christianity, another, demystified, deconstructed—and I would say a de-Paulinized—Christianity that turns on the notions of giving and for-giving, of for-giving and for-getting, about which I will have more to say below. Such a Christianity does not turn on an economy of salvation but on the "kingdom of God." It does not view the crucifixion in Pauline terms as the retribution God exacted for sin, or as the reason Jesus was born—Jesus came to live, not to die—but as a fate visited upon a just man who told the truth on the powers that be. It does not turn on making earthly payments on long-term, deferred celestial returns.

In fact, such a (deconstructed) Christianity looks a great deal more like what is contained in some of the most authentic Jesus-sayings about the "kingdom," in which the kingdom is not the deferred reward for present sacrifice but the future present, the kingdom now, begun in Jesus' proclamation that the kingdom of God is at hand. It merits noting that the expression "kingdom of heaven" (*basileia ton ouranon*) is a distinctively Matthean innovation on the older phrase "kingdom of God" (*basileia tou theou*), which is very likely *ipsissima verba*. With the "kingdom of heaven" the kingdom of God is given just the economic twist that Derrida exposes, even as Matthew has also redacted "the poor" (*hoi ptochoi*) into "poor in spirit" (*pneumeati*). By thus interiorizing poverty, *Matthew* gives comfort to post-Constantinian Christianity, for in the Matthean account a heavenly reward need not be bought at the price of external earthly treasures, so long as one remained poor in one's heart, in secret, for which one will earn heavenly return. It was also in *Matthew* that the Pharisees are maligned, reflecting rather more the polemics between the emerging Christian movement and the established Jewish religion in the last quarter of the first Christian century than anything historical about the Pharisees themselves.

The kingdom of God does not turn on pain and re-pentance, which is a more Baptist (as in John the Baptist) rendering of *metanoia*, but on joy, which is a more Jesus-minded version of *metanoia*. Jesus did not play a dirge but a dance, and he does not mourn but pipes (Matthew 11:17–18). These kingdom sayings are not organized around the infinite debt of sin, and gathering infinite resources to pay it off. They do not speak of guilt and punishment, of satisfying the wrath of an infinitely offended deity, but of for-giveness, on giving debt away, on the loving care of *abba* ("dad" or "mom") for his children, however prodigal they may be. Far from demanding infinite retribution for the prodigal son's offense, the father forgives him immediately and celebrates his return. The kingdom is organized around giving and forgiving, not debt and sacrifice, above all not the hypersacrifice of a God, of a divine immolation, to pay off an infinite, bottomless debt.

The kingdom sayings are woven into all the early Christian texts, along with the characteristically Markan, Matthean, Lukan, Johannine, and Pauline redactions, and we can still feel their power and hear them resonating.

So *Matthew*, too, means many things, and cannot be reduced to the machinations of a "celestial economy," to a higher, more sublime, more calculating system of accounting. Matthew 6 contains the little sermon on worrying (*merimnatein*), which is one of the most Zen-like discourses of Jesus, in which Jesus urges the disciples not to count, not to worry, and to be maddeningly uncalculating (6:25–34). Be not concerned (*merimnate*), have no *Sorge* for yourselves or your *conatus essendi*, don't go around counting up what you need. You should live without care (*sine cura, secura*). The "opthalmology" here is to look, to see—birds and lilies and grasses—and to live like them, to live like the rose, *ohne Warum*, as Angelus Silesius said.[26] The celestial here is not a heavenly reward but the realm of the birds of "the air" (*ouranos*): see (*emblepsate*) how they neither sow nor reap but God gives them what they need, as if they were utterly non-productive things who live purely off gifts from God. The kingdom is a kingdom of gifts. Consider the lilies of the field. What productive work do they do?—and yet the garments of Solomon himself are no rival to their raiments. But if God cares this greatly about birds and lilies and grasses, how much more will God care for you, you whose very tears he has counted, you *oligopistoi*, you who are too much given to counting up (*créanciers*) and not enough given to faith (*croyance*). For faith means to live without keeping count, without taking account (*sine ratione*), and to say yes, a number of yeses, *oui, oui*, again and again, each day, day by day. Each day (*epiousios*) (6:11), comes, *viens*. For religion is something to be deconstructed, just as faith, if there is such a thing, cannot be deconstructed. Live without why, without demanding or rendering accounts, *sine ratione*. Have the madness not to ask what you shall eat or drink or wear, not to ask where your next meal is coming from, not to seek job security, medical insurance, or guaranteed housing. Seek the kingdom (*basileian*)—which is today, the kingdom is now, today—and seek justice (*dikaiosynen*) and do not worry (*merimnesote*) about tomorrow. Stop thinking about tomorrow. Let tomorrow worry about itself.

This is quite mad. It violates everything we mean by "tenure," and it would make it extraordinarily difficult to find a permanent pastor who would accept these terms.

Everything in these sayings turns on God's love and God's gift-giving, on the appeal to the disciples to trust God, to have a little more faith, to turn their concerns over to God, to let God do the worrying. This is not because God, who keeps secret books, will reward us infinitely more than men can, but because in the kingdom of God, where God rules, God will give us just enough of what we *need* today, and not so much as to burden us with wealth or with seeking wealth. If we have given everything up, unconditionally and not as part of a bargain, God will give us the time, *donner le temps*, which will free us for our true concern, which is justice. (Unless a man lose his life he will not have it given back.) If we give up the search for security, if we live *sine cura* (*ohne Sorge*), if we acquire what Heidegger calls the free relationship to things—in the famous discourse on *Gelassenheit*[27]—then we will be freed. The time will be given to us, not just for the thinging of the thing, but for justice, for seeking justice, for the kingdom of justice, which is the kingdom of God.

So faith is linked here not with building credit (*créancier*) but with trust, and trust is inseparable from love: have faith and trust in God's love for you, which is at least as great as his love for the lilies of the field. For God is love and what God gives is the best, because God's will, God's heart, is good through and through. The kingdom of God: *viens!*

That is not a way to calculate in a more cunning, celestial, and long-range way, but a way to love and trust and seek justice, to seek the kingdom, which is here and now, which is for the lame and the leper, the outcast and the sinner, the widow and the orphan, in short, to use a word whose time has come, for the "other." The kingdom is not like a long-term bond, not a wise form of estate planning for a vault of heavenly treasures. The kingdom is the call of the other, and the kingdom is here and now.

None of this is to say that the evangelical life is absolutely safe from what it can turn into: a caste of priestly bourgeoisie, well kept and well fed, who have made a profitable business out of the crucifixion. That is precisely what set the wheels of the Kierkegaardian writing machine in motion. Nothing is safe. You *should* worry that *not* worrying will turn into a life of bourgeois ease, which is the counterfeit side of the coin of letting God do the worrying, the counterfeit of the kingdom, a counterfeit kingdom. That is why fear and trembling are permanent features of biblical trust, and part of the meaning of not worrying.

Have fear and trembling—but don't worry.

Deconstruction is a theory, if it is a theory, that nothing is safe, pure, clean, uncontaminated, monochromatic, unambiguous; it is thus a quasi-theory of undecidability, and it works well for everything from architecture to literary criticism, from religion to politics. Deconstruction is an exploration of as many "instants" of undecidability as it has time (as it is given time) to study. Its "solution" to the question of undecidability shows a trend: it always tends to say that the undecidability is permanent, that undecidability precedes, follows, and permeates the decision, that the undecidability is first, last, and always, but that decisions must be made and indecision broken. By definition, it is impossible to *know* what one's secret, unconscious motives are, or when one is trading with counterfeit coins (which are only "good counterfeits" so long as they are not known to be counterfeit), whether in one's heart one is pharisaical or not, whether one is living like the lilies of the field or just enjoying a comfortable living with good benefits, like Trollopean parsons in Barsetshire. One begins where one is and does all that one can; the rest is beyond us. The pure gift is im/possible, a condition of possibility and impossibility.

That is what Derrida means by beginning "*by* the impossible," which is "the gift as the first mover of the circle," the pure gift even though and when it may finally, inevitably, "contract itself into a circular contract":

> For finally, the overrunning of the circle by the gift, if there is any, does not lead to a simple, ineffable exteriority that would be transcendent and without relation. It is this exteriority that sets the circle going, it is this exteriority that puts the economy in motion.[28]

That is what is possible and impossible—if and when there are any subjects. For the ultimate, radical logic of the pure gift is to remove the gift entirely from the field of intentionality and willing, from pure hearts and cunning deceivers, from good will and bad, from human will or divine. That is to shift to a giving that is not human at all, neither Abrahamic nor pharisaical nor Matthean, neither selfish nor altruistic, neither ethical nor religious, and so to pass beyond *L'Éthique du don*, both the book and the concept. This "pure" giving, which is discussed at length in *Donner le temps*, in which everything "humanistic" or "subjectivistic" is disseminated, is a lot more like Heidegger's *es gibt*, the impersonal giving that gives being and time, or like the anonymous rumblings of *il y a* in Levinas. In this purely anonymous giving, no one gives anything ("present") to anyone, and giving subsides into a middle-voice impersonality. That is the deeper "context" of Derrida's study of Abraham's gift of Isaac's death. *"Donner la mort"* is an instance, one of the "instants," of *Donner le temps*. There is no giving outside the context of this *il y a*, if there is any (*s'il y en a*).

My present purposes are served by returning to the essentials of *"Donner la mort,"* "Giving Death," which is to underline the significance of singularity, obligation, responsibility, justice, the unconditional gift in the work of Derrida. It is enough for me to scandalize the knights of good conscience. (I need nothing more; the rest will be added.) The singularity that captures Derrida's attention is not that of the aesthete, as it is widely taken by the officials of anti-deconstruction, but is rather an ethico-religious singularity that crosses the lines of the ethical and the religious, a singularity situated in the intersection or crossfire between Kierkegaard and Levinas. Far from being unethical, anethical, or antiethical, deconstruction has to do with the *Seelenfünklein* of ethics, exploring the fine tip of the ethical soul, analyzing the most delicate effects and reversibilities that infiltrate obligation and responsibility. Such reversibilities ought to fill those who rush to judgment—on deconstruction, on others, on anything—with a certain trepidation. Shall we say, with a certain fear and trembling?

Notes

1. Derrida, "Passions: 'An Oblique Offering'," p. 15.
2. Derrida, "*Donner la mort*," in *L'Éthique du don*, p. 67; hereafter "DM."
3. M. C. Taylor, *Altarity*, chap. 10; "Secretions," in *Tears*; Agacinski, *Aparté*; Mackey, "Slouching Toward Bethlehem"; Caputo, "Beyond Aestheticism." More recently, my *Against Ethics* is an attempt to restage *Fear and Trembling* in Derridean terms; unfortunately, "*Donner la mort*" appeared only after this book was completed.
4. Kierkegaard, FT 7.
5. Economic metaphors recur continually in *Fear and Trembling*, framing the book at the beginning and end (FT 5, 121).
6. Derrida, *Given Time.*
7. It was Mark Taylor, before Derrida, who noticed the deconstructionistic implications of Abraham's secret; see Taylor, "Secretions."
8. I follow the Greek text and the New International Version translation found in *The NASB-NIV Parallel New Testament.*
9. The French *me voici*, here I am, see me here, a centerpiece of Levinas's thought, appears to be a remarkably felicitous translation of the Hebrew *hinneni* which means, "behold, here am I." I have been particularly helped on this and other matters with the story of Abraham by Trible, *Genesis 22.*
10. See Westphal, "The Teleological Suspension of the Religious." See DM 88, where Derrida points out that Kierkegaard seems to come back to a kind of Kantianism; if Kierkegaard is a critic of Kantian universalizability, he is an advocate of the Kantian notion of "sacrificing" sensibility to duty.
11. This is Lyotard's objection to trying to reinscribe the Nazi genocide within the genre of sacrifice, by calling it a "holocaust." Did the Nazi executioners love the Jews? Did they offer them up to God in fear and trembling? See Lyotard, *The Differend*, no. 168, p. 109.
12. In *Against Ethics*, my more Derridean version of *Fear and Trembling*, I make everything turn on a distinction between "ethics," as a philosophical discourse, and "obligation," which I treat as "fact as it were," something that happens (*arrive*), but something that lacks the deeper backup of a reassuring philosophical discourse, which is what Kierkegaard calls the comfort of universality.
13. Levinas, *Noms Propres*, p. 86.
14. For bibliographies, see Westerman, *Genesis 12-36: A Commentary*; and Crenshaw, ed., *A Whirlpool of Torment.*
15. Caputo, *Demythologizing Heidegger*, chap. 2.

16. See Heidegger's famous discussion of ethics in "A Letter on Humanism" in *Heidegger: Basic Writings*, pp. 323–33. The constant references to the *ratio reddenda* in "*Donner la mort*" are allusions to Heidegger's *The Principle of Reason*.

17. Kierkegaard (and with him Derrida) ignores the earlier chapters of Genesis, in which Abraham haggles with God over the price of saving Sodom and Gomorrah. Suppose he can come up with fifty just men? Well, if fifty, then why not forty-five? etc. (18:23–33). Abraham eventually gets the price down to ten, which he cannot come up with.

18. While this may be, as Derrida says (DM 84), a little shibboleth, a secret of the French language, it can be detected in other languages. In English, the closest one can come to this formula is "all others are all-other"; in Latin, *omnis alter est omni-alter*. It is not a mere quirk of French.

19. Levinas, *Otherwise than Being*, p. 185.

20. Derrida, "Force of Law," pp. 3–67.

21. For more on denegrating secrets, see Derrida, "How to Avoid Speaking" in Budick and Wolfgang, eds., *Languages of the Unsayable*.

22. This is a central motif in *Circumfessions* in Bennington and Derrida, *Jacques Derrida*, trans. Geoffrey Bennington (Chicago: University of Chicago Press, 1993).

23. This point is developed in Derrida, *Given Time*, pp. 1–33.

24. Nietzsche, *"The Birth of Tragedy" and "The Genealogy of Morals,"* second essay, chap. xxi, p. 225.

25. In terms of giving death, there always was a fine line between martyrdom and the death wish. Historically, the Church's condemnation of suicide arose from the growing desire among early Christians to take one's life in order to be with Christ, which seemed like a good deal to the early Christians, and also to Nietzsche who likewise encouraged the latter-day saints to be done with it and join their Savior. The Church's response to this wave of violence against oneself was to tell the faithful (*les croyances*) to leave death-dealing to God, to leave giving life and giving death in God's hands, not to deal in death. That too is the point of another, non-Kierkegaardian, less macho reading of the story of the binding of Isaac. The Lord is rubbing Abraham's nose in the bloodiness of sacrifice: take this son whom you dearly love—and he tells Abraham to lay off, not to deal in (human) death.

26. See Heidegger, *The Principle of Reason*, pp. 32–40.

27. Heidegger, *Discourse on Thinking*, pp. 54–55.

28. Derrida, *Given Time*, pp. 30–31.

14 Kierkegaard's Radical Existential Praxis, or

*Why the Individual Defies
Liberal, Communitarian, and
Postmodern Categories*

Martin J. Matuštík

THERE IS A received view of the Kierkegaard who resists Hegel's communitarian nation-state on the platform of an anti-social or apolitical, if not possessive, individualism. This received wisdom tends to overlook that Kierkegaard's critique of reason and society exposes specifically the truncated instrumental rationality and the atomistic individualism found in modern politics and economies. It is, then, not surprising that to such a chorus of interpreters has been recently added the new celebratory tune of another Kierkegaard, the prophet of deconstructive transgressions who writes under the erasure of all normative agency. Many of these sympathizers mistake Kierkegaard's attack on reified modern rationality and on the self-certain, let us add masculinist, notions of autonomy as if this were his wholesale abdication of all care for ethico-political universals. I argue that Kierkegaard's dialogue with the present age delivers troubles equally to certain strains of modernism and postmodernism. This Kierkegaard jests where modernists expect unreasonably much from critical rationality and autonomous self-determination, and he is earnest where postmoderns sidestep the difficulty of life into a transgressive gesture about the undecidability of self-choice. He unmasks the oversights of both views: the former's foundationalist, abstract, and absolutist reason and the latter's jargon of textuality and abstract death of the self-transparent author/subject. What is common to both is that they prescind from existing. Kierkegaard's attack on the leveling trends in modernity, however, propels the individual neither into a premodern communitarianism nor into nominalist aloofness but empowers one to envision an equality of communicative praxis.[1]

My aim goes beyond a polemical claim that some post/modern positions pass one another as so many ships in the dark: Kierkegaard points to the next step to be taken beyond this unfruitful divide. I characterize such a step as existential praxis and situate it by this question: How to speak of dying to decontextualized rationality and its possessive individualism but still allow for the individual as the category of ethico-politically responsible self-choice? Kierkegaard invites us to consider a form of critical theory and action that would solicit radical honesty about limits and motives informing concept-formation and activism.

I will argue, first, against three sets of category mistakes that Kierkegaard's individual is neither a communitarian, nor a possessive liberal, nor an anti-normative proto-postmodernist. The category of the individual is missing both from the liberal-communitarian controversy and from many a post/modern debate. Second, my proposal takes the path of the individual as an opening to that radical existential praxis which is crucial if democratic multiculture in the present age can be made possible. Third, my conclusion presents Kierkegaard's individual, not as someone offering a total withdrawal from the ethico-political, but as a concrete universal, wherein radical existential praxis enhances and embodies critical social theory.

I. Rethinking the Existential Individual

There are statements in his 1846 critique of the present age which put the brakes on the internationalist call to a proletarian union issued only two years later in Marx's *Communist Manifesto*: Kierkegaard is rather suspicious that "the age will be saved by the idea of sociality, of association." While both the early Marx and Kierkegaard are very much preoccupied with the demise of the human individual, not unlike later Adorno and Marcuse, Kierkegaard argues that the leveling of the individual by the herd mentality of the present age cannot be resisted directly through social union. "[N]ot until the single individual has established an ethical stance despite the whole world, not until then can there be any question of genuinely uniting" (TA 106). For all the arguments about the progressive role of the nation-state in 1848 and now in some Third World post-colonial opposition to Western hegemony, Kierkegaard is as much critical of nationalism as he is of those revolutionaries who attack the philistine bourgeois only through quantitative equality. In his essay, "The Individual," Kierkegaard restates this oversight most emphatically: " 'The individual' is the category through which . . . this age, all history, the human race as a whole, must pass" (PV 128).[2]

Does Kierkegaard's one-sided passion for the individual and his critique of the present age turn him into a possessive individualist, into a communitarian harnessing the substantive sources of the self or, on the flip side, into an ally of the postmodern suspensions of normative discourse? It is ironic that he was hired to legitimate all three positions but both jests about their responses to the crises of modernity and remains earnest about individual responsibility. Yet what can this category bespeak if it is neither an atomistic path to autonomous agency, nor a prevalent convention, nor a nominal gesture bereft of compelling solidarity? Let me examine how Kierkegaard prompts us to rethink each of these three problem areas.

Westphal has demonstrated that a classical liberal reading of Kierkegaard's category of the individual is a mistake. This becomes more obvious when we examine how Kierkegaard's concern with the individual begins where Hegel's ends. Had Kierkegaard wanted to return from Hegel's ethical totality of the rational state to premoral contract relations among disencumbered individuals *qua* property owners, then he would have exchanged holistic "dialectical individualism" for "compositional individualism." We would then place Kierkegaard within the early stage of Hegel's *Philosophy of Right* and classify him as a possessive individualist. But Kierkegaard commences on the grounds of Hegel's ethical reformation of liberal atomism, wherein Hegel's holistic argument wants to get one at the end of the day. The minimalist view of Kierkegaard's critique of Hegel is, thus, insupportable.[3]

A more accurate reading is that Kierkegaard accepts Hegel's full view of the self as relational, situated, and linguistic. If every I-individual is always-already embedded in some cultural we-universal, then Kierkegaard's objection to Hegel is holistic, not atomistic. Unless we wish to deify the nation-state, Kierkegaard objects to Hegel and Heidegger alike. The most concrete universal is achieved not by the hermeneutically given cultural whole but by the individuals who take responsible relation to and choose themselves to be this or that whole which they already descriptively are (TA 62f.).[4]

Kierkegaard's objection is obvious in Johannes de Silentio's relation to the Hegelian view of language and community. *Fear and Trembling* accepts that language harnesses the ethical-universal, while the individual remains that positionality which is not sayable and which cannot be mediated directly by this universal (FT 54–57, 60, 70, 82). Yet the text does not defend fundamentalism. De Silentio's defense of the knight of faith presents a strong critique of fundamentalism along with an attack on the Cartesian view of autonomous agency and on the moral and socio-political privileging of conventional ethics (*Sittlichkeit*). That the single individual is higher than the universal (FT 55) does not prove private self-ownership which knows no fear and trembling. And that Abraham cannot speak about his ordeal with Isaac and Sarah does not mean that anything goes. Depicting the individual in possessive or in purely anarchistic terms misses the target: to revel in the textual undecidability of *Fear and Trembling* would mean to make a virtue out of one's aesthetic self-relation to fear and trembling or to retreat into the resignation of pure textuality which stoically checks out from any embodied risk of having to fear and tremble. Such heroic transgressions of the present age are not what de Silentio has in mind when he calls us back to inhabit the universal in fear and trembling. His earnest jest is that he speaks of agency in terms not clearly recognizable in our liberal-communitarian and post/modern debates. The jest is that one is to act responsibly towards others in the world even when neither one's self-transparency nor conventions (Abraham's patriarchy or the promise that he is the father of the human race) secures action. De Silentio's earnestness about the death of self-possessive agency becomes more clearly socio-political in Anti-Climacus who does not offer us blind faith in the total transgression of the ethical-universal but rather invites us to dissent against the nation-state, the established orthodoxies, and prevalent powers (FT 55, 59, 74, 79; PC 88).[5]

Fear and trembling embody a jesting spirit of seriousness. They occur for the one who chooses herself as a responsible actor in the world yet who can rely neither on the dominant cultural models (TA, PC, KAUC) nor on one's will to be or not to be an agent (SUD) as the criteria for moral action. The jest shows that agency is indeed in trouble; the earnestness plays a joke on the joker who mistook the jargon of agency-in-trouble for the pathos of living in it. However, even if Kierkegaard's individual need not be a possessive individualist, is not the transgressive positionality (i.e., the teleological suspension of the ethical) plagued by decisionism? Can such an individual, like Abraham, sustain her claims otherwise than by arbitrary self-assertions or by the particular narrations of the good life, or by nothing at all?

What Kierkegaard teaches us is that radical self-choice cannot be identified with self-assertions, communitarian visions of the good, or value skepticism. The latter group represents an undecidability about the sources of good and bad, but self-choice stands for an act prior to having such a value dilemma. While the Kierkegaardian individual is always-already a well socialized member of a society, to become such an individual it is insufficient to be individuated via socialization alone. (I.e., to become this individual I cannot rest satisfied with being socialized as a good American; indeed, Kierkegaard invites one to be at times quite un-American!) True, I choose myself not *in abstracto* but as I already am. And yet this is not a choice of this or that tradition or this or that value-sphere but of myself as someone who is capable of responsible, radically honest choosing. Self-choice is qualitative for Kierkegaard; it modifies how I embody my choices but does not justify what I choose (see EO, II, 204).

This characterization of radical self-choice as, so to speak, prior to good and evil explains why Kierkegaard's concerns defy and baffle those of a liberal or neo-existentialist individualist, communitarian, or postmodernist alike, in spite of their differences. He not only defies and baffles but also earnestly jests with all three ideal types (EO, II, 219–24). From a Kierkegaardian perspective, the possessive individualist confuses various aesthetic choices of this or that with one's "choosing to will" (EO, II, 157–77). The communitarian conflates the value spheres of culture or the eudaimonistic domains of the good with the existential sources of the self (CUP 420–31). And the postmodernist mis/reads the death of the author and the end of the book as if these mean that one has no responsibility to oneself and others—i.e., authoring one's always-already living text (CUP 251–300; PV).

All three ideal types remain overly preoccupied with the indeterminacy of modernity. The individualist, Kierkegaard's aesthete (EO, I, *passim*), gets paralyzed by the dizzy freedom of possibilities (CA): if anything goes, nothing matters. The communitarian decries this modern virtueless situation: MacIntyre lectures Kierkegaard about the existentialist and emotivist maleducation of the young, while Charles Taylor tries to retrieve some enduring forms of the good that would define our path. The postmodernist celebrates this ethical undecidability of what to choose. In place of becoming Kierkegaard's "dear reader" (see prefaces to EUD and PV) who asks the how of choosing, this one makes his or her life too easy by jettisoning the other side of transgressions, namely normative agency itself (CUP 202–204, 323).[6]

Radical self-choice lies neither in the cultural nor eudaimonistic valuespheres, nor needs to be lost in signifiers. Self-choice of oneself as the existing individual locates the chooser in a subject-positionality which Climacus calls truth (CUP 189–250). This truth, subjectivity, is not a retreat into navel-gazing (or into self-possession apart from the social) but a venture into an uncertainty of the "chasmic abyss" (CUP 423). The charges of subjectivism, just as those of decisionism, overlook the difference between choices pertaining to validity and those pertaining to identity claims. The charges would apply to Kierkegaard if the category of self-choice directly determined validity claims, e.g., claims about the good life or the moral right. This is not so: both charges against and celebrations of Kierkegaard's anti-normativism are category mistakes.[7]

How, then, are existential questions related to ethical and moral questions? What is the rationale for the distinction between radical self-choice, on the one hand, and the value spheres of ethical life (eudaimonia and *Sittlichkeit*) and procedural morality (*Moralität*) on the other? Is not this distinction between the existential how (I embody choices) and the validity domains of what (I choose) dodging the problem of decisionism?[8] It would be a vicious dodge if no relation were thematized since we could never speak about the importance of Kierkegaard's category of the individual for ethical, moral, and socio-political universals. I claim that Kierkegaard's category does something very important for a normative social theory and practice even though not directly. Kierkegaard's ethical totality is the concrete individual (CUP 529, 534, 537), but this holism is neither derivable from Hegel's *Sittlichkeit*, nor from Kant's moral rigorism, nor from procedural justice alone. Because the individual is the most concrete and the most ideal vanishing point of conceivable difference (i.e., non-identity), the positionality of Kierkegaard's existential ethics cannot be communicated directly through universalizing speech-acts but only via radical self-choice.

For this reason, we get Kierkegaard's existential, not possessive individualist or communitarian, ethics. The latter two types admit a degree of direct communication. Radical self-choice, however, is not directly sayable through the universalizing aims of language. (It is after all the suspension of the ethi-cal-universal in fear and trembling that places individuals *and* communities in the chasmic abyss of distancing from any positivism of values or any tradition-ally received view.) Thus, it constitutes a modal condition of the possibility that we can reflect critically on the normative ideals of the good and right at all. A Kierkegaardian unsayable venture of becoming positioned as this indi-vidual indeed defies liberal, communitarian, and postmodern categories: I transgress both the cocksure, let's say masculinist, subject of instrumental modernity and the conventional guides to the good life, but nowhere do I meet the death of my responsibly positioned agency of personal and social change. Although self-choice presupposes critical distance from the given social norms, this is no excuse for justifying positively private or authoritarian exceptions within the ethical and moral domains. To the contrary, self-choice operates as the condition of the possibility that I can think normatively and act morally in the public sphere.

II. Rethinking Radical Existential Praxis

One striking attempt at rethinking the category of the individual occurs in 1929 when the young Marcuse adopts Kierkegaard's activist critique of Christendom as an example of critical theory rooted in concrete existential praxis. Kierkegaard's pamphlets against Danish Christendom and his street ac-tivism serve as models of social theory rooted in an individually embodied ac-tion. In Marcuse's early view, existential and socio-economic critiques are not opposed (to be existentially concrete is not, then, to dodge the social whole) but two necessarily complementary forms of materially concrete philosophy. The mature Marcuse rejects the German political existentialism that abstracts from historical concretion and, so, plays into the hands of Nazi nationalists. Marcuse's 1960s new sensibility and radical subjectivity, unlike later Conti-nental and Anglo-American thinkers, shows some moderate success in socially integrating Kierkegaard's existential approach into the activist notion of the Great Refusal.[9]

If the individual is reducible to neither a liberal nor a communitarian nor a postmodernist view, but is an existential voice missing from all these posi-tions, then what implications can we derive from Kierkegaard in dialogue with contemporary social theory? Taking cues from some recent returns to Kierke-gaard, I want to examine whether or not the category of the individual can support our striving for societies with democratic multicultures. The common question that emerges from various shipwrecking voyages with Kierkegaard's category is the following: If the individual is the frontier of the teleological suspension of the ethical-universal, what would it mean to translate this posi-tionality (without a dodge) back into this very ethical and socio-political universal, to view it as a concretely individual universal? I will discuss two such translation efforts, even as I find each incomplete without the other, that of Habermas, in relation to Charles Taylor, and Derrida.[10]

The Category of the Individual in Discourse Ethics

In his recent returns to Kierkegaard, Habermas makes two innovative moves: first, he harnesses the category of the individual into what he calls post-metaphysical thinking. Habermas depicts existential positionality under the rubric of the performative claim to identity. In the latter term, he finds an opening for translating the Kierkegaardian verticality or inwardness into the horizontal or the publicly available linguistic forum of communication. Second, he adopts a Kierkegaardian self-reflexive attitude in order to evaluate those traditions that have become morally and socio-politically problematic. Habermas's originality lies in translating the existential either/or, typical for radical self-choice, into public debates on our choices of the vital elements in our inherited traditions. But in both ways of translating the individual back into the universal, I argue, Habermas nonetheless collapses a Kierkegaardian transgressive attitude into local narratives about the good life: he invents a hybrid concept of existential-communitarian discourse and subsumes it under the normative questions of the moral right. Even though this latter subsumption of the good under the right is made for otherwise cogent reasons, the former association of radical self-choice with the communitarian questions of the good entails a category mistake. Habermas overlooks that the earnestly jesting individual acts as a locus of resistance to those local narratives and homogenizing universalisms whose ideological motives might absolutize or distort our very identity, theory, and consensual constructions.[11]

Habermas's first move is made possible by Kierkegaard's characterization of "self-relation as a relating-to-oneself, wherein I relate myself at the same time to an antecedent Other on whom this relation depends." This Other, unlike in German idealism and in later existential phenomenology, is no longer a transcendental, absolute or apodictic ego cogito "qua the subject of the original act of self-positing." Rather it is the "performative attitude of the subject who chooses himself" while situated in concrete life histories of existing individuals. There are no private selves apart from the historical and linguistic facticity of relating in one's self-relation to others. And yet I am responsible for the self which I posit in my identity-claim and present to others. How can this be? Habermas provides the transcription of Kierkegaard's ethical self-and-other relation into communicative ethics: responsibility, to either drift or to become a self, is awakened in the ego by its self-relation related to an alter. Ego's responsible yes and no attitude to the claims raised by alter in dialogue is marked by the doubly reflexive contingency of dialogic reciprocity among responsible speakers. Habermas takes Kierkegaard's postsecular or "vertical axis" of self-relation before the wholly Other and tips it "into the horizontal axis of interhuman communication." In place of this wholly Other, the horizontal axis functions as the idealized speech condition which allows ego and alter each to maintain their performative continuity. To be sure, this is no longer a substantive continuity but a performative positionality in communication which itself allows for ethical self-understanding of what it takes to be a speaker and a hearer. Habermas projects this formal condition of felicitous speech-acts as the generalized other, i.e., the regulative ideal of linguistic community. This ideal envisions neither a given historical community nor disencumbered selves. Neither ego nor alter can rely on "the possessive individualism" or on the descriptively narrative "reconstructive appropriation of [his or her] life history." In concrete dialogue, each in relation to the other, authenticates and negotiates the performative "guarantee" to a continuity of such ethical reconstructions. "The self of an ethical self-understanding is dependent upon recognition by addressees because it generates itself as a response to the demands of an other in the first place."[12]

Second, from the formal-pragmatic structure of communicative ethics Habermas proceeds to translate the Kierkegaardian self-reflexive attitude toward tradition into deliberative democracy. Again, he corrects what he perceives to be the normative deficits of Kierkegaard's position: if formal-pragmatics allows Habermas to bring the responsible individual back into the linguistic universal, democratic theory reveals the socio-political import of this publicly anchored existential attitude. It is obvious that his latter move is aimed at offsetting the decisionistic character of some existentialist versions of the either/or: if we integrate the self-choosing individual into deliberative democracy, then it is the public debate, not subjectivist value-choices, which serves as the normative guide for action. Yet it is less apparent from Habermas's approach that he appeals to Kierkegaard in order to prevent rooting universal democracy in national or religious traditionalism.[13]

Habermas's appeal is possible because Kierkegaard's individual already knows that no social convention and no tradition disposes with innocent origins: Climacus's existential pathos teaches us the difficulty of beginnings (CUP 525–55); Johannes de Silentio, Vigilius Haufniensis, and Anti-Climacus show us that there is no way out of facticity, out of passing through anxiety, despair, and fear and trembling (FT *passim*; CA; PC 85–94); and Kierkegaard's critique of the present age (TA) and his rereading of his own authorship testify that the pathway of subjectivity throws individuals and communities into an ongoing objective uncertainty (PV; cf. CUP 203). This individual is earnestly responsible and yet jestingly defies the expectations of possessive individualism, group ethos, and the ethics of anarchy alike. Kierkegaard's critique of the present age exposes both the melancholy leftists of the 1840s, whose liberal clubs of mutual admiration lost the pathos of critical theory and praxis for the human rights of 1789, and the aristocratic Hegelians, who sought an unholy alliance between nationalism and Christian orthodoxy. While Kirmmse finds Kierkegaard's position supportive of the liberal political agenda of the revolutionary age, this support comes much closer to Marcuse's radical subjectivity than to the lukewarm liberalism we are used to in our Western establishmentarianism. Further, Kirmmse has argued insightfully that the standpoint of Kierkegaard's critique does not pine for yet another nomenklatura of the Golden Age but rather reveals a radically egalitarian concern for the common misery of ordinary citizens. Kierkegaard is keenly aware that what follows the death of the instrumental modernist subject and of meaningful cultural signifiers need not be the end of ideology and history but more acute leveling. As Tolić recently put it, the modernist grand narratives symbolized by Gulag and Auschwitz give way to the postmodern wars of local narratives symbolized by Dubrovnik and Sarajevo. The carnival end of Eurocentric metanarratives dissipates into the new world disorder of nationalisms and fundamentalisms—with no exit. Yet Kierkegaard's individual is not someone who easily gets high on becoming a leveler at will or for whom the undecidability of the age provides an alibi, whereby one need not become a responsible self (TA 60–112).[14]

Habermas turns to Kierkegaard's critique of the Hegelian nation-state and of Christendom in order to confront present day nationalism and fundamentalism. Transposed into communicative ethics, one's existential self-choice takes on the character of a public debate on the future of our traditions. Habermas originally thought of this use of Kierkegaard in his 1987 paper given in Copenhagen, where he criticizes some German historians for wanting to revise Germany's responsibility for its Nazi past. This innovation has become since then even more timely in the context of post-1989 Europe.[15]

Let me consider the debate about the Czechoslovak "velvet revolution." Whereas Habermas shares with Havel the view that guilt cannot be apportioned to groups, there is ample room for negotiating our present relationship to the past and, thus, to our choices for the future by which we define who we are and want to be. Some people in the post-communist countries (presumably those whom Michnik ironically calls the clean hands) have become disaffected with the velvet character of the change. Given that former communists not only sit on stolen monies but, as the communists-cum-capitalists, have legitimated their old market monopolies in today's unabashed apologetic for the capital-logic; some charge Havel's humanism with being at best the failure of a naïve intellectual and at worst a conspiracy that secured for the past regime the punishment-free transfer of power. Yet the tragic irony of these charges is that the amorality of the market itself stands under this accusation along with the former state socialist orthodoxy. Without acknowledging the lack of genuine democracy in the present markets as much as in past communism, both of which promised to give all equal chances, what guarantee is there that a bloody change or more severe purges ("lustrace") of the old structures would have dealt a decisive blow to totalitarianism?[16]

The call for a strong hand discloses the revolutionary impatience of those whom Michnik characterizes as the anti-communists with the faces of Bolsheviks: they dream that a collectively assignable guilt can grant us a clean slate. I agree that some intermediate position should exist between Havel's untimely meekness vis-à-vis the Stalinist past and the authoritarian fascist reaction to it. Will not our failure to find such a medium way lead to collapsing responsible self-choice, before the transition to new civil societies, into anti-democratic leveling? Don't we meet this confusion in its most cynical form within some extreme right-left or black-red nationalist coalitions in the Russian Federation or in the division of Bosnia's territory among Croats and Serbs? To secure the possibility of forging democratic structures where there were none, I would take any day Havel's or Michnik's Kierkegaardian critiques of disciplinary power (their non-political politics rather unpopular now in the East) over joining the nationalists or the black shirt skinheads. That the former nomenklatura now wears the coats of the free market or the colors of the nation-state should strip our illusions about capitalistic or any other innocent origins. Democracy with a human face is as difficult a task under the market economy as it was in the reform socialism of the Prague Spring of 1968.[17]

This is not the right place to take sides with or against the velvet nature of the current Czech and Slovak social transformations. The debate about 1989 serves here as an example of what is meant by the postnational and post-traditional character of Habermas's translation of Kierkegaard's radical existential praxis into forming a radically democratic republic. Perhaps the complaints against Havel's and Michnik's non-violence are misaddressed; for in spite of non-violence (on the balance sheet of the post-1989 era) there is more blood and authoritarianism than civility. New countries learn to live in the void of existential self-choice only with difficulty.

But this learning is indispensable for ongoing openness to others, even though it cannot be legislated and even though it can regress into new uncritical narratives of beginnings. Briefly put, we need to form democratic public spheres. In a civic forum, whereby received traditions become self-reflexively available in practical discourse, Habermas rightly argues that self-choice takes on an incisively normative character. In place of nationalist worship of symbols and flags, citizens ought to come together in constitutional patriotism, under the sober procedures of the linguistified sacred. In communicative ethics all socio-political and economic needs are on the table. To decide what will become normative, we may appeal to the deliberative competence of other participants and accept as legitimate what can be agreed upon by all concerned. In complex societies this model solicits radical economic, multicultural, multiracial, and multigender democracy.[18]

Now it is my contention that in the process of his translation, Habermas has lost some important aspects of the transgressive role of Kierkegaard's individual. Radical existential praxis cannot be given over to public policy choices alone, since these require that citizens are capable of responsible self-choice in the first place. Deliberative democracy presupposes the Kierkegaardian individual in order to sustain itself against cultural (nationalist, fundamentalist, sexist, racist) and imperial (internationalist, systemic, consensually totalitarian) homogenizations alike. Kierkegaard's individual both lives in the ethical-universal (this defies individualist atomism) and yet is not commensurable with it (this defies a Hegelian holism or any communitarian ethos). Inscribing the individual in this dual movement, Kierkegaard fosters human rights (the liberal concerns) and communal solidarity (the communitarian requirements) alike while always defying any universalist or regionalist forms of homogenization. I believe that here, in this individual dissent to totality in responsible citizenship, lies the meaning of Havel's term existential revolution as he applies the category of self-choice to human rights and deliberative democracy. In its transgressive role this category provides a check and balance on any totalitarian drive that might emerge from individuals or groups when these take up some value-domains of the universal and try to make other individuals commensurate with them. Therefore, while sympathetic with Habermas's procedural model of democracy, I suggest that we need the distinction between the communitarian and existential categories of self-choice.[19]

I want now to examine Habermas's position in relation to Charles Taylor's *Sources of the Self.* Taylor, in holding with Hegel that the I and the We are reciprocal, raises two issues: he incorporates into his neo-Hegelianism Habermas's communicative turn, and he finds in Kierkegaard one of the modernist sources for new, subtler languages of "personal resonance." In sum, he argues for a personally indexed entry to the traditional sources of the self in order to sustain modern identity under the experiential and ecological demands of the age. Under the first issue, he defines identity as one's capacity to answer for oneself within the discursive space of questions. Identity offers moral orientation in modernity no longer reducible to one dominant identity-frame. He identifies among the moral sources of modernity theism, Enlightenment rationality, and romantic expressivism. The question of identity is meaningful only "in the interchange of speakers." Taylor adopts Habermas's insight that identity is linguistic. The linguistification of inwardness marks the "original position of identity-formation." "The full definition of someone's identity . . . usually involves not only his stand on moral and spiritual matters but also some reference to a defining community."[20]

Under the second issue, Taylor explores the personally indexed access to mythology, metaphysics, and theology. Yet he insists that today one cannot return to the classicist world-view or simply retreat to subjectivism. Both turning to inwardness and decentering the subject are the moments of the same non-subjectivist and non-objectivist want of self-affirmation. "[The] turn inward may take us beyond the self as usually understood, to a fragmentation of experience which calls our ordinary notions of identity into question . . . or beyond that to a new kind of unity, a new way of inhabiting time. . . . " He argues that the plurality of our experiences is accompanied by reflexivity and acts of creative self-transformation. The poet becomes "the bringer of epiphanies." Against the postmodernism of Derrida and Foucault, he proposes that "[d]ecentering is not the alternative to inwardness; it is its complement." The reflexive turn "intensifies our sense of inwardness," but this intensification does not mean a fall into subjectivism, just as post/modern decentering does not imply that we must resort to objectivist frames: "The modernist multilevelled consciousness is . . . frequently 'decentered': aware of living on a transpersonal rhythm which is mutually irreducible in relation to the personal. But for all that it remains inward; and is the first only through being the second."[21]

Taylor retrieves Kierkegaard's, Dostoyevsky's, and Nietzsche's dynamic, non-metaphysical transformations of personal, inward vision. For him, these thinkers share the modernist creative imagination: I transform what I interpret and affirm; my relation to the world and others are changed through my self-relation. The difference between a MacIntyre longing for the Aristotelian polis and a Kierkegaard who chooses the self within a tradition is that if I am the latter, "[a]ll the elements in my life may be the same, but they are now transfigured because chosen in the light of the infinite. . . . Through choice we attain self-love, self-affirmation." Through this self-choice, I attain a transformed posture toward myself and tradition. Where Kierkegaard projects self-affirmation before the vertical other, Nietzsche's yes to the world is a self-overcoming. Yet both are speaking within a tradition where they articulate a discourse of transfiguration, "a vision which doesn't alter any of its contents but the meaning of the whole."[22]

Poets bespeak these traditional sources—divine, worldly, aesthetic—but they can never offer us a "regression . . . to a new age of faith." They do not raise positive public claims but rather the performative, "invocative uses of language; those whereby we bring something about or make something present by what we say." Taylor seeks not a formal moral point of view but an ethic of the good in a mode of invocative, epiphanic language.[23]

Given his partial yes to Habermas, by a new language of "personal resonance," Taylor ought to mean that life-form in which the post-traditional individual inhabits the communicative space of existential questioning. True, he envisions a concrete narrative identity which has the quality of an "epiphany," a "moral source," and a new language that would "make crucial human goods alive for us again." Yet he reads this disclosive language in communitarian

(Hegelian and Aristotelian), but not existential (Kierkegaardian) terms. I suspect that this communitarian retreat conflicts with the call for radical self-choice, unless one interprets the latter through the former in a non-Kierkegaardian fashion. Rather than working from within a category of the self-reflexive individual, Taylor attaches his narrative to the authority of a *Sittlichkeit*. Because he seeks a normative priority of the 'We' to the 'I,' and not like Kierkegaard merely a descriptive priority of a hermeneutical we, he reduces the language of inwardness or self-choice to eudaimonistic ethics. But in order to enter the mode of personal resonance that a post-traditional world demands of our identity, Taylor would have to effect his return to local narratives through one's existential reflexivity, and not through an uncritical security of group ethos.[24]

True, with Hegel, Taylor retrieves the value sources of identity within a postconventional, modern ethic. Yet, Taylor argues that the role of philosophy is not merely to elucidate the moral point of view but to orient us to viable projects of the good life. Habermas notes that Taylor, unlike his communitarian kin, MacIntyre, is neither a metaphysician nor an antimodernist. Taylor, he says, is a Catholic skeptic who seeks the whole of morality in larger existential meanings. Taylor is a genealogist of morals who nonetheless directs his neo-existentialist skepsis to constitutive, substantive goods.[25]

Habermas asks Taylor: Can modern identity be defended within an ethic of the substantive good and still with postmetaphysical means? He answers no to Taylor's affirmative answer. Let us keep in mind that Habermas agrees with Kierkegaard's articulation of the identity-crises of the present age and, thus, he should not have implicated Kierkegaard in Taylor's position. Unfortunately, neither Taylor nor Habermas distinguishes an existential category of the individual from the question of the good or even from theological dogmatics. Both thinkers set the question of moral legitimacy (right) and existential authenticity (read by them as the question of the good) against one another. Taylor's reasons are that authenticity is intelligible only as a communitarian quest: he proceeds to orient modern identity not on the basis of self-choice but rather via objective sources of the good which are to constitute our identity. He wants to find a substantive ethic of authentic personal resonances that could include all these goods. Habermas's reasons are neo-Kantian: he celebrates the plurality of gods and demons—the many goods of modernity—on the basis of moral legitimation or autonomous self-determination. But both thinkers, in their two opposing emphases, engage in reductionism that waters down the category of existential, qualitative identity. Taylor absorbs the transgressive individual into universal goods; Habermas subsumes the existential, as if it were already Taylor's eudaimonistic category of communitarian value-choices of the good, under the procedural moral right.[26]

Taylor like Habermas finds in Kierkegaard a resource for an articulation of modern identity. Both also view Kierkegaard under what Habermas ascribed to a communitarian/neo-existentialist category of "ethical-existential" discourse: in this transcript of the existential categories into the clinical or evaluative questions of the good life both, for opposing reasons, abandon that transgressive individual who challenges the very communitarian ethos of the leveling age. Taylor, unlike Habermas, is eager to bring Kierkegaard back under the ethical fold of *eudaimonia*: he extends the perceived modern sources of the good into a new social ethos (neo-Hegelian *Sittlichkeit*). Habermas, however, reforms the possessive individualist by inviting him or her into a procedural public forum (intersubjectively reformulated Kantian *Moralität*) where raising normative issues is possible.[27]

Taking Kierkegaard's side in this Habermas-Taylor debate, I object to both moves for shared reasons: I think that it is a mistake to transcribe the category of radical self-choice into the questions of the good or bad life (self-choice is the mode of existence, whereby I relate self-reflexively to my tradition and choose myself as someone capable of good and bad in the first place). If this is true, then we can neither domesticate this category by a prior or future communitarian solidarity (Taylor) nor simply subordinate it along with other questions about the good (ethical life-projects) under the right (the procedural morality of Habermas). The term "ethical-existential"—if it stands for eudaimonia or social ethos—is a Kierkegaardian misnomer.[28]

Taylor argues for a substantive democracy. Yet, we can ask, is not this longing for democracy, anchored in a national vision of the good, a convex mirror of wanting some objectively positivist domain of eudaimonia by which an aesthete can secure self-choice before he or she ventures any choice? Do not both the communitarian and the neo-existentialist starting points, not unlike the nominalist readings of Kierkegaard, begin with an arbitrary set of sources of solidarity or value-choice, thereby begging the question whether one can account for such beginnings in the first place?

I tend to agree with Habermas's misgivings that genuine democracy can be built on the basis of the overlapping substantive sources of the good.[29] But unlike Habermas, I distinguish the existential from the communitarian categories, existential ethics from an ethic of the substantive life-projects. It is interesting that Habermas approximates this distinction when he unleashes on Taylor the negating Adorno and the deconstructive Derrida: the personal resonance sought for by Taylor lies in the epiphanic value-domain of art; but aesthetics cannot provide the substantive utopia of the good. Adorno teaches us that there is no aesthetic substitute for religious epiphany or premodern substantive unity. Likewise for Derrida, modern art is bereft of the good and the true and hence cannot be the normative source of morality. Should then modern philosophers choose an aesthetic way or an aesthetic critique? One cannot privilege aesthetic over practical and theoretical rationality in order to affirm the positive ethic of the good. Adorno's critique discloses a negative epiphany of the damaged life (the materially negative utopia or aesthetic critique), yet it cannot replace the disenchanted materially positive, religious or metaphysical utopias. Moreover, even Marcuse's positive appeal to the aesthetic dimension is never a nostalgic glance to a golden age since it provides the source of critical social theory and revolutionary praxis. Taylor is unsatisfied with aesthetics conceived as a source of critique, but the aesthetic way alone lacks the critical, to be sure, for Habermas non-quietist, force of a valid claim.[30]

The Category of the Individual in Post/Modernity

I conclude here by discussing Derrida's option for the transgressive Kierkegaard, i.e., for the politics of the impossible. While I am critical of that "Derrida" (D1) who finds home mainly in the mainstream North American academic receptions of deconstruction, I affirm the "Derrida" (D2) whose transgressions empower the marginalized agency of the oppressed. I am in no fashion undecidable on this issue of which of the *two "Derridas"* can help us build coalitions against the neocolonial discourses of power. I opt for (D2), along the lines of my reading of Kierkegaard's radical existential praxis, as the cogent pathway that allows for a politically relevant dialogue with critical social theory.

In Derrida's Kierkegaardian "hope, fear, and trembling," we encounter the crisis of European (read: modern) identity as such. Derrida transgresses the ethical-universal, i.e., the idea of Europe. Yet some readings of this transgression do not allow us to return there even in the limited sense admitted by Adorno's negatively apprehended material utopia or Marcuse's positively oriented social critique. In the anti-Enlightenment uses of Derrida (D1), there is no dialectical link with the ethical-universal left open. But must Derrida's insistence on remaining in the moment of "imminence," which is "at once a chance and a danger," situate him vis-à-vis the category of the individual wholly on the other side and even against Habermas's defense of critical Enlightenment? I want to read "Derrida" (D2) in service of an intensified, radicalized promise of the Enlightenment: both Derrida and Habermas are confronting nationalism, xenophobia, and racism; and both envision some form of radical multiculture as a corrective. True, Habermas translates Kierkegaard's fear and trembling into a normative public debate about our disastrous traditions, whereas Derrida translates this same urgency into a transgressive gesture that is to resist any procedural co-optation. Do we have to view Habermas's and Derrida's failures to encounter one another at the end of the day as a proof that Kierkegaard's category of the individual is philosophically and politically useless since it cannot be harnessed into democratic procedures where alone its transgressive dissent is morally and socio-politically relevant? There is no normative argument *in Derrida*, nor in the politically retrograde uses of him, that prevents me from bringing his transgressions and Habermas's stress on procedural agency into mutual collaboration. If my ambition is not to make Habermas and Derrida reconcile their differences, still my entire argument points to such a missing positionality between liberals and communitarians as well as between modernists and postmodernists. And I argue that admitting this possibility through Kierkegaard's earnest jesting with modernity and postmodernity is not a dodge of the issue between singular and universal perspectives but rather a genuine alternative to the parameters in which these debates are now structured.[31]

If Derrida's critique of nationalism and racism were not to be normative in either the liberal or communitarian or discourse-ethical senses, how are we to communicate its political import? Derrida operates here with a conceptually broad sense of the political. He calls for overcoming the binary opposition between Eurocentrism and anti-Eurocentrism and for adopting the posture that disrupts all capital headings, whether in their power-centers or in their economic capital-logic. And yet, his attack on the homogenizing logic of the proper name (i.e., the capital as Europe's heading and capital as private property) aspires to a revisioning, not a rejection of the promise of reciprocal recognition. I wish to propose here that this reading of Derrida's Kierkegaardian particularized interventions (D2), just as Foucault, in his debate with Habermas on Kant's "What is Enlightenment?," decenters the Habermasian universalism for the sake of a more intense Marxian politics of inclusion. How else can we grasp Derrida's hope for, his fear and trembling about, multiculturalism without ethnic, racial, gender, and economic cleansing? What else could an openness to refugees without the destruction of their alterity mean? Can we in good faith leave out Derrida's deconstructive Marx from his deconstructive Kierkegaard? Can we afford to leave out Marx from Kierkegaard, and *vice versa*?[32]

Again, the particularized element of Derrida's critique of Eurocentric rationality lies in adopting the transgressive method first originated by Johannes de Silentio against Hegel's ethical totality. If Derrida were arguing for a pluralized collage of diverse headings, then he would be a postmodern liberal, e.g., in an edifying conversation of the West. If his transgression gave us just another, albeit anti-Eurocentrically postmodern, communitarian locus (his Paris over Aquinas's), then one could only abstractly fantasize, but not truly trespass Hegel's ethical-universal. But Derrida's other of the heading differs from many other headings and from the masculinist logic of the head. He attacks the capital-head as the root Western metaphor of power and of money. The other of cultural and economic domination is the netherside of the heading. This can be intimated in a perpetually transgressive gesture that keeps the promise of democracy open, never settling its context, not even consensually closing it as a substantive regulative ideal.[33]

In his well argued and nuanced defense of Derridean politics, Caputo depicts how deconstructive transgressions operate a shuttle between the universal (deconstructible laws) and the singular (undeconstructible justice). This politics is not, then, Caputo insists, an anarchistic retreat to a total deconstruction. Rather, a deconstructionist, just as de Silentio's Abraham, can keep one foot in the political sphere of democratic institutions and with the other foot transgress the laws of this sphere for the sake of justice. The transgressive gesture "moves within the space of two impossibles," i.e., "the failed universal and the inaccessible singular." "[T]hat twofold impossibility constitutes the condition of its possibility."[34]

Hence is not there a sense in which Kierkegaard's individual defies likewise that version of "Derrida" (D1) whose postmodern categories, for all their conceptual expansion of the political, do not show us how (at times even forbid us) to link the hope, fear, and trembling of transgressions with the existential and institutional agencies of social change? Let's say we hold, like Caputo, Kierkegaardian sympathies with Derrida's project and read the deconstructive transgressions of the ethical-universal as radical existential acts. There are questions that will not go away, especially if raised by voices from the colonized margins: Is Abrahamic silence the positive meaning of radical transgression? Or do these gestures invite us to an *undecidable* postmodern epoch? Or do they lure us to retreat into a premodern if not antimodern *Denken*? Or perhaps the unsayable transgressions and the undecidable gestures mean that Kierkegaard's individual *must* be mis/read in all this normative questioning? Yet is not *this* undecidability or *this* 'must' a dodge? Should not we ask whether in all the attention to the mis/reading of texts it is rather self-misreading that matters to a radical existential praxis? Is it not the critique of all neocolonial comfort in the undecidability of social change that matters to the issues of race?[35]

Some versions of "Derrida" (D1), unlike Marx and unlike Kierkegaard in his authorship and in his attack on the establishment, do not always return to take a yes-and-no stance within the ethical-universal. And when this "Derrida" (D1) does come back, not in his silence, but only to read the very transgression as already a proto-normative condition of the impossible ethical-universal. What if this very celebrated postmodern impossibility turns politically neocolonial? What if the same notion of textual undecidability becomes now existential and social undecidability, thereby blocking the needed agency of personal and social change? And what if this blockage conveniently prevents any unmasking of the ideological role that notions such as impossibility and undecidability might play in the neocolonial discourse? What then becomes of their celebrated radicality? My version of "Derrida" (D2), read along with Kierkegaard and Marx, disrupts any donkey who is stuck with these types of undecidable stacks of hay: the decisive either/or posture shows the individual inhabiting the transgression of the ethical-universal in existing—prior but related to normative questions as the lived condition of their possibility. It seems that the marginalized deserve a concrete historical hope in possibilities, their fear and trembling translate transgressions into a yes-and-no stance on oppression. And I find nothing in Derrida's own moves that would prevent me (normatively or by coercion) from unmasking that privileged jargon of textual transgressions which even in our postmodern times acquiesces to the impossibility of social change on behalf of the underprivileged. Short of talking abstractly and in bad faith about transgressions within texts, I am prompted to embrace, e.g., Fanon's reading of existential categories as embodied transgressions of all racially motivated impossibilities.[36]

Without this existential and material embodiment of transgression, how can we differentiate between MacIntyre's antimodern and Derrida's postmodern Paris? Again, it seems that the objection usually raised to Kierkegaard's antinormative posture applies better to any reified talk of transgressions, impossible or double binds, undecidable gestures, etc. And it is this reified rendition of "Derrida" (D1) and of fear and trembling that disallows us from articulating the dialectical link of radical self-choice to the moral and socio-political universals. That Kierkegaard's Abraham cannot speak is not positively normative for his obligations to the community. Rather the unsayable pertains to his individual positionality. In this latter sense transgressions can become negatively normative as correctives to the community's demand that the individual conform to the social whole (FT 82ff.). If the silence of hidden inwardness (cf. CUP with PC) were directly normative, then the heroic posture or quietist resignation would give us a proper Kierkegaardian politics. Judging from Anti-Climacus's and Kierkegaard's appeals to fear and trembling in their attacks on the established order, this is a false conclusion about the extent of his or any contemporary existential or even deconstructive praxis (PC 85–94 and xv–xvii; JP 6:6690, 6699; PV; and KAUC).[37]

Marcuse comes closer to Kierkegaard's truth of radical subjectivity that one is to be both an active agent in the community and an individual positioned in refusal at its limits, both responsible to the social domain and reflectively distant from it. What is missing from certain nominalist readings of Derrida is Kierkegaard's and Marcuse's dialectic, whereby the latter two invert Hegel's mediation but unlike in nominalism retain both the positionality of transgressive movement (the single individual) and of the agential movement (the universal). Both the "Derrida" of the pure transgressive textual gestures (D1 severed from the ethical-universal) and Habermas on the side of normative discourse (apart from sustaining communicating individuals existentially) bypass radical existential praxis. I argued that the category of the concrete individual decisively binds the transgressive "Derrida" (D2) with the existential and critical-social agency of deliberative change.

III. Conclusion: Rethinking Critical Theory and Existential Philosophy

Some might object that I have shown how Kierkegaard earnestly jests with both sides of the post/modern divide and how he ironizes what in the present fragmented age are legitimate concerns for community, but that the joke is on Kierkegaard. How does the individual lead us to a critical theory beyond both homogenizing universalism and xenophobic particularism? What kind of politics is possible with radical existential praxis? What does the rethinking of these categories do for us that the other positions cannot?

One instance where the double movement of transgressive positionality and normative agency played a key role, and where the failure to develop their linkage partly accounts for new forms of nationalist and fundamentalist hatred, is the development of post-1989 Europe. The Kierkegaardian element was best articulated in the dissenting communities of individuals who, not wholly unlike in Los Angeles of the April 1992 rebellion and far from tenured radicals, functioned as so many disruptive positionalities on the urban outskirts of totalitarian regimes. The normative moment enters in when dissenting individuals are to be translated into new democratic structures. The need for both movements of transgression and agency is given by the historically concrete lack of transitional civil societies that can carry the burden of forging the new institutions and at the same time take some stock of the past while resisting the desires to define the present by a strong hand. To focus on the pure transgressive moment of dissent feeds into quietist defeatism, so typical for reactions to political setbacks, and into elitism, which reinforces the desire for some authority. These two regressions lead to the eclipse of democratic institutions. The ethics of anarchy, while a welcome tool against a totally administered society, if left without the normative agency of change, supports such reactionary trends in these new historical conditions. If we want to do social theory, we cannot abstract from concrete material history into grand conceptual schemes alone, even where these are no longer meta-philosophies of history but textual deconstructions.

In contrast, we can thematize the double positionality of transgression and agency in a less historically linear and more dialectical manner: there is a need for singular and social agency in the moment of dissent as much as we require the transgressive corrective during supposedly normal times of identity formation and democratic institutionalization. This is true for theory and practice alike. Dissidents were not merely theoreticians of the ethics of anarchy, and they were not pure anarchists either. Let's have "Charta 77" serve as an example: this was issued in 1977 as a dissenting act against a very repressive post-1968 normalization by Gustav Husák's Czechoslovak government. At the time the action was ridiculed as a politically ineffective gesture of arrogant and self-serving intellectuals by the officials as well as by some dissidents. But the manifesto interpreted the transgression itself in terms of radical individual and social responsibility, given by Levinas and Patočka alike, that we as humans and citizens are called to bear toward others. Citizenship and the courage to act at the time of common need were brought together existentially. This was also a call for human rights: the group placed concrete demands upon the government, appealed to international charters, and generally articulated a normative argument that the legitimacy of governments originates in the deliberation of its citizens, not vice versa. This existentially grasped civic responsibility became the basis for many later theoretical documents of "Charta 77" leading up to the pathbreaking November 1989.[38]

The changes after 1989 raised the question what to do with the transgressive moment when it comes to a functioning democracy. Should powerless dissidents now become the powerful? Should they give way to professional politicians? Again, the most theoretically and practically innovative appears in the moments when transgression and agency, both understood in individual and social settings alike, come to collaborate in the new situation. There is plenty of space for transgressive performances. They meet the needs which are not satisfied by building democratic institutions alone because nationalism, racism, and fundamentalism exercise too strong an appeal for individual and group identity-formations in transition as to yield voluntarily the stage to democratic deliberations. The problem in the new Europe is precisely that we lack those types of citizens who are ready to relate reflexively to their traditions. Without individuals formed as transgressive positionalities in unoppressive communities,[39] rather than hardened by the national or religious intransigencies of regional hatreds, we cannot benefit from the normative agency of mass democratic procedures.

Habermas, on the one hand, offers a public debate in the style of Kierkegaard's either/or but, bereft of existential distance from our origins, the new myths of blood and soil have already decided what we choose as normative for us. On the other hand, if we read selectively and adopt the one-sided "Derrida" of pure transgressions (D1), then the other of the heading will remain abstract and will lack any normative stage in which to enact our noble gestures. I argued that to fear and tremble calls us to engage both individual and social transgression of oppressive traditions and communities; and that to hope invites us to envision an agency of individual and social change. One cannot be adopted ahead of the other, against or at the expense of the other, but both movements of transgression and agency are to act in sync.

Note that this *both* is not, however, a Hegelian both/and. The two movements retain the either/or logic insofar as they project the category of the individual into the Kierkegaardian concrete universal. Because the category of the individual represents the 'how' of the singular and universal alike, it makes little sense to thematize it as the "inner" subjectivity in opposition to the "outer" sociality. This existential category represents the "how" of both the personal and social domains of culture. Shortly, the said category is necessary if we are to thematize and practically effect a distanciation from one's already socialized existence in a culture. How are, e.g., Fanon's transgressions of the racist society possible at all? Both Fanon and Marcuse understood and lived the import of the existential categories within critical social theory and praxis: one learns here that the "how" both explains and allows for Marcuse's and Fanon's great refusals since it shows us how one can live in a culture but also not be of culture *qua* culture—especially if it happens to be the white or patriarchal or bourgeois philistine mainstream. In that sense the "how" qualifies (though does not descriptively or normatively replace) both the personal and social domains of the "what." The "how" then pertains to the individual and universal alike since in its material concretion this category, as the most radical point of difference, leaves open the avenue for the community of diversity and confluence. Radical praxis emerges as a middle term, let's say here, binding the positionalities of Habermas and Derrida. We meet at this crossroad an ecologically sound environment integrating the positionalities of existentially and socially responsible transgressive resistance with those of deliberative and procedurally just, multicultural, multigendered, and multiracial agency. With such self-corrective loci of openness, we may be able to prevent in common the homogenization of universalizing democratic procedures and at the same time the fragmentation of the particular regional habitats.

Kierkegaard transgresses both disencumbered, possessive individualism (instrumental modernity) and the substantive ideals of the ethical-universal (communitarian critique of liberalism). Both transgressions inhabit that positionality from which we can dramatize the full role of the individual. They also seek to secure the consensual aims against totalitarian distortions. But this individual, rather than offering a nominalist suspension of all ethico-political universals, engenders a concretely responsible agency. In this sense Kierkegaard's transgression defies some academically prevalent postmodern sensibilities; indeed, arrives in earnest jest after post/modern existential and social undecidability. Kierkegaard—just as that "Derrida" (D2) who can help us to empower the feminist, anti-heterosexist, and anti-racist agency of change— does not long for an immaculate space of transgression or transparent agency. The radical existential praxis for this present age invites us to resist both xenophobic particularisms and imperial universalisms. A dialogue with Kierkegaard suggests that we meet this task when we present multigendered and multiculturally positioned individuals with questions on how to become responsible for a more just world. Put otherwise, the task is to link historically concrete postmodern and critical theory with new multilevel movements for social change.[40]

Notes

1. See, on Kierkegaard and modernism: Adorno, Horkheimer, Marcuse, Lukács, Apel, Habermas, Wolin, Kellner, Marsh, and Perkins; and postmodernism: M. Taylor, Caputo, Derrida, Lorraine, Brown; and communitarianism: MacIntyre and C. Taylor. Cf. Westphal, *Kierkegaard's Critique of Reason and Society*; Hall, *Word and Spirit*; Macpherson, *The Political Theory of Possessive Individualism*; Adorno, *The Jargon of Authenticity*.

2. Marcuse, *An Essay On Liberation*; Horkheimer and Adorno, *Dialectic of Enlightenment*.

3. Westphal, *Kierkegaard's Critique of Reason and Society*, 31–33.

4. On Sartre's singular universal, see McBride's essay in this volume. On Kierkegaard's critique of Heidegger, see Huntington in this volume.

5. Kierkegaard's authorship "seduces" not only the secular public from aesthetical into ethical life but also the religious public from the quietist and piously fundamentalist Christendom into a liberation theology and radical praxis.

6. MacIntyre, *After Virtue*, on Kierkegaard, 5, 39–49, 73, 203, 242; on C. Taylor, see section II below; Caputo, *Radical Hermeneutics* and "Hermeneutics"; M. Taylor, *Altarity* and series, "Kierkegaard and Postmodernism" (Florida State University Press).

7. See Emmanuel, "Reading Kierkegaard." On decisionism, see Habermas's key essay, "Diskursethik"/"Discourse Ethics." (Cf. Huntington in this volume.)

8. The objection was raised in these words to my position by Richard J. Bernstein during my doctoral dissertation defense (April 18, 1991).

9. Apart from Marcuse's project of the Great Refusal and Sartrean existential Marxism, we have mostly various readings of Kierkegaard through what I above indicated as the ideal-typical category mistakes. To give only a synoptic glance at some examples of such readings: in the group of critical theorists, the later Lukács depicts Kierkegaard as a decadent beneath whose despairing, perhaps even atheistic, religiosity is masked, on the one extreme, a romantic dandy and, on the other, a proto-fascist. While Lukács himself made a passage from a youthful romantic infatuation with Kierkegaard and mysticism to a leap into the arms of the revolutionary Communist Party, he abstracted from his own difficulty when he insinuated that the way from Kierkegaard's destruction of reason leads to the Nazi Führer principle. Wolin does not advance much from this tendentious leftism when he confines the entire existential philosophy to a decisionist and quietist corner in light of Heidegger's politics of being which in the 1930s translated an individual resolve into a nationalist destiny. Adorno views Kierkegaard's care for inwardness as a privatist concern by someone who has the financial luxury to withdraw from the economic strife of his age into an idealistically constructed bourgeois *intérieur*. This type of critique is echoed in Buber and Levinas who attack a presumed one-sided religious individualism in Kierkegaard's stress on one's posture before God at the exclusion of one's ethical relationship to others. Critical theorists like Horkheimer, Adorno, and Marcuse often defend the individual as the last resort for revolutionary dissent against the mass culture industry and the one-dimensional, totally administered society. And so it is surprising that neither Wolin, nor Best and Kellner, nor Apel ap-

preciate these deep affinities between the early Frankfurt School's dialectic of enlightenment and Kierkegaard's critique of the present age. Best and Kellner reject Marsh's and Westphal's uses of Kierkegaard to critique instrumental rationality and one-dimensional society. And in Apel's Weberian reading of existential thought, Kierkegaard becomes a subjectivist complement to the objectivist value-free scientist rationality, whether in its Western liberal or in state socialist systems. Best and Kellner, just as Caputo and M. C. Taylor, read Kierkegaard as proto-postmodern insofar as they focus on his critique of reason and society. While Best and Kellner resolve for Marx over Kierkegaard, and while Caputo and M. Taylor celebrate in Kierkegaard's individual an opening for an ethics of anarchy, MacIntyre and C. Taylor choose to fill this opening with local communitarian narratives. But neither possessive individualism, nor ethical anarchism, nor some group ethos can genuinely sustain Kierkegaard's category of the individual. In her book on gender identity, Lorraine admits that Kierkegaard's individual allows for the possibility of receptive reciprocity vis-à-vis God but digresses into a self-mastering relation to other humans. She calls the former a feminine and the latter a masculine positionality. Thus, in her view, de Silentio's fear and trembling disrupt the gender ceiling in the vertical dimension of faith but leave the masculinist ratio intact on the horizontal plane among the individuals where Abraham relates from a patriarchal position to both Isaac and Sarah. Similarly, Brown argues that Climacus's view of indirect communication, if it were to complement socio-political theory and practice, would have to relinquish the individual solipsism of hidden inwardness. Both authors find Kierkegaard, or better, his pseudonyma, deficient for pursuing a critical social and feminist theory. [For the authors cited, see Marcuse, "Über konkrete Philosophie"; his works between 1928-1933: "Beiträge zu einer Phänomenologie des Historischen Materialismus," "Transzendentaler Marxismus?," "Zum Problem der Dialektik," "Neue Quellen zur Grundlegung des Historischen Materialismus," and *Hegels Ontologie*; on new sensibility and radical subjectivity, see Marcuse's *One-Dimensional Man* and *An Essay On Liberation*; further, Kosík, *Dialectics of the Concrete*; Sartre, "Kierkegaard: The Singular Universal"; Matuštík, "Merleau-Ponty's Phenomenology of Sympathy" and "Merleau-Ponty On Taking the Attitude of the Other"; Adorno, *Kierkegaard*; Buber, "The Question to the Single One"; Levinas, *Collected Philosophical Papers*, 133, 143f., 150; Lukács, *Die Zerstörung der Vernunft*, 219-69; Wolin, *The Terms of Cultural Criticism*, 89, 128; Horkheimer and Adorno, *Dialectic of Enlightenment*; Best and Kellner, "Modernity, Mass Society, and the Media"; Kellner, *Herbert Marcuse*, 66; Marsh, "The *Corsair* Affair and Critical Social Theory" and "Marx and Kierkegaard on Alienation"; Westphal, *Kierkegaard's Critique of Reason and Society*, 105-25; Matuštík, "Kierkegaard as Socio-Political Thinker and Activist," and review of Perkins, ed., *International Kierkegaard Commentary: The Corsair Affair*; Wolin, *The Terms of Cultural Criticism*; C. Taylor, *Sources of the Self*; MacIntyre, *After Virtue*; M. C. Taylor, *Altarity*; Apel, *Diskurs und Verantwortung*, 24, 26-29, 32f., 34-41, 56, 103-216; Lorraine, *Gender*, 115f., 118f.; and Brown, "Grave Voices."]

10. This portion of the chapter further develops the themes first introduced in Matuštík, *Postnational Identity* and "Derrida and Habermas."

11. Habermas, *Nachmetaphysisches Denken*, 209 / *Postmetaphysical Thinking*, 170; and his 1987 Copenhagen lecture, "Geschichtsbewußtsein und posttraditionale Identität" / "Historical Consciousness and Post-Traditional Identity."

12. Habermas, *Nachmetaphysisches Denken*, 202-209 / *Postmetaphysical Thinking* 164-70. On the "vertical" and "horizontal," see also Habermas in this volume.

13. See C. Taylor, *Sources of the Self* and "The Liberal-Communitarian Debate." For a critique of Taylor's move to ground morality in communitarian ethics, see Habermas, *Erläuterungen zur Diskursethik*, 176-85, 188, 203f. / *Justification and Application*, 69-76,

78f., 91f., and for his opposition to Apel's ultimate transcendental grounding of morality 185–99/76–88. Habermas views both Taylor's and Apel's positions as convex mirrors of neo-existentialist decisionism.

14. Kirmmse, *Kierkegaard*, 245–47, 264–78, 400–404, 408–22, and 449–81; Tolib, "Im ersten postmodernen Krieg"; and Fukuyama, *The End of History*.

15. See Habermas's Copenhagen paper (n. 11 above) and Matuštík *Postnational Identity*.

16. Havel, "The Post-Communist Nightmare"; Michnik, "An Embarrassing Anniversary." The sad irony of Havel's existential position is that after his unsuccessful opposition to the "lustrace" law, he signed the new Czech law that criminalizes groups *per se* for collaborating with the past regime, and yet this most recent attempt at political de-Stalinization does not even touch the capital stolen and now "legitimately" disposed of by the former nomenklatura.

17. Michnik, "Bojím sa antikomunistov."

18. See Habermas, "Volkssouveruntität als Verfahren," his Copenhagen lecture (n. 11 above), and his "Diskursethik" / "Discourse Ethics," section 7. I am thankful to Lewis R. Gordon for the following clarification: even if we depict both race and culture as social constructs, it is wise (e.g., in political struggle against the racial state) to keep race formation distinct from the questions of nation, ethnos, and culture broadly understood. While these distinctions are not explicitly brought up in my discussion of the individual, their use would only further strengthen my critique of liberal, communitarian, and postmodern renditions of radical existential praxis. For a very helpful discussion of race as the political category of the "racial formation" within the "racial state," see Outlaw, "Towards a Critical Theory of 'Race.'"

19. Havel, "The Power of the Powerless."

20. Taylor, *Sources of the Self*, 27ff., 34–36, 495, 524 n.12, 508–13.

21. Ibid., 462, 465, 480, and 481; cf. 456, 459, 461.

22. Ibid., 449f., 453.

23. Ibid., 490–93.

24. Ibid., 508–21.

25. Habermas, *Erläuterungen zur Diskursethik*, 176–85 / *Justification and Application*, 69–76. On the other side of Taylor, Habermas critiques Apel for wanting to elucidate the moral point of view by strong transcendental warrants, i.e., *Letztbegründung* (see n. 13 above).

26. Habermas, *Erläuterungen zur Diskursethik*, 176–84 / *Justification and Application*, 69–76.

27. See Habermas, on "ethical-existential," *Die nachholende Revolution*, 118–26, 141, and 144 with reference to Kierkegaard; "Vom pragmatischen, ethischen und moralischen Gebrauch der praktischen Vernunft," 103ff., 109, 111 / "On the Pragmatic, the Ethical, and the Moral Employment of Practical Reason," 4ff., 9, 11; and 112/12 with a cryptic reference to Kierkegaard's SUD; further, specifically on Kierkegaard, "Kommunikative Freiheit," 31f.; cf. with "Über Moralität und Sittlichkeit" 221, 225f.; *Theorie des kommunikativen Handelns*, 2:167f. / *The Theory of Communicative Action*, 109f.; "Transzendenz von innen," 149f. / "Transcendence from Within," 242f., as well as Fiorenza's ed. intro. 10f. referring to this essay; and Habermas, *Faktizität und Geltung*, 125f.

28. See Ferrara, "Postmodern Eudaimonia," "Justice and the Good from a Eudaimonistic Standpoint," and *Modernity and Authenticity*. He argues both for the post-traditional ethics of the good and exemplary universalism (here justice is conceived along *eudaimonistic* lines as the largest and most comprehensive context of the good, i.e., humankind). With these two moves, he wants to sidestep the split between procedural legitimacy (e.g., Haber-

mas) and authenticity (e.g., Kierkegaard). While this approach does important work reconciling the Kantian and the Hegelian-Aristotelian perspectives in moral theory, it does little to clarify existential self-choice as understood by Kierkegaard. My argument is that the latter's concern with authenticity is about the mode of choosing which qualifies both eudaimonistic or clinical questions of the good and the moral procedures of legitimation.

See also Cooke's "Realizing the post-conventional self," and "Habermas, Autonomy and the Identity of the Self." Similarly to Ferrara, I think that Cooke's insightful attempt to improve on Habermas's proceduralism is still too dependent on the debate about the priority of right and the good and on Habermas's characterization of existential authenticity in the communitarian categories of ethical self-realization. Cf. the arguments for post-conventional *Sittlichkeit* in Benhabib's *Situating the Self*, 11f., 68–88, 146, and Honneth's *Kampf um Anerkennung*, 274–87.

29. This point is brought up also by Young who argues that the substantive notions of community cannot form the basis of democratic politics, *Justice and the Politics of Difference*, esp. chap. 8.

30. Habermas, *Erläuterungen zur Diskursethik*, 183f. / *Justification and Application*, 74; Adorno, *Negative Dialectics*; and Marcuse, *The Aesthetic Dimension*.

31. Derrida, *The Other Heading*, 6 and 5. Cf. Habermas, "Staatsbürgerschaft und nationale Identität." I am thankful to Derrida for discussing with me his pedagogical and theoretical interests in Kierkegaard's *Fear and Trembling* during a visit at Prague's Central European University (February 28–March 9, 1992); on Kierkegaard and deconstruction, see also Caputo's essay in this volume and his "Hyperbolic Justice" and *Against Ethics*.

32. Derrida, *The Other Heading*, 77–80. Cf. Foucault, "What Is Enlightenment?" For such a sympathetic reading, see also Matuštík, "Habermas and Derrida." As I suggested in "Kierkegaard as Socio-Political Thinker," 224 n.18, I continue to hold that Derrida's reading of Kierkegaard (*L'Éthique du don*) is implied in his reading of Marx (*Spectres de Marx*), and vice versa. This is brought up by his *Other Heading*, where fear and trembling become inscribed into a hope for a solidarity among the oppressed. In his text on Marx this solidarity takes on the affinity of a new International.

33. See Caputo, "Beyond Aestheticism: Derrida's Responsible Anarchy."

34. Caputo, "Hyperbolic Justice," 16; on Derrida and Kierkegaard, 10f., 15, and 19 n.11. (See also n. 31 above.)

35. West, *Race Matters*. (See also n.40 below.)

36. See Fanon, *Black Skin, White Masks*. Cf. Bhabha's postmodern view in "Interrogating Identity," that portrays Fanon as "the purveyor of the transgressive and transitional truth" (183). Yet even he admits that Fanon's is not a pure transgression bereft of an agency for social change: "his Hegelianism restores hope to history; his existentialist evocation of the 'I' restores the presence of the marginalized; his psychoanalytic framework illuminates the madness of racism . . . " (184). Cf. Gordon, *Fanon and the Crisis of European Man*, and *Bad Faith and Antiblack Racism*.

37. Martin, *Matrix and Line*, on MacIntyre's and Derrida's Paris, 142, on the unnameable community, chap. 5., on transgressive politics, 193f., and on Jameson's critique of "postmodern pastiche," 162. See also Jameson, *Postmodernism*, 16–19, 21, 25, 34. After revoking the pseudonym, Kierkegaard takes over Anti-Climacus's posture in PC as his own attack on the established order.

38. On these themes from Levinas, see Havel, *Dopisy Olze*, letters 122–44; cf. Patočka, Kacírské eseje, and Matuštík, *Postnational Identity*, part III.

39. I expand Young's notion of unoppressive city (*Justice and the Politics of Difference*) to allow for both urban and rural political solidarities.

40. *Postscriptum*: During my presentation of "The Specters of Deconstruction," a criti-

cal commentary on Derrida's *Spectres de Marx* (an invited panel on Derrida's *Spectres de Marx*, with two other commentaries by Simon Critchley and Rebecca Comay, Seattle: Meeting of the Society for Phenomenology and Existential Philosophy, Oct. 1, 1994), John Caputo characterized my reading of the concept of undecidability in Derrida as a serious misreading if not just a street version of deconstruction. Briefly, Caputo defended Derrida against identifying undecidability with existential and social irresponsibility. I have never had any problems with this defense as far as the general issue is concerned. But in this particular usage my point is not about the scholarship concerning the undecidability of Derrida's or Kierkegaard's authorship. Rather, I raise an existential issue about certain practices in deconstruction and authoring. Simon Critchley suggested that we distinguish between two senses of undecidability (U1) and (U2) in order to further clarify my distinction between my "two readings of Derrida," (D1) and (D2). (U1) refers to the impossibility of deciding the meaning of an authorship (textual undecidability), whereas (U2) designates the impossibility of deciding how to be existentially and socially responsible for one's authoring and acting (practical undecidability). Hence, Caputo's worry about misreading becomes serious only insofar as this distinction between (U1) and (U2) is leveled down. The counterfactual condition of Caputo's valid defense on Derrida's behalf presupposes some affirmation that (U1) could not legitimate (U2). If (U1) is to function as an enabling occasion for individual responsibility or social praxis, it can never come to mean also (U2). And if this distinction holds, then it must be true that while ethical significance of (U1) is clear enough from reading Derrida and other deconstructive analyses of texts, this ethic remains insufficient to provide us with a mature critical social theory. To equate the ethical significance of deconstruction with a developed critical social theory and praxis equals leveling (U1) into (U2), opting solely for (D1), and watering down the urgency of (D2). Caputo's well-taken point seems to be addressed more readily to certain readings and practices in deconstruction than to the needed joint venture in postmodern and critical social theory. With Derrida's book on Marx, there even emerges the urgency that a certain street version of deconstruction and critical theory might make both more concrete: going to the street corner might be after all what Kierkegaard and Marcuse did, as well as what the present age could now require of us existentially and politically. (On philosophy becoming concrete, see Marcuse, "Über konkrete Philosophie" and Kierkegaard's last writings.)

15 | The Transparent Shadow
Kierkegaard and Levinas in Dialogue
Merold Westphal

For how transparent is the shadow that troubles the clarity of coherent speech![1]

I. Can Two Walk Together . . .

IN HIS SPLENDID book, *To the Other*, Adriaan Peperzak presents Levinas's 1957 essay, "Philosophy and the Idea of Infinity" as the best brief introduction to *Totality and Infinity* (1961). A similar case could be made for the 1965 essay, "Phenomenon and Enigma" in relation to *Otherwise than Being or Beyond Essence* (1974). It has been described as the most Kierkegaardian of Levinas's essays,[2] which gives it special interest in the present context. What makes this description apt is not merely the fact that its latter half contains four of the rather rare references to Kierkegaard in Levinas's writings; it is rather the fact that "the Kierkegaardian God" (66–67) plays the role in this essay that the Cartesian God plays in the 1957 essay, the infinity that is an "inassimilable alterity" (71).

Actually, this is a more theological essay than the earlier one. For while the Cartesian God serves to provide a formal structure of transcendence and heteronomy over against the totality and autonomy of the ontological tradition, in terms of which the face of the human Other can be understood to address me from on high, the Kierkegaardian God is not just a foil for introducing the neighbor. The face of the neighbor is by no means forgotten (64–65, 70), for this infinite signifies "not by opening [itself] to the gaze to inundate it with light, but in being extinguished in the incognito in the face that faces" (72). And when we read that Kierkegaard's "properly philosophical work seems to us to lie in the *formal* idea of a truth persecuted in the name of a universally evident truth" (67, my emphasis), we might assume that the strategy of this essay recapitulates that of "Philosophy and the Idea of the Infinite."

But the formality of the Kierkegaardian idea that interests Levinas here signifies only that he will abstract from the specifically Christian "salvation drama" (67) that provides the content of Kierkegaard's challenge to the speculative tradition. It does not signify a shift of emphasis from the divine transcendence to human transcendence. For this reason, it is the shadow of God, however transparent it may turn out to be, that makes this a disturbing essay. For "absolute alterity" turns out to be an "absolute disturbance" (64) to every order, semantic or social, by means of which human reason seeks to make itself lord of the earth. This disturbance is thematized on virtually every page of the essay. It signifies that to go "beyond being" (62, 73) is to go "beyond reason" (61). Like Kierkegaard's Climacus, who insists that reality may indeed be a system for God (CUP 118), Levinas denies that it can be such for us, precisely because the infinite that is other to us continually disturbs, disrupts, and, if you like, deconstructs each totality we seek to construct, every logos into which we try to make everything fit (61).[3]

The Kierkegaardian overtones are more overt when Levinas speaks of this move "beyond reason" as a kind of madness or folly (61–62).[4] But beyond this "quotation," and beyond the generic role God plays as the Great Disturber, there is an even more specific Kierkegaardian element to this essay. Long before any explicit reference to Kierkegaard, its strategy mirrors that of Johannes Climacus in *Philosophical Fragments*. In the thought experiment that occupies his first two chapters, Climacus identifies Reason as the Socratic assumption that knowledge is recollection, meaning that the human knower has the capacity to recognize the truth, and then sets out to find what it would take to generate a genuinely different understanding of human knowledge. Without saying just what motivates his effort, other than the hints of the preface that he is critical of the Hegelian mindset of his contemporary culture, he devotes considerable energy to working out the details of his alternative hypothesis. He does not argue for the superiority of his alternative, just that it is truly different from the Socratic assumption.[5]

In the third chapter the two accounts of human knowledge confront each other as Reason and the Paradox[6] and the point of the project begins to emerge. Reason is proud of having excluded the Paradox, which it considers to be absurd, since it (the Paradox) does not play the game by Reason's rules. But this "discovery, if it may be put this way, does not belong to Reason but to the Paradox," and in announcing their mutual incompatibility "Reason merely parrots the Paradox, . . . " which replies to Reason, "It is just as you say, and the amazing thing is that you think that it is an objection" (PF 50, 52). The fact that Reason excludes the Paradox only proves that it is exclusionary, not that what it excludes is by that fact discredited. The point of the apparently trivial thought experiment, looking for an alternative to the assumption that knowledge is recollection, is Augustinian. It is to raise the question whether the Platonic propagation of the Socratic suggestion is not a form of "presumption."[7] By what authority (*quid juris*) does the thinking that calls itself Reason exclude other kinds of thinking and claim for itself exclusive title to the highest truth? This question is already a form of madness, for in the return of the repressed that it represents, the calm and complacent sanity of exclusionary Reason is disturbed.

Given the linguistic turn of contemporary philosophy and Levinas's own increasingly linguistic orientation as he moves toward *Otherwise than Being*,[8] it is not surprising that his version of the *Fragments*' thought experiment, or, if you prefer, his brilliant commentary thereon, begins under the heading "Rational Speech and Disturbance" (61). Like Climacus he defines rational speech quite briefly and spends most of his time and energy seeking to clarify the disturbance that "troubles the clarity of coherent speech!" (71).

> As rational speech, philosophy is taken to move from evidence to evidence, directed to what is seen, to what shows itself, thus directed to the present. The term *present* suggests both the idea of a privileged position in the temporal series and the idea of manifestation. The idea of being connects them. . . . Being is a manifestation in which the uncertain memory and the aleatory anticipation are moored; being is a presence to the gaze and to speech, an appearing, a phenomenon.
>
> As speech directed upon the present, philosophy is an understanding of being, or an ontology, or a phenomenology. In the order of its speech it encompasses and situates even what seemed first to contain this speech or overflow it, but which, when present, that is, discovered, fits into this logos. . . . To utter a speech that would not be anchored in the present would be to go beyond reason. (61)

This linguistic account of philosophy as Reason makes it clear 1) how the target of Levinas's critique[9] can be designated more or less equivalently as the metaphysics of presence, logocentrism, ontology, or ontotheology, 2) why he describes this style of philosophy as the reduction of the other to the same, 3) how he conceives of the phenomenologies of Husserl and Heidegger to belong to this tradition rather than to be its overcoming,[10] and 4) how nothing short of the enigma that disturbs this logos can turn ontology's world of phenomena into the phenomenal world and the God of ontotheology into an idol. By contrast "with the indiscreet and victorious appearing of a phenomenon," what he calls enigma is "this way of manifesting himself without manifesting himself" (66), that which "signifies itself without revealing itself" (73).

Like Climacus's pursuit of the Paradox, Levinas's engagement with enigma is a form of critique directed, like the earlier critiques of Augustine and Kant, against the hubris of a human reason that would be autonomous and self-sufficient.[11] It is motivated in part by the sense that logocentric Reason is dogmatically atheistic, that it arbitrarily excludes God from its world or, what is worse, domesticates God by transforming the divine into a (visible or intelligible) phenomenon, a process in which "the divinity of God dissipates" (62).

"Phenomena, apparition in the full light, the relationship with being, ensure immanence as a totality and philosophy as atheism" (70).[12]

It is also motivated by the sense that the transcendence thus reduced to immanence properly belongs to philosophy. In pursuit of enigma he takes as his guide "the notion of God, which a thought called faith succeeds in getting expressed and introduces into philosophical discourse" (62). To affirm this thought requires that one "endure the contradiction between the existence in-cluded in the essence of God and the scandalous absence of this God ... [and] to suffer an initiation trial into religious life which separates philosophers from believers" (62).

But this thought that faith manages to introduce into philosophical dis-course is not entirely eccentric to the latter. In the first place it is a thought, not simply an image or a feeling. There is no hint that what distinguishes this thought from the thoughts of logocentric ontology or phenomenology is that it is an undergraduate *mythos* that has not yet learned the doctoral level lan-guage of the *logos*, a minor league *Vorstellung* not yet good enough to join the Big Show and its superstar *Begriffe*. The distinguishing mark of this thought is simply that it radically disturbs the thoughts by which we construct the worlds of nature and history.

Second, "to think more than one thinks, to think of what withdraws from thought, is to desire, and with a desire that, unlike need, is renewed and be-comes ardent the more it is nourished with the desirable" (72).[13] It is precisely this desire that Levinas takes to be, rather than either wonder or doubt, the origin of philosophy. That is why, when he speaks of "the contradiction be-tween the existence included in the essence of God and the scandalous absence of this God" (62), he presents it as what separates philosophers from believers "unless the obstinate absence of God were one of those paradoxes that call to the highways."[14] It is the affirmation of this possibility with which Levinas concludes his essay, speaking of "the antecedence of God relative to a world which cannot accommodate him" as involving "the One, which every philoso-phy would like to express, beyond being" (73).

In *Philosophical Fragments*, Climacus's critique has the same dual motiva-tion. On the one hand, it is directed against what is perceived to be a dogmatic and arbitrary exclusion without which human understanding could not abso-lutize itself as Reason. In his case the God whom the world cannot accommo-date is the specifically Christian God become human in Jesus of Nazareth. What his thought experiment (PF, chapters 1–2) is designed to show is that the Socratic assumption that knowledge is recollection excludes this possibility *a priori* (as Lessing clearly saw).[15] An incarnation is not the sort of reality avail-able to recollection.

At the same time, Climacus thinks human understanding has a built-in desire for an absolute that will relativize it. He says that "the thinker without the paradox is like the lover without passion" and that "the ultimate paradox of thought [is] to *want* to discover something that thought itself cannot think" (PF 37, my emphasis).[16] The human understanding, when not deluding itself into thinking it is Reason, has a "paradoxical passion that *wills* the collision . . . and, without really understanding itself, *wills* its own downfall." Concretely speaking, God incarnate is "this unknown against which the understanding in its paradoxical passion collides and which even *disturbs* man and his self-knowledge" (38–39, my emphasis). Abstractly speaking, the unknown against which human understanding in its paradoxical passion continuously collides, is "the absolutely different. . . . Defined as the absolutely different, it seems to be at the point of being disclosed, but not so, because the understanding cannot even think the absolutely different" (PF 44–45).

Levinas's own account has its concrete side in the theory of the neighbor as the face that commands us from on high. But in the essay before us, the emphasis falls, more abstractly in a theory of enigma as semantic alterity. Phenomena signify, that is, they enter into the domain of human meaning, by appearing. "To appear, to seem, is forthwith to resemble terms of an *already familiar order*, to *compromise* oneself with them, to *be assimilated* to them. Does not the invisibility of God belong to another play, to an approach which does not polarize into a *subject-object correlation* but is deployed as a drama with several personages? . . . Everything depends on the possibility of vibrating with a meaning that is not synchronized with the speech that *captures* it and cannot *be fitted into* its order" (62–63, my emphasis).[17] The semantic disturbance Levinas has in mind is "the entry into a given order of another order which does not *accommodate* itself with the first. Thus we exclude from disturbance the simple parallelism of two orders that would be in a relationship of sign to signified, of appearance to thing in itself, and between which, as we have said, the relationship would reestablish the simultaneity of one single order" (67, my emphasis).

Since the other cannot appear "without renouncing his radical alterity, without entering into an order" (64), only that will be transcendent (and thus disturbing) which can show itself without appearing. It cannot allow itself to be tied down to the "unbreakable chain of significations" (64) that make up the "triumphant, that is, primary truths" (70) of a given cultural order if it would signify as enigma rather than phenomenon. It must "tear itself" free from "the public order of the disclosed and triumphant significations of nature and history" (70).[18]

It would seem to follow that the gods who are the keystones of these humanly created orders of intelligibility, say the God of Aquinas in relation to the structures of nature and the *Geist* of Hegel in relation to the structures of history, are phenomenal and not enigmatic, ontotheological and not truly transcendent. This is why a God like Kierkegaard's who is quite thoroughly enigmatic, is "essential in a world which can no longer believe that the books about God attest to transcendence *as a phenomenon* and to the Ab-solute *as an apparition. And without the good reasons atheism brings forth, there would have been no enigma*" (67, my emphasis).

In other words, the "atheism" of Hume and Kant in relation to the God of Aquinas and the atheism of Feuerbach and Marx in relation to the Hegelian *Geist* need not be seen as the vindication of dogmatic secularism but can be construed as a kind of prophetic protest against every project of domesticating the divine.[19] They can be read as opening the question whether the absence of God from self-evidence and the "scandalous absence" of God from "the moral conduct of the world" (62) points to the abyss or to revelation as disturbance.

Levinas takes his semantics of the enigma, his answer to the question, "How could such a disturbance occur?" (63), to be at odds with the traditional theory of the sign.[20] As we have already seen, he sees the orders of sign and of signified as being parts of a larger whole in which the play between them is undisturbed by any real difference (67). (There is always an ambiguity when speaking of the signified, for writers often slide between the strict meaning, *Sinn* (concept), and the looser meaning, *Bedeutung* (object referred to by the concept and thus by the sign as grapheme or phoneme). It seems to be the latter notion that is primary in Levinas, but since his concept of phenomenon is one of a kind of Kantian adequation between thing and concept, the difference may not be too important.)

The problem with the sign, according to Levinas, is its re-presentational character. It assumes that the signified has been present, has appeared, and serves to recall that appearance to mind. By definition, the enigma cannot be such a signified. "But how refer to an irreversible past, that is, a past which this very reference would not bring back, like memory which retrieves the past, like signs which recapture the signified? . . . But in a face before signifying as a sign it is the very emptiness of an irrecuperable absence. The gaping open of emptiness is not only the sign of an absence . . . but the very emptiness of a passage. And what has withdrawn is not evoked, does not return to presence, not even to an indicated presence" (65–66).

In place of the sign Levinas would put the trace, giving the following correlations: sign | phenomenon = trace | enigma. What is distinctive about the trace is its temporality, since it refers to "an irreversible, immemorial, unrepresentable past" (65), or to a past "which no memory could resurrect as a present" since "the past of the other must never have been present" (68).

This notion of a past that has never been present is by no means an easy one. But one thing is clear—it precludes, as it is intended to preclude, the notion that knowledge is recollection.[21] In his semantics of the trace Levinas is on the side of Climacus as he seeks an alternative both to the recollection theory (PF, chapters I and II) and to its existential correlate, the notion that one can back out of temporal existence into eternity by means of such knowledge (CUP 207–10, 217, 226).[22] This is why it is possible to read "Phenomenon and Enigma" as one of the most insightful and illuminating commentaries on the *Fragments* and *Postscript* ever written.

Recollection presupposes the essential kinship or likeness of subject and object. Thus Kierkegaard, referring to the *Phaedo's* doctrine of the divinity of the soul, speaks of how "Socrates so beautifully binds men firmly to the divine by showing that all knowledge is recollection" (CI 30). The goal of philosophical ascesis is the "pure knowledge" we gain when we "get rid of the body and contemplate things by themselves with the soul by itself" (*Phaedo* 66e). On the recollection theory this sheer presence, the linkage of total manifestation with total presentness, is a future possibility because it has been a past actuality. Knowledge as re-presentation (the classical theory of the sign) is possible and deserving to be called knowledge, if not Knowledge, because its Alpha is a past presence and its Omega a future presence. The wound of each present presence, in which representation signifies absence as much as presence, is healed by its archeological and teleological linkage to sheer presence.[23]

It is this immanence and totality that Kierkegaard and Levinas seek to deconstruct with their notions of divine transcendence and infinity. The closeness of their thought on this point is especially clear in one form of Levinas's complaint about the atheism of what he calls the ontological tradition. "Philosophy is atheism, or rather unreligion, negation of a God that reveals himself and puts truths into us."[24] The God Levinas has in mind is precisely the God whom Climacus presents in the *Fragments* as giving to the learner not just the truth, but the very condition for recognizing the truth (PF 14). (For what the slave boy in the *Meno* had within him was not the truth of the geometrical theorem Socrates "teaches" him, but the ability to recognize its truth once it is set before him, however that may be occasioned.) This is the God whose self revelation is the antithesis to the situation where "self-knowledge is God-knowledge" (PF 11).

If Climacus describes such an act of revelation as the decisive Moment of Conversion and Rebirth (PF 18–19), the transition from "not to be" to "to be" that can only be grasped as Wonder or Miracle (PF 30, 36), it is to signify the radical disruption of ordinary time that is involved. However, since he calls the Moment *"the fullness of time"* (PF 18), it may seem as if he has something in mind quite different from the trace, which Levinas describes in terms of "the withdrawal of the indicated" and "the very emptiness of an irrecuperable absence" (65). But the fullness of time is not the Husserlian filling in intuition of a previously empty intention; it is rather the kairotic moment which disturbs the continuity of quotidian chronology. Like Kant before him and Heidegger after him, Climacus insists on temporality as the horizon of human thought. It is just because the Moment of revelation disturbs the temporality of recollection so deeply that the God who "appears" in it is the unknown (PF 39, 44), the absolutely different (PF 44-46).

It is not that God is simply absent from the world of human experience. It is rather that in every self-presentation God remains incognito, like Jesus to the disciples on the road to Emmaus (Luke 24:13-35). "For how transparent is the shadow that troubles the clarity of coherent speech!" (71). Except that it is cast in terms of speech rather than thought, this might easily have been a comment on Climacus's paradox rather than Levinas's enigma. Here is how Levinas describes it: "A God was revealed on a mountain or in a burning bush, or was attested to in Scriptures. And what if it were a storm! And what if the Scriptures come to us from dreamers! . . . It is up to us, or, more exactly, it is up to *me* to retain or to repel this God . . . this way of manifesting himself without manifesting himself, we call enigma" (66).[25]

In the *Fragments* Climacus focuses on God incarnate as the paradox, the transparent shadow that shows itself while remaining invisible. But he talks of God as being incognito in the created world as well. Can I prove God's existence from the works of creation? Yes, but only if I have already decided to retain rather than to repel God's presence in the world, to interpret it as revelation and not, to return to Levinas, as a storm. "Therefore, from what works do I demonstrate [God's existence]? From the works regarded ideally—that is, as they do not appear directly and immediately. But then I do not demonstrate it from the works, after all, but only develop the ideality [interpretation] I have presupposed; trusting in *that* I even dare to defy all objections, even those that have not yet arisen" (PF 42). The argument of chapter IV that the eyewitness follower of Jesus has no advantage over those of subsequent generations because "the god cannot be known directly" (PF 63) or because "the teacher of whom we speak could not be known immediately" (PF 68) is an argument *a fortiori*. Simply to watch him at work is not to eliminate the possibility, to return to Levinas again, that he is a dreamer.

II. . . . Unless They Be Agreed?

Up to this point I have focused on the agreements between Kierkegaard and Levinas, which I take to be both extensive and deep. Along the road they travel together, two dialogues take place. The first is between the two of them and thinkers like Nietzsche, Heidegger, Foucault, and Derrida,[26] who operate on the assumption that a serious critique of metaphysics can only occur outside the framework of Judeo-Christian faith,[27] either on the soil of some pagan cult or in the ether of a radical secularism. Together Kierkegaard and Levinas challenge the identification of these faith traditions with the ontotheologies often embraced within them, and they expose as a *non sequitur* the often presupposed but rarely stated assumption that to offer a critique of logocentrism is to legitimate the exclusion of the voices of these traditions from the domain of serious thought, to absolve philosophy from any need either to listen to them or to listen for the voice they purport to have heard. Together, Kierkegaard and Levinas raise the question whether prominent forms of the postmodern challenge to the Enlightenment project are simply variations of the same theme of excluding radical alterity so as to make philosophy (human reason in its reflective mode) the final arbiter of truth. The quarrel over whether truth should be spelled with an upper case or lower case t appears, from their perspective, to be a domestic dispute among those who have excluded any truly personal transcendence. They raise the possibility of a challenge to the Enlightenment project and the larger philosophical tradition to which it belongs from within "a tradition at least as ancient,"[28] which also spells (human) truth with a lower case t, but in order to signify a divine reality that disturbs postmodern as well as modern philosophy.[29]

The other dialogue that takes place on the road I have been trying to map is the one between Kierkegaard and Levinas themselves. It is, I have been suggesting, the kind that takes place in half sentences and partially expressed thoughts. The deep inner kinship between the two makes it possible for each to anticipate what the other will say, and at times to complete the other's sentence, saying even better what the other was trying to say.

But this is true only up to a point, and the agreement between these two thinkers is limited in such a way as to make each the other's Other. They can walk together only so far, and then their paths diverge. I want now to turn to two of the places where this happens and the dialogue between them becomes debate.

Levinas writes, "The infinite is a withdrawal like a farewell which is signified not by opening oneself to the gaze to inundate it with light, but in being extinguished in *the incognito in the face that faces*" (72, my emphasis). Although he immediately reaffirms the importance of Kierkegaardian subjectivity vis-à-vis the infinite, a subjectivity embodied in "someone who is no longer agglutinated in being, who, at his own risk, responds to the enigma and grasps the allusion" (72), the two part company at this point.

To begin with, for Kierkegaard it is first and foremost "the face of Jesus Christ" (2 Cor. 4:6) in whom God "appears" incognito. This cannot be "the face that faces" for Levinas, who has abstracted "from the salvation drama whose play in existence Kierkegaard, a Christian thinker, fixed and described" (67), and it is both obvious and unsurprising that Levinas has in mind the face of the human neighbor.

But there is a deeper divergence here than this most obvious difference between a Jewish and a Christian thinker. For Levinas, recognizing the infinity of the neighbor is an essential prior condition to recognizing the infinity of God, while for Kierkegaard it seems to be the other way around (WL 26–27).

Whereas Kierkegaard would repeat Jesus' summary of the Torah, that the first commandment is to love God and the second to love one's neighbor as oneself (Mark 12:28–34), Levinas reverses the order.[30] For him ethics is first, then religion, and the neighbor always stands between me and God, while for Kierkegaard religion is first, then ethics, and God always stands between me and my neighbor. To be sure, in the theory of the stages of existence we move from the ethical to the religious, but this is in order to discover the ultimacy of the latter and the relativity of the former.

Which must be given primacy, the relation to God or the relation to the neighbor? Both Kierkegaard and Levinas seek to develop a non-Marxian form of ideology critique, and it is their difference on this point that primarily distinguishes their respective strategies. So politics is at issue, along with personal ethics and piety. This is a huge and multifaceted issue, whose proper exploration requires more space than is available here. I shall here address only the one aspect of it that comes especially into view in the essay before us, what Levinas calls illeity.

"We hear this way to signify—which does not consist in being unveiled nor in being veiled, absolutely foreign to the hide-and-seek characteristic of cognition . . . —under the third person personal pronoun, under the word *He* [*Il*]. The enigma comes to us from Illeity" (71). Why is this? An enigma "is a plot with three personages: the I approaches the infinite by going generously toward the you, who is still my contemporary, but, in the trace of illeity, presents himself out of a depth of the past, faces, and approaches me" (72). For the human face can appear as such "only if it enigmatically comes from the infinite and its immemorial past. And the infinite . . . solicits across a face, the term of my generosity and my sacrifice. A you is inserted between the I and the absolute He." Because of this triangle it is "vain to posit an absolute you" (73).

We know why Levinas wants to keep the human neighbor between God and the religious self. He believes this is the only protection against religion becoming ideology, the ally of a dehumanizing violence that desecrates in one and the same moment the infinity of both divine and human persons, reducing both to mere means in the service of some individual or community will to power.[31] History becomes war, and war all but inevitably becomes holy war.

The denial of an absolute You raises the question of prayer. If God is an absolute He but not an absolute You, if, in other words, I can speak to you about Him but not to Him, as another You, about you, what happens to prayer?[32] Here are some of the questions Kierkegaard, who so often in his writings addresses God in the second person, will want to ask. Does it make sense to insist on the personal character of divine infinity and then restrict it to the third person? Is there not some other way to work against idolatry and inhumanity, given the high price of this strategy? Surely the Jewish Scriptures know no such qualms against addressing God in the second person. Does Levinas want his distinction between his "Greek" and his "Hebrew" writings to become the gap between the God of the philosophers and the God of Abraham, Isaac, and Jacob? Is he, in this respect, much closer to the ontological tradition than he realizes? Has he made the world safe for ethics by sacrificing something utterly essential to religion, at least to the biblical traditions that Jews and Christians share? It is not that Levinas either repudiates or ignores prayer, which he acknowledges to be "one of the most difficult subjects for a philosopher."[33] But in one of his "Hebrew" writings he says "the Judaism of reason must take precedence over the Judaism of prayer: the Jew of the Talmud must take precedence over the Jew of the Psalms."[34]

What is the nature of this "must"? If it is that religion must not be too offensive, too disturbing to the modern *Zeitgeist* to make assimilation, and thus sociological survival, possible, then Kierkegaard, who makes the offense of faith an essential part of it,[35] will ask, What is the point of insisting on the disturbing role of infinity only to give priority to the Talmud over the Psalms because it is less disturbing to modern sensibility? Is it sufficient, or even possible, to challenge the violence of ontological totality without challenging its prayerlessness? Or, to put it just a little differently, can the community of faith be a light to the nations (Isa. 42:6) without grounding its life in the prayerfulness of the Psalms?

In another essay, Levinas approaches the problem of prayer differently. We begin, as we might expect, with ethics. "This responsibility for others therefore comes to be for man the meaning of his own self-identity. His self (*son moi*) is not originally *for itself* (*pour soi*). . . . " The *conatus essendi* of our egoistic self-assertion must be inverted or converted until we become *"the one for the others"* that forgets itself in " 'fear and trembling' for the other. . . . "[36] The conclusion is that "prayer means that, instead of seeking one's own salvation, one secures that of others." Levinas summarizes the treatise he is expounding quite categorically. "True prayer, then, is never for oneself, never 'for one's needs. . . . ' "[37]

Here Kierkegaard will have two questions. First, does not the Torah command me to love my neighbor *as myself* (Lev. 19:18, 34)? The self-concern of my natural *conatus essendi* is to be the measure of my "fear and trembling for the other." But if I cannot pray for my own needs, how can I pray for my neighbor's? Second, leaving myself aside and focusing just on my neighbors, how can I pray for their needs, material or spiritual, if I cannot address God in the second person, if the only legitimate speech about God is that which mentions Him to some human you?

A second point at which the dialogue between Kierkegaard and Levinas turns into debate involves the notion of the trace. While phenomena are signified by signs, that which indicates the enigma is the trace. What is essential to the trace is that it "signifies" a past that has never been present (68, 73). Levinas is fond of the story in Exodus 33 of Moses being allowed to see God only from behind. He uses it here (69) to suggest that what makes the enigma enigmatic is that we always arrive too late to encounter it face to face. If we catch a glimpse of it, it is always already departing, withdrawing. For us it never is (here), but always has been (here). The spatial image for this temporal definition of the trace is the transparent shadow.

The trace "signifies" what is beyond being, "a beyond borne by a time is different from that in which the overflowings of the present flow back to this present across memory and hope. Could faith be described then as a glimpse into a time whose moments are no longer related to the present as their term or their source?" (62). Such a faith, it would seem, is cut off from hope just as much as it is cut off from memory. Just as we cannot access transcendence through recollection, since its past has never been present, so we cannot await transcendence in hope, since its future will never be present either. That is why the infinite cannot be given to desire "as an end . . . cannot be incarnated in a desirable, cannot, qua infinite, be shut up in an end" (72–73).

By contrast, the Climacus writings link faith tightly to hope. The whole problematic of faith is portrayed in terms of the hope for eternal happiness. Although he does not put it just this way, Climacus's critique of speculation is a continuous meditation on the Pauline reminder that for now "we see in a mirror, dimly" (1 Cor. 13:12), while the orientation of faith to eternal happiness expresses its hope that "then we will see face to face." The critique of the metaphysics of presence in the *Fragments* and *Postscript* is intended to open the door to such a hope, not to preclude it, as Levinas seems to do.

If we go back and take a closer look at the two respective critiques of recollection, we will find the difference that underlies this disagreement. Levinas writes, "The impossibility of manifesting itself in an experience [that defines enigma] can be due not to the finite or sensible essence of this experience, but to the structure of *all thought*, which is correlation. Once come into correlation, the divinity of God dissipates" (62, my emphasis), or, in other words, God ceases to be disturbingly different. "An enigma is beyond not finite cognition, but *all cognition*" (71, my emphasis).

On the surface these claims appear to be dogmatically Hegelian; for they make human thought in its present capacity the ultimate measure of thought as such. This, I believe, is how Climacus would see them. His lack of enthusiasm for them stems both from his anti-Hegelianism, which one would have expected Levinas to share, and from his giving a different diagnosis of why we are cut off from recollection. The paradox (enigma) is the unknown because it is "absolutely different" and "the understanding cannot even think the absolutely different. . . . But if the god is to be absolutely different from a human being, this can have its basis not in that which man owes to the god (for to that extent they are akin) but in that which he owes to himself or in that which he himself has committed. What, then, is the difference? Indeed, what else but sin. . . . We stated this in the foregoing by saying that the individual is untruth and is this through his own fault" (PF 44–47; cf. 28, 31, 34).

Climacus agrees with Levinas that the flaming sword east of Eden that bars any recollective return to the presence of paradise (Gen. 3:24) does not bear the name of creaturely finitude. Creation may generate absolute dependence, but not absolute difference, since "to that extent they are akin." But in his view it is not "all thought" or "all cognition" that are cut off from the presence of God, but sinful thought and sinful cognition. Radical alterity is not to be found in an ontological interpretation of finitude vis-à-vis infinity, but in a moral interpretation of evil vis-à-vis goodness.

This has important consequences for the possibility of presence. If there were to be a "salvation drama" in which sin and its consequences were eliminated from our experience, restoring us to what was intended in creation, the hope of seeing God face to face would not be unrealistic. It is to such a drama that Climacus refers when he describes the Paradox as manifesting itself "negatively, by bringing into prominence the absolute difference of sin and, positively, by wanting to annul this absolute difference in the absolute equality" (PF 47).

Climacus might put his critique of speculation this way. Ontology is the utopian moment of human thought, the longing for salvation. The trouble with ontology, from Plato to Hegel, is that by insisting prematurely on replacing faith with sight it converts utopia into ideology, claiming to possess now a presence for which we have only the right to hope. But the critique of ontology that responds by eliminating even the hope of sight, thereby reducing ontological utopianism to political utopianism, is a counsel of despair. Is not this despair, that is to say, political utopianism devoid of both the sense of sin and the hope of divine salvation, the major source of the violence of our most recent history?

It now appears that Levinas has abstracted not just from the specifically Christian "salvation drama" of Kierkegaard, but from any drama which gives to God a decisive agency in human affairs and envisages a fundamental alteration of experience as we now endure it. He seems to share with Hegel and with the secular postmodernists the conviction that "it doesn't get any better than this."

Ironically, on one point Levinas is closer to Kierkegaard in "Philosophy and the Idea of Infinity" than in his "most Kierkegaardian" essay, "Phenomenon and Enigma." There, too, he is concerned with radical alterity. But there he links the idea of infinity with "the collapse of the good conscience of the same" and repeatedly describes the experience of the otherness of the Other as one of guilt and shame in which I know myself to be wicked and unjust.[38] Just as for Climacus it is sin that generates absolute difference, in this context what makes the absolutely other absolutely other is fault, not the conditions of "all thought" or "all cognition." Most immediately this is fault in relation to my neighbor. But if the human face has its moral appeal "only if it enigmatically comes from the infinite and its immemorial past" and if the absolute He "solicits across a [human] face" (73), then injustice toward my neighbor is sin against God as well.

Taking the two essays together, we might say that Levinas has a philosophy of sin without salvation. Of course the reality of sin is no guarantee of divine deliverance. But to exclude such a possibility from philosophic reflection at the outset by restricting reflection ("all thought . . . all cognition") to the domain of what is conceivable (and achievable) in the circumstances of our present fallenness—is that not to reduce the other to the same? Is it not to abandon "the original antecedence of God [as Savior] relative to a world which cannot accommodate him" (73), compelling him to accommodate himself to that world so as to fit in to the conditions of our present experience?

Notes

1. Emmanuel Levinas, "Phenomenon and Enigma," in *Collected Philosophical Papers*, p. 71. Page references without sigla in the text are to this essay. "Philosophy and the Idea of Infinity" is also included in this volume, as well as in Peperzak's, *To the Other*.

2. By Robert Bernasconi, in personal correspondence.

3. For Kierkegaard this logos is most immediately the Hegelian Logic. For Levinas it includes, as he surprisingly but stubbornly insists, Heidegger's *Lichtung*. See p. 73, n. 19. Cf. "Philosophy and the Idea of Infinity," *Collected Philosophical Papers*, pp. 51–53 for but one of the many places where Levinas turns Heidegger's Nietzsche thesis against him, arguing that he (Heidegger) is the most powerful recent expression of logocentric thinking rather than its overcoming. For Levinas's relation to Hegel, see Robert Bernasconi, "Levinas Face to Face—with Hegel."

4. I shall use the name Kierkegaard to refer to a body of texts written by Søren Kierkegaard, often under one or another pseudonym. This does not involve attributing to Kierkegaard himself the views expressed by his pseudonyms, with whom he does not always agree and from whom he wishes to distance himself even when he does. The notion of faith, in its opposition to human reason, as a kind of (divine) madness is especially important in *Fear and Trembling, Philosophical Fragments*, and *Concluding Unscientific Postscript*. On the New Testament roots of Kierkegaard's interest in the Socratic notion of divine madness, see my *Kierkegaard's Critique of Reason and Society*, pp. 87–88.

5. For the significance of this curious strategy, see my "Johannes and Johannes: Kierkegaard and Difference," in *International Kierkegaard Commentary: Philosophical Fragments and Johannes Climacus.*

6. Here I stick with the 1962 translation of Swenson and Lowrie. In the 1985 translation the Hongs have replaced Reason with understanding, weakening the rhetorical force of the passage considerably. Accordingly, I have altered the translation to restore Reason.

7. See *Confessions*, VII, 20 in relation to VII, 9.

8. But already in "Philosophy and the Idea of Infinity" we read, "The epiphany of a face is wholly language" (p. 55), and *Totality and Infinity* gives a thoroughly semantic analysis of the alterity expressed in the human face that commands us from on high.

9. As we can learn from either Climacus's thought experiment or from Kant, simply to raise the question of right (*quid juris*) is to engage in critique. See *Critique of Pure Reason*, A84 = B116.

10. Levinas is more careful than some in referring to the philosophical tradition he seeks to undermine. We are not dealing here with Western philosophy as a seamless totality but with its "dominant tradition," with characteristics it has "most often" exhibited. "Philosophy and the Idea of Infinity," pp. 57 and 48.

11. To put it this way is to suggest that there is an ethical as well as an epistemological dimension to critique. Derrida would agree, claiming that even before ethics is the theme of reflection, deconstruction is already the work of justice. See "Force of Law: The 'Mystical Foundation of Authority.' "

12. Levinas speaks of the atheism of philosophy on p. 70 in terms of immanence and totality, blind or deaf to enigma and transcendence. Cf. p. 49. At p. 53, he specifically addresses the atheism of Heidegger, which is discussed in some detail in chapters 2 and 3 of Marion's *God Without Being*. The atheism Levinas here seeks to escape is different from the atheism affirmed in *Totality and Infinity*, pp. 57–58 and 77 as a "break with participation" that permits the interiority of the self as I.

13. This distinction between desire and need, fundamental to the argument of *Totality and Infinity*, is introduced in "Philosophy and the Idea of Infinity," pp. 54–57.

14. The Kierkegaardian overtones of these references to contradiction, paradox, and scandal (offense) are clear. But when Levinas speaks of the "scandalous absence" of God there is an unmistakable reference to the holocaust. See the dedication of *Otherwise than Being*, p. v, "To the memory of those who were closest among the six million assassinated by the National Socialists, and of the millions on millions of all confessions and all nations, victims of the same hatred of the other man, the same anti-Semitism." In the light of Auschwitz, he holds that all theodicy is probably "indecent." *Nine Talmudic Readings*, p. 187. Cf. "Loving the Torah more than God" in *Difficult Freedom*.

15. Lessing's claim that "contingent historical truths can never become a demonstration of eternal truths of reason" (CUP 93) is the crucial stimulus for both *Philosophical Fragments* and *Concluding Unscientific Postscript*. In other words, Johannes Climacus represents Kierkegaard's attempt to come to grips with the Socratic assumption as reformulated by Lessing. Lessing's famous essay, "On the Proof of the Spirit and of Power" is found in Chadwick, *Lessing's Theological Writings*.

16. Cf. Levinas's formulation in "Philosophy and the Idea of Infinity," p. 54, " . . . the idea of infinity is exceptional in that its ideatum surpasses its idea. . . . The intentionality that animates the idea of infinity is not comparable with any other; it aims at what it cannot embrace. . . . In thinking infinity the I from the first *thinks more than it thinks*. Infinity does not enter into the *idea* of infinity, is not grasped; this idea is not a concept. The infinite is radically, absolutely, other."

17. Cf. p. 63, "If the other is presented to the same, the copresence of the other and the same in a phenomenon forthwith constitutes an order."

18. To describe significations as "triumphant" is to call attention to their historical contingency. It is also to point to the triumph of structure over event, for they represent the said that has broken free from the saying that gave them birth. It is on p. 65, where this central theme of *Otherwise than Being* first appears in the essay, that Levinas identifies this order of temporarily fixed meaning as the "context" of signification. In *Totality and Infinity*

Levinas presents ethics as presupposing a semantics of *"signification without context"* (p. 23). This is what he means when he says that the Other signifies καθ᾽ αὐτό. My interpretation of these themes is found in "Levinas and the Immediacy of the Face."

19. This would be to give an interesting twist to the Hegelian thesis that a proper skepticism is the necessary preparation for a proper metaphysics. See ¶¶79–82 of *The Encyclopaedia Logic* and "Relationship of Skepticism to Philosophy."

20. This puts him in conversation with Derrida, who repudiates the traditional sign as metaphysical in the pejorative sense. See *Positions*, especially the interview with Kristeva, "Force and Signification," and "Structure, Sign, and Play," in *Writing and Difference*, "The Pit and the Pyramid" and "Différance," in *Margins of Philosophy*, part I of *Of Grammatology*, and, perhaps before all else, *Speech and Phenomena*. Derrida's argument that signs are radically ambiguous because the context of their employment can never be either closed or (*a fortiori*) fully thematized, is weaker than Levinas's claim that both God and neighbor disturb the complicity of sign and signified that constitutes every human order or context.

21. Probably the most Kierkegaardian feature of *Totality and Infinity* is the sustained polemic against knowledge as recollection. See, for example, pp. 43, 51, 61, 171, 180, and 204.

22. John D. Caputo skillfully develops this same theme from *Repetition* in the Kierkegaard chapter of *Radical Hermeneutics*. In *Fragments* he simply associates this idea with Socrates, but in *Postscript* he follows Kierkegaard's own *The Concept of Irony* in distinguishing Socrates from Plato and attributing this speculative idea to the latter.

23. In Levinas's linguistic formulation this view ignores the difference between the saying and the said, reducing event to essence, and reduces language to a doubling up of phenomena "so that men could point them out to one another." In fact, however, "significations said offer a hold to the *saying* which 'disturbs' them. . . . All speaking is an enigma" (69–70; cf. 65).

24. Levinas, "Philosophy and the Idea of Infinity," p. 49.

25. It is just this feature of the enigmatic that leads Levinas to speak of inwardness and to say that "subjectivity is enigma's partner, partner of the transcendence that disturbs being" (70; cf. 72). It is just this essential link to subjectivity, "whereas the disclosure of Being occurs open to universality" (70), that removes the enigma from ordinary communication. Readers of Kierkegaard need not be reminded of the chiasmic relation of inwardness and indirect communication.

26. It is these four whose common ground Allan Megill seeks to articulate in *Prophets of Extremity*.

27. The importance given to Abraham in *Fear and Trembling* and to Job in *Repetition* is an indication of the degree to which the Kierkegaardian project presents Christianity as a Jewish sect rather than a footnote to Plato.

28. See Levinas, "Philosophy and the Idea of Infinity," p. 53.

29. For an interpretation of Kierkegaard along these lines, see Hall, *Word and Spirit*.

30. Is this the meaning of loving the Torah more than God? See Levinas, *Difficult Freedom*, pp. 142–45. I have introduced this difference between Kierkegaard and Levinas in "Levinas' Teleological Suspension of the Religious," but the exploration of its significance awaits another occasion. I also leave unaddressed the question whether this is a Jewish-Christian issue, as Levinas suggests in "Ideology and Idealism." See *The Levinas Reader*, p. 247.

31. For details see Westphal, "Levinas' Teleological Suspension of the Religious."

32. Like Levinas, Kierkegaard will focus on the difference between the second and third person pronouns, leaving to others the question of the masculine form of the latter.

33. "Education and Prayer," in Levinas, *Difficult Freedom*, p. 269.

34. Ibid., p. 271.

35. See the appendix to chapter III of PF; SUD 83, 87, 113–31; and PC 23–26, 36–40, and 69–144. That we should expect a gap between any of society's norms (*Sittlichkeit*) and the will of God is the point of the teleological suspension of the ethical in *Fear and Trembling*.

36. "Prayer without Demand," in *The Levinas Reader*, pp. 230–32.

37. Ibid., p. 233.

38. Levinas, "Philosophy and the Idea of Infinity," pp. 50–53, 57–59.

Works Cited

Adorno, Theodor W. *The Jargon of Authenticity*. Trans. Knut Tarnowski and Frederic Will. Evanston: Northwestern University Press, 1973.

——. *Kierkegaard: Construction of the Aesthetic*. Trans. Robert Hullot-Kentor. Minneapolis: University of Minnesota Press, 1989.

——. *Minima Moralia*. Trans. E. F. Jephcott. London: New Left, 1974.

——. *Negative Dialectics*. New York: Seabury, 1973.

Adorno, Theodor W., and Max Horkheimer. *Dialectic of Enlightenment*. Trans. John Cumming. New York: Seabury, 1972.

Agacinski, Sylviane. *Aparte: Conceptions and Deaths of Søren Kierkegaard*. Trans. Kevin Newmark. Tallahassee: University Presses of Florida, 1988.

Anscombe, Elizabeth. "Modern Moral Philosophy." *Philosophy* 33 (1958):1–19.

Apel, Karl-Otto. *Diskurs und Verantwortung: Das Problem des Übergangs zur postkonventionellen Moral*. Frankfurt a/M: Suhrkamp, 1988.

Arens, Edmund, ed. *Habermas und die Theologie: Beiträge zur theologischen Rezeption, Diskussion und Kritik der Theorie kommunikativen Handelns*. Düsseldorf: Patmos, 1989. [Trans. with an additional reply by Habermas in Browning et al., eds. *Habermas, Modernity, and Public Theology*.]

Aristotle. *Nichomachean Ethics*. Trans. Terence Irwin. Indianapolis: Hackett, 1985.

Baier, Annette. "Why Honesty Is a Hard Virtue." *Identity, Character, and Morality: Essays in Moral Psychology*. Ed. O. Flanagan and A. Rorty. Cambridge: MIT Press, 1990. 259–82.

Baker-Fletcher, Karen Elene. "A Womanist Ontology of Freedom and Equality." Presented to the Womanist Approaches to Religion and Society Group, American Academy of Religion, 24 Nov. 1992.

Ballard, B. W. "Marxist Challenges to Heidegger on Alienation and Authenticity." *Man and World* 23 (1990):121–41.

Barnes, Hazel. "Sartre's War Diaries: Prelude and Postscript." *Bulletin de la Société Américaine de Philosophie de Langue Française* IV/2–3 (1992):93–111.

Baudrillard, Jean. *Jean Baudrillard: Selected Writings*. Ed. Mark Poster. Stanford: Stanford University Press, 1988.

Bell, Linda. *Sartre's Ethics of Ambiguity*. Tuscaloosa: University of Alabama Press, 1989.

Benhabib, Seyla. "Feminism and Postmodernism: An Uneasy Alliance." *Praxis International* 11/2 (July 1991):137–49.

——. *Situating the Self: Gender, Community and Postmodernism in Contemporary Ethics*. New York: Routledge, 1992.

Benjamin, Walter. *Passagen-Werk, Volume 1.* Ed. Rolf Tiedman. Frankfurt a/M: Suhrkamp, 1982.

Bernasconi, Robert. "Levinas Face to Face—with Hegel." *Journal of the British Society for Phenomenology* 13 (1982):267–76.

Berry, Donald. *Mutuality: The Vision of Martin Buber.* Albany: SUNY Press, 1985.

Berry, Wanda Warren. "Finally Forgiveness: Kierkegaard as a 'Springboard' for a Feminist Theology of Reform." *Foundations of Kierkegaard's Vision of Community: Religion, Ethics, and Politics in Kierkegaard.* Ed. George B. Connell and C. Stephen Evans. Atlantic Highlands, NJ: Humanities Press, 1992. 196–217.

———. "The Heterosexual Imagination and Aesthetical Existence in *Either/Or, Part One.*" Presented to the Kierkegaard Seminar of the American Academy of Religion, 1988.

———. "Images of Sin and Salvation in Feminist Theology." *Anglican Theological Review* 60 (1978):25–54.

———. "Judge William Judging Woman: Existentialism and Essentialism in *Either/Or, Part Two.*" Presented to the Kierkegaard Seminar of the American Academy of Religion, 1989.

———. "Kierkegaard's Existential Dialectic: The Temporal Becoming of the Self." *Journal of Religious Thought* 38/1 (spring–summer 1981):20–41.

———. "Wresting and Jesting Silence: A Feminist Dialogue with *For Self-Examination.*" Presented to the Søren Kierkegaard Society, 1992.

Berthold-Bond, Daniel. "A Kierkegaardian Critique of Heidegger's Concept of Authenticity." *Man and World* 24 (1991):119–42.

Best, Steven, and Douglas Kellner. "Modernity, Mass Society, and the Media: Reflections on the *Corsair* Affair." In Perkins, ed., *International Kierkegaard Commentary: The* Corsair *Affair.* 23–61.

Bhabha, Homi K. "Interrogating Identity: The Postcolonial Prerogative." In Goldberg, ed., *Anatomy of Racism.* 183–209.

Brandt, Richard B. "The Structure of Virtue." *Midwest Studies in Philosophy,* vol. XIII, *Ethical Theory: Character and Virtue.* Ed. P. A. French, T. E. Uehling, Jr., and H. K. Wettstein. Notre Dame: University of Notre Dame Press, 1988. 64–82.

———. "Traits of Character: A Conceptual Analysis." *American Philosophical Quarterly* 7 (1970):23–37.

Brennan, Teresa. *The Interpretation of the Flesh: Freud and Femininity.* New York: Routledge, 1992.

Brown, Alison. "Grave Voices: A Discussion about Praxis." *Man and World* 25 (1992):5–19.

Brown, James. *Kierkegaard, Heidegger, Buber and Barth: Subject and Object in Modern Theology.* New York: Crowell-Collier, 1962.

Browning, Don S., and Francis Schüssler Fiorenza, eds. *Habermas, Modernity, and Public Theology.* New York: Crossroad, 1992.

Buber, Martin. "Autobiographical Fragments." In Schilpp and Friedman, eds., *The Philosophy of Martin Buber.*

———. *I and Thou.* Trans. Walter Kaufmann. New York: Scribner's, 1970.

———. *Pointing the Way.* Ed. and trans. Maurice S. Friedman. New York: Schocken, 1974; repr. Harper and Row, 1975.

———. "The Question to the Single One." In Buber, *Between Man and Man.* New York: Macmillan, 1965. 40–82.

———. "Reply to My Critics." *Martin Buber's Life and Work*. 3 vols. Ed. Maurice Friedman. New York: Dutton, 1982.

Butler, Judith. *Gender Trouble: Feminism and the Subversion of Identity*. New York: Routledge, 1990.

———. *Subjects of Desire*. New York: Columbia University Press, 1987.

Caputo, John D. *Against Ethics: Contributions to a Poetics of Obligation with Constant Reference to Deconstruction*. Bloomington: Indiana University Press, 1993.

———. "Beyond Aestheticism: Derrida's Responsible Anarchy." *Research in Phenomenology* 18 (1988):59–73.

———. *Demythologizing Heidegger*. Bloomington: Indiana University Press, 1993.

———. "Hermeneutics as the Recovery of Man." *Hermeneutics and Modern Philosophy*. Ed. Brice R. Wachtarhauser. Albany: SUNY Press, 1986. 416–45.

———. "Hyperbolic Justice: Deconstruction, Myth, and Politics." *Research in Phenomenology* 21 (1991):3–20.

———. *Radical Hermeneutics: Repetition, Deconstruction, and the Hermeneutic Project*. Bloomington: Indiana University Press, 1987.

Caws, Peter. *Sartre*. London/Boston/Henley: Routledge & Kegan Paul, 1979.

Chomsky, Noam, and Edward Herman. *Manufacturing Consent*. New York: Pantheon, 1988.

———. *Year 501: The Conquest Continues*. Boston: South End Press, 1993.

Clair, André. *Pseudonymie et Paradoxe: Le Pensée Dialectique de Kierkegaard*. Paris: J. Vrin, 1976.

Connell, George B., and C. Stephen Evans, eds. *Foundations of Kierkegaard's Vision of Community*. Atlantic Highlands, NJ/London: Humanities Press, 1992.

Cooke, Maeve. "Habermas, Autonomy and the Identity of the Self." *Philosophy and Social Criticism* 18/3–4 (1992):269–91.

———. "Realizing the Post-conventional Self." *Philosophy and Social Criticism* 20/1–2 (1994):87–101.

Crenshaw, James, ed. *A Whirlpool of Torment*. Philadelphia: Fortress Press, 1984.

Culpepper, Emily. "The Spiritual, Political Journey of a Feminist Freethinker." In *After Patriarchy: Feminist Transformations of the World Religions*. Ed. Paula M. Cooey, William R. Eakin, and Jay B. McDaniel. Maryknoll, NY: Orbis, 1991.

Cumming, Robert D. "Existence and Communication." *Ethics* LXV, 2 (1955):79–101.

Daly, Mary. *Beyond God the Father*. Boston: Beacon Press, 1973.

———. *GYN/ECOLOGY: The Metaethics of Radical Feminism*. Boston: Beacon Press, 1978.

———. *PURE LUST: Elemental Feminist Philosophy*. Boston: Beacon Press, 1984.

Davaney, Sheila Greeve. "Problems with Feminist Theory: Historicity and the Search for Sure Foundations." *Embodied Love: Sensuality and Relationship as Feminist Values*. Ed. Paula M. Cooey, Sharon Farmer, and Mary Ellen Ross. San Francisco: Harper and Row, 1987. 79–95.

Derrida, Jacques. *"Donner la mort." L'Éthique du don: Jacques Derrida et la pensée du don*. Paris: Métailié-Transition, 1992.

———. "Force of Law: The 'Mystical Foundation of Authority.' " *Deconstruction and the Possibility of Justice*. Ed. Drucilla Cornell, Michael Rosenfeld, and David Gray Carlson. New York: Routledge, 1992.

———. *Given Time: I. Counterfeit Money*. Trans. Peggy Kamuf. Chicago: University of Chicago Press, 1992.

———. "How to Avoid Speaking: Denials." *Languages of the Unsayable*. Ed. Sanford Budick and Wolfgang Iser. New York: Columbia, 1989.

———. *L'Éthique du don: Jacques Derrida et la pensée du don*. Paris: Métailié-Transition, 1992.

———. *Margins of Philosophy*. Trans. Alan Bass. Chicago: University of Chicago Press, 1982.

———. *Of Grammatology*. Trans. Gayatri Chakravorty Spivak. Baltimore: Johns Hopkins University Press, 1976.

———. *The Other Heading: Reflections on Today's Europe*. Trans. Pascale-Anne Brault and Michael B. Naas, intro. M. B. Nass. Bloomington: Indiana Univ. Press, 1992.

———. "Passions: 'An Oblique Offering.' " *Derrida: A Critical Reader*. Trans. and ed. David Wood. Oxford: Basil Blackwell, 1992.

———. *Positions*. Trans. Alan Bass. Chicago: University of Chicago Press, 1981.

———. *Spectres de Marx: L'Etat de la dette, le travail du deuil et la nouvelle Internationale*. Paris: Éditions Galilée, 1993. [*Specters of Marx*. Trans. Peggy Kamuf. New York: Routledge, 1994.]

———. *Speech and Phenomena and Other Essays on Husserl's Theory of Signs*. Trans. David B. Allison. Evanston: Northwestern University Press, 1973.

———. *Writing and Difference*. Trans. Alan Bass. Chicago: University of Chicago Press, 1978.

Ding, Zijiang. "An Examination of the Concept of Socio-Political Deviation." Purdue University, unpublished Ph.D. thesis, July 1989.

Doran, Robert M. *Theology and the Dialectics of History*. Toronto: University of Toronto Press, 1989.

Dostal, Robert J. "The World Never Lost: The Hermeneutics of Trust." *Philosophy and Phenomenological Research* XLVII/3 (March 1987):413–34.

Dunning, Stephen N. *Kierkegaard's Dialectic of Inwardness: A Structural Analysis of the Theory of Stages*. Princeton: Princeton University Press, 1985.

Dussel, Enrique. *Ethics and Community*. Trans. Robert R. Barr. Maryknoll, NY: Orbis, 1988.

Eagleton, Terry. *The Ideology of the Aesthetic*. Cambridge, MA: Basil Blackwell, 1990.

Earle, William, James M. Edie, and John Wild. *Christianity and Existentialism*. Evanston: Northwestern University Press, 1963.

Eliot, T. S. "The Four Quartets," in *The Complete Poems and Plays*. New York: Harcourt, Brace, and World, 1952.

Elrod, John. *Being and Existence in Kierkegaard's Pseudonymous Works*. Princeton: Princeton University Press, 1975.

———. *Kierkegaard and Christendom*. Princeton: Princeton University Press, 1981.

———. "Kierkegaard on Self and Society." *Kierkegaardiana* XI, 178–96.

Emmanuel, Steven M. "Reading Kierkegaard." *Philosophy Today* 36/3-4 (fall 1992):240–55.

Epictetus. *Enchiridion*. Trans. Thomas W. Higginson. Indianapolis: Bobbs-Merrill, 1948. XVI.

Evans, C. Stephen. *Kierkegaard's "Fragments" and "Postscript": The Religious Philosophy of Johannes Climacus*. Atlantic Highlands, NJ: Humanities Press, 1983.

———. *Passionate Reason: Making Sense of Kierkegaard's Philosophical Fragments*. Bloomington: Indiana University Press, 1992.

Ewen, Stuart. *Captains of Consciousness: Advertising and the Roots of Consumer Culture*. New York: McGraw Hill, 1976.

Fairbairn, W. D. *Psychoanalytic Studies of the Personality*. London: Tavistock, 1952.

Faludi, Susan. *Backlash: The Undeclared War against American Women*. New York: Doubleday, 1991.

Fanon, Frantz. *Black Skin, White Masks*. New York: Grove Press, 1967.

Feick, Hildegard, ed. 2nd ed. *Index zu Heideggers' Sein und Zeit*. Tübingen: Niemeyer, 1968.

Fenger, Henning. *Kierkegaard, The Myths and Their Origins: Studies in the Kierkegaardian Papers and Letters*. Trans. George C. Schoolfield. New Haven: Yale University Press, 1976.

Ferrara, Alessandro. "Justice and the Good from a *Eudaimonistic* Standpoint." *Philosophy and Social Criticism* 18/3–4 (1992):333–54.

———. *Modernity and Authenticity: A Study in the Social and Ethical Thought of Jean-Jacques Rousseau*. Albany: SUNY Press, 1993.

———. "Postmodern Eudaimonia." *Praxis International* 11/4 (January 1992):387–411.

Flax, Jane. *Psychoanalysis, Feminism, and Postmodernism in the Contemporary West*. Berkeley: University of California Press, 1990.

Foucault, Michel. "What Is Enlightenment?" *The Foucault Reader*. Paul Rabinow, ed. New York: Pantheon, 1984. 32–50.

Fraser, Nancy. "False Antitheses: A Response to Seyla Benhabib and Judith Butler." *Praxis International* 11:2 (July 1991):166–77.

———. "The Uses and Abuses of French Discourse Theories for Feminist Politics." *Revaluing French Feminism: Critical Essays on Difference, Agency, and Culture*. Ed. Nancy Fraser and Sandra Lee Bartky. Bloomington: Indiana University Press, 1992. 177–94.

Freud, Sigmund. *Civilization and Its Discontents*. Trans. James Strachey. New York: Norton, 1961.

———. *The Ego and the Id*. London: Woolf, 1935.

———. *An Outline of Psycho-Analysis*. Trans. James Strachey. New York: Norton, 1949.

Friedeburg, L. V., and Jürgen Habermas, eds. *Adorno-Konferenz 1983*. Frankfurt a/M: Suhrkamp, 1983.

Friedman, Maurice, ed. *Martin Buber's Life and Work*. 3 vols. New York: Dutton, 1982.

Fukuyama, Francis. *The End of History and the Last Man*. New York: Free Press, 1992.

Gadamer, Hans-Georg. *Wahrheit und Methode*, 4th ed. Tübingen: J. C. B. Mohn (Paul Siebeck), 1975. [*Truth and Method*, 2nd ed. Trans. Joel Weinsheimer and Donald G. Marshall. New York: Crossroad, 1990.]

Gavi, P., J.-P. Sartre, and P. Victor (pseudonym). *On a raison de se révolter*. Paris: Gallimard, 1974.

Gill, Jerry H. "Faith Is as Faith Does." *Kierkegaard's* Fear and Trembling: *Critical Appraisals*. Ed. Robert L. Perkins. Tuscaloosa: University of Alabama Press, 1981. 204–17.

Glass, James M. *Shattered Selves: Multiple Personality in a Postmodern World*. Ithaca: Cornell University Press, 1993.

Goldberg, David Theo, ed. *Anatomy of Racism*. Minneapolis: University of Minnesota Press, 1990.

Gordon, Haim. "Existential Guilt and Buber's Social and Political Thought." In Gordon and Bloch, eds., *Martin Buber*.

———. "The Sheltered Aesthete: A New Appraisal of Martin Buber's Life." In Gordon and Bloch, eds., *Martin Buber*.

Gordon, Haim, and Jochannan Bloch, eds. *Martin Buber: A Centenary Volume*. N.p.: KTAV Publishers, 1984.

Gordon, Lewis R. *Bad Faith and Antiblack Racism*. Atlantic Highlands: Humanities Press, 1994.

———. "Commentary on Phyllis S. Morris' 'Sartre and de Beauvoir on Objectification: A Feminist Perspective' and Robert Bernasconi's 'A White Problem: Sartre's Analysis of Racism.' " unpublished ms.

———. *Fanon and the Crisis of European Man*. Forthcoming.

Gramsci, Antonio. *Selections from the Prison Notebooks*. Ed. and trans. Quintin Hoare and Geoffrey Nowell Smith. New York: International, 1971.

Grant, Jacquelyn. *White Women's Christ and Black Women's Jesus: Feminist Christology and Womanist Response*. Atlanta: Scholars Press, 1989.

Green, Ronald M. "Deciphering *Fear and Trembling*'s Secret Message." *Religious Studies* 22/1 (March 1986):95–111.

———. *Kant and Kierkegaard: The Hidden Debt*. Albany: SUNY Press, 1992.

Guntrip, Harry. *Psychoanalytic Theory, Therapy, and the Self*. New York: Basic, 1971.

Habermas, Jürgen. *Communication and the Evolution of Society*. Trans. Thomas McCarthy. Boston: Beacon Press, 1979.

———. *Die nachholende Revolution: Kleine politische Schriften VII*. Frankfurt a/M: Suhrkamp, 1990.

———. "Discourse Ethics: Notes on a Program of Philosophical Justification." *Moral Consciousness and Communicative Action*. Trans. Christian Lenhardt and Shierry Weber Nicholsen. Cambridge: MIT Press, 1990. 43–115.

———. "Diskursethik—Notizen zu einem Begründungsprogramm." In Habermas, *Moralbewußtsein und kommunikatives Handeln*. 53–126. ["Discourse Ethics: Notes on a Program of Philosophical Justification." In Habermas, *Moral Consciousness and Communicative Action*. 43–115.]

———. *Eine Art Schadensabwicklung: Kleine Politische Schriften VI*. Frankfurt a/M: Suhrkamp, 1987. [Partially trans. in Habermas, *New Conservatism*.]

———. *Erläuterungen zur Diskursethik*. Frankfurt a/M: Suhrkamp, 1991. [Partially translated in Habermas, *Justification and Application*.]

———. *Faktizität und Geltung: Beiträge zur Diskurstheorie des Rechts und des demokratischen Rechtstaats*. Frankfurt a/M: Suhrkamp, 1992.

———. "Gerechtigkeit und Solidarität: Eine Stellungnahme zur Diskussion über 'Stufe 6.' " *Zur Bestimmung der Moral: Philosophische und sozialwissenschaftliche Beiträge zur Moralforschung*. Ed. Wolfgang Edelstein and Gertrud Nunner-Winkler. Frankfurt a/M: Suhrkamp, 1986. 291–318. ["Justice and Solidarity: On the Discussion Concerning 'Stage 6.' " *Hermeneutics and Critical Theory in Ethics and Politics*. Ed. Michael Kelly. Cambridge: MIT Press, 1990. 32–52.]

———. "Geschichtsbewußtsein und posttraditionale Identität: Die Westorientie rung der Budesrepublik." In Habermas, *Eine Art Schadensabwicklung*. 161–79. ["Historical Consciousness and Post-Traditional Identity: The Federal Republic's Orientation to the West." In Habermas, *The New Conservatism.* 249-67.]

———. "Historical Consciousness and Post-Traditional Identity: The Federal Republic's Orientation to the West." *The New Conservatism: Cultural Criticism and the Historians' Debate.* Ed. and trans. Shierry Weber Nicholsen. Cambridge: MIT Press, 1989. 249-67.

———. "An Intersubjectivist Concept of Individuality." Paper presented at Brighton: World Congress of Philosophy, 24 Aug. 1988. [This is a partial draft from Habermas, *Nachmetaphysisches Denken.* 187-241, which does not yet include Habermas's Kierkegaard discussion.]

———. *Justification and Application: Remarks on Discourse Ethics.* Trans. Ciaran P. Cronin. Cambridge: MIT Press, 1993.

———. "Kommunikative Freiheit und Negative Theologie." *Dialektischer Negativismus: Michel Theunissen zum 60. Geburtstag.* Ed. Emil Angehrn, Hinrich Fink Eitel, Christian Iber, and Georg Lohmann. Frankfurt a/M: Suhrkamp, 1992. 15-34. [See the trans. in this volume.]

———. *Moralbewußtsein und kommunikatives Handeln.* Frankfurt a/M: Suhrkamp, 1983. [*Moral Consciousness and Communicative Action.* Trans. Christian Lenhardt and Shierry Weber Nicholsen. Cambridge: MIT Press, 1990.]

———. "Moralität und Sittlichkeit. Treffen Hegels Einwände gegen Kant auch die Diskursethik zu?" *Moralität und Sittlichkeit: Das Problem Hegels und die Diskursethik.* Ed. Wolfgang Kuhlmann. Frankfurt a/M: Suhrkamp, 1986. 16-37. ["Morality and Ethical Life: Does Hegel's Critique of Kant Apply to Discourse Ethics?" In Habermas, *Moral Consciousness and Communicative Action.* 195-215.]

———. *Nachmetaphysisches Denken: Philosophische Aufsätze.* Frankfurt a/M: Suhrkamp, 1988. [*Postmetaphysical Thinking: Philosophical Essays.* Trans. William Mark Hohengarten. Cambridge: MIT Press, 1992.]

———. *The New Conservatism: Cultural Criticism and the Historians' Debate.* Ed. and trans. Shierry Weber Nicholsen. Intro. Richard Wolin. Cambridge: MIT Press, 1989. [This a partial trans. of Habermas, *Eine Art Schadensabwicklung,* with additional essays from other works.]

———. *The Philosophical Discourse of Modernity.* Trans. Frederick Lawrence. Cambridge: MIT Press, 1987.

———. *Postmetaphysical Thinking.* Trans. William Mark Hohengarten. Cambridge: MIT Press, 1992.

———. "Staatsburgerschaft und nationale Identität. Überlegungen zur Europäischen Zukunft" (1990). In Habermas, *Faktizität und Geltung.* 632-60.

———. *Texte und Kontexte.* Frankfurt a/M: Suhrkamp, 1991.

———. *Theorie des kommunikativen Handelns.* Frankfurt a/M: Suhrkamp. Band 1: *Handlungsrationalität und gesellschaftliche Rationalisierung,* 1981; Band 2: *Zur funktionalistichen Vernunft,* 1985. [*The Theory of Communicative Action.* Two volumes. Trans. Thomas McCarthy. Boston: Beacon Press. Vol. 1: *Reason and the Rationalization of Society,* 1984; vol. 2: *Lifeworld and System: A Critique of Functionalist Reason,* 1987.]

———. *The Theory of Communicative Action.* Vols. I & II. Trans. Thomas McCarthy. Boston: Beacon Press, 1984.

———. *Toward a Rational Society.* Trans. Jeremy Shapiro. Boston: Beacon Press, 1970.

———. "Transzendenz von innen, Transzendenz ins Diesseits." In Habermas, *Texte und Kontexte*. 127–56. ["Transcendence from Within, Transcendence in this World." Trans. Eric Crump and Peter P. Kenny. *Habermas, Modernity, and Public Theology*. Ed. Don S. Browning and Francis Schüssler Fiorenza. New York: Crossroad, 1992. 226–50.]

———. "Über Moralität und Sittlichkeit—Was macht eine Lebensform rational?" *Rationalität: Philosophische Beiträge*. Ed. Herbert Schnädelbach. Frankfurt a/M: Suhrkamp, 1984. 218–35.

———. *Vergangenheit als Zukunft*. Zürich: Pendo, 1990, 1991.

———. "Volkssouverentität als Verfahren" (1988). In Habermas, *Faktizität und Geltung*. 600–31.

———. "Vom pragmatischen, ethischen und moralischen Gebrauch der praktischen Vernunft." In Habermas, *Erläuterungen zur Diskursethik*. 100–18. ["On the Pragmatic, the Ethical, and the Moral Employment of Practical Reason." In Habermas, *Justification and Application*. 1–17.]

———. "Work and Weltanschauung: The Heidegger Controversy from a German Perspective." *Critical Inquiry* 15 (winter 1989):431–56.

Hall, Ronald L. *Word and Spirit: A Kierkegaardian Critique of the Modern Age*. Bloomington: Indiana University Press, 1993.

Hampson, Daphne. "Luther on the Self: A Feminist Critique." *Feminist Theology: A Reader*. Ed. Ann Loades. Louisville: Westminster/John Knox, 1990. 215–25.

———. *Theology and Feminism*. Oxford: Blackwell, 1990.

Harries, Karsten. "Heidegger as Political Thinker." *Review of Metaphysics* 29 (1975–76):642–69.

Havel, Václav. *Dopisy Olze*. [Letters To Olga.] Praha: Atlantis, 1990.

———. "The Post-Communist Nightmare." *The New York Review of Books* 27 May 1993:8, 10.

———. "The Power of the Powerless." Trans. P. Wilson. *Living in Truth: Twenty-Two Essays Published on the Occasion of the Award of the Erasmus Prize to Václav Havel*. Ed. Jan Ladislav. London: Faber & Faber, 1986, 1990.

Hegel's Philosophy of Right. Trans. T. M. Knox. London: Oxford University Press, 1967.

Hegel, G. W. F. *The Encyclopaedia Logic*. Trans. T. F. Geraets, W. A. Suchting, and H. S. Harris. Indianapolis: Hackett, 1991.

———. *Phenomenology of Spirit*. Trans. A. V. Miller. New York: Oxford University Press, 1977.

———. "Relationship of Skepticism to Philosophy." *Between Kant and Hegel*. Trans. George di Giovanni and H. S. Harris. Albany: SUNY Press, 1985.

Heidegger, Martin. "A Letter on Humanism." *Heidegger: Basic Writings*. Ed. David Krell. New York: Harper and Row, 1977.

———. *Being and Time*. Trans. John Macquarrie and Edward Robinson. New York: Harper and Row, 1962.

———. *Discourse on Thinking*. Trans. John Anderson and E. Hans Freund. New York: Harper and Row, 1966.

———. *An Introduction to Metaphysics*. Trans. Ralph Manheim. New Haven: Yale University Press, 1959.

———. *The Metaphysical Foundations of Logic*. Trans. Michael Heim. Bloomington: Indiana University Press, 1984.

——. *On the Way to Language.* Trans. Peter D. Hertz. New York: Harper and Row, 1971.

——. *The Principle of Reason.* Trans. Reginald Lilly. Bloomington: Indiana University Press, 1991.

Hohlenberg, Johannes. *Kierkegaard.* Trans. T. H. Croxall. New York: Pantheon, 1954.

Holmer, Paul L. *The Grammar of Faith.* San Francisco: Harper and Row, 1978.

Honneth, Axel. *Kampf um Anerkennung: Zur moralischen Grammatik sozialer Konflikte.* Frankfurt a/M: Suhrkamp, 1992.

Horkheimer, Max. *Gesammelten Schriften,* vol. 7. Frankfurt a/M: Fischer, 1985.

Horkheimer, Max and Theodor W. Adorno. *Dialectic of Enlightenment.* Trans. John Cumming. New York: Continuum, 1987.

Huntington, Patricia J. *Autonomy, Community, and Solidarity: Some Implications of Heidegger's Thought for the Feminist Alliance with Poststructuralism.* Unpublished MS.

Irigaray, Luce. *Elemental Passions.* Trans. Collie and Still. New York: Routledge, 1992.

——. *je, tu, nous.* Trans. Martin. New York: Routledge, 1993.

——. *Marine Lover of Friedrich Nietzsche.* Trans. Gill. New York: Columbia University Press, 1991.

Jameson, Fredric. *Postmodernism, or The Cultural Logic of Late Capitalism.* Durham: Duke University Press, 1991.

Janik, Allan. "Haecker, Kierkegaard and the Early Brenner: A Contribution to the History of the Reception of *Two Ages* in the German Speaking World." In Perkins, ed., *International Kierkegaard Commentary: Two Ages,* 189–222.

Jay, Martin. *Marxism and Totality: The Adventures of a Concept from Lukács to Habermas.* Berkeley: University of California Press, 1984.

Kant, Immanuel. *Religion within the Limits of Reason Alone.* Trans. Theodore M. Greene and Hoyt H. Hudson. LaSalle: Open Court, 1934.

Kaufmann, Walter. "Buber's Failure and Triumphs." In Gordon and Bloch, eds., *Martin Buber.*

Keller, Catherine. *From a Broken Web: Separation, Sexism, and Self.* Boston: Beacon Press, 1986.

Kellner, Douglas. *Herbert Marcuse and the Crisis of Marxism.* Macmillan and University of California Press, 1984.

——. *Jean Baudrillard: From Marxism to Postmodernism and Beyond.* Stanford: Stanford University Press, 1989.

——. *The Persian Gulf TV War.* Boulder: Westview Press, 1993.

Kirmmse, Bruce H. *Kierkegaard in Golden Age Denmark.* Bloomington: Indiana University Press, 1990.

Kisiel, Theodore. "Heidegger's Apology: Biography as Philosophy and Ideology." *The Heidegger Case: On Philosophy and Politics.* Ed. Tom Rockmore and Joseph Margolis. Philadelphia: Temple University Press, 1992. 11–51.

Kosík, Karel. *Dialectics of the Concrete: A Study on Problems of Man and World.* Trans. Karel Kovanda with James Schmidt. Dodrecht and Boston: D. Reidel, 1976.

Kristeva, Julia. *Black Sun.* Trans. Leon Roudiez. New York: Columbia University Press, 1989.

——. *Desire in Language.* Trans. Gora, Jardine, and Roudiez. New York: Columbia University Press, 1980.

———. *Revolution in Poetic Language.* Trans. Margaret Waller. New York: Columbia University Press, 1984.

———. *Strangers to Ourselves.* Trans. Leon Roudiez. New York: Columbia University Press, 1991.

———. *Tales of Love.* Trans. Leon Roudiez. New York: Columbia University Press, 1987.

Kruschwitz, R. B., and R. C. Roberts. *The Virtues: Contemporary Essays on Moral Character.* Belmont, CA: Wadsworth, 1986.

Kupperman, Joel. "Character and Ethical Theory." *Midwest Studies in Philosophy*, vol. XIII. 115-25.

Kuykendall, Eléanor. "Toward an Ethic of Nurturance: Luce Irigaray on Mothering and Power." *Mothering: Essays in Feminist Theory.* Ed. Joyce Trebilcot. Totowa: Rowman & Allenheld, 1983. 263-74.

Lamblin, Bianca. *Mémoires d'une jeune fille dérangée.* Paris: Balland, 1993.

Lerner, Gerda. *The Creation of Feminist Consciousness: From the Middle Ages to Eighteen-Seventy.* New York & Oxford: Oxford University Press, 1993.

Lessing, Gotthold. *Lessing's Theological Writings.* Ed. Henry Chadwick. Stanford: Stanford University Press, 1957.

Levinas, Emmanuel. *Collected Philosophical Papers.* Trans. Alphonso Lingis. Dodrecht: Martinus Nijhoff, 1987.

———. *Difficult Freedom: Essays on Judaism.* Trans. Seán Hand. Baltimore: Johns Hopkins University Press, 1990.

———. *The Levinas Reader.* Ed. Seán Hand. Oxford: Blackwell, 1989.

———. *Nine Talmudic Readings.* Trans. Annette Aronowicz. Bloomington: Indiana University Press, 1990.

———. *Noms Propres.* Paris: Fata Morgana, 1976.

———. *Otherwise than Being or Beyond Essence.* Trans. Alphonso Lingis. The Hague: Martinus Nijhoff, 1981.

———. *Totality and Infinity.* Trans. Alphonso Lingis. Pittsburgh: Duquesne University Press, 1969.

Lindbloom, Ernst. *Politics and Markets.* New York: Basic, 1977.

Lohmann, G. *Indifferenz und Gesellschaft.* Frankfurt a/M: Suhrkamp, 1991.

Lorde, Audre. *Sister Outsider.* New York: Crossing Press, 1984.

Lorraine, Tamsin E. *Gender, Identity, and the Production of Meaning.* Boulder: Westview Press, 1990.

Louden, Robert B. *Morality and Moral Theory: A Reassessment and Reaffirmation.* New York: Oxford University Press, 1992.

Löwith, Karl. *Heidegger: Denker in Dürftiger Zeit.* Frankfurt a/M: S. Fischer, 1953.

Lowrie, Walter. " 'Existence' as Understood by Kierkegaard and/or Sartre." *Sewanee Review* LVIII (July 1950):379-401.

———. *Kierkegaard.* London: Oxford University Press, 1938.

———. *A Short Life of Kierkegaard.* Princeton: Princeton University Press, 1942 and 1970.

Lukács, Georg. "Existentialism or Marxism?" *Existentialism versus Marxism: Conflicting Views of Humanism.* Ed. George Novack. New York: Dell, 1966. 134-53.

———. *Die Zerstörung der Vernuft, Werke 9* (1954). Darmstadt: Luchterhand, 1974.

Lyotard, Jean-François. *The Differend: Phrases in Dispute.* Trans. G. Van Den Abbeele. Minneapolis: University of Minnesota Press, 1988.

MacIntyre, Alasdair. *After Virtue,* 2nd ed. Notre Dame: University of Norte Dame Press, 1984.

Mackey, Louis. "Slouching Toward Bethlehem: Deconstructive Strategies in Theology." *Anglican Theological Review* 65 (1983):255-72.

MacKinnon, Catharine. "Feminism, Marxism, Method, and the State: Toward Feminist Jurisprudence." *Critical Legal Studies.* Ed. Allan C. Hutchinson. Totowa: Rowman & Littlefield, 1989. 56-76.

Macpherson, C. B. *The Political Theory of Possessive Individualism.* Oxford: Clarendon Press, 1962.

Malantschuk, Gregor. *Kierkeqaard's Thought.* Ed. and trans. Howard V. Hong and Edna H. Hong. Princeton: Princeton University Press, 1971.

Mannheim, Karl. *Ideology and Utopia.* Trans. Louis Wirth and Edward Shils. New York: Harcourt, Brace, and World, n.d.

Marcuse, Herbert. *The Aesthetic Dimension: Towards a Critique of Marxist Aesthetics.* Boston: Beacon Press, 1978.

———. "Beiträge zu einer Phänomenologie des Historischen Materialismus," *Philosophische Hefte* 1/1 (Berlin, 1928):45-68.

———. *An Essay on Liberation.* Boston: Beacon Press, 1969.

———. *Hegel's Ontologie und die Grundlegung einer Theorie der Geschichtlichkeit.* Frankfurt a/M: V. Klosterman, 1932.

———. "Neue Quellen zur Grundlegung des Historischen Materialismus," *Die Gesellschaft,* 9 (part 2), 8 (Berlin, 1932):136-74.

———. *One-Dimensional Man: Studies in the Ideology of Advanced Industrial Society,* with a new introduction by Douglas Kellner. Boston: Beacon Press, c.1964, 1991.

———. "Transzendentaler Marxismus?" *Die Gesellschaft,* 7 (part 2), 10 (Berlin, 1930):304-26.

———. "Über konkrete Philosophie," *Archiv für Sozialwissenschaft und Sozialpolitik,* 62 (Tübingen, 1929):111-28.

———. "Zum Problem der Dialektik" *Die Gesellschaft,* 7 (part 1), 1 (Berlin, 1930):15-30 and *Die Gesellschaft,* 8 (part 2), 12 (Berlin, 1931):541-57.

Marion, Jean-Luc. *God Without Being.* Trans. Thomas A. Carlson. Chicago: University of Chicago Press, 1991.

Marsh, James L. "The *Corsair* Affair and Critical Social Theory." In Perkins, ed. *International Kierkegaard Commentary: The* Corsair *Affair,* 63-83.

———. "Marx and Kierkegaard on Alienation." In Perkins, ed. *International Kierkegaard Commentary: Two Ages,* 155-74.

———. *Post-Cartesian Meditations.* New York: Fordham University Press, 1988.

———. "Praxis and Ultimate Reality: Intellectual, Moral, and Religious Conversion as Radical Political Conversion." *Ultimate Reality and Meaning* 13 (1990):222-40.

———. "The Religious Significance of Habermas." *Faith and Philosophy* (October 1993):521-38.

Martin, Bill. *Matrix and Line: Derrida and the Possibilities of Postmodern Social Theory.* Albany: SUNY Press, 1992.

Marx, Karl. *Capital.* Volume 1. Trans. Ben Fowkes. New York: Vintage, 1976.

———. *Economic and Philosophical Manuscripts of 1844.* Ed. Dirk J. Struik. Trans. Martin Milligan. New York: International, 1964.

———. *Grundrisse.* Trans. Martin Nicolaus. New York: Vintage, 1973.

———. *Selected Writings*. Ed. David McClellan. New York: Oxford, 1976.

Matuštík, Martin J. "Derrida and Habermas on the Aporia of the Politics of Identity and Difference: Towards Radical Democratic Multiculturalism." *Constellations: International Journal of Critical and Democratic Theory* 1/3 (former *Praxis International*, forthcoming 1994).

———. "Kierkegaard as Socio-Political Thinker and Activist." *Man and World* 27/2 (April 1994):211–24.

———. "Merleau-Ponty on Taking the Attitude of the Other." *Journal of the British Society for Phenomenology* 22/1 (January 1991):44–52.

———. "Merleau-Ponty's Phenomenology of Sympathy." *Auslegung* 17/1 (January 1991):41–65.

———. *Postnational Identity: Critical Theory and Existential Philosophy in Habermas, Kierkegaard, and Havel*. New York & London: Guilford Press, 1993. Series "Critical Perspectives," Douglas Kellner gen. ed.

———. Review of Perkins. Ed. *International Kierkegaard Commentary: The Corsair Affair*. *Man and World* 26 (1993):93–97.

———. "The Specters of Deconstruction: Critical Social Theory without Apologies." A critical commentary on Derrida's *Spectres de Marx* (q.v.). Seattle: 33rd Annual Meeting of Society for Phenomenology and Existential Philosophy, Oct 1, 1994. Ms.

McBride, William L. "Community: The Dialectic of Abandonment and Hope in Sartre's Last Words." *Bulletin de la Société Américaine de Philosophie de Langue Française* IV/2–3 (1992):218–31.

———. "Power and Empowerment: Reflections on Thomas Wartenberg's *The Forms of Power* and the Feminist Movement." Unpublished ms.

———. "Sartre and His Successors: Existential Marxism and Postmodernism at Our Fin de Siècle." *Praxis International* 11/1 (April 1991):78–92.

———. *Sartre's Political Theory*. Bloomington and Indianapolis: Indiana University Press, 1991.

McKinnon, Alastair. "Kierkegaard: Paradox and Irrationalism." *Essays on Kierkegaard*. Ed. Jerry H. Gill. Minneapolis: Burgess, 1969. 102–12.

Megill, Allan. *Prophets of Extremity: Nietzsche, Heidegger, Foucault, Derrida*. Berkeley: University of California Press, 1985.

Metz, Johann Baptist. "Anamnetische Vernunft." In Axel Honneth, et al., *Zwischenbetrachtungen*. Frankfurt a/M: Suhrkamp, 1989.

Michnik, Adam. "Bojím sa antikomunistov s tvárami bolševikov" [I am Afraid of the Anticommunists with the Faces of Bolsheviks] (Interview). *Kultúrny život* (Bratislava), 11 June 1992:3.

———. "An Embarrassing Anniversary." *The New York Review of Books* 10 June 1993:19–21.

Mills, Jane. *Womanwords: A Dictionary of Words about Women*. New York: Free Press, 1989.

Morris, Phyllis S. "Sartre and de Beauvoir on Objectification: A Feminist Perspective." unpublished ms.

NASB-NIV Parallel New Testament in Greek and English. Grand Rapids: Regency Reference Library, 1986.

Nietzsche, Friedrich. *"The Birth of Tragedy" and "The Genealogy of Morals."* Trans. Francis Golffing. Garden City: Doubleday Anchor, 1956.

Oakley, Justin. *Morality and the Emotions*. New York: Routledge, 1992.

Outlaw, Lucius. "Towards a Critical Theory of 'Race.' " In Goldberg, *Anatomy of Racism*. 58–82.
Paci, Enzo. *The Function of the Sciences and the Meaning of Man*. Trans. Paul Piccone and James Manson. Evanston: Northwestern University Press, 1972.
Parenti, Michael. *Inventing Reality*. New York: St. Martin's Press, 1986.
———. *Make-Believe Media: The Politics of Entertainment*. New York: St. Martin's Press, 1992.
Patočka, Jan. *Kacírské eseje o filosofii dějin*. [Heretical Essays About the Philosophy of History.] Intro. Ivan Dubský. Praha: Academia, 1990.
Peperzak, Adriaan. *To the Other: An Introduction to the Philosophy of Emmanuel Levinas*. West Lafayette: Purdue University Press, 1993.
Perkins, Robert L. "Buber and Kierkegaard: A Philosophic Encounter." In Gordon and Bloch, eds., *Martin Buber*. 275–304.
———. "Kierkegaard's Critique of the Modern State." *Inquiry* 27 (1984):207–18.
———. Ed. *International Kierkegaard Commentary: The Corsair Affair*, vol. 13. Macon: Mercer University Press, 1990.
———. Ed. *International Kierkegaard Commentary: Philosophical Fragments and Johannes Climacus*, vol. 7. Macon: Mercer University Press, 1994.
———. Ed. *International Kierkegaard Commentary: Two Ages, the Present Age and the Age of Revolution, A Literary Review*, vol. 14. Macon: Mercer University Press, 1984.
———. *International Kierkegaard Commentary: The Sickness unto Death*, vol. 19. Macon: Mercer University Press, 1987.
Phillips, D. Z. *Faith after Foundationalism*. London: Routledge, 1988, 241.
Plaskow, Judith. *Sex, Sin and Grace: Women's Experience and the Theologies of Reinhold Niebuhr and Paul Tillich*. Washington: University Press of America, 1980.
Plaskow, Judith, and Carol P. Christ, eds. *Weaving the Visions: New Patterns in Feminist Spirituality*. San Francisco: Harper and Row, 1989.
Plekhanov, George. *The Role of the Individual in History*. New York: International, 1940.
Ramsey, Ian T. *Religious Language: An Empirical Placing of Theological Phrases*. New York: Macmillan, 1957.
Raynova, Ivanka. *From Existentialist Philosophy to Post-Personalism* (translation of Bulgarian title). Sofia: Apis '90, 1992.
Roberts, Robert C. "Aristotle on Emotions and Virtues." *Philosophical Studies* 56 (1989):293–306.
———. *Faith, Reason, and History: Rethinking Kierkegaard's* Philosophical Fragments. Macon: Mercer University Press, 1986.
———. "Virtues and Rules." *Philosophy and Phenomenological Research* 51 (1991):325–43.
———. "What an Emotion Is: A Sketch." *Philosophical Review* 97 (1988):183–209.
Rorty, Amélie. "Virtues and Their Vicissitudes." *Midwest Studies in Philosophy*, vol XIII. 136–48.
Rorty, Richard. "Habermas and Lyotard on Postmodernity," *Habermas and Modernity*. Ed. Richard Bernstein. Cambridge: MIT Press, 1985.
Rousseau, Jean-Jacques. *Discours sur l'Origine de l'Inégalité*. In *Du Contrat Social*, etc. Paris: Éditions Garnier, 1954. 25–122.
Saiving [Goldstein], Valerie. "The Human Situation: A Feminine View." *Journal of Religion* 40 (April 1960).

Sartre, Jean-Paul. *Being and Nothingness*. Trans. Hazel E. Barnes. New York: Philosophical Library, 1956.

——. *The Critique of Dialectical Reason*. Ed. Jonathan Ree. Trans. Alan Sheridan-Smith. London: New Left, 1976.

——. "Kierkegaard: The Singular Universal" (1972). *Between Existentialism and Marxism*. New York: New Left, 1974.

——. *Les Mots*. Paris: Gallimard, 1964.

——. *Lettres au Castor et à quelques autres 1940-1963*. Paris: Gallimard, 1983.

——. "L'Espoir, maintenant." *Le Nouvel Observateur* 10 Mar. 1980:26; 17 Mar. 1980:52; 24 Mar. 1980:55.

——. *L'être et le néant: Essai d'ontologie phénoménologique*. Paris: Gallimard, 1957.

——. "L'Universel singulier." In *Situations*, IX. Paris: Gallimard, 1972. 152-90.

——. *The War Diaries: November 1939-March 1940*. Trans. Quintin Hoare. New York: Pantheon, 1984.

——. "What's Jean-Paul Sartre Thinking Lately?" Interview with Pierre Bénichou. *Esquire*, Dec. 1972:204-208, 280-86.

Sausser, Bernard. *Existence and Utopia: The Social and Political Thought of Martin Buber*. Rutherford: Fairleigh Dickinson University Press, 1981.

Schilpp, Paul, ed. *The Philosophy of Jean-Paul Sartre*. Library of Living Philosophers, La Salle: Open Court, 1981.

Schilpp, Paul Arthur, and Maurice Friedman, eds. *The Philosophy of Martin Buber*. Library of Living Philosophers. La Salle: Open Court, Cambridge: Cambridge University Press, 1967.

Schrag, Calvin O. *Existence and Freedom: Towards an Ontology of Human Finitude*. Evanston: Northwestern University Press, 1961.

——. "Note on Kierkegaard's Teleological Suspension of the Ethical." *Ethics*, vol. 70 (1959).

Søe, N. H. "Kierkegaard's Doctrine of the Paradox." Trans. Margaret Grieve. *A Kierkegaard Critique*. Ed. Howard A. Johnson and Niels Thulstrup. Chicago: Henry Regnery, 1962. 207-27.

Sölle, Dorothee. *Death by Bread Alone*. Philadelphia: Fortress Press, 1978.

——. *Political Theology*. Philadelphia: Fortress Press, 1974.

——. *The Window of Vulnerability: A Political Spirituality*. Minneapolis: Fortress Press, 1990.

Spiegelberg, Herbert. *The Phenomenological Movement*. 3rd revised and enlarged edition. The Hague/Boston/London: Martinus Nijhoff, 1982.

Sponheim, Paul. *Kierkegaard on Christ and Christian Coherence*. London: SCM Press, 1968.

Stern (Anders), Guenther. "On the Pseudo-Concreteness of Heidegger's Philosophy." *Philosophy and Phenomenological Research* 8/2 (December 1947):337-71.

Stocker, Michael. "The Schizophrenia of Modern Ethical Theories." In Kruschwitz and Roberts. 36-45.

Stone, Robert, and Elizabeth Bowman. "Dialectical Ethics: A First Look at Sartre's Unpublished 1964 Rome Lecture Notes." *Social Text* 13-14 (winter/spring 1986):195-215.

Strasser, Bernard. *Existence and Utopia: The Social and Political Thought of Martin Buber*. Rutherford: Fairleigh Dickinson University Press, 1981.

Taylor, Charles. "The Liberal-Communitarian Debate." *Liberalism and the Moral Life*. Ed. Nancy Rosenblum. Cambridge: Harvard University Press, 1989.

——. *Sources of the Self: The Making of the Modern Identity*. Cambridge: Harvard University Press, 1989.

Taylor, Marc C. *Altarity*. Chicago: University of Chicago Press, 1987.

——. *Kierkegaard's Pseudonymous Authorship: A Study of Time and the Self*. Princeton: Princeton University Press, 1975.

——. "Secretions." *Tears*. Albany: SUNY Press, 1990.

Theunissen, Michael. *Das Selbst auf dem Grund der Verzweiflung*. Frankfurt a/M: Suhrkamp, 1991.

——. *Der Andere: Studien zur Sozialontologie der Gegenwart*. 2nd ed. Berlin: Walter de Gruyter, 1977. [*The Other: Studies in the Social Ontology of Husserl, Heidegger, Sartre, and Buber*. Trans. Christopher Macann, with an intro. by Fred R. Dallmayr. Cambridge: MIT Press, 1984.]

——. *Der Begriff Verzweiflung: Korrekturen an Kierkegaard*. Frankfurt a/M: Suhrkamp, 1993.

——. *Kritische Gesellschafttheorie*. Berlin, 1981.

——. *Negative Theologie der Zeit*. Frankfurt a/M: Suhrkamp, 1991.

——. *Sein und Schein*. Frankfurt a/M: Suhrkamp, 1978.

——. *Selbstverwirklichung und Allgemeinheit*. Frankfurt a/M: Suhrkamp 1982.

Theunissen, Michael, and Wilfred Greve, eds. *Materialien zur Philosophie Sören Kierkegaards*. Frankfurt a/M: Suhrkamp, 1979.

Tillich, Paul. "The Lost Dimension in Religion." *Decisions in Philosophy of Religion*. Ed. W. B. Williamson. Columbus, Ohio: Merrill, 1976.

Tolib, Dubravka Oraib. "Im ersten postmodernen Krieg befindet sich Europa jenseits von Gut und Böse." Trans. Ulrich Dronske, PEN-Congress, Dubrovnik 1993. *Frankfurter Allgemeine Zeitung*, no. 113, 17 May 1993. 13.

Trible, Phyllis. *Genesis 22: The Sacrifice of Sarah*. Gross Memorial Lecture. Valparaiso: Valparaiso University Press, 1989.

Troeltsch, Ernst. *The Social Teaching of the Christian Churches*, vol. I & II. New York: Macmillan, 1931.

UNESCO. *Kierkegaard Vivant* (colloque). Paris: Gallimard, 1966.

van Buren, John. "The Young Heidegger and Phenomenology." *Man and World* 23 (1990):239–72.

Vergil (P. Vergilius Maro). *Aeneidos*. From *The Aeneid of Vergil*, Books I-VI, etc. Chicago/Atlanta/Dallas/New York: Scott, Foresman, 1928.

Wahl, Jean. *Etudes Kierkegaardiennes*. Paris: Librairie J. Vrin, 1938. 2nd edition, 1951.

——. "Existentialism: A Preface." *New Republic* CXIII, 1 Oct. 1945:442-44.

——. *Vers le concret*. Paris: Librairie J. Vrin, 1932.

Walker, Alice. *In Search of Our Mothers' Gardens: Womanist Prose*. San Diego: Harcourt Brace Jovanovich, 1983.

Wallace, James. *Virtues and Vices*. Ithaca: Cornell University Press, 1978.

Walsh, Sylvia (Perkins). "On 'Feminine' and 'Masculine' Forms of Despair." In Perkins, ed. *The International Kierkegaard Commentary: The Sickness unto Death*. 121-34.

Wartenberg, Thomas E. *The Forms of Power: From Domination to Transformation*. Philadelphia: Temple University Press, 1990.

Watkin, Julia. "Serious Jest? Kierkegaard as Young Polemicist in 'Defence' of Women." Presented to Søren Kierkegaard Society, American Academy of Religion, 1992.

Weir, Allison. "From the Subversion of Identity to the Subversion of Solidarity? Feminism in the Age of Gender Trouble." Excerpted from Ed. Linda J. Nicholson. *Thinking Gender* series. New York: Routledge, forthcoming.

Weltsch, Robert. "Buber's Political Philosophy." In Schilpp and Friedman, eds. *The Philosophy of Martin Buber*. 435–50.

West, Cornel. *Race Matters*. Boston: Beacon Press, 1993.

Westerman, Claus. *Genesis 12–36: A Commentary*. Minneapolis: Augsburg, 1985.

Westphal, Merold. "Johannes and Johannes: Kierkegaard and Difference." In Perkins, ed. *International Kierkegaard Commentary: Philosophical Fragments*.

———. *Kierkegaard's Critique of Reason and Society*. Macon: Mercer University Press, 1987, reprinted by Pennsylvania State University Press, 1991.

———. "Kierkegaard's Psychology and Unconscious Despair." In Perkins, ed. *International Kierkegaard Commentary: The Sickness unto Death*.

———. "Levinas and the Immediacy of the Face." *Faith and Philosophy* 10 (1993).

———. "Levinas' Teleological Suspension of the Religious." Forthcoming with the papers of the International Levinas Conference, Loyola University of Chicago, 1993.

White, Stephen K. "Heidegger and the Difficulties of a Postmodern Ethics and Politics." *Political Theory* 18/1 (February 1990):80–103.

Williams, Bernard. "A Critique of Utilitarianism." *Utilitarianism: For and Against*. B. Williams and J. J. C. Smart. Cambridge: Cambridge University Press, 1973.

Wills, Gary. *Reagan's America: Innocents at Home*. Garden City: Doubleday, 1987.

Winson, Jonathan. *Brain and Psyche*. New York: Random House, 1986.

Wittgenstein, Ludwig. *Philosophical Investigations*. Trans. G. E. M. Anscombe. New York: Macmillan, 1953.

Wolin, Richard. *The Politics of Being: The Political Thought of Martin Heidegger*. New York: Columbia University Press, 1990.

———. *The Terms of Cultural Criticism: The Frankfurt School, Existentialism, Poststructuralism*. New York: Columbia University Press, 1992.

Woocher, Jonathan S. "Martin Buber's Politics of Dialogue." *Thought* 53 (1978):241–57.

Wood, Robert E. *Martin Buber's Ontology: An Analysis of* I and Thou. Evanston: Northwestern University Press, 1969.

Young, Iris Marion. *Justice and the Politics of Difference*. Princeton: Princeton University Press, 1990.

Zimmerman, Michael E. "On Discriminating Everydayness, Unownedness, and Falling in *Being and Time*." *Research in Phenomenology* 5 (1975):109–27.

Žižek, Slavoj. *Enjoy Your Symptom!* New York: Routledge, 1992.

Contributors

Wanda Warren Berry is associate professor of philosophy and religion at Colgate University in Hamilton, New York.

Alison Leigh Brown is assistant professor of philosophy at Northern Arizona University in Flagstaff, Arizona.

John D. Caputo is the David R. Cook Professor of Philosophy at Villanova University in Villanova, Pennsylvania.

Stephen N. Dunning is associate professor of religious studies at the University of Pennsylvania in Philadelphia, Pennsylvania.

C. Stephen Evans is professor of philosophy at Calvin College in Grand Rapids, Michigan.

Jürgen Habermas is professor of philosophy at J. W. Goethe-Universität in Frankfurt am Main, Germany.

Patricia J. Huntington is assistant professor of philosophy at Moravian College in Bethlehem, Pennsylvania.

Tamsin Lorraine is assistant professor of philosophy at Swarthmore College in Swarthmore, Pennsylvania.

James L. Marsh is professor of philosophy at Fordham University in Bronx, New York.

Martin J. Matuštík is assistant professor of philosophy at Purdue University in W. Lafayette, Indiana.

William L. McBride is professor of philosophy at Purdue University in W. Lafayette, Indiana.

Robert L. Perkins is professor of philosophy at Stetson University in DeLand, Florida.

Robert C. Roberts is professor of philosophy at Wheaton College in Wheaton, Illinois.

Calvin O. Schrag is the George Ade Distinguished Professor of Philosophy at Purdue University in W. Lafayette, Indiana.

Merold Westphal is professor of philosophy at Fordham University in Bronx, New York.

Index